W9-DGF-323

WITHDRAWN

Other *Baby Blues*® Books from Andrews McMeel Publishing

Guess Who Didn't Take a Nap?

I Thought Labor Ended When the Baby Was Born

We Are Experiencing Parental Difficulties . . . Please Stand By

Night of the Living Dad

I Saw Elvis in My Ultrasound

One More and We're Outnumbered!

Check, Please . . .

threats, bribes & videotape

If I'm a Stay-at-Home Mom, Why Am I Always in the Car?

Lift and Separate

I Shouldn't Have to Scream More Than Once!

Motherhood Is Not for Wimps

Baby Blues®: Unplugged

Dad to the Bone

Never a Dry Moment

Two Plus One Is Enough

Playdate: Category 5

Our Server Is Down!

Something Chocolate This Way Comes

Briefcase Full of Baby Blues®

Night Shift

The Day Phonics Kicked In

My Space

The Natural Disorder of Things

We Were Here First

Ambushed! In the Family Room

Cut!

Treasuries

The Super-Absorbent Biodegradable Family-Size Baby Blues®

Baby Blues®: Ten Years and Still in Diapers

Butt-Naked Baby Blues®

Wall-to-Wall Baby Blues®

Driving Under the Influence of Children

Framed!

X-Treme Parenting

Gift Books

It's a Boy

It's a Girl

eat my poop

BABY BLUES® 28 SCRAPBOOK

By Rick Kirkman & Jerry Scott

Andrews McMeel
Publishing, LLC

Kansas City • Sydney • London

Baby Blues® is syndicated internationally by King Features Syndicate, Inc. For information, write King Features Syndicate, Inc., 300 West Fifty-Seventh Street, New York, New York 10019.

Eat, Cry, Poop copyright © 2011 by Baby Blues Partnership. All rights reserved. Printed in the United States of America. No part of this book may be used or reproduced in any manner whatsoever without written permission except in the case of reprints in the context of reviews.

Andrews McMeel Publishing, LLC
an Andrews McMeel Universal company
1130 Walnut Street, Kansas City, Missouri 64106

www.andrewsmcmeel.com

11 12 13 14 15 RR2 10 9 8 7 6 5 4 3 2 1

ISBN: 978-1-4494-1458-0

Library of Congress Control Number: 2011932609

Find *Baby Blues*® on the Web at
www.babyblues.com.

ATTENTION: SCHOOLS AND BUSINESSES

Andrews McMeel books are available at quantity discounts with bulk purchase for educational, business, or sales promotional use. For information, please e-mail the Andrews McMeel Publishing Special Sales Department: specialsales@amuniversal.com

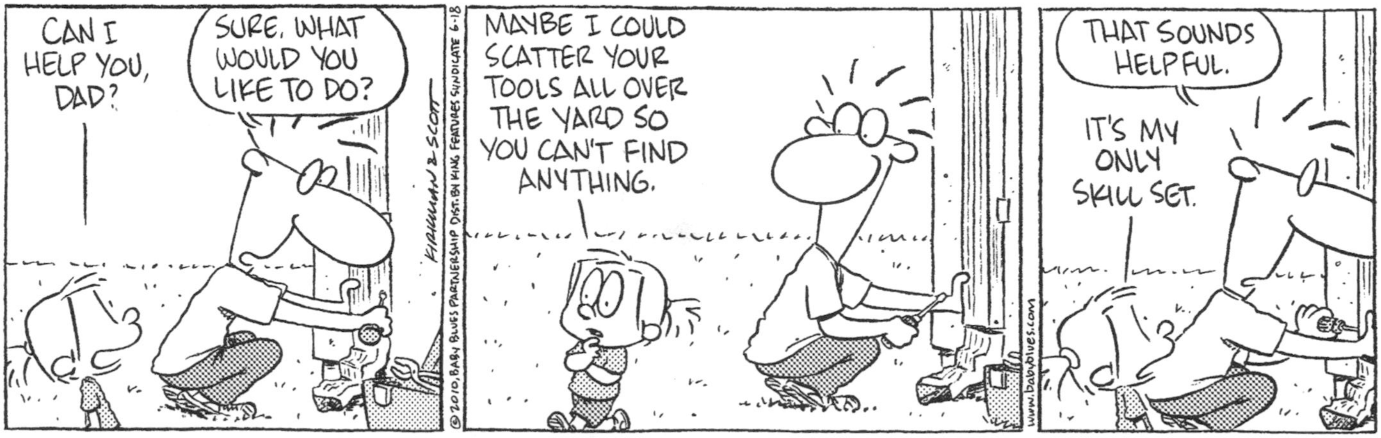
CAN I HELP YOU, DAD?
SURE. WHAT WOULD YOU LIKE TO DO?
MAYBE I COULD SCATTER YOUR TOOLS ALL OVER THE YARD SO YOU CAN'T FIND ANYTHING.
THAT SOUNDS HELPFUL.
IT'S MY ONLY SKILL SET.
KIRKMAN & SCOTT
© 2010, BABY BLUES PARTNERSHIP DIST. BY KING FEATURES SYNDICATE 6-18
www.babyblues.com

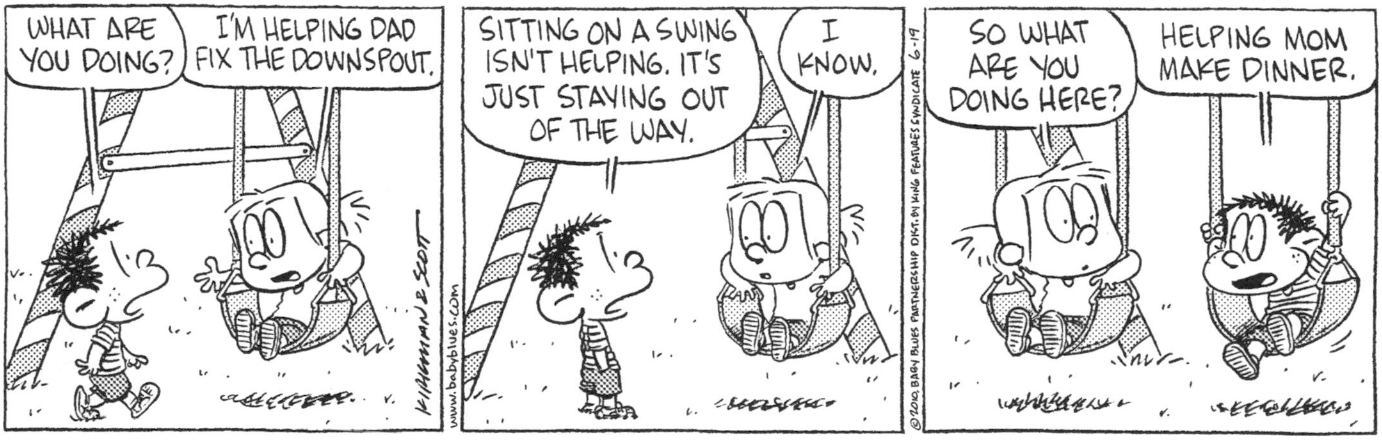
WHAT ARE YOU DOING?
I'M HELPING DAD FIX THE DOWNSPOUT.
SITTING ON A SWING ISN'T HELPING. IT'S JUST STAYING OUT OF THE WAY.
I KNOW.
SO WHAT ARE YOU DOING HERE?
HELPING MOM MAKE DINNER.
KIRKMAN & SCOTT
www.babyblues.com
© 2010, BABY BLUES PARTNERSHIP DIST. BY KING FEATURES SYNDICATE 6-19

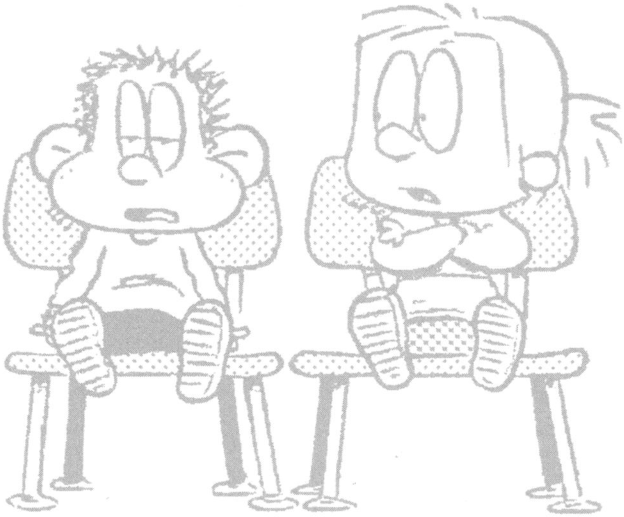

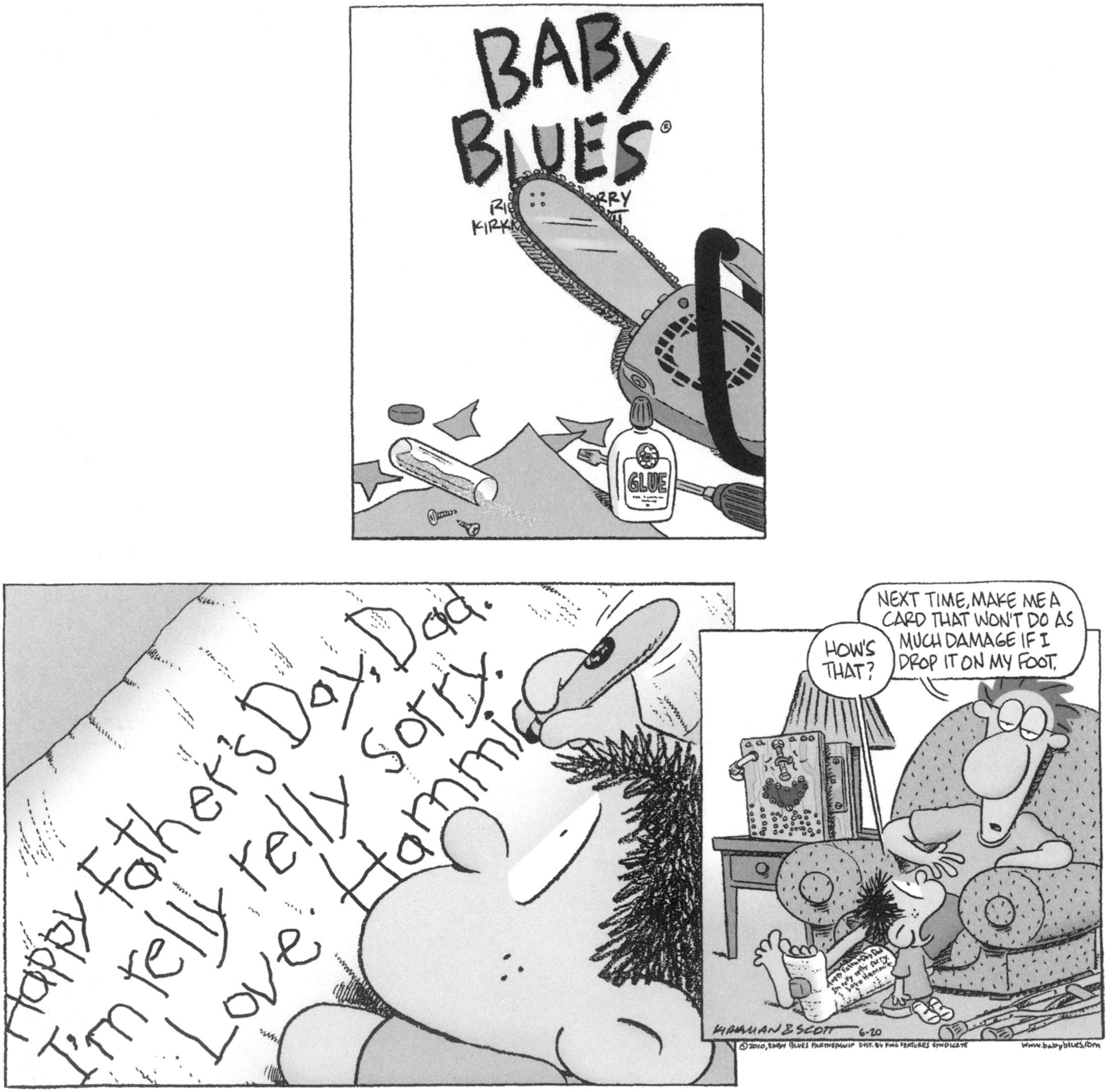
BABY BLUES®
GLUE
Happy Father's Day, Dad.
I'm relly relly sorry.
Love: Hammi
HOW'S THAT?
NEXT TIME, MAKE ME A CARD THAT WON'T DO AS MUCH DAMAGE IF I DROP IT ON MY FOOT.
KIRKMAN & SCOTT 6-20
©2010, BABY BLUES PARTNERSHIP DIST. BY KING FEATURES SYNDICATE
www.babyblues.com

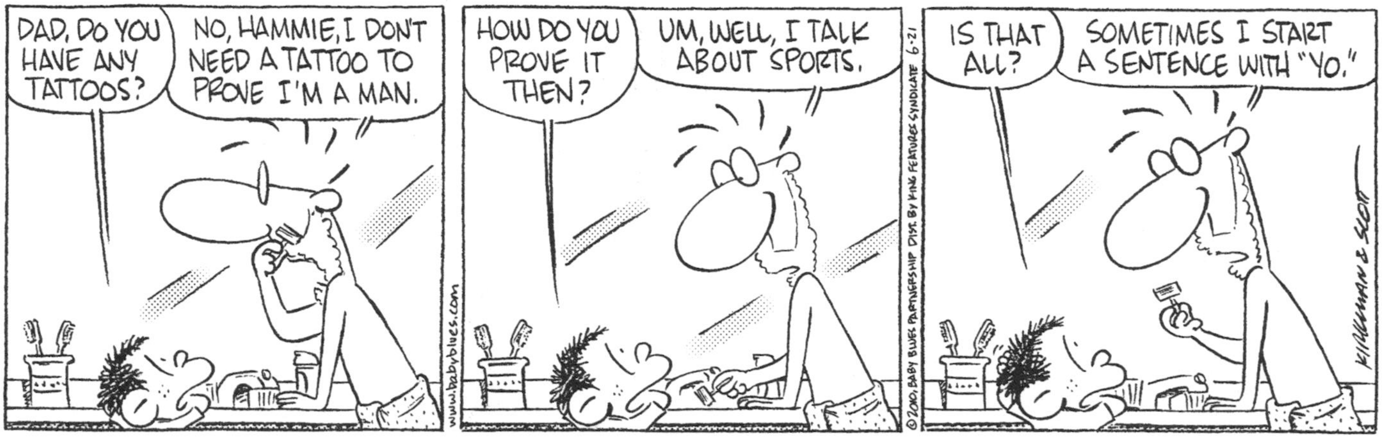
DAD, DO YOU HAVE ANY TATTOOS?
NO, HAMMIE, I DON'T NEED A TATTOO TO PROVE I'M A MAN.
www.babyblues.com
HOW DO YOU PROVE IT THEN?
UM, WELL, I TALK ABOUT SPORTS.
©2010, BABY BLUES PARTNERSHIP DIST. BY KING FEATURES SYNDICATE 6-21
IS THAT ALL?
SOMETIMES I START A SENTENCE WITH "YO."
KIRKMAN & SCOTT

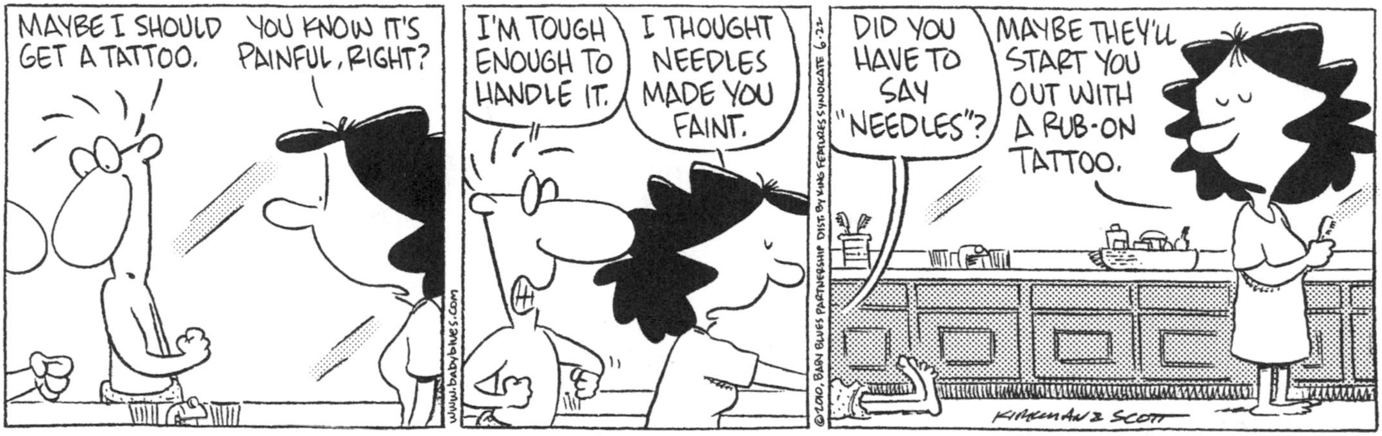
MAYBE I SHOULD GET A TATTOO.
YOU KNOW IT'S PAINFUL, RIGHT?
www.babyblues.com
I'M TOUGH ENOUGH TO HANDLE IT.
I THOUGHT NEEDLES MADE YOU FAINT.
©2010, BABY BLUES PARTNERSHIP DIST. BY KING FEATURES SYNDICATE 6-22
DID YOU HAVE TO SAY "NEEDLES"?
MAYBE THEY'LL START YOU OUT WITH A RUB-ON TATTOO.
KIRKMAN & SCOTT

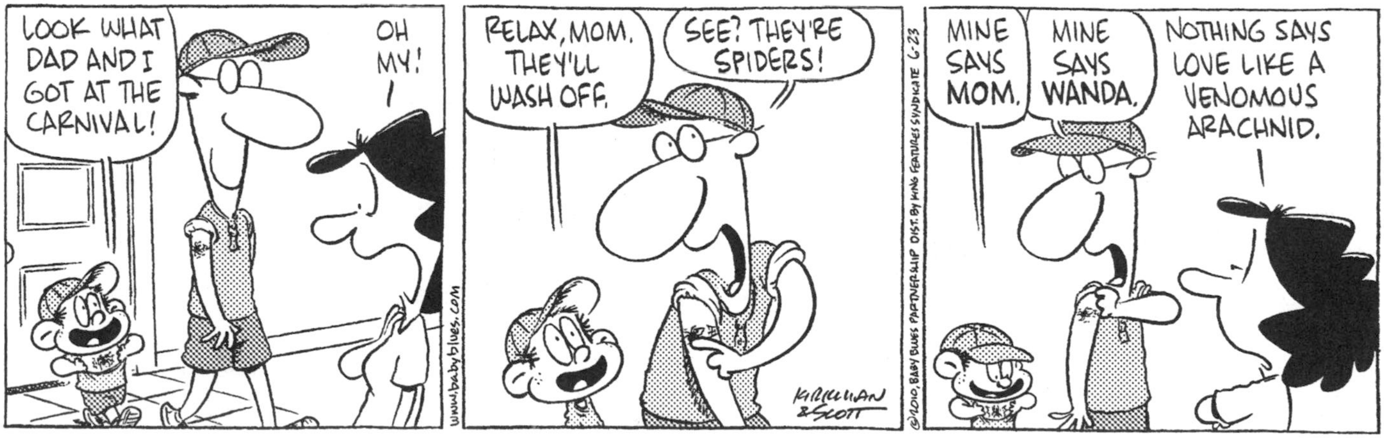
LOOK WHAT DAD AND I GOT AT THE CARNIVAL!
OH MY!
www.babyblues.com
RELAX, MOM. THEY'LL WASH OFF.
SEE? THEY'RE SPIDERS!
KIRKMAN & SCOTT
©2010, BABY BLUES PARTNERSHIP DIST. BY KING FEATURES SYNDICATE 6-23
MINE SAYS **MOM.**
MINE SAYS **WANDA.**
NOTHING SAYS LOVE LIKE A VENOMOUS ARACHNID.

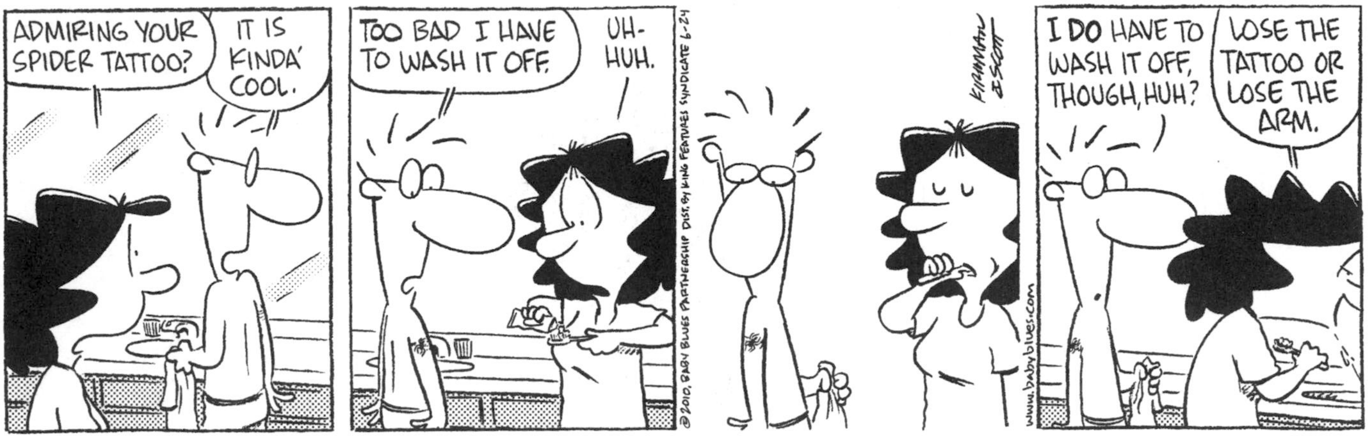
ADMIRING YOUR SPIDER TATTOO?
IT IS KINDA' COOL.
TOO BAD I HAVE TO WASH IT OFF.
UH-HUH.
© 2010, BABY BLUES PARTNERSHIP DIST. BY KING FEATURES SYNDICATE 6-24
KIRKMAN & SCOTT
www.babyblues.com
I DO HAVE TO WASH IT OFF, THOUGH, HUH?
LOSE THE TATTOO OR LOSE THE ARM.

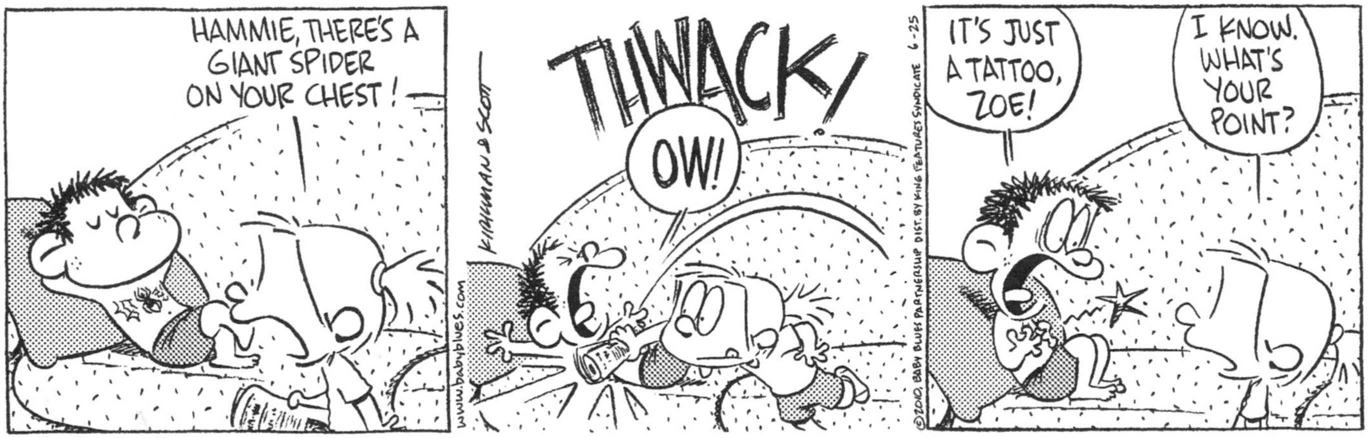
HAMMIE, THERE'S A GIANT SPIDER ON YOUR CHEST!
www.babyblues.com
KIRKMAN & SCOTT
THWACK!
OW!
© 2010, BABY BLUES PARTNERSHIP DIST. BY KING FEATURES SYNDICATE 6-25
IT'S JUST A TATTOO, ZOE!
I KNOW. WHAT'S YOUR POINT?

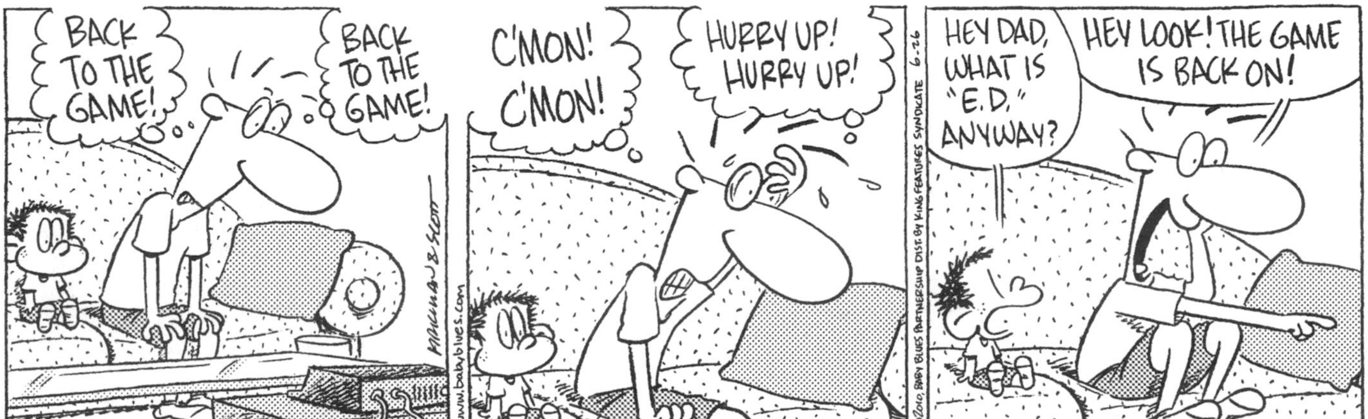
BACK TO THE GAME!
BACK TO THE GAME!
KIRKMAN & SCOTT
www.babyblues.com
C'MON! C'MON!
HURRY UP! HURRY UP!
© 2010, BABY BLUES PARTNERSHIP DIST. BY KING FEATURES SYNDICATE 6-26
HEY DAD, WHAT IS "E.D." ANYWAY?
HEY LOOK! THE GAME IS BACK ON!

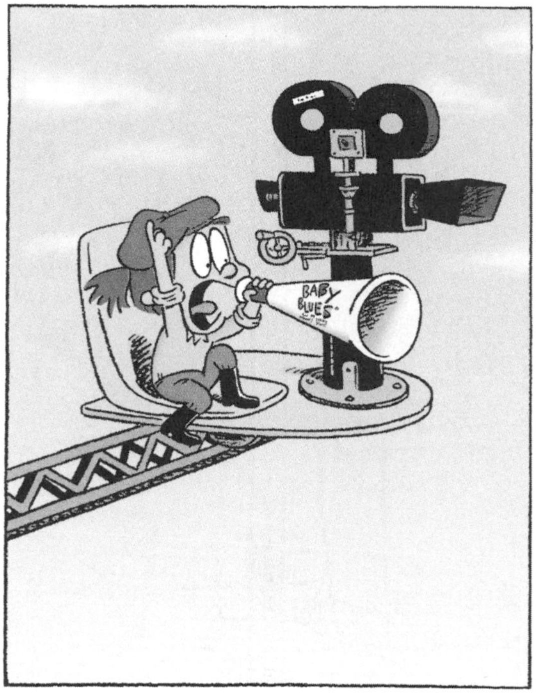
BABY BLUES

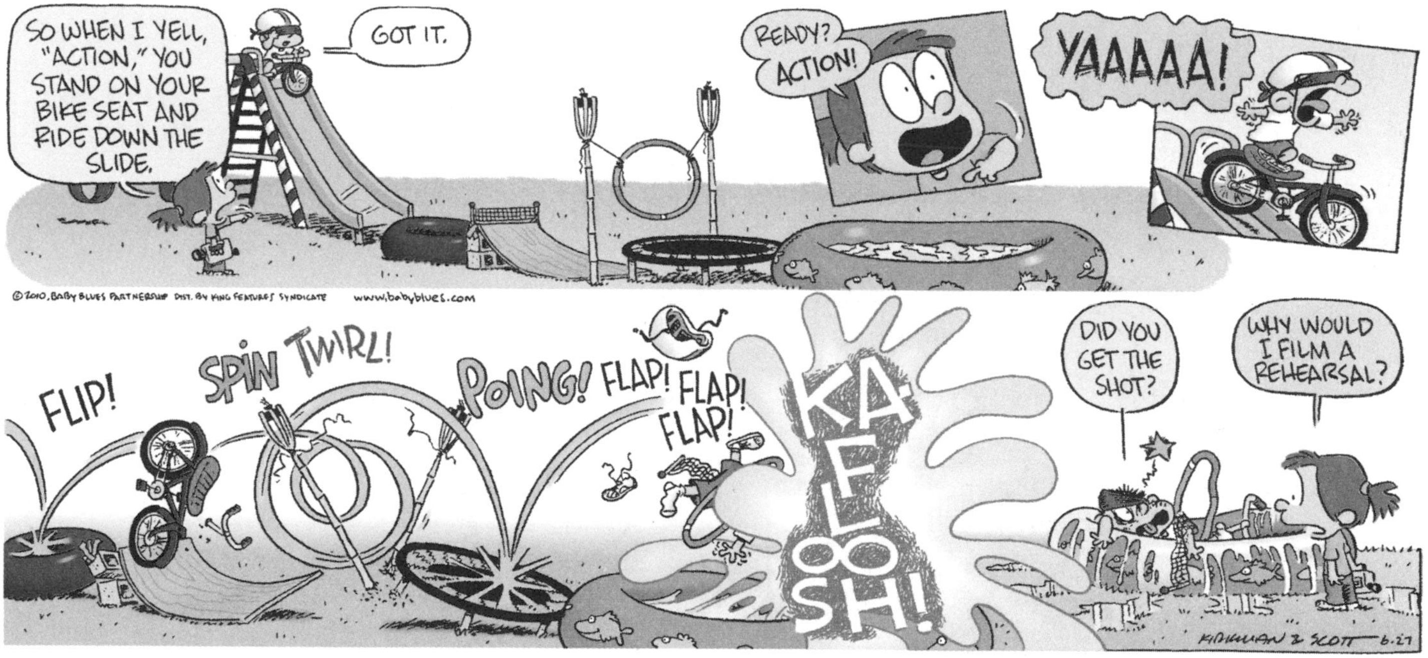
SO WHEN I YELL, "ACTION," YOU STAND ON YOUR BIKE SEAT AND RIDE DOWN THE SLIDE.
GOT IT.
READY?
ACTION!
YAAAAA!
© 2010, BABY BLUES PARTNERSHIP DIST. BY KING FEATURES SYNDICATE
www.babyblues.com
FLIP!
SPIN TWIRL!
POING! FLAP! FLAP! FLAP!
KA-FLOOSH!
DID YOU GET THE SHOT?
WHY WOULD I FILM A REHEARSAL?
KIRKMAN & SCOTT 6-27

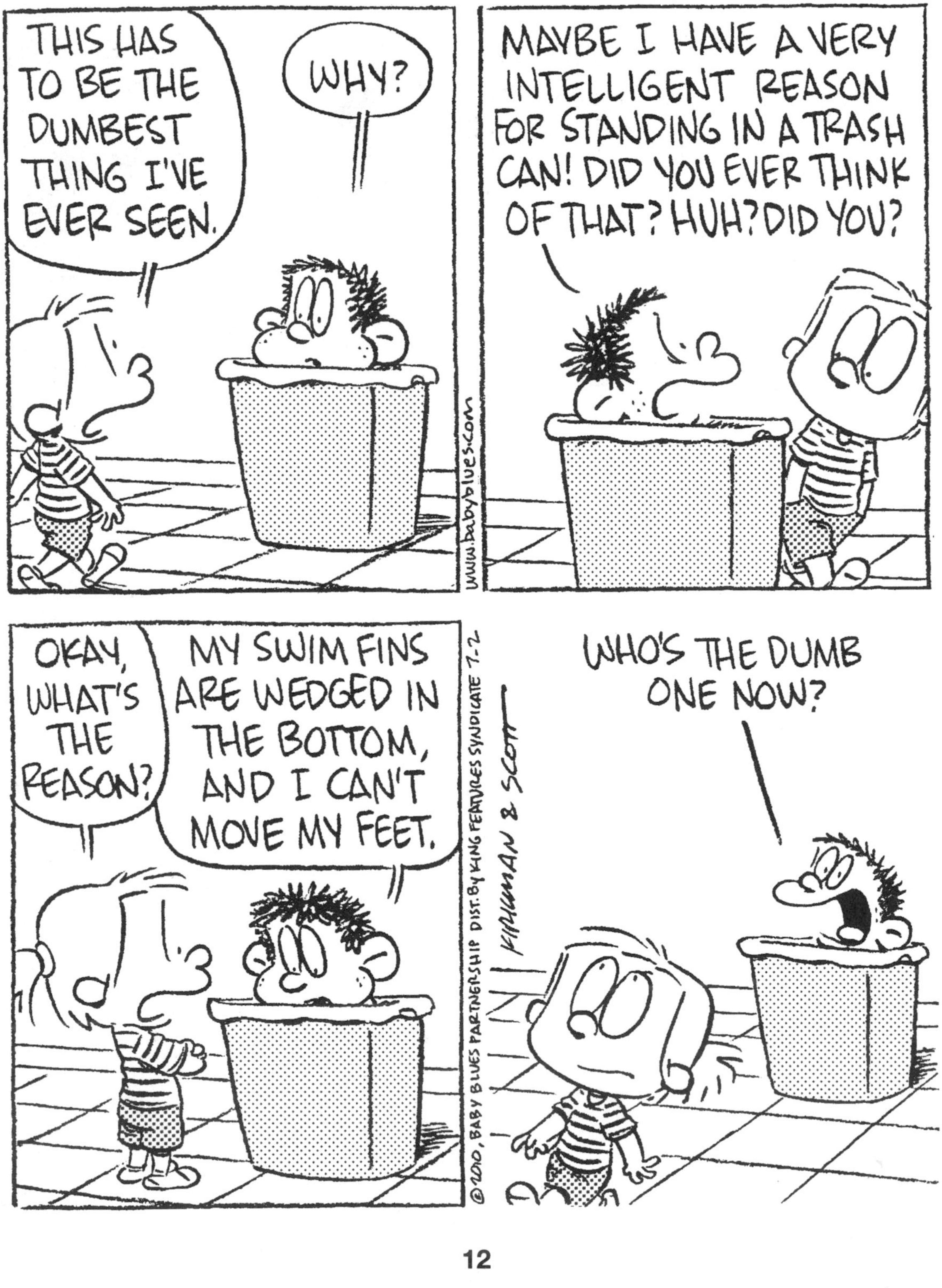
THIS HAS TO BE THE DUMBEST THING I'VE EVER SEEN.
WHY?
MAYBE I HAVE A VERY INTELLIGENT REASON FOR STANDING IN A TRASH CAN! DID YOU EVER THINK OF THAT? HUH? DID YOU?
www.babyblues.com
OKAY, WHAT'S THE REASON?
MY SWIM FINS ARE WEDGED IN THE BOTTOM, AND I CAN'T MOVE MY FEET.
©2010, BABY BLUES PARTNERSHIP DIST. BY KING FEATURES SYNDICATE 7-2
KIRKMAN & SCOTT
WHO'S THE DUMB ONE NOW?

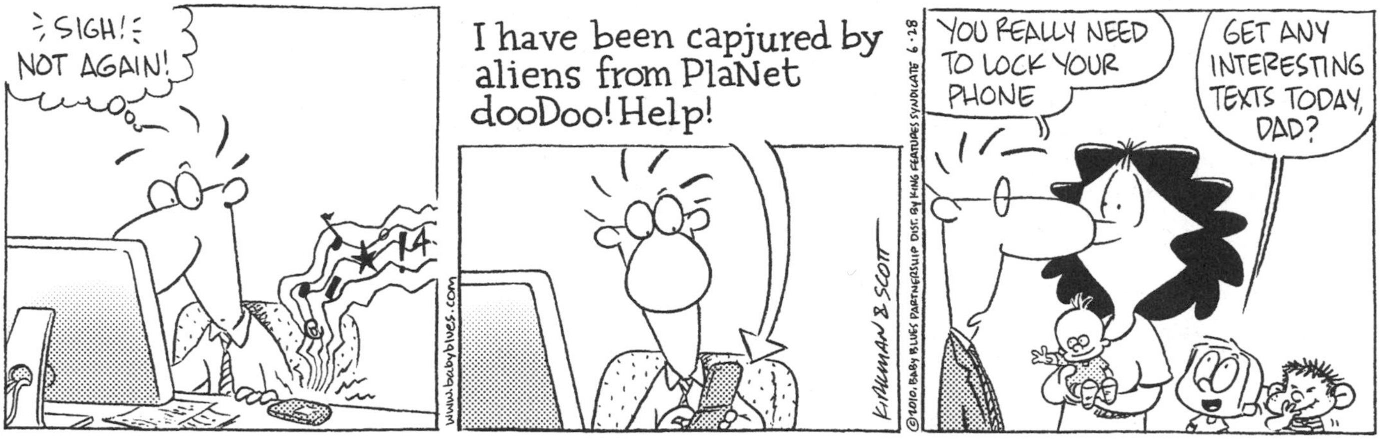
SIGH! NOT AGAIN!
www.babyblues.com
I have been capjured by aliens from PlaNet dooDoo! Help!
KIRKMAN & SCOTT
©2010, BABY BLUES PARTNERSHIP DIST. BY KING FEATURES SYNDICATE 6·28
YOU REALLY NEED TO LOCK YOUR PHONE
GET ANY INTERESTING TEXTS TODAY, DAD?

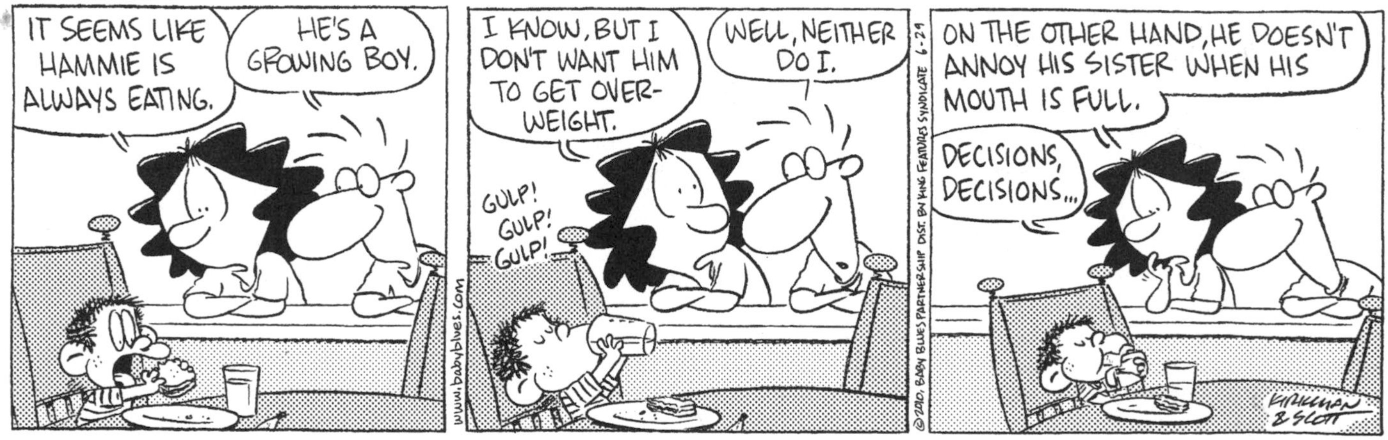
IT SEEMS LIKE HAMMIE IS ALWAYS EATING.
HE'S A GROWING BOY.
www.babyblues.com
I KNOW, BUT I DON'T WANT HIM TO GET OVER-WEIGHT.
WELL, NEITHER DO I.
GULP! GULP! GULP!
©2010, BABY BLUES PARTNERSHIP DIST. BY KING FEATURES SYNDICATE 6·29
ON THE OTHER HAND, HE DOESN'T ANNOY HIS SISTER WHEN HIS MOUTH IS FULL.
DECISIONS, DECISIONS...
KIRKMAN & SCOTT

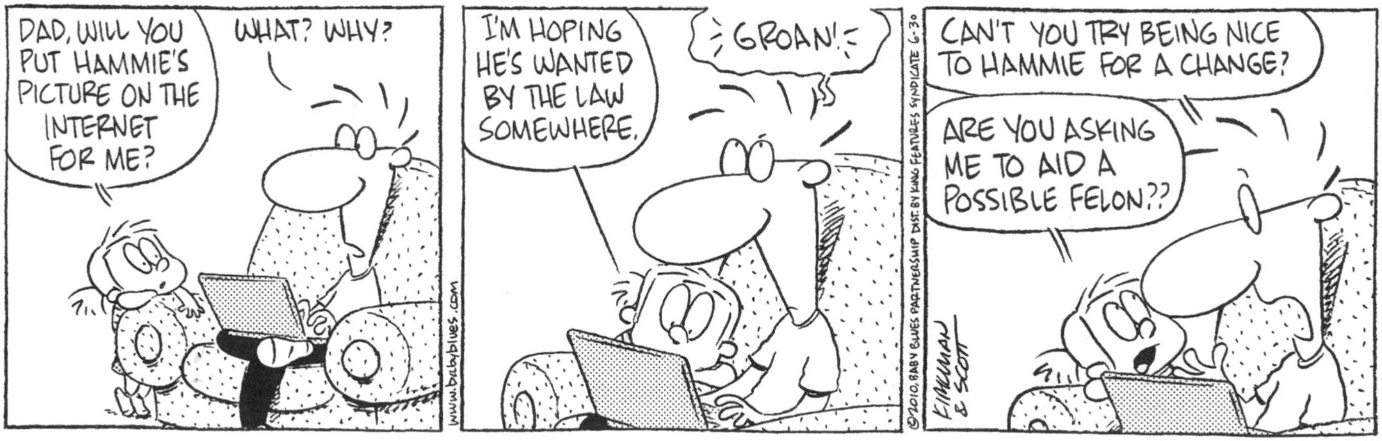
DAD, WILL YOU PUT HAMMIE'S PICTURE ON THE INTERNET FOR ME?
WHAT? WHY?
www.babyblues.com
I'M HOPING HE'S WANTED BY THE LAW SOMEWHERE.
GROAN!
©2010, BABY BLUES PARTNERSHIP DIST. BY KING FEATURES SYNDICATE 6·30
KIRKMAN & SCOTT
CAN'T YOU TRY BEING NICE TO HAMMIE FOR A CHANGE?
ARE YOU ASKING ME TO AID A POSSIBLE FELON??

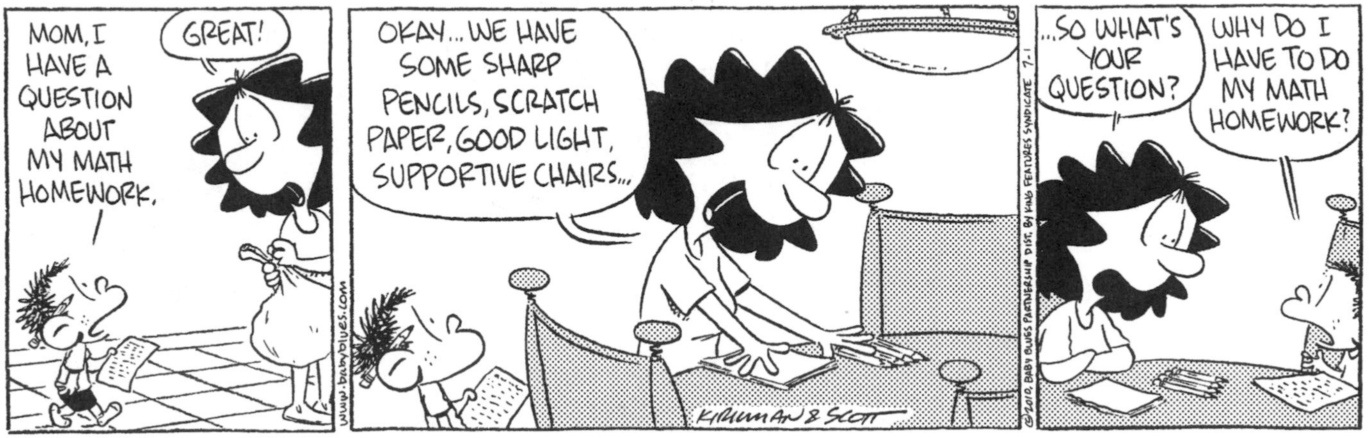
MOM, I HAVE A QUESTION ABOUT MY MATH HOMEWORK.
GREAT!
www.babyblues.com
OKAY... WE HAVE SOME SHARP PENCILS, SCRATCH PAPER, GOOD LIGHT, SUPPORTIVE CHAIRS...
KIRKMAN & SCOTT
©2010, BABY BLUES PARTNERSHIP DIST. BY KING FEATURES SYNDICATE 7-1
...SO WHAT'S YOUR QUESTION?
WHY DO I HAVE TO DO MY MATH HOMEWORK?

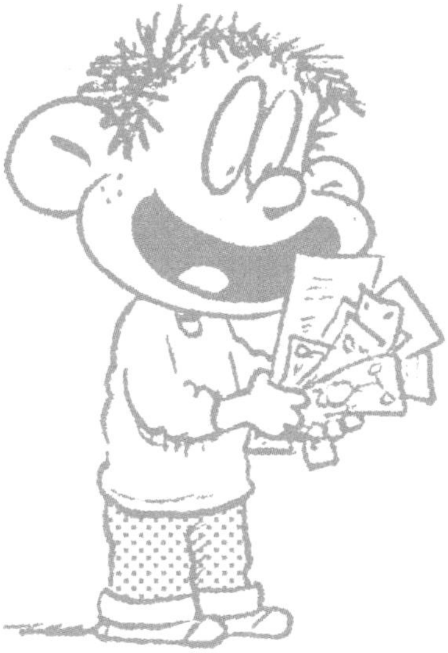

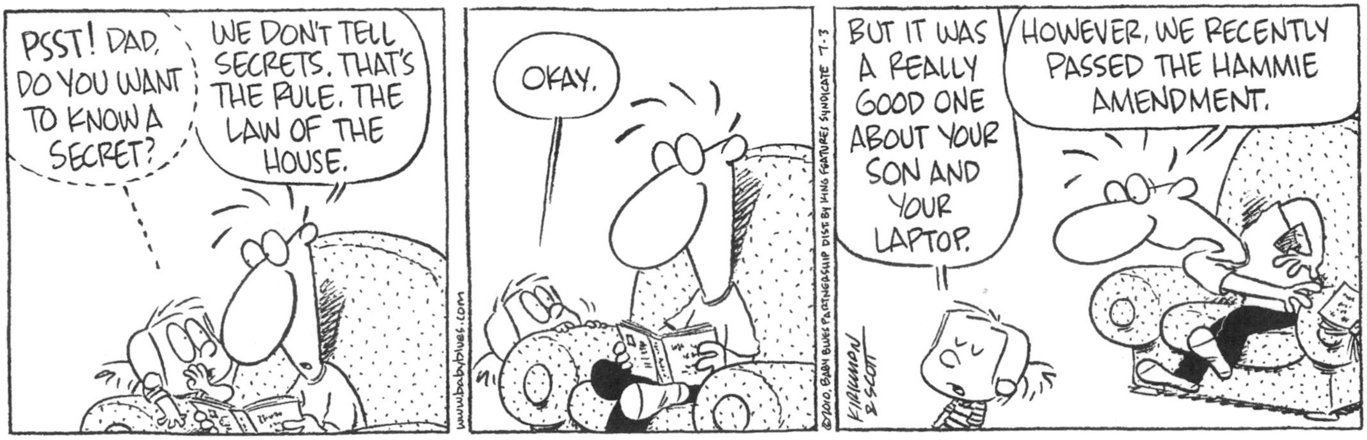
PSST! DAD, DO YOU WANT TO KNOW A SECRET?
WE DON'T TELL SECRETS. THAT'S THE RULE. THE LAW OF THE HOUSE.
www.babyblues.com
OKAY.
©2010, BABY BLUES PARTNERSHIP DIST. BY KING FEATURES SYNDICATE 7-3
KIRKMAN & SCOTT
BUT IT WAS A REALLY GOOD ONE ABOUT YOUR SON AND YOUR LAPTOP.
HOWEVER, WE RECENTLY PASSED THE HAMMIE AMENDMENT.

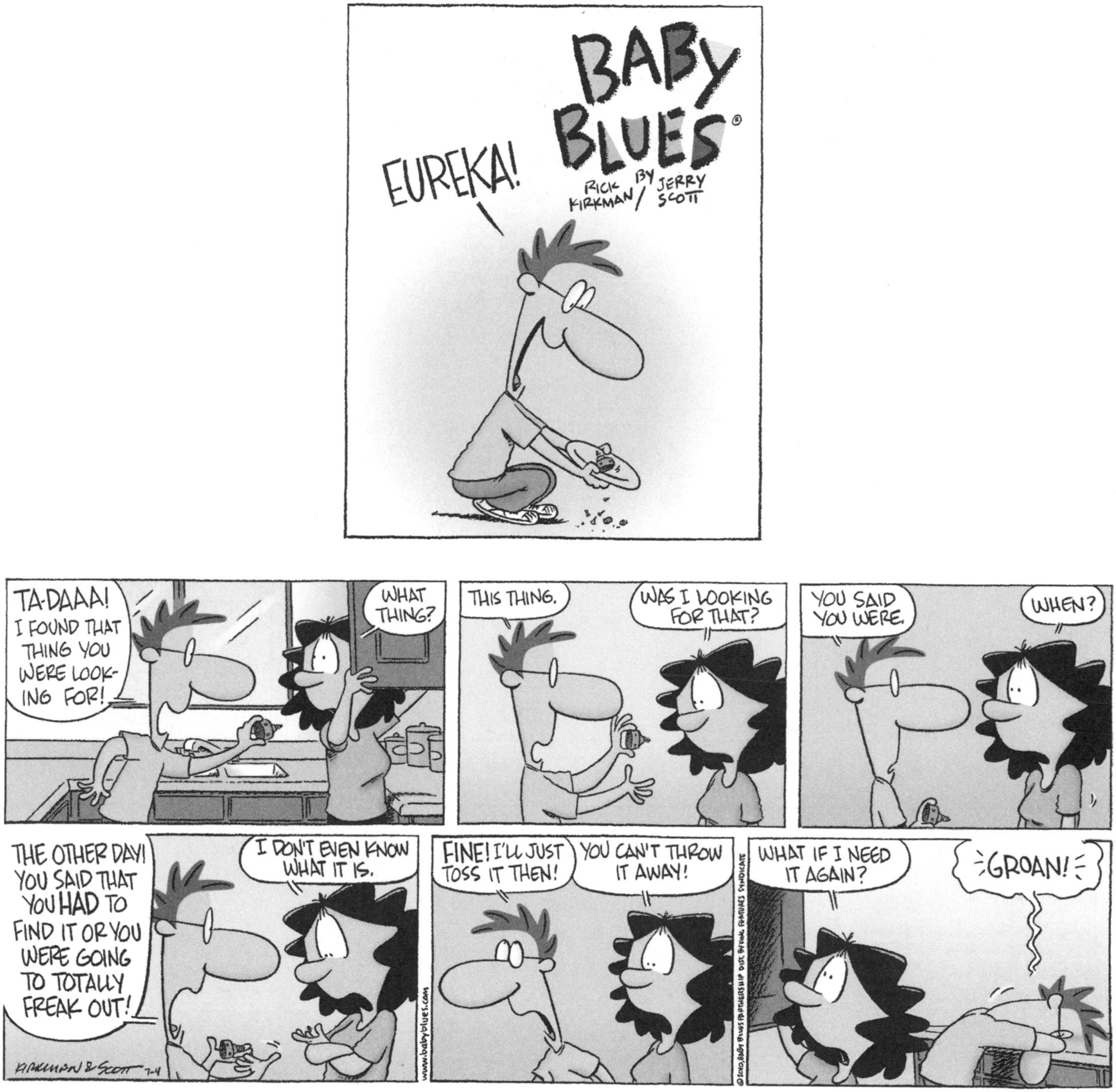
BABY BLUES®
EUREKA!
BY RICK KIRKMAN / JERRY SCOTT
TA-DAAA! I FOUND THAT THING YOU WERE LOOKING FOR!
WHAT THING?
THIS THING.
WAS I LOOKING FOR THAT?
YOU SAID YOU WERE.
WHEN?
THE OTHER DAY! YOU SAID THAT YOU HAD TO FIND IT OR YOU WERE GOING TO TOTALLY FREAK OUT!
I DON'T EVEN KNOW WHAT IT IS.
KIRKMAN & SCOTT 7-4
www.babyblues.com
FINE! I'LL JUST TOSS IT THEN!
YOU CAN'T THROW IT AWAY!
WHAT IF I NEED IT AGAIN?
GROAN!

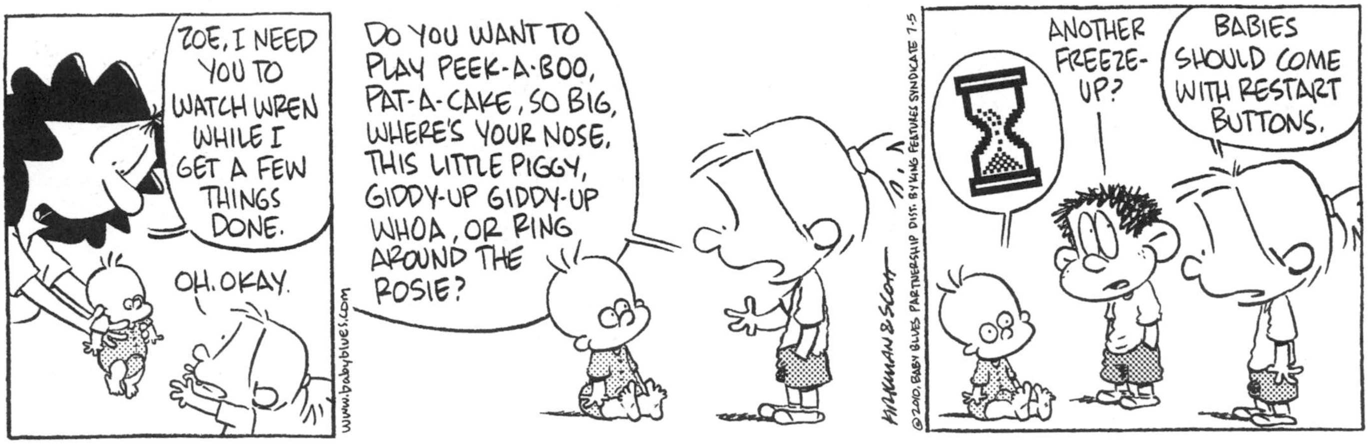

ZOE, I NEED YOU TO WATCH WREN WHILE I GET A FEW THINGS DONE.
OH. OKAY.
www.babyblues.com
DO YOU WANT TO PLAY PEEK-A-BOO, PAT-A-CAKE, SO BIG, WHERE'S YOUR NOSE, THIS LITTLE PIGGY, GIDDY-UP GIDDY-UP WHOA, OR RING AROUND THE ROSIE?
KIRKMAN & SCOTT
©2010, BABY BLUES PARTNERSHIP DIST. BY KING FEATURES SYNDICATE 1-5
ANOTHER FREEZE-UP?
BABIES SHOULD COME WITH RESTART BUTTONS.

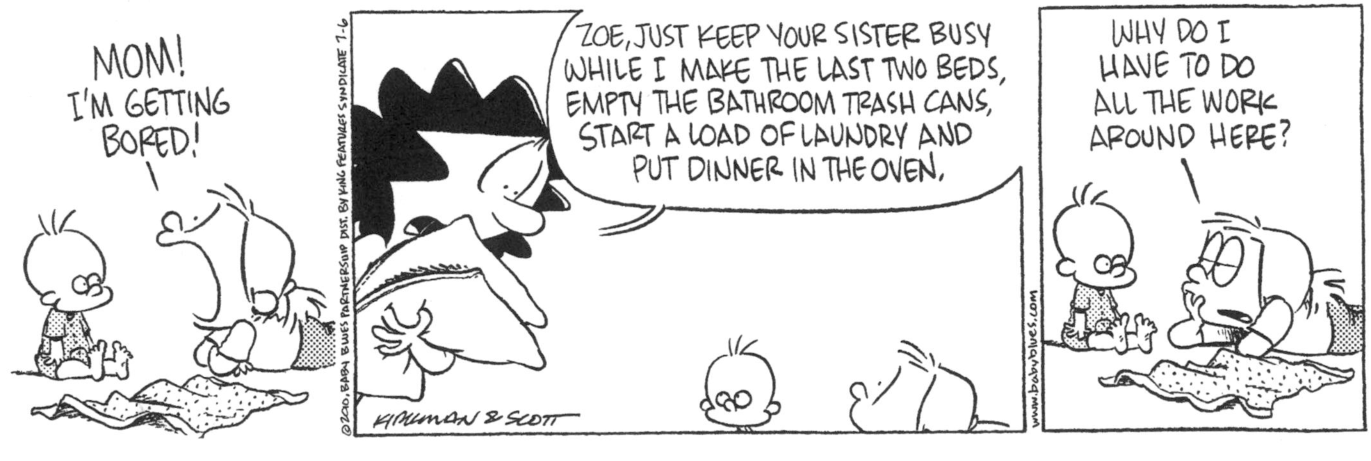

MOM! I'M GETTING BORED!
©2010, BABY BLUES PARTNERSHIP DIST. BY KING FEATURES SYNDICATE 1-6
ZOE, JUST KEEP YOUR SISTER BUSY WHILE I MAKE THE LAST TWO BEDS, EMPTY THE BATHROOM TRASH CANS, START A LOAD OF LAUNDRY AND PUT DINNER IN THE OVEN.
KIRKMAN & SCOTT
www.babyblues.com
WHY DO I HAVE TO DO ALL THE WORK AROUND HERE?

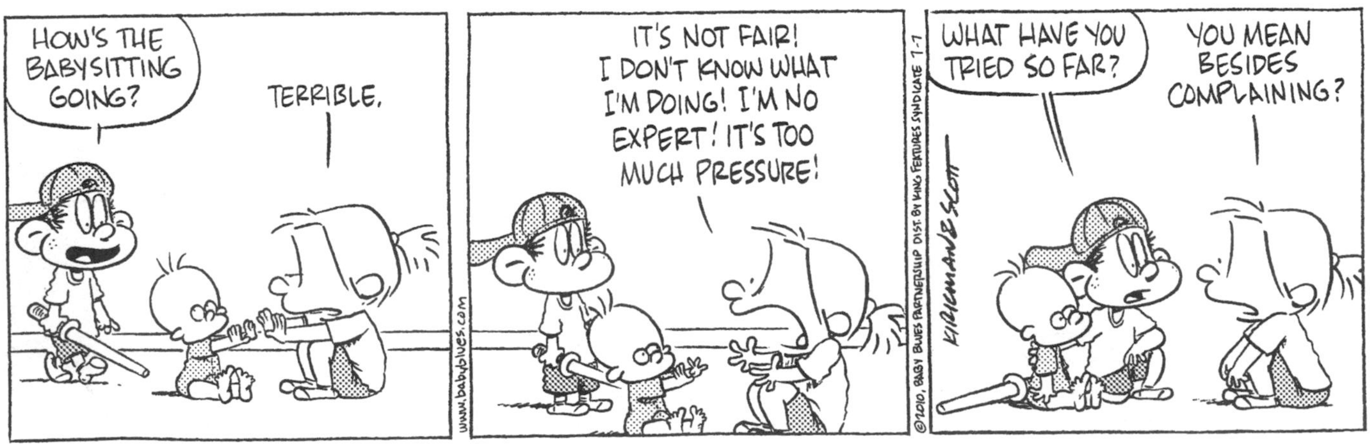

HOW'S THE BABYSITTING GOING?
TERRIBLE.
www.babyblues.com
IT'S NOT FAIR! I DON'T KNOW WHAT I'M DOING! I'M NO EXPERT! IT'S TOO MUCH PRESSURE!
©2010, BABY BLUES PARTNERSHIP DIST. BY KING FEATURES SYNDICATE 1-7
KIRKMAN & SCOTT
WHAT HAVE YOU TRIED SO FAR?
YOU MEAN BESIDES COMPLAINING?

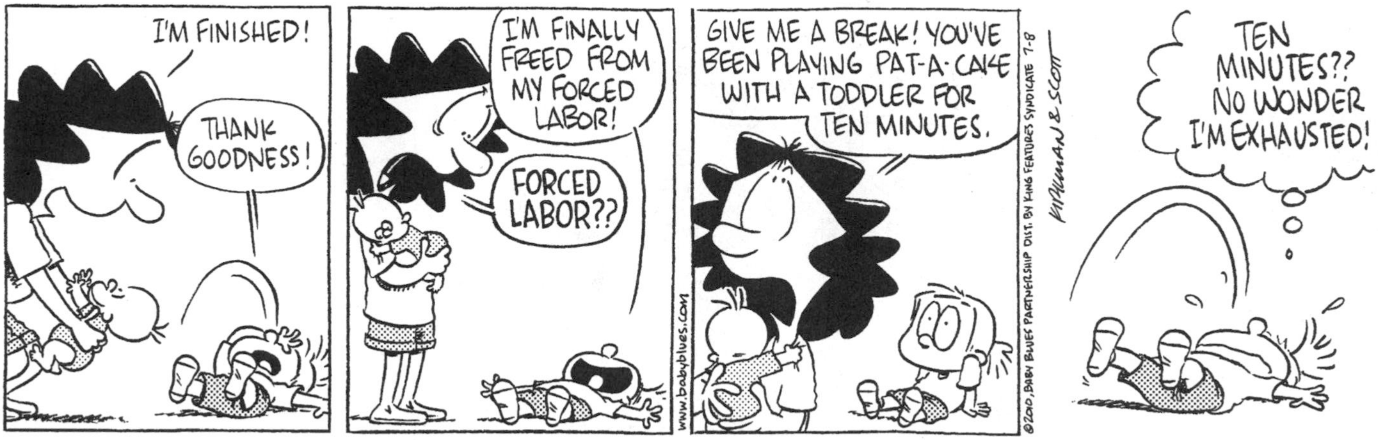
I'M FINISHED!
THANK GOODNESS!
I'M FINALLY FREED FROM MY FORCED LABOR!
FORCED LABOR??
www.babyblues.com
GIVE ME A BREAK! YOU'VE BEEN PLAYING PAT-A-CAKE WITH A TODDLER FOR TEN MINUTES.
©2010, BABY BLUES PARTNERSHIP DIST. BY KING FEATURES SYNDICATE 7-8
KIRKMAN & SCOTT
TEN MINUTES?? NO WONDER I'M EXHAUSTED!

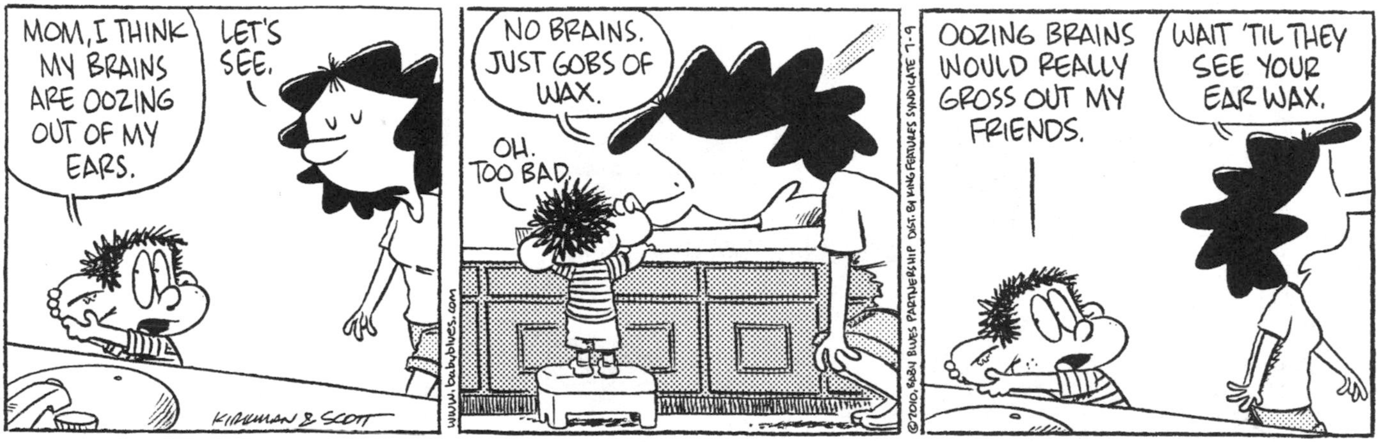
MOM, I THINK MY BRAINS ARE OOZING OUT OF MY EARS.
LET'S SEE.
KIRKMAN & SCOTT
www.babyblues.com
NO BRAINS. JUST GOBS OF WAX.
OH. TOO BAD.
©2010, BABY BLUES PARTNERSHIP DIST. BY KING FEATURES SYNDICATE 7-9
OOZING BRAINS WOULD REALLY GROSS OUT MY FRIENDS.
WAIT 'TIL THEY SEE YOUR EAR WAX.

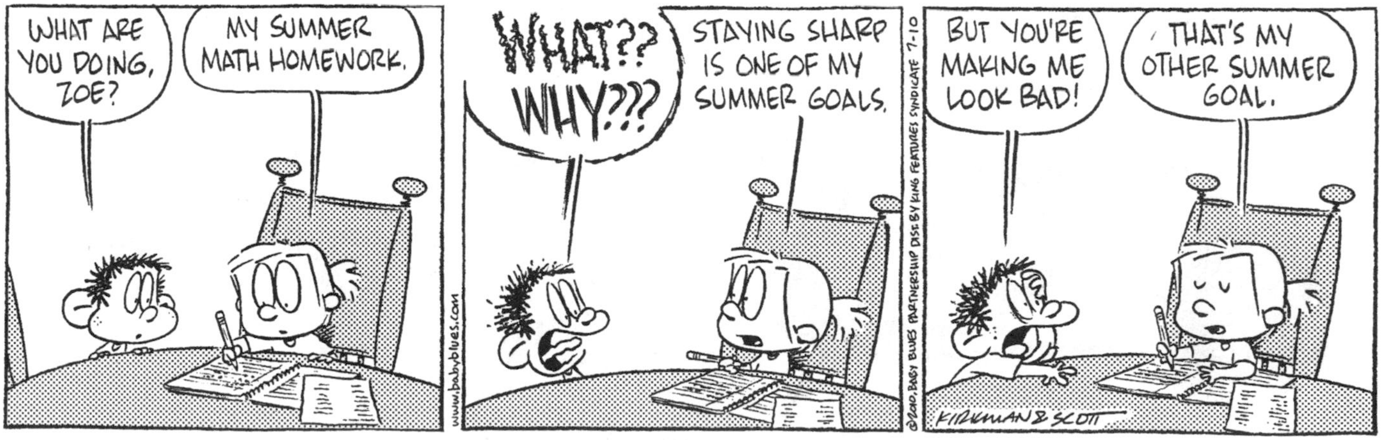
WHAT ARE YOU DOING, ZOE?
MY SUMMER MATH HOMEWORK.
www.babyblues.com
WHAT?? WHY???
STAYING SHARP IS ONE OF MY SUMMER GOALS.
©2010, BABY BLUES PARTNERSHIP DIST. BY KING FEATURES SYNDICATE 7-10
BUT YOU'RE MAKING ME LOOK BAD!
THAT'S MY OTHER SUMMER GOAL.
KIRKMAN & SCOTT

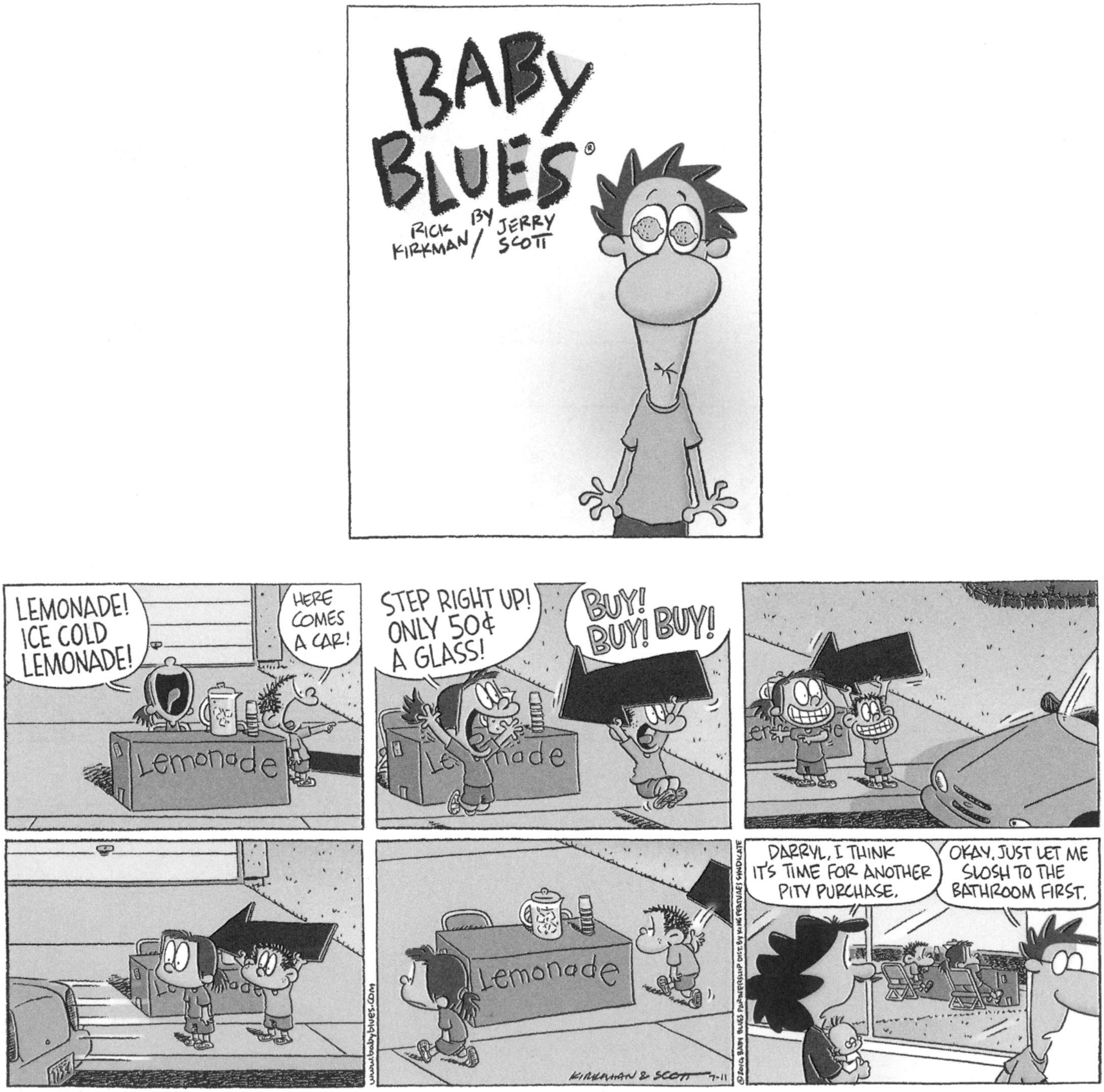
BABY BLUES®
BY RICK KIRKMAN / JERRY SCOTT
LEMONADE! ICE COLD LEMONADE!
HERE COMES A CAR!
Lemonade
STEP RIGHT UP! ONLY 50¢ A GLASS!
BUY! BUY! BUY!
www.babyblues.com
KIRKMAN & SCOTT 7-11
©2010, BABY BLUES PARTNERSHIP DIST. BY KING FEATURES SYNDICATE
DARRYL, I THINK IT'S TIME FOR ANOTHER PITY PURCHASE.
OKAY. JUST LET ME SLOSH TO THE BATHROOM FIRST.

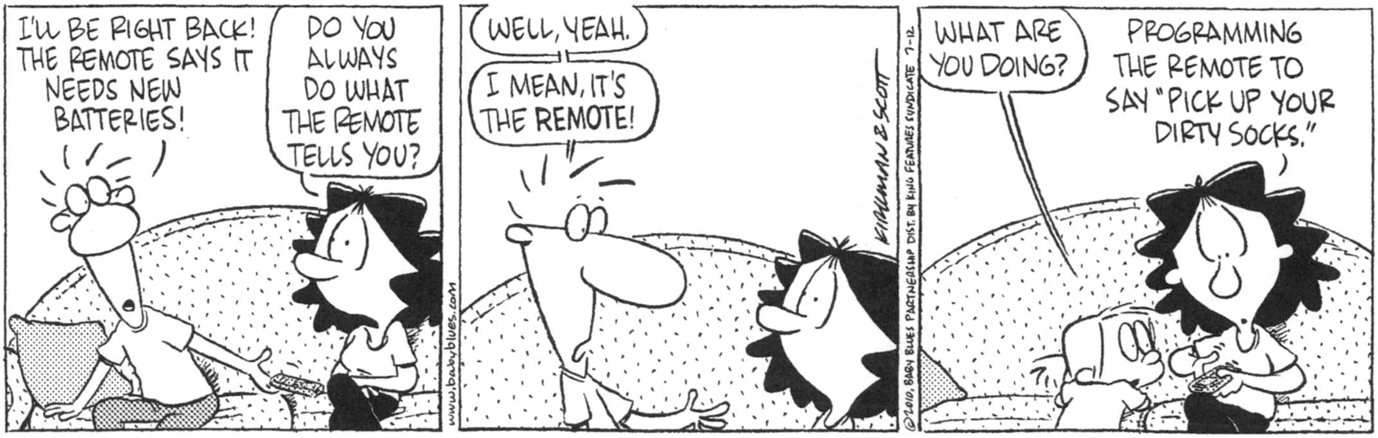
I'LL BE RIGHT BACK! THE REMOTE SAYS IT NEEDS NEW BATTERIES!
DO YOU ALWAYS DO WHAT THE REMOTE TELLS YOU?
WELL, YEAH.
I MEAN, IT'S THE REMOTE!
WHAT ARE YOU DOING?
PROGRAMMING THE REMOTE TO SAY "PICK UP YOUR DIRTY SOCKS."
www.babyblues.com
KIRKMAN & SCOTT
© 2010, BABY BLUES PARTNERSHIP DIST. BY KING FEATURES SYNDICATE 7-12

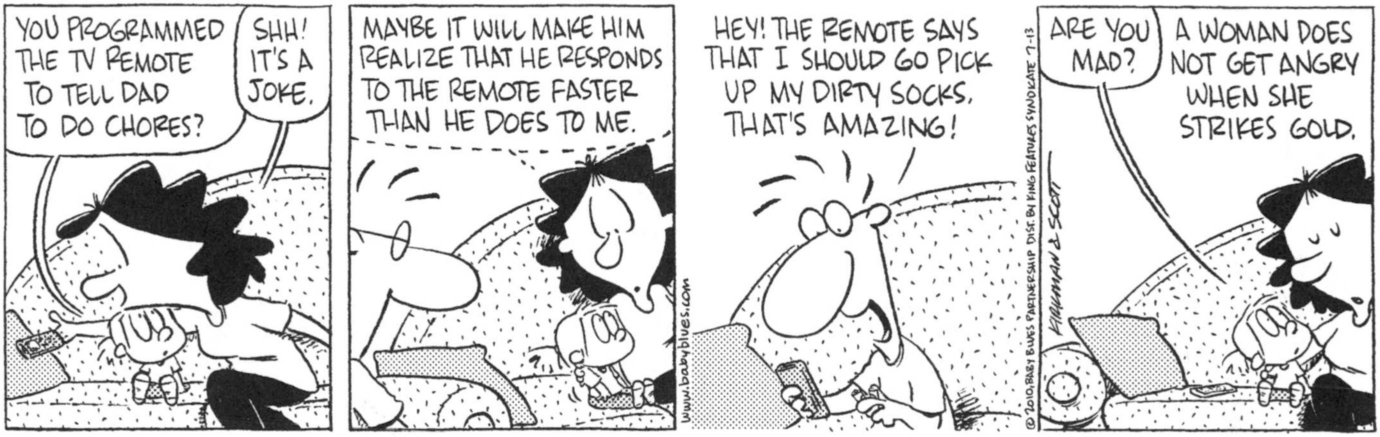
YOU PROGRAMMED THE TV REMOTE TO TELL DAD TO DO CHORES?
SHH! IT'S A JOKE.
MAYBE IT WILL MAKE HIM REALIZE THAT HE RESPONDS TO THE REMOTE FASTER THAN HE DOES TO ME.
HEY! THE REMOTE SAYS THAT I SHOULD GO PICK UP MY DIRTY SOCKS. THAT'S AMAZING!
ARE YOU MAD?
A WOMAN DOES NOT GET ANGRY WHEN SHE STRIKES GOLD.
www.babyblues.com
KIRKMAN & SCOTT
© 2010, BABY BLUES PARTNERSHIP DIST. BY KING FEATURES SYNDICATE 7-13

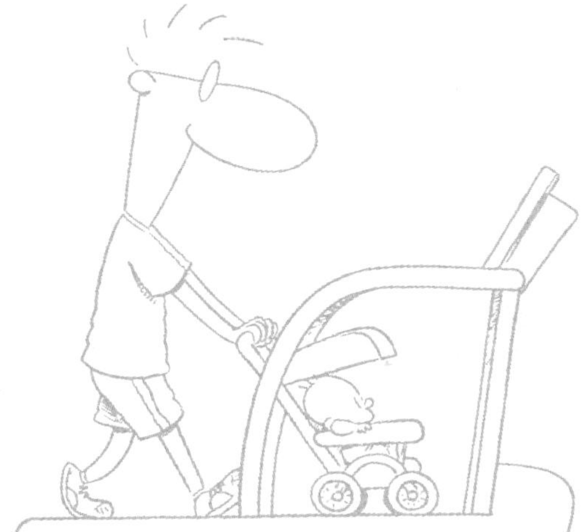

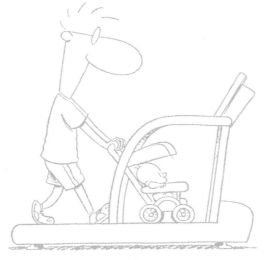

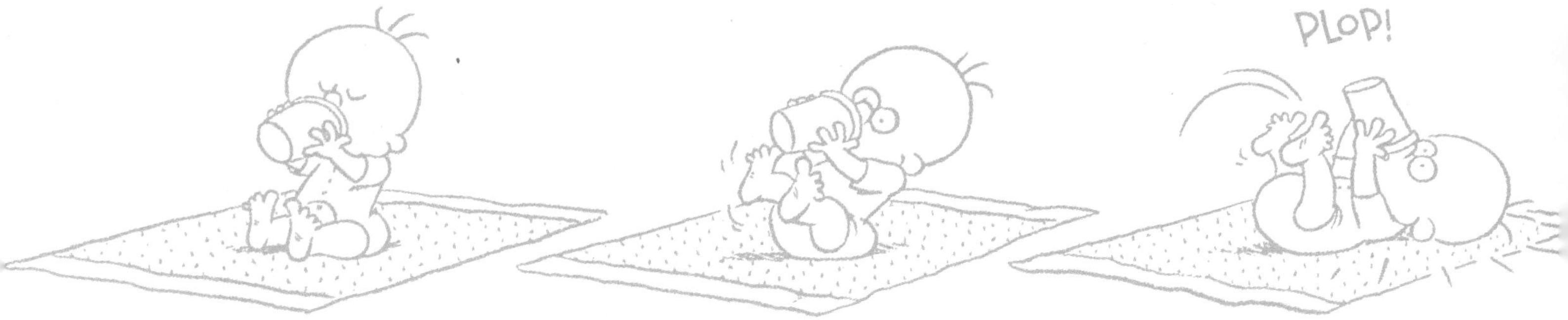
PLOP!

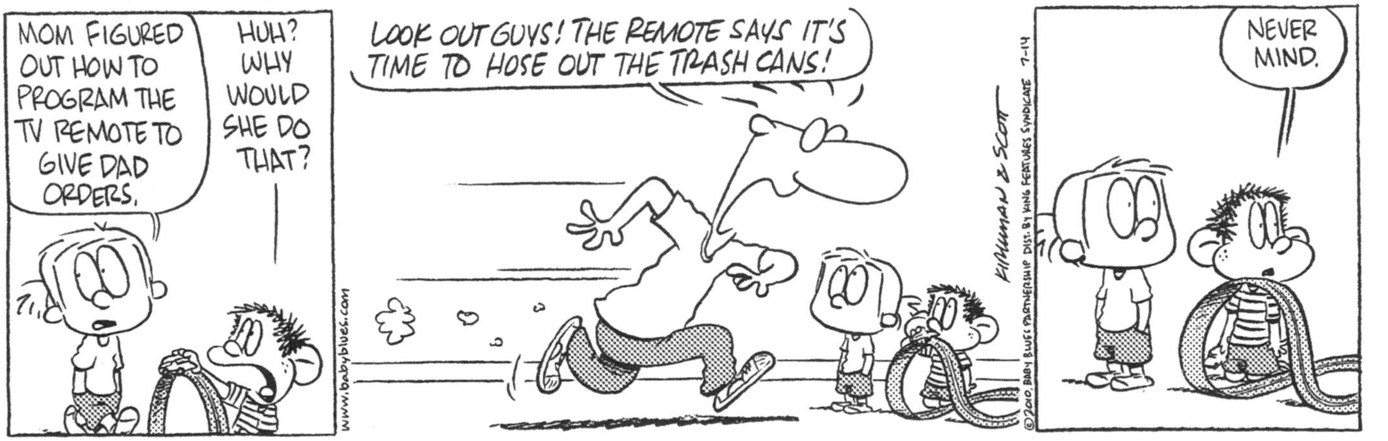
MOM FIGURED OUT HOW TO PROGRAM THE TV REMOTE TO GIVE DAD ORDERS.
HUH? WHY WOULD SHE DO THAT?
www.babyblues.com
LOOK OUT GUYS! THE REMOTE SAYS IT'S TIME TO HOSE OUT THE TRASH CANS!
KIRKMAN & SCOTT
7-14
©2010, BABY BLUES PARTNERSHIP DIST. BY KING FEATURES SYNDICATE
NEVER MIND.

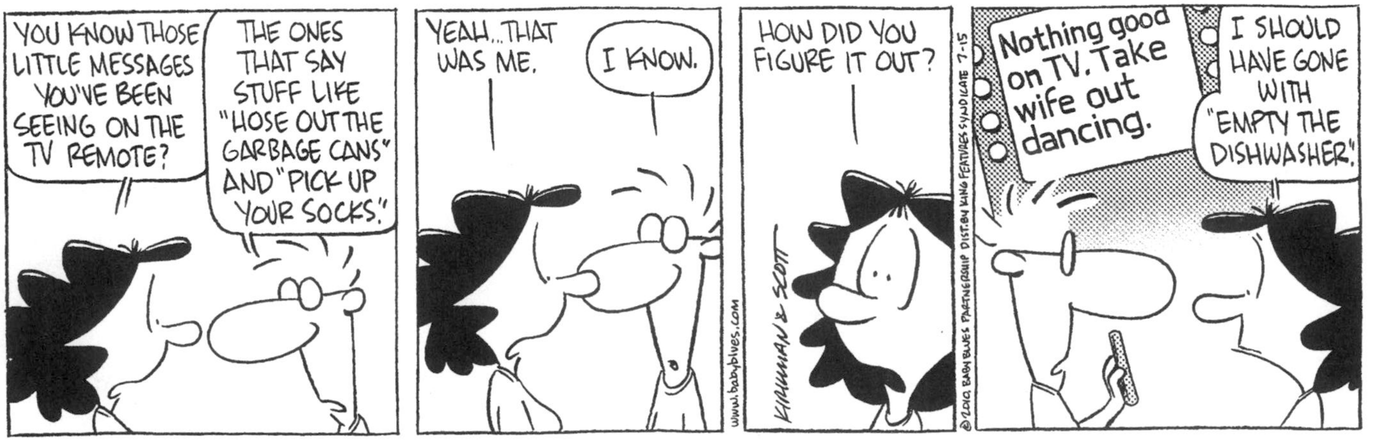
YOU KNOW THOSE LITTLE MESSAGES YOU'VE BEEN SEEING ON THE TV REMOTE?
THE ONES THAT SAY STUFF LIKE "HOSE OUT THE GARBAGE CANS" AND "PICK UP YOUR SOCKS."
YEAH...THAT WAS ME.
I KNOW.
www.babyblues.com
HOW DID YOU FIGURE IT OUT?
KIRKMAN & SCOTT
7-15
©2010, BABY BLUES PARTNERSHIP DIST. BY KING FEATURES SYNDICATE
Nothing good on TV. Take wife out dancing.
I SHOULD HAVE GONE WITH "EMPTY THE DISHWASHER."

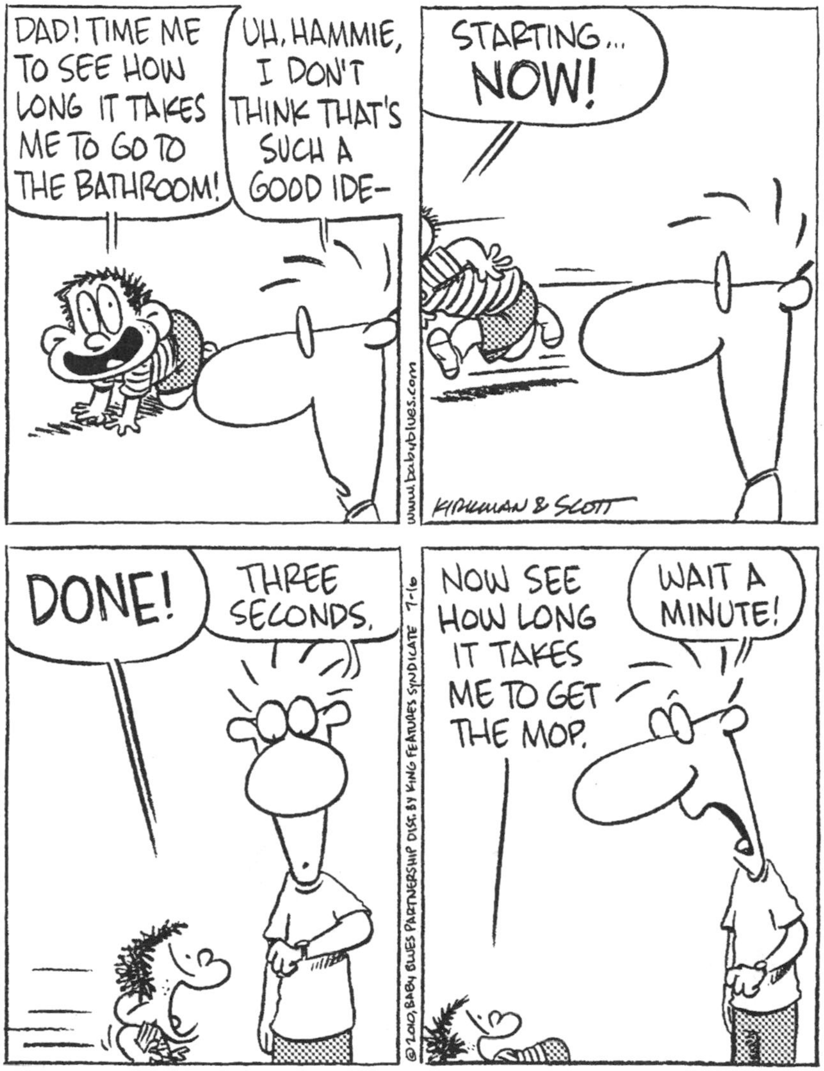
DAD! TIME ME TO SEE HOW LONG IT TAKES ME TO GO TO THE BATHROOM!
UH, HAMMIE, I DON'T THINK THAT'S SUCH A GOOD IDE-
STARTING... NOW!
www.babyblues.com
KIRKMAN & SCOTT
DONE!
THREE SECONDS.
NOW SEE HOW LONG IT TAKES ME TO GET THE MOP.
WAIT A MINUTE!
© 2010, BABY BLUES PARTNERSHIP DIST. BY KING FEATURES SYNDICATE 7-16

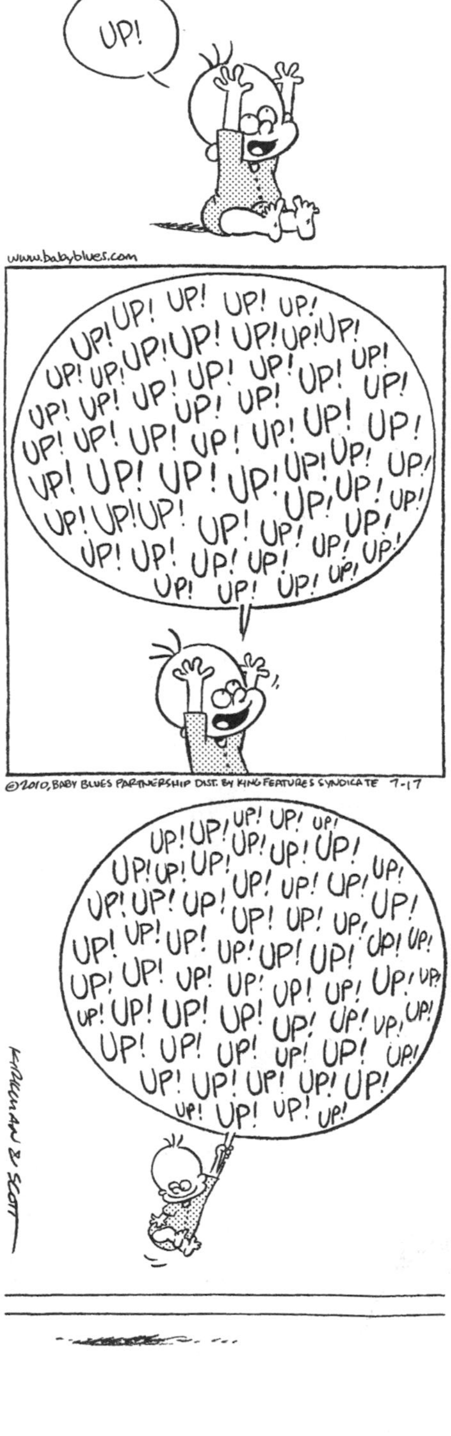
UP!
www.babyblues.com
UP! UP! UP! UP! UP!
UP! UP! UP! UP! UP! UP! UP!
UP! UP! UP! UP! UP! UP! UP! UP!
UP! UP! UP! UP! UP! UP! UP! UP!
UP! UP! UP! UP! UP! UP! UP! UP!
UP! UP! UP! UP! UP! UP! UP! UP!
UP! UP! UP! UP! UP! UP! UP! UP!
UP! UP! UP! UP! UP! UP! UP!
UP! UP! UP! UP!
© 2010, BABY BLUES PARTNERSHIP DIST. BY KING FEATURES SYNDICATE 7-17
UP! UP! UP! UP! UP!
UP! UP! UP! UP! UP! UP! UP!
UP! UP! UP! UP! UP! UP! UP!
UP! UP! UP! UP! UP! UP! UP!
UP! UP! UP! UP! UP! UP! UP! UP!
UP! UP! UP! UP! UP! UP! UP! UP!
UP! UP! UP! UP! UP! UP! UP! UP!
UP! UP! UP! UP! UP! UP!
UP! UP! UP! UP! UP!
UP! UP! UP! UP!
KIRKMAN & SCOTT

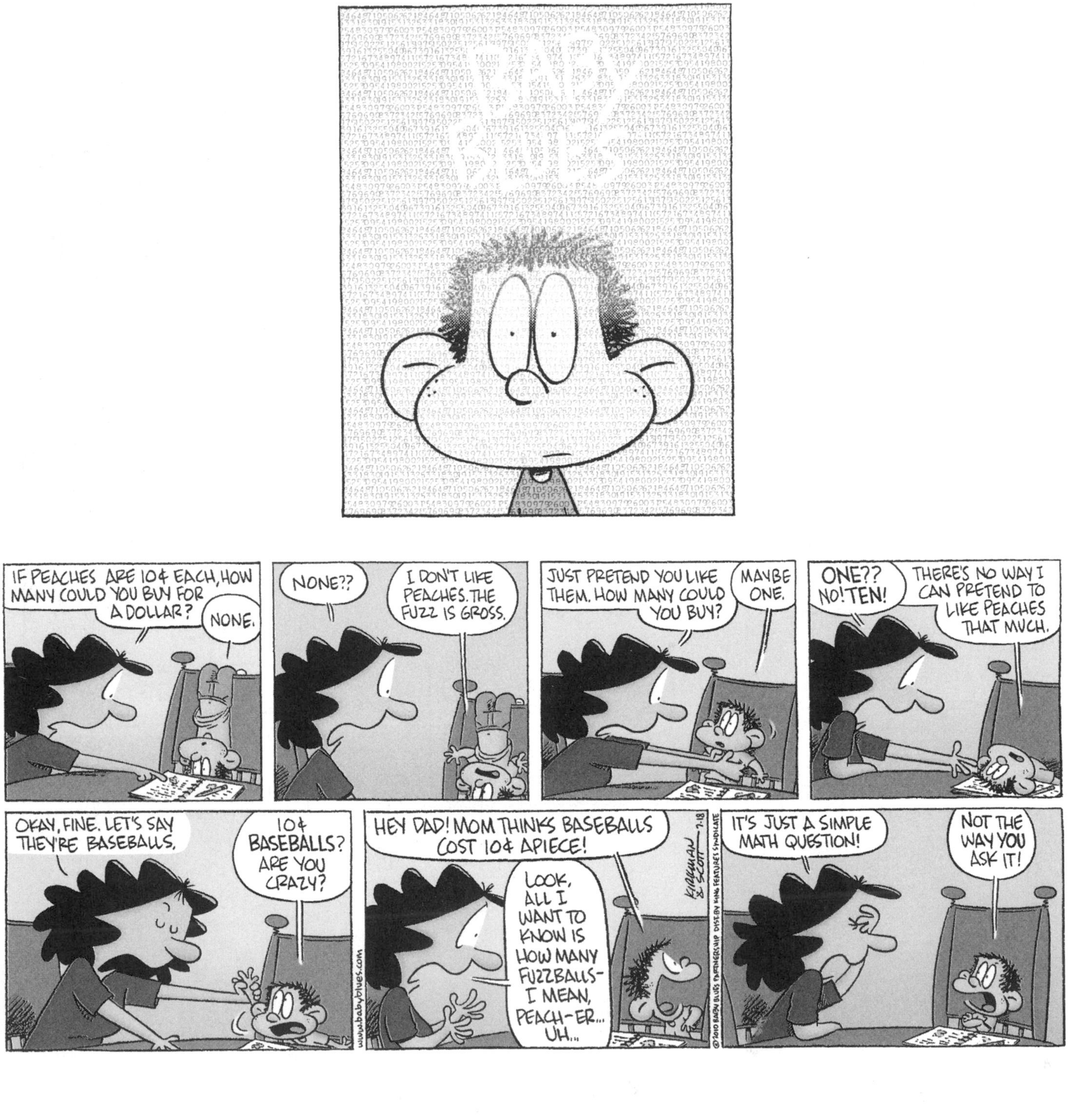
IF PEACHES ARE 10¢ EACH, HOW MANY COULD YOU BUY FOR A DOLLAR?
NONE.
NONE??
I DON'T LIKE PEACHES. THE FUZZ IS GROSS.
JUST PRETEND YOU LIKE THEM. HOW MANY COULD YOU BUY?
MAYBE ONE.
ONE?? NO! TEN!
THERE'S NO WAY I CAN PRETEND TO LIKE PEACHES THAT MUCH.
OKAY, FINE. LET'S SAY THEY'RE BASEBALLS.
10¢ BASEBALLS? ARE YOU CRAZY?
www.babyblues.com
HEY DAD! MOM THINKS BASEBALLS COST 10¢ APIECE!
LOOK, ALL I WANT TO KNOW IS HOW MANY FUZZBALLS- I MEAN, PEACH-ER... UH...
KIRKMAN & SCOTT
7-18
©2010 BABY BLUES PARTNERSHIP DIST. BY KING FEATURES SYNDICATE
IT'S JUST A SIMPLE MATH QUESTION!
NOT THE WAY YOU ASK IT!

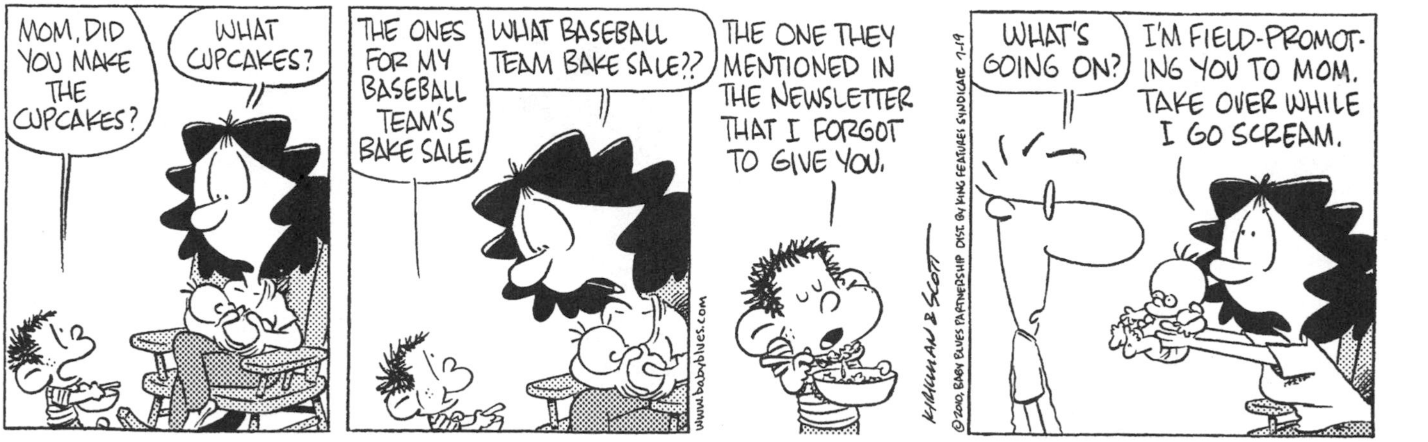
MOM, DID YOU MAKE THE CUPCAKES?
WHAT CUPCAKES?
THE ONES FOR MY BASEBALL TEAM'S BAKE SALE.
WHAT BASEBALL TEAM BAKE SALE??
www.babyblues.com
THE ONE THEY MENTIONED IN THE NEWSLETTER THAT I FORGOT TO GIVE YOU.
KIRKMAN & SCOTT
©2010, BABY BLUES PARTNERSHIP DIST. BY KING FEATURES SYNDICATE 7-19
WHAT'S GOING ON?
I'M FIELD-PROMOTING YOU TO MOM. TAKE OVER WHILE I GO SCREAM.

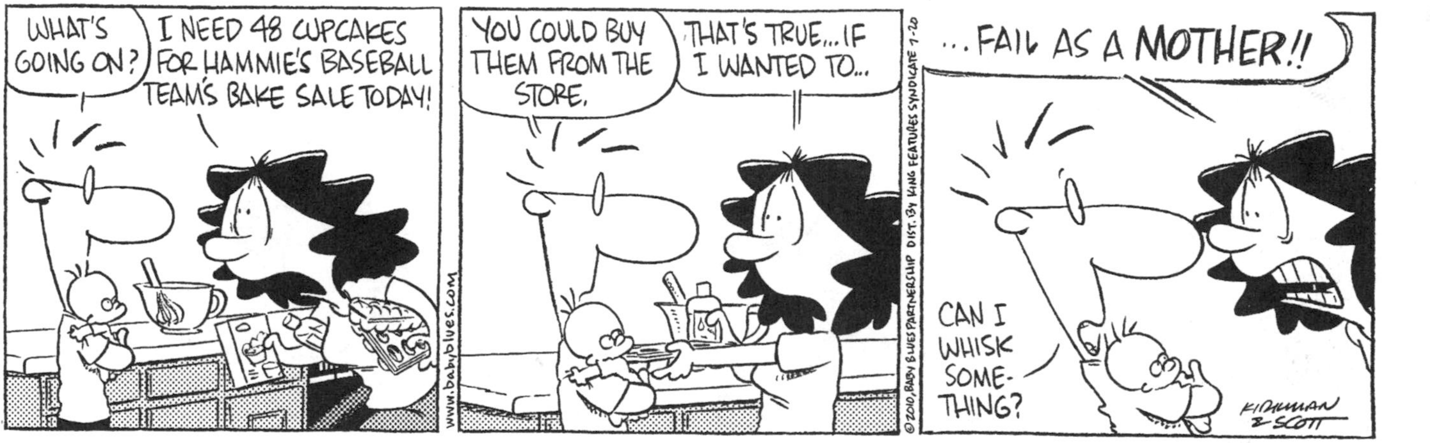
WHAT'S GOING ON?
I NEED 48 CUPCAKES FOR HAMMIE'S BASEBALL TEAM'S BAKE SALE TODAY!
www.babyblues.com
YOU COULD BUY THEM FROM THE STORE.
THAT'S TRUE... IF I WANTED TO...
©2010, BABY BLUES PARTNERSHIP DIST. BY KING FEATURES SYNDICATE 7-20
... FAIL AS A MOTHER!!
CAN I WHISK SOMETHING?
KIRKMAN & SCOTT

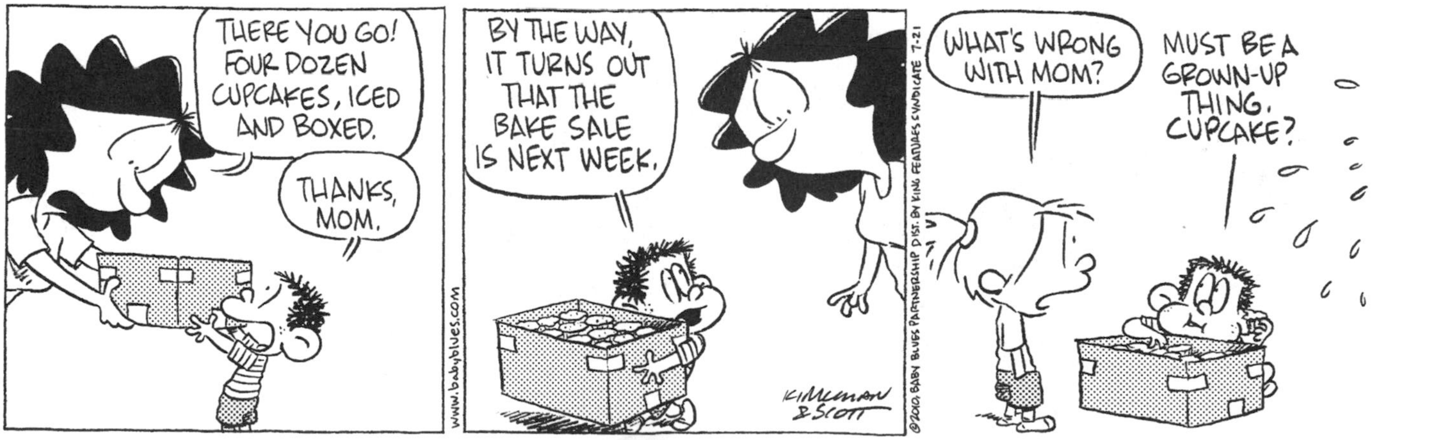
THERE YOU GO! FOUR DOZEN CUPCAKES, ICED AND BOXED.
THANKS, MOM.
www.babyblues.com
BY THE WAY, IT TURNS OUT THAT THE BAKE SALE IS NEXT WEEK.
KIRKMAN & SCOTT
©2010, BABY BLUES PARTNERSHIP DIST. BY KING FEATURES SYNDICATE 7-21
WHAT'S WRONG WITH MOM?
MUST BE A GROWN-UP THING. CUPCAKE?

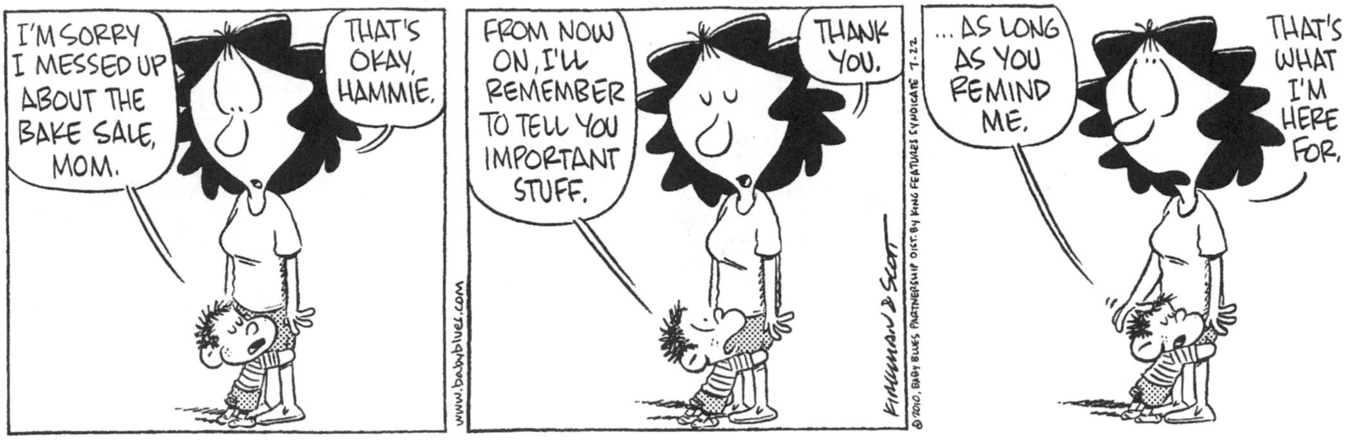
I'M SORRY I MESSED UP ABOUT THE BAKE SALE, MOM.
THAT'S OKAY, HAMMIE.
www.babyblues.com
FROM NOW ON, I'LL REMEMBER TO TELL YOU IMPORTANT STUFF.
THANK YOU.
KIRKMAN & SCOTT
©2010, BABY BLUES PARTNERSHIP DIST. BY KING FEATURES SYNDICATE 1-22
... AS LONG AS YOU REMIND ME.
THAT'S WHAT I'M HERE FOR.

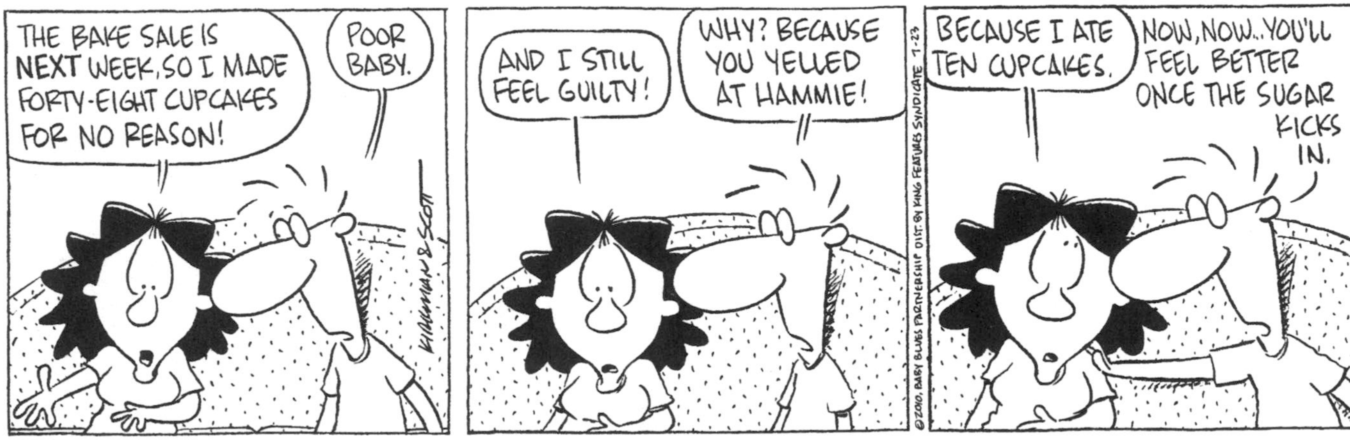
THE BAKE SALE IS NEXT WEEK, SO I MADE FORTY-EIGHT CUPCAKES FOR NO REASON!
POOR BABY.
KIRKMAN & SCOTT
AND I STILL FEEL GUILTY!
WHY? BECAUSE YOU YELLED AT HAMMIE!
©2010, BABY BLUES PARTNERSHIP DIST. BY KING FEATURES SYNDICATE 1-23
BECAUSE I ATE TEN CUPCAKES.
NOW, NOW... YOU'LL FEEL BETTER ONCE THE SUGAR KICKS IN.

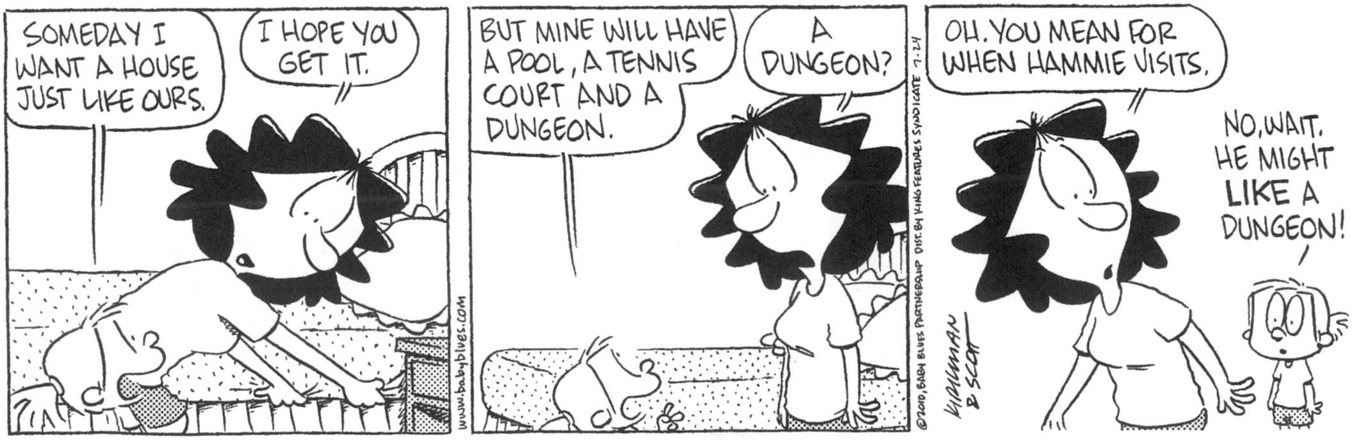
SOMEDAY I WANT A HOUSE JUST LIKE OURS.
I HOPE YOU GET IT.
www.babyblues.com
BUT MINE WILL HAVE A POOL, A TENNIS COURT AND A DUNGEON.
A DUNGEON?
©2010, BABY BLUES PARTNERSHIP DIST. BY KING FEATURES SYNDICATE 1-24
KIRKMAN & SCOTT
OH. YOU MEAN FOR WHEN HAMMIE VISITS.
NO, WAIT. HE MIGHT LIKE A DUNGEON!

BABY BLUES®
BY RICK KIRKMAN / JERRY SCOTT
TUNA

:AHEM!: MOM IS CURRENTLY IN THE KITCHEN.
FLIP!
ACCORDING TO REPORTS, SHE HAS GATHERED THE FOLLOWING ITEMS.
•Box of noodles
•bag of frozen peas
•little onyons
•mushroom soup
•can of tuna
GIVEN THESE FACTS, WE HAVE NO CHOICE BUT TO MOVE THE BAD DINNER THREAT LEVEL FROM ORANGE...
KIRKMAN & SCOTT
©2010, BABY BLUES PARTNERSHIP DIST. BY KING FEATURES SYNDICATE 7-25
...TO RED!!!
FLIP!
www.babyblues.com
YOU GUYS REALLY DON'T LIKE MOM'S TUNA CASSEROLE, DO YOU?
AT THIS POINT, TAKEOUT IS OUR ONLY HOPE.
SAVE US, DAD!

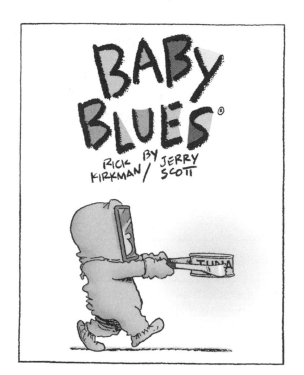

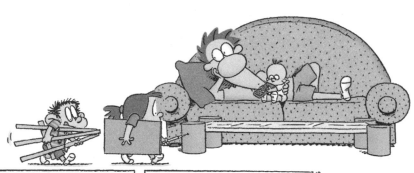

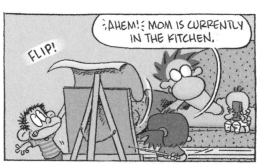

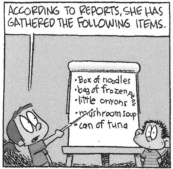

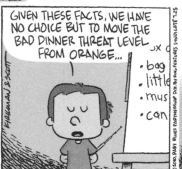

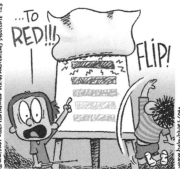

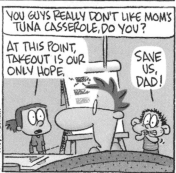

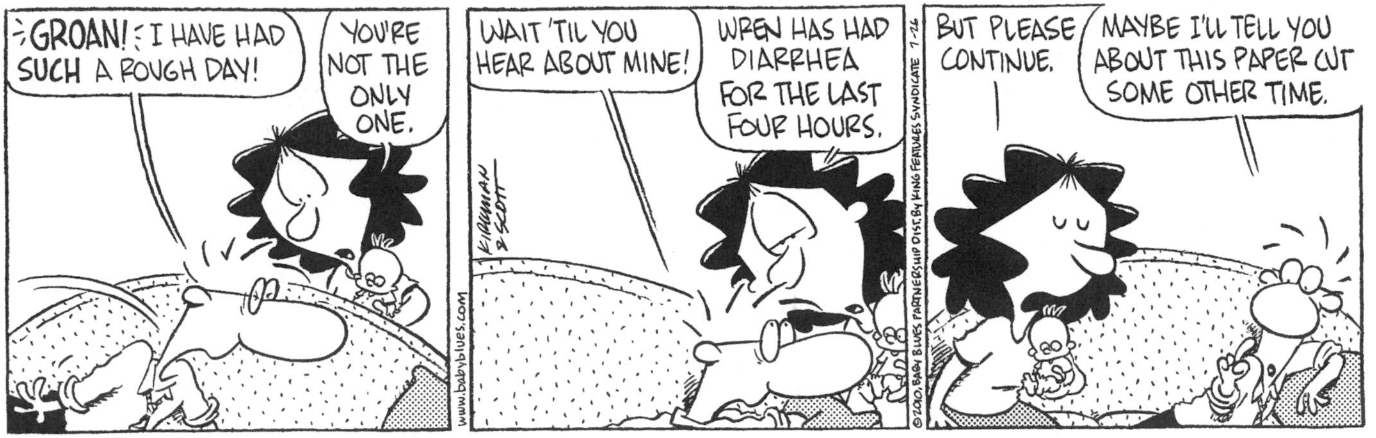
GROAN! I HAVE HAD SUCH A ROUGH DAY!
YOU'RE NOT THE ONLY ONE.
WAIT 'TIL YOU HEAR ABOUT MINE!
WREN HAS HAD DIARRHEA FOR THE LAST FOUR HOURS.
BUT PLEASE CONTINUE.
MAYBE I'LL TELL YOU ABOUT THIS PAPER CUT SOME OTHER TIME.
KIRKMAN & SCOTT
www.babyblues.com
©2010, BABY BLUES PARTNERSHIP DIST. BY KING FEATURES SYNDICATE 1-26

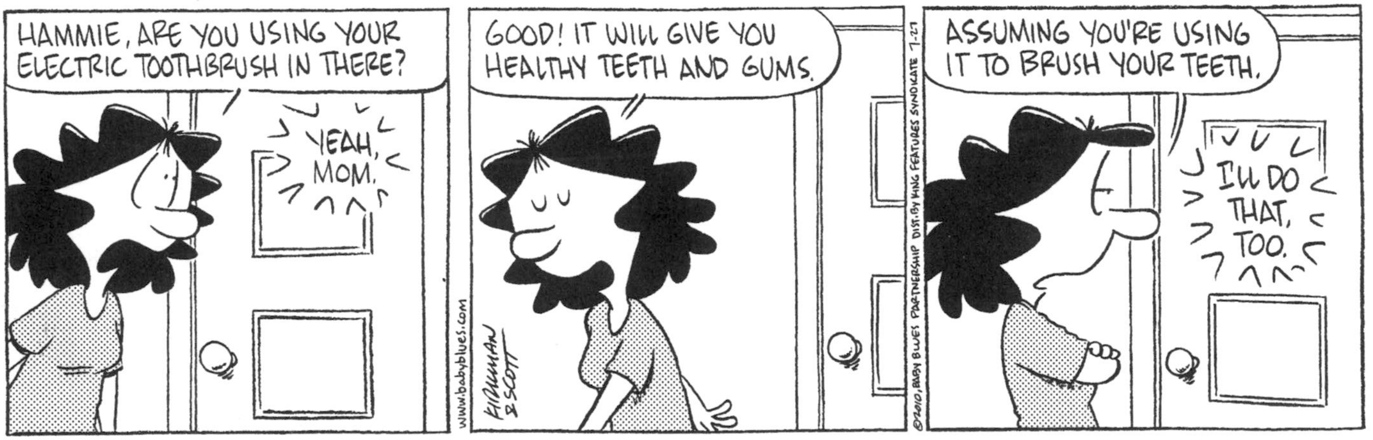
HAMMIE, ARE YOU USING YOUR ELECTRIC TOOTHBRUSH IN THERE?
YEAH, MOM.
GOOD! IT WILL GIVE YOU HEALTHY TEETH AND GUMS.
ASSUMING YOU'RE USING IT TO BRUSH YOUR TEETH.
I'LL DO THAT, TOO.
KIRKMAN & SCOTT
www.babyblues.com
©2010, BABY BLUES PARTNERSHIP DIST. BY KING FEATURES SYNDICATE 1-27

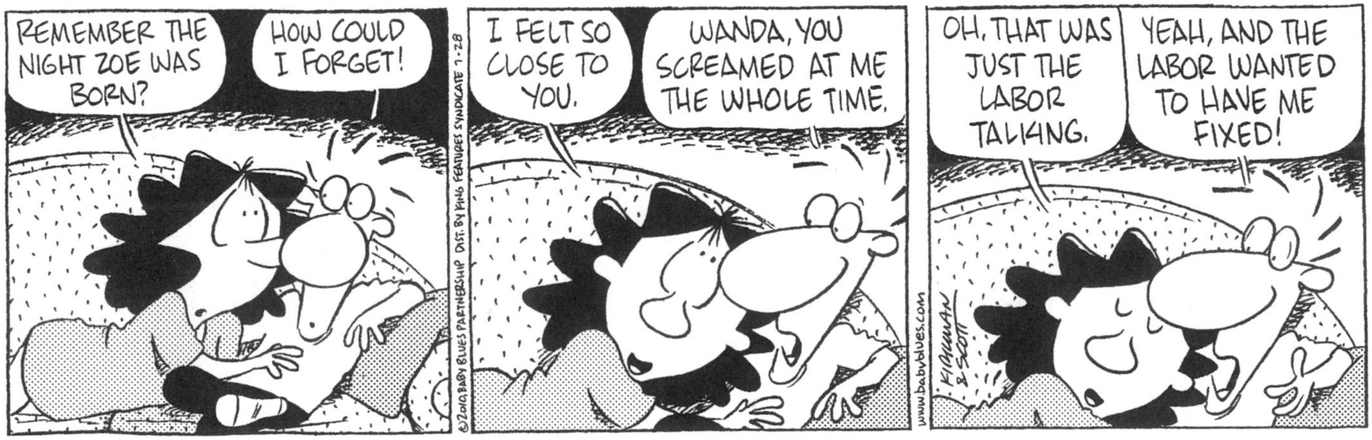
REMEMBER THE NIGHT ZOE WAS BORN?
HOW COULD I FORGET!
I FELT SO CLOSE TO YOU.
WANDA, YOU SCREAMED AT ME THE WHOLE TIME.
OH, THAT WAS JUST THE LABOR TALKING.
YEAH, AND THE LABOR WANTED TO HAVE ME FIXED!
KIRKMAN & SCOTT
www.babyblues.com
©2010, BABY BLUES PARTNERSHIP DIST. BY KING FEATURES SYNDICATE 1-28

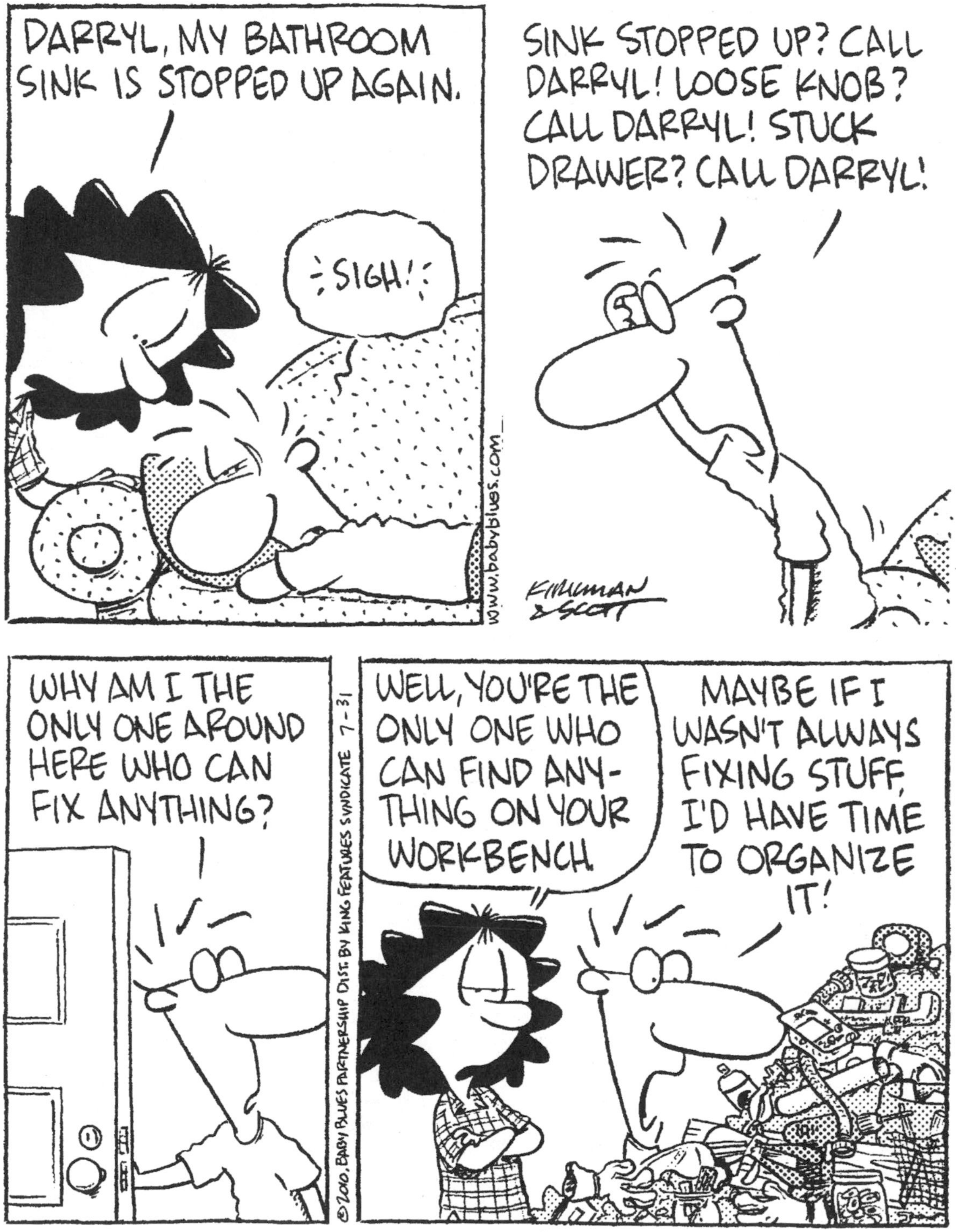
DARRYL, MY BATHROOM SINK IS STOPPED UP AGAIN.
SIGH!
www.babyblues.com
SINK STOPPED UP? CALL DARRYL! LOOSE KNOB? CALL DARRYL! STUCK DRAWER? CALL DARRYL!
KIRKMAN & SCOTT
WHY AM I THE ONLY ONE AROUND HERE WHO CAN FIX ANYTHING?
7-31
© 2010, BABY BLUES PARTNERSHIP DIST. BY KING FEATURES SYNDICATE
WELL, YOU'RE THE ONLY ONE WHO CAN FIND ANYTHING ON YOUR WORKBENCH.
MAYBE IF I WASN'T ALWAYS FIXING STUFF, I'D HAVE TIME TO ORGANIZE IT!

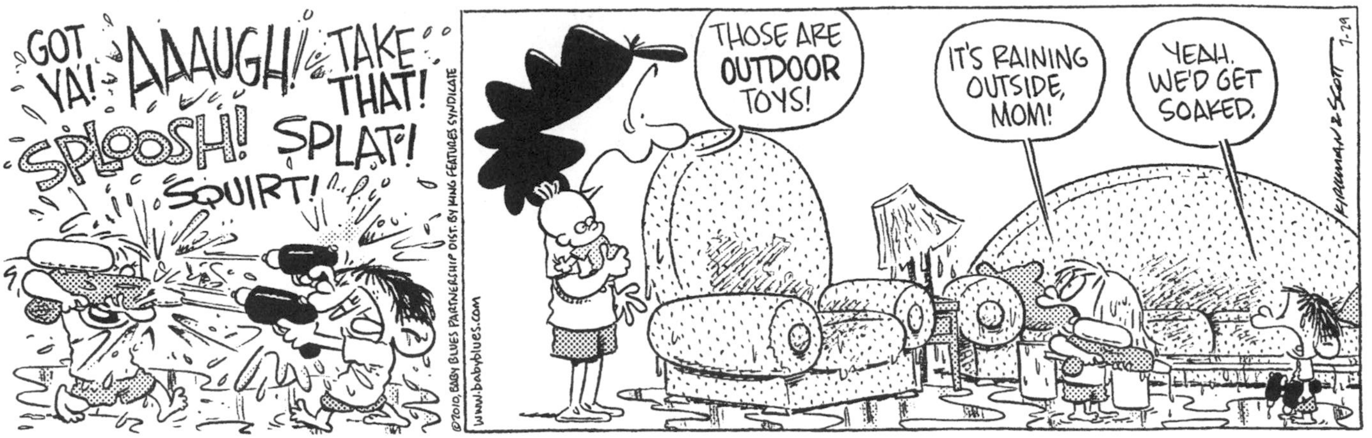
GOT YA!
AAAUGH!
TAKE THAT!
SPLOOSH!
SPLAT!
SQUIRT!
©2010, BABY BLUES PARTNERSHIP DIST. BY KING FEATURES SYNDICATE
www.babyblues.com
THOSE ARE OUTDOOR TOYS!
IT'S RAINING OUTSIDE, MOM!
YEAH. WE'D GET SOAKED.
KIRKMAN & SCOTT
7-29

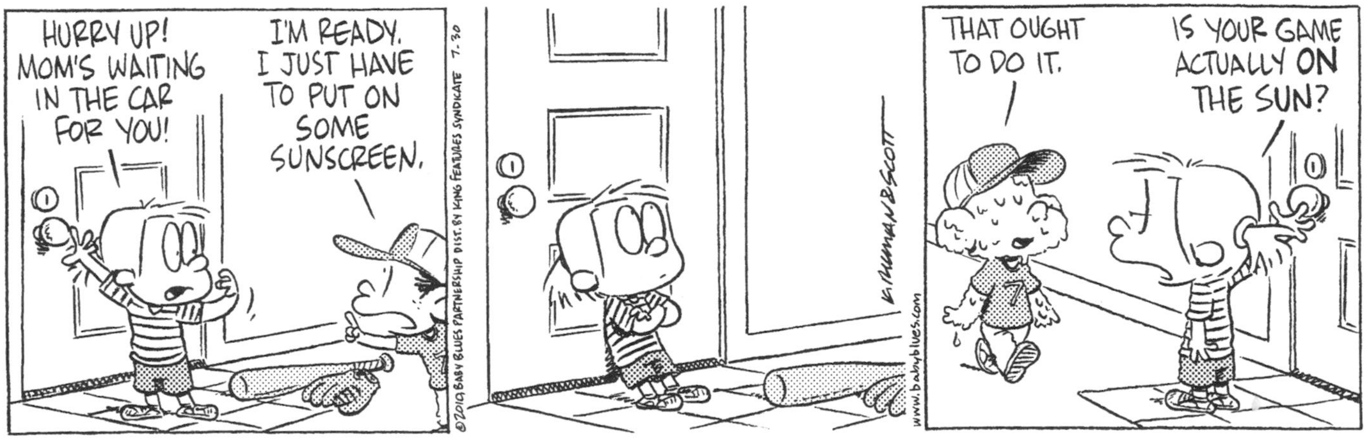
HURRY UP! MOM'S WAITING IN THE CAR FOR YOU!
I'M READY. I JUST HAVE TO PUT ON SOME SUNSCREEN.
7-30
©2010 BABY BLUES PARTNERSHIP DIST. BY KING FEATURES SYNDICATE
KIRKMAN & SCOTT
www.babyblues.com
THAT OUGHT TO DO IT.
IS YOUR GAME ACTUALLY ON THE SUN?

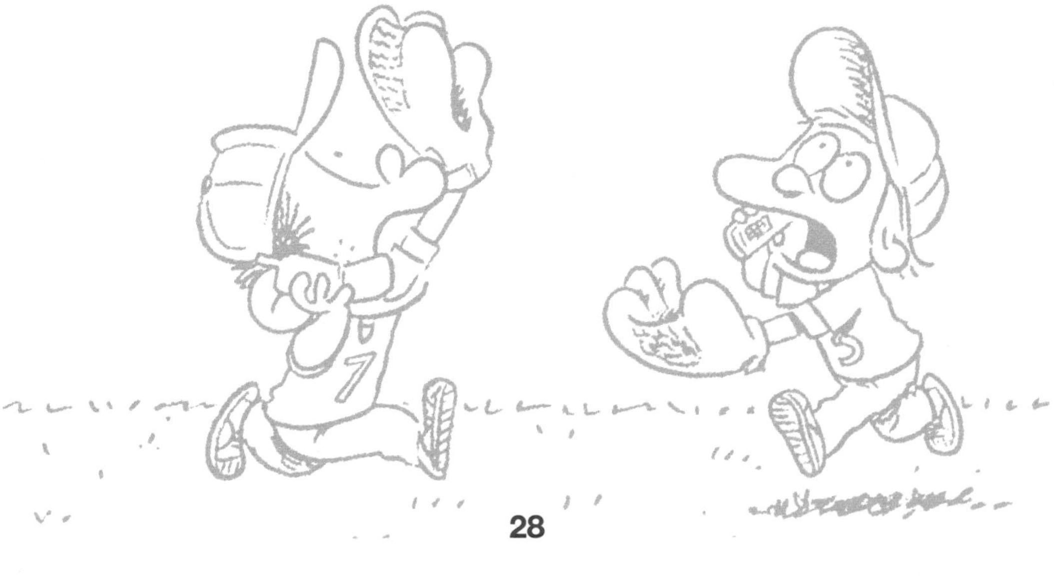

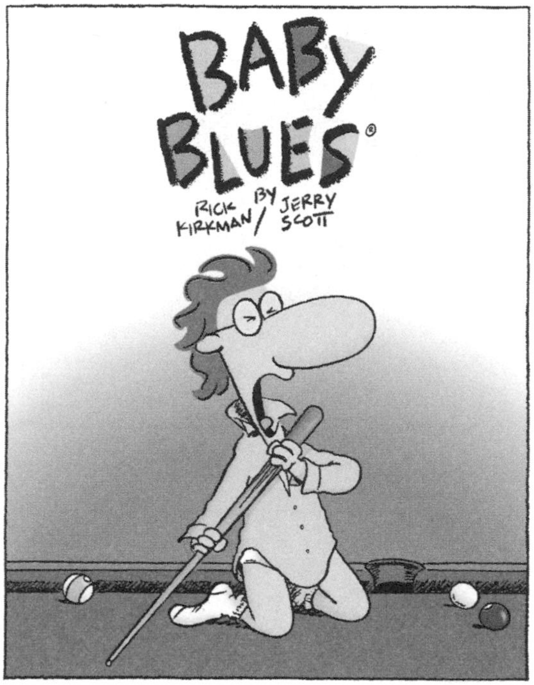
BABY BLUES®
BY RICK KIRKMAN / JERRY SCOTT

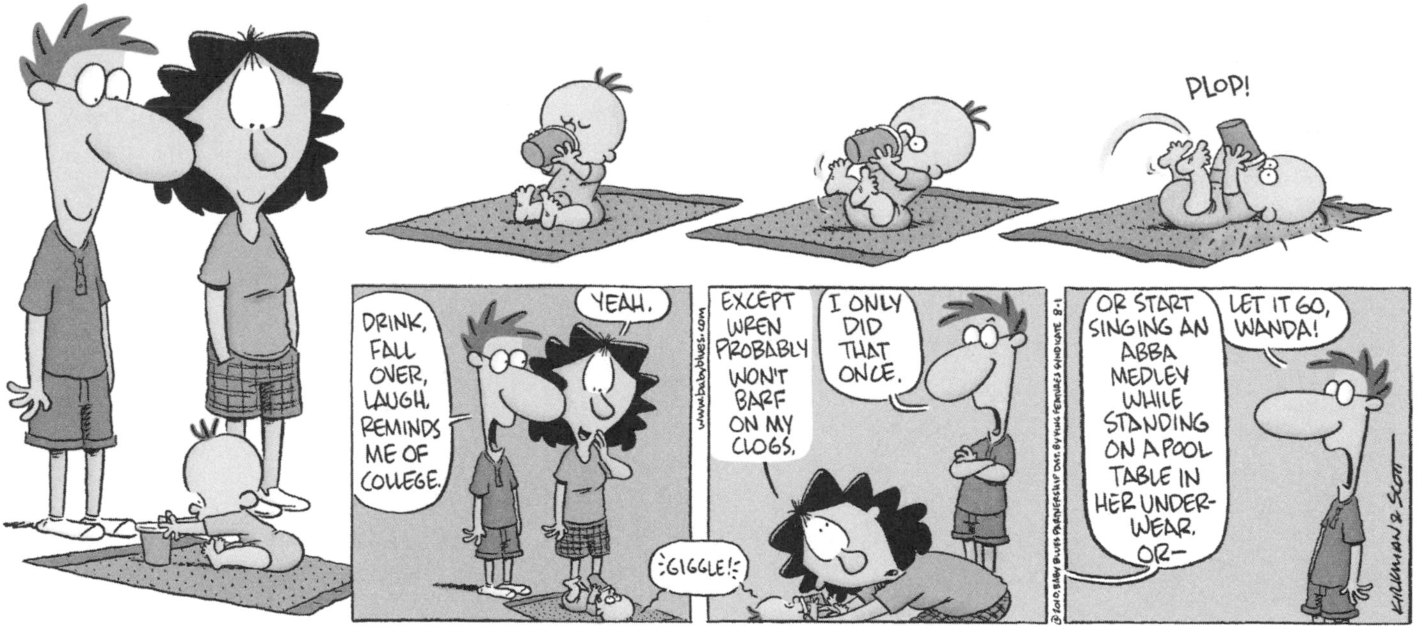
PLOP!
DRINK, FALL OVER, LAUGH. REMINDS ME OF COLLEGE.
YEAH.
www.babyblues.com
GIGGLE!
EXCEPT WREN PROBABLY WON'T BARF ON MY CLOGS.
I ONLY DID THAT ONCE.
© 2010, BABY BLUES PARTNERSHIP DIST. BY KING FEATURES SYNDICATE 8-1
OR START SINGING AN ABBA MEDLEY WHILE STANDING ON A POOL TABLE IN HER UNDER-WEAR. OR—
LET IT GO, WANDA!
KIRKMAN & SCOTT

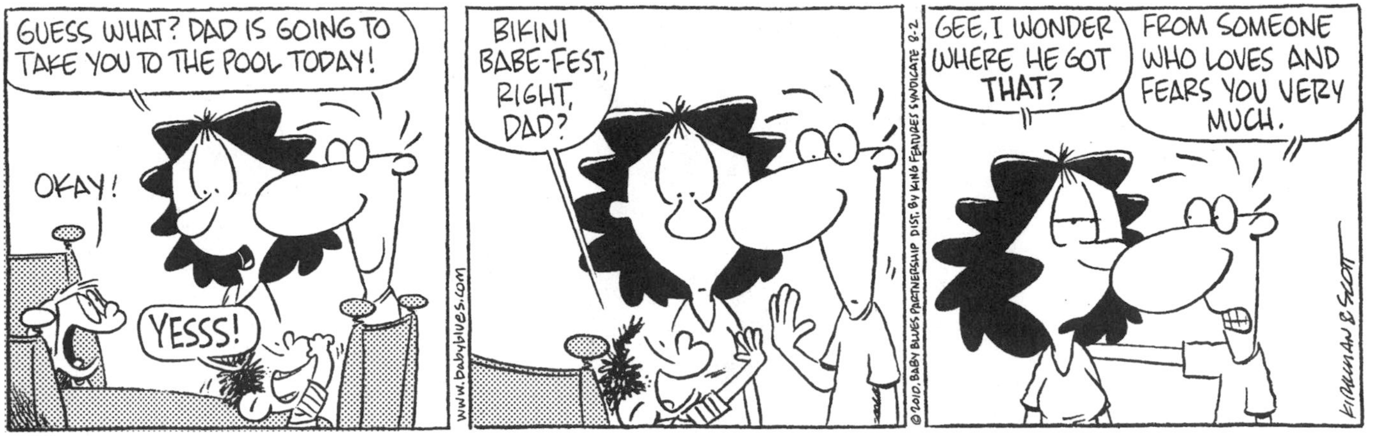
GUESS WHAT? DAD IS GOING TO TAKE YOU TO THE POOL TODAY!
OKAY!
YESSS!
www.babyblues.com
BIKINI BABE-FEST, RIGHT, DAD?
©2010, BABY BLUES PARTNERSHIP DIST. BY KING FEATURES SYNDICATE 8-2
GEE, I WONDER WHERE HE GOT THAT?
FROM SOMEONE WHO LOVES AND FEARS YOU VERY MUCH.
KIRKMAN & SCOTT

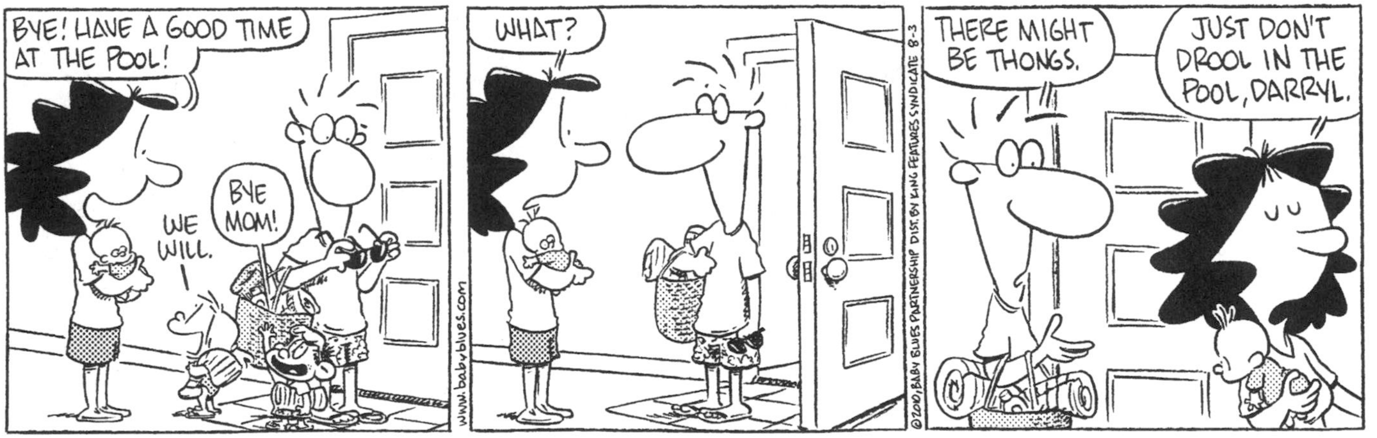
BYE! HAVE A GOOD TIME AT THE POOL!
WE WILL.
BYE MOM!
www.babyblues.com
WHAT?
©2010, BABY BLUES PARTNERSHIP DIST. BY KING FEATURES SYNDICATE 8-3
THERE MIGHT BE THONGS.
JUST DON'T DROOL IN THE POOL, DARRYL.

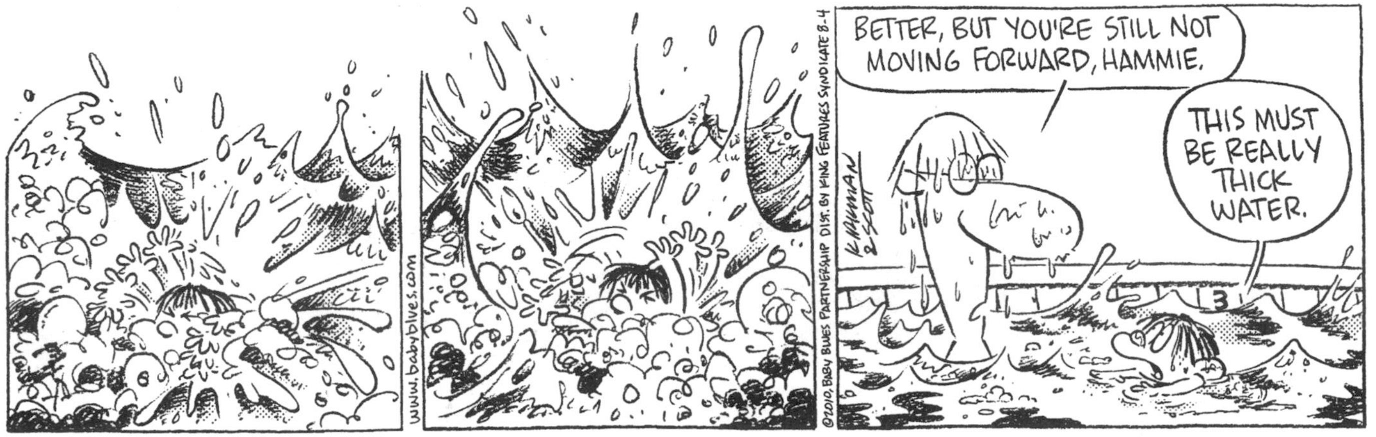
www.babyblues.com
©2010, BABY BLUES PARTNERSHIP DIST. BY KING FEATURES SYNDICATE 8-4
KIRKMAN & SCOTT
BETTER, BUT YOU'RE STILL NOT MOVING FORWARD, HAMMIE.
THIS MUST BE REALLY THICK WATER.
3

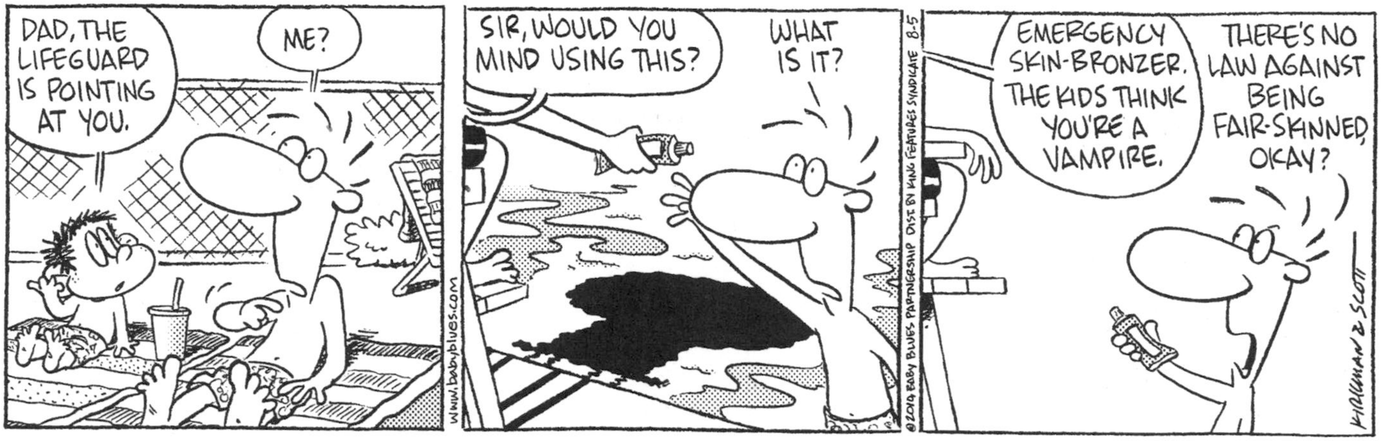
DAD, THE LIFEGUARD IS POINTING AT YOU.
ME?
www.babyblues.com
SIR, WOULD YOU MIND USING THIS?
WHAT IS IT?
©2010 BABY BLUES PARTNERSHIP DIST. BY KING FEATURES SYNDICATE 8-5
EMERGENCY SKIN-BRONZER. THE KIDS THINK YOU'RE A VAMPIRE.
THERE'S NO LAW AGAINST BEING FAIR-SKINNED, OKAY?
KIRKMAN & SCOTT

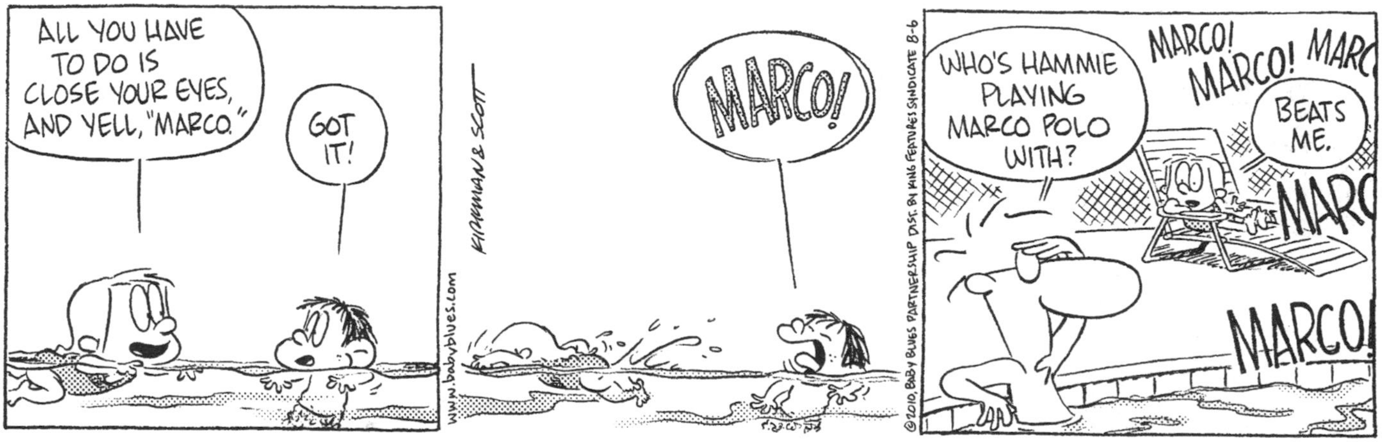
ALL YOU HAVE TO DO IS CLOSE YOUR EYES, AND YELL, "MARCO."
GOT IT!
www.babyblues.com
KIRKMAN & SCOTT
MARCO!
©2010 BABY BLUES PARTNERSHIP DIST. BY KING FEATURES SYNDICATE 8-6
WHO'S HAMMIE PLAYING MARCO POLO WITH?
MARCO!
MARCO!
BEATS ME.
MARCO!

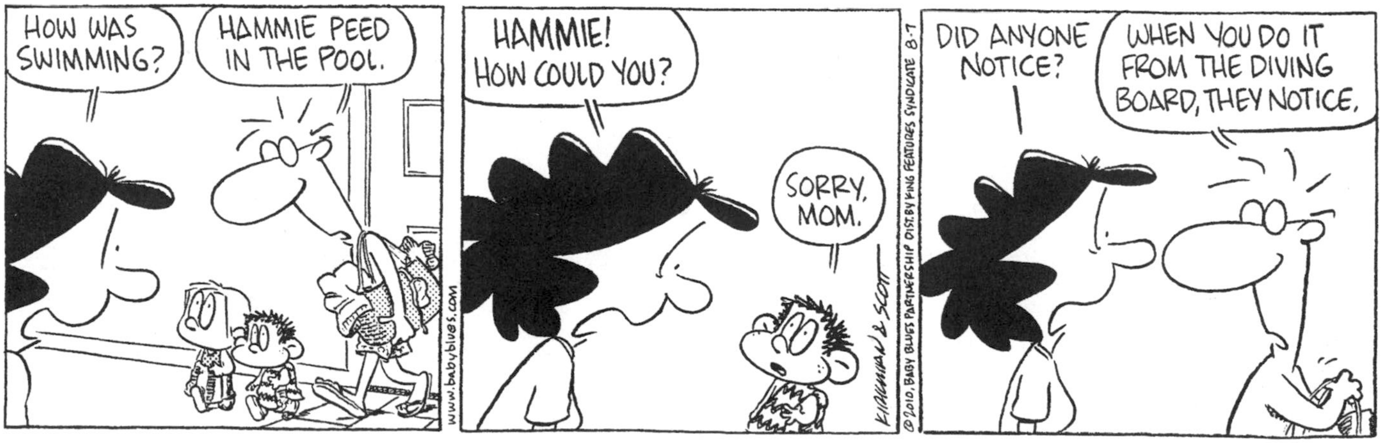
HOW WAS SWIMMING?
HAMMIE PEED IN THE POOL.
www.babyblues.com
HAMMIE! HOW COULD YOU?
SORRY, MOM.
KIRKMAN & SCOTT
©2010 BABY BLUES PARTNERSHIP DIST. BY KING FEATURES SYNDICATE 8-7
DID ANYONE NOTICE?
WHEN YOU DO IT FROM THE DIVING BOARD, THEY NOTICE.

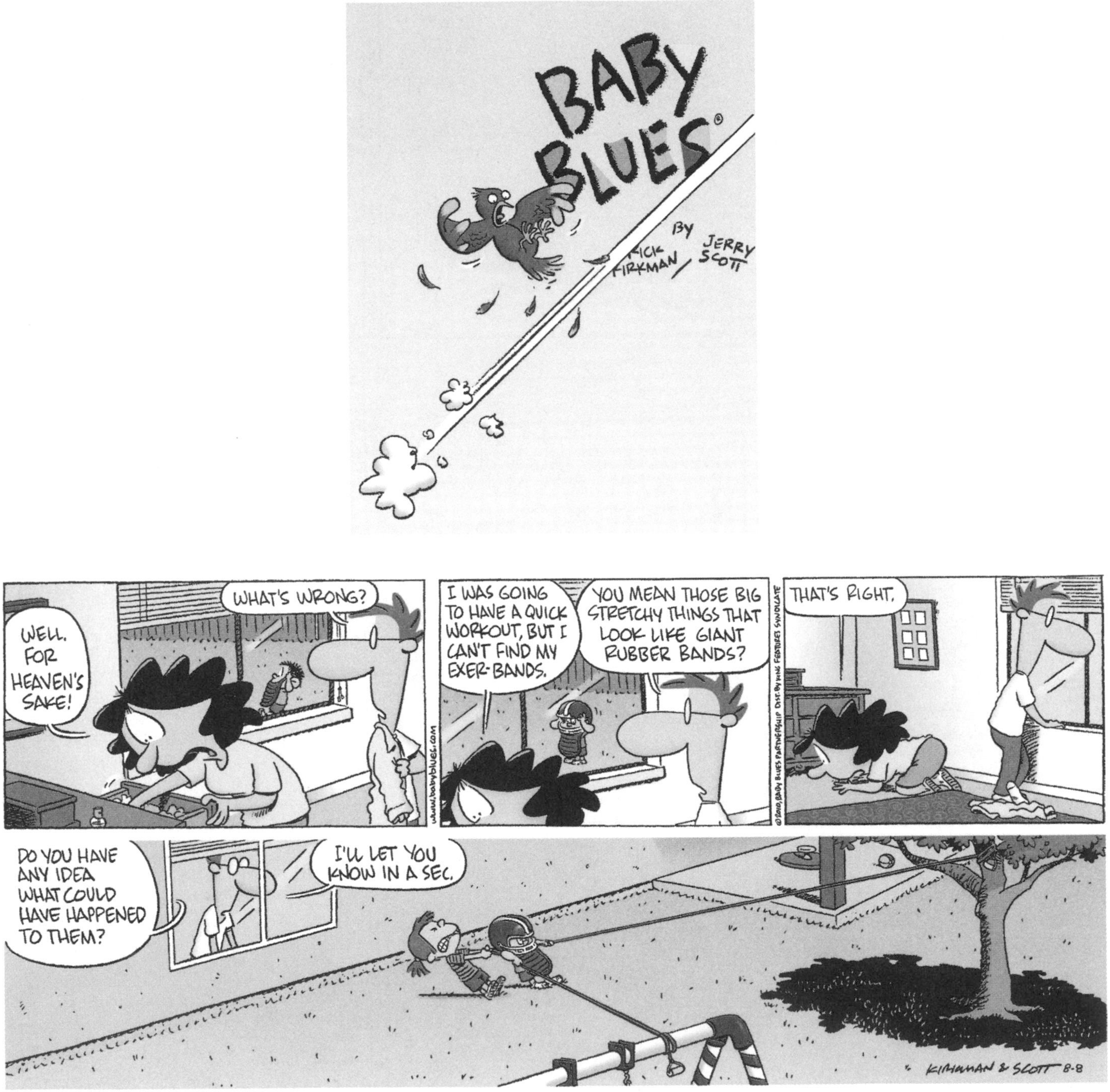

BABY BLUES®
BY RICK KIRKMAN / JERRY SCOTT
WHAT'S WRONG?
WELL. FOR HEAVEN'S SAKE!
www.babyblues.com
I WAS GOING TO HAVE A QUICK WORKOUT, BUT I CAN'T FIND MY EXER-BANDS.
YOU MEAN THOSE BIG STRETCHY THINGS THAT LOOK LIKE GIANT RUBBER BANDS?
©2010, BABY BLUES PARTNERSHIP DIST. BY KING FEATURES SYNDICATE
THAT'S RIGHT.
DO YOU HAVE ANY IDEA WHAT COULD HAVE HAPPENED TO THEM?
I'LL LET YOU KNOW IN A SEC.
KIRKMAN & SCOTT 8-8

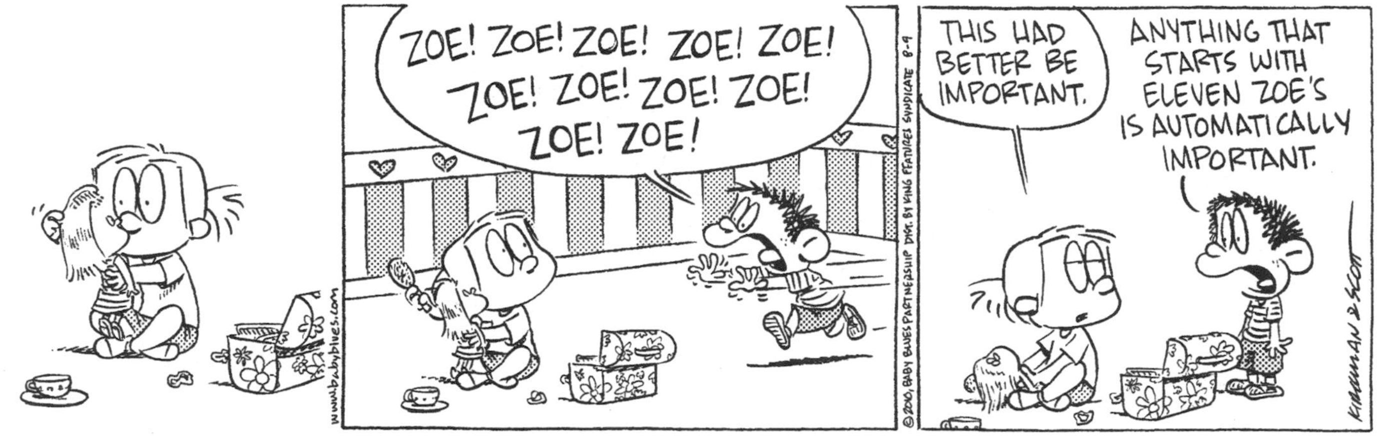
ZOE! ZOE! ZOE! ZOE! ZOE! ZOE! ZOE! ZOE! ZOE! ZOE! ZOE!
THIS HAD BETTER BE IMPORTANT.
ANYTHING THAT STARTS WITH ELEVEN ZOE'S IS AUTOMATICALLY IMPORTANT.
www.babyblues.com
©2010, BABY BLUES PARTNERSHIP DIST. BY KING FEATURES SYNDICATE 8-9
KIRKMAN & SCOTT

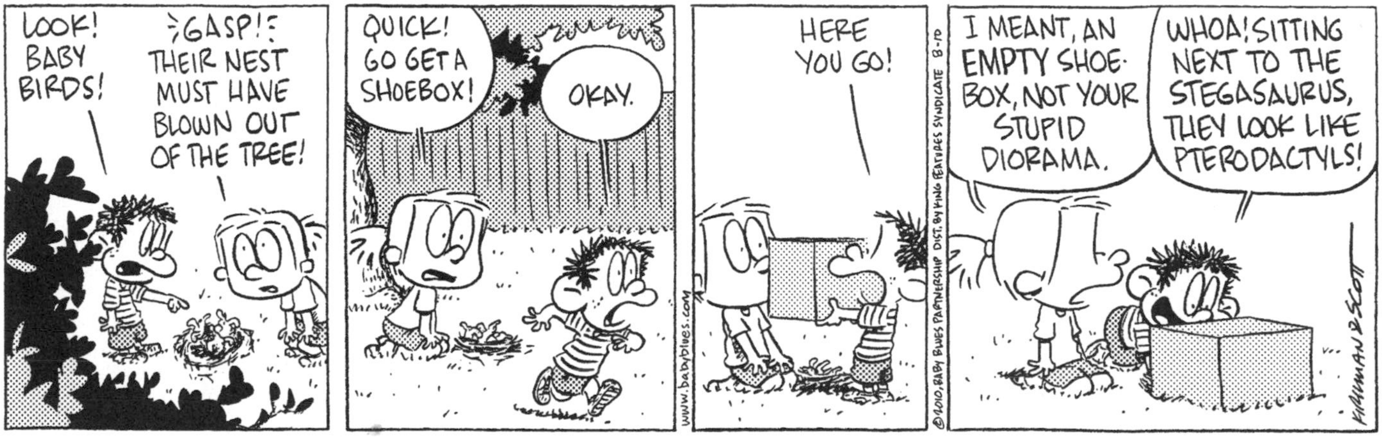
LOOK! BABY BIRDS!
GASP!
THEIR NEST MUST HAVE BLOWN OUT OF THE TREE!
QUICK! GO GET A SHOEBOX!
OKAY.
HERE YOU GO!
I MEANT, AN EMPTY SHOE-BOX, NOT YOUR STUPID DIORAMA.
WHOA! SITTING NEXT TO THE STEGASAURUS, THEY LOOK LIKE PTERODACTYLS!
www.babyblues.com
©2010, BABY BLUES PARTNERSHIP DIST. BY KING FEATURES SYNDICATE 8-10
KIRKMAN & SCOTT

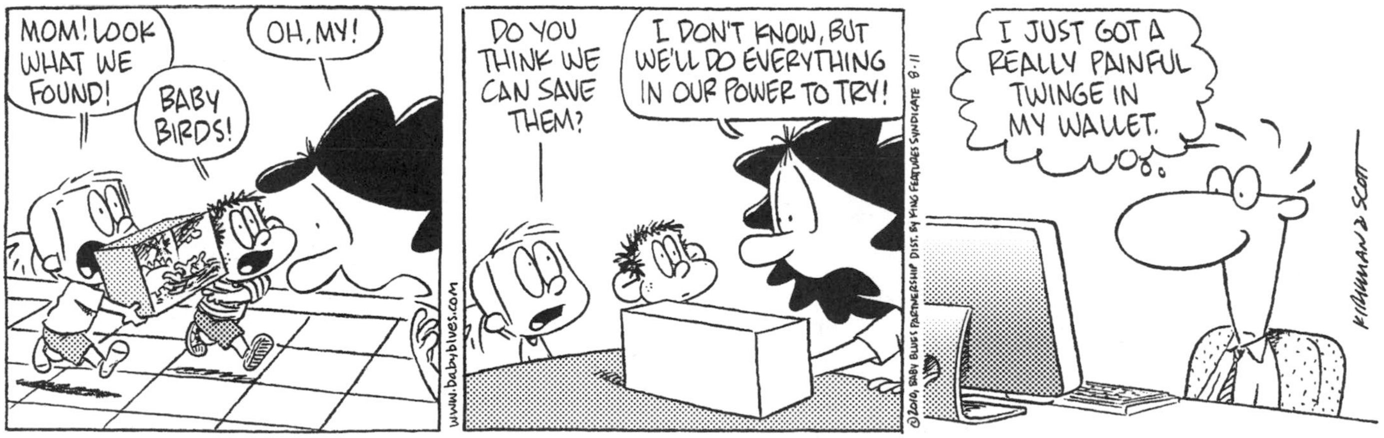
MOM! LOOK WHAT WE FOUND!
BABY BIRDS!
OH, MY!
DO YOU THINK WE CAN SAVE THEM?
I DON'T KNOW, BUT WE'LL DO EVERYTHING IN OUR POWER TO TRY!
I JUST GOT A REALLY PAINFUL TWINGE IN MY WALLET.
www.babyblues.com
©2010, BABY BLUES PARTNERSHIP DIST. BY KING FEATURES SYNDICATE 8-11
KIRKMAN & SCOTT

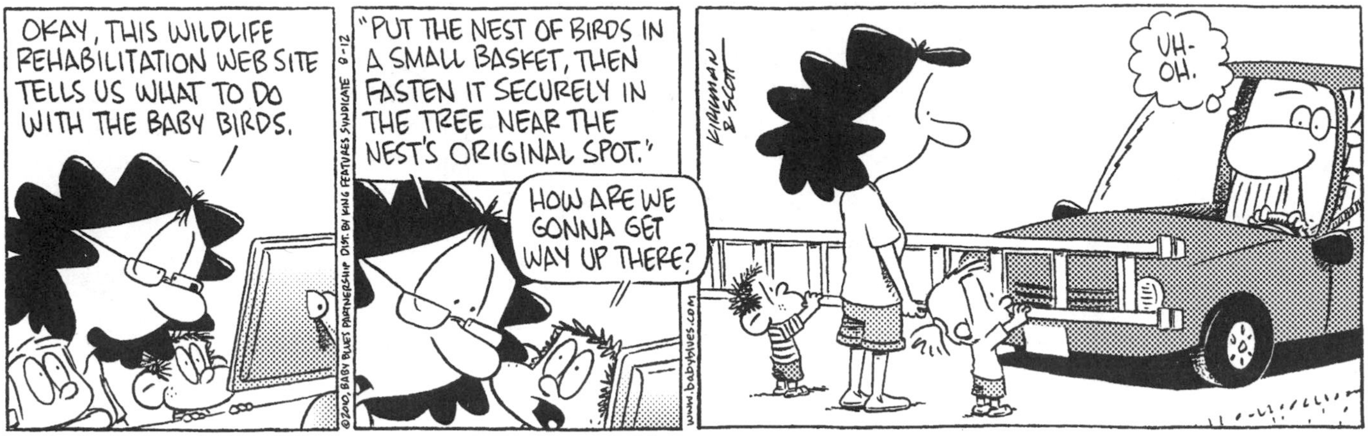
OKAY, THIS WILDLIFE REHABILITATION WEB SITE TELLS US WHAT TO DO WITH THE BABY BIRDS.
©2010, BABY BLUES PARTNERSHIP DIST. BY KING FEATURES SYNDICATE 8-12
"PUT THE NEST OF BIRDS IN A SMALL BASKET, THEN FASTEN IT SECURELY IN THE TREE NEAR THE NEST'S ORIGINAL SPOT."
HOW ARE WE GONNA GET WAY UP THERE?
www.babyblues.com
KIRKMAN & SCOTT
UH-OH.

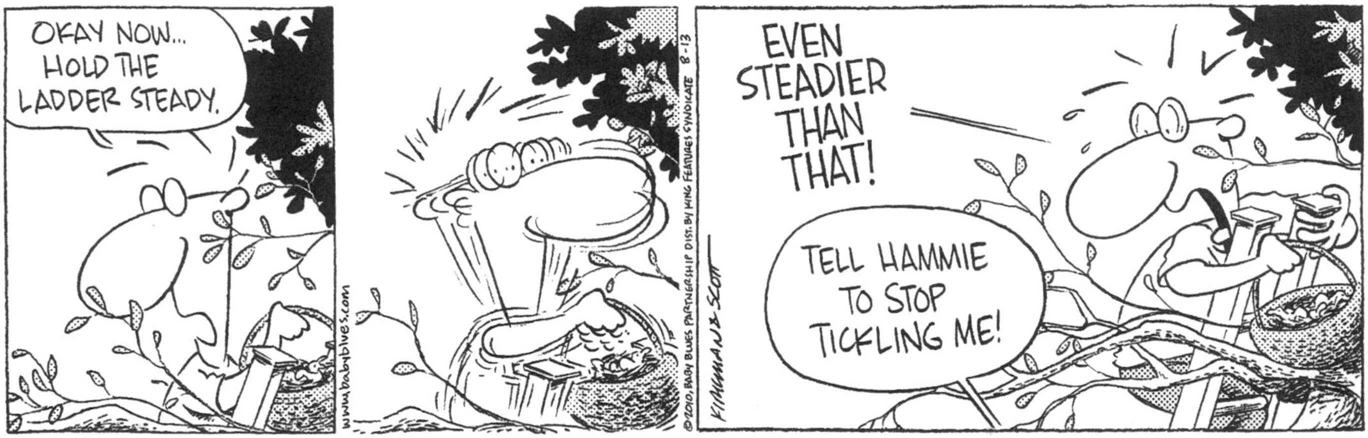
OKAY NOW... HOLD THE LADDER STEADY.
www.babyblues.com
©2010, BABY BLUES PARTNERSHIP DIST. BY KING FEATURES SYNDICATE 8-13
KIRKMAN & SCOTT
EVEN STEADIER THAN THAT!
TELL HAMMIE TO STOP TICKLING ME!

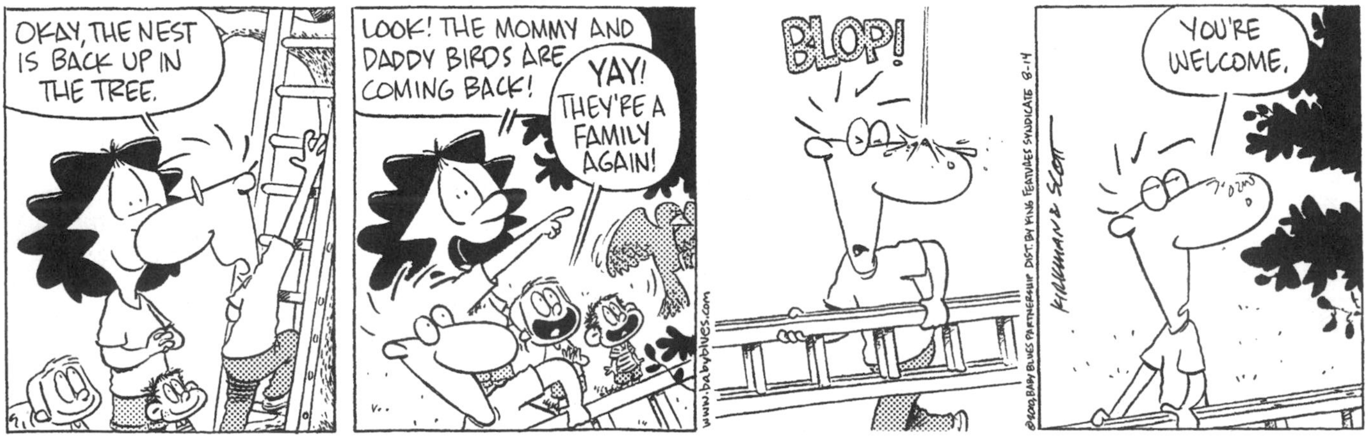
OKAY, THE NEST IS BACK UP IN THE TREE.
LOOK! THE MOMMY AND DADDY BIRDS ARE COMING BACK!
YAY! THEY'RE A FAMILY AGAIN!
www.babyblues.com
BLOP!
©2010 BABY BLUES PARTNERSHIP DIST. BY KING FEATURES SYNDICATE 8-14
KIRKMAN & SCOTT
YOU'RE WELCOME.

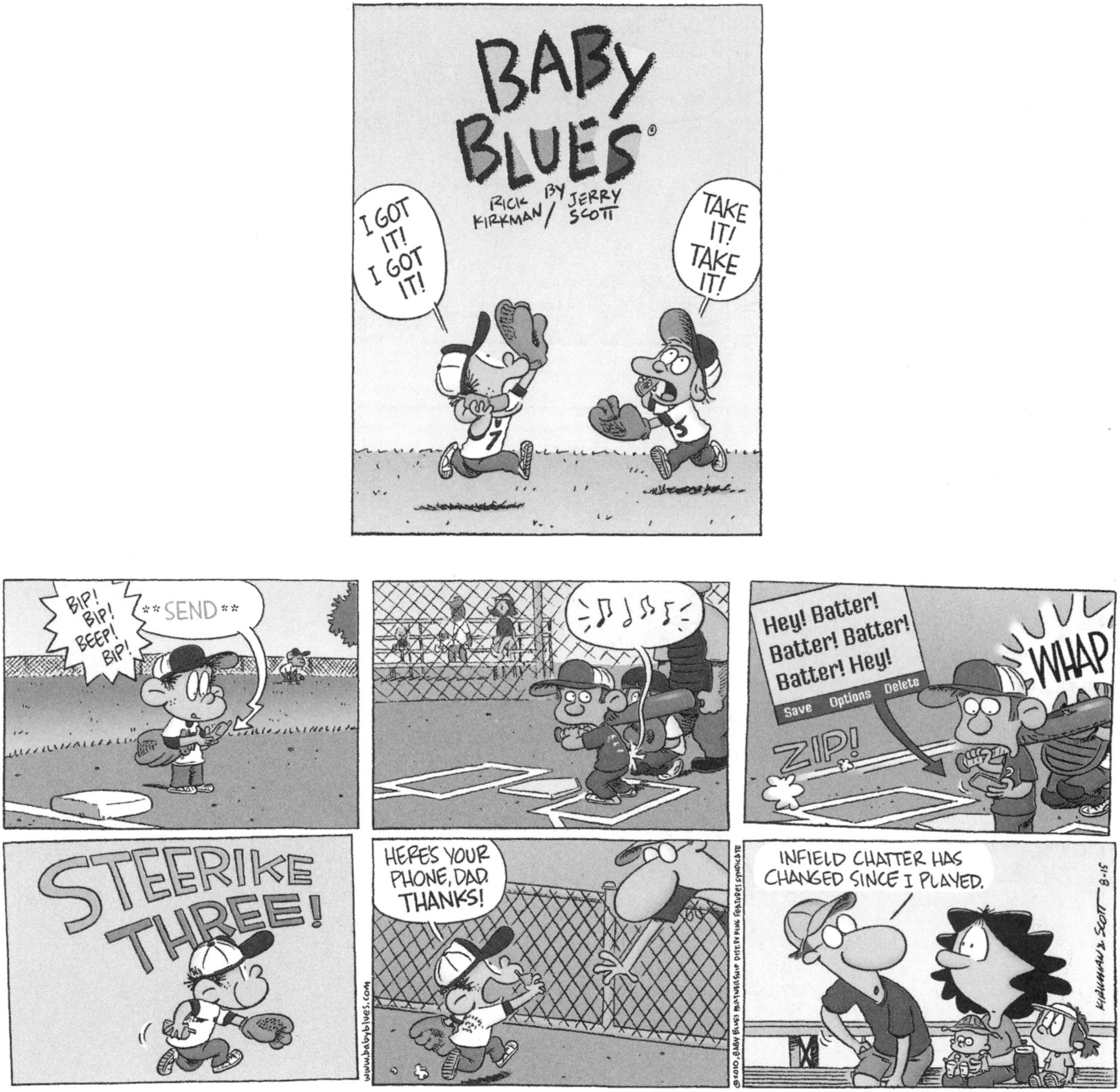
BABY BLUES®
BY RICK KIRKMAN / JERRY SCOTT
I GOT IT! I GOT IT!
TAKE IT! TAKE IT!
BIP! BIP! BEEP! BIP!
** SEND **
Hey! Batter! Batter! Batter! Batter! Hey!
Save Options Delete
ZIP!
WHAP
STEERIKE THREE!
www.babyblues.com
HERE'S YOUR PHONE, DAD. THANKS!
©2010, BABY BLUES PARTNERSHIP DIST. BY KING FEATURES SYNDICATE
INFIELD CHATTER HAS CHANGED SINCE I PLAYED.
KIRKMAN & SCOTT 8-15

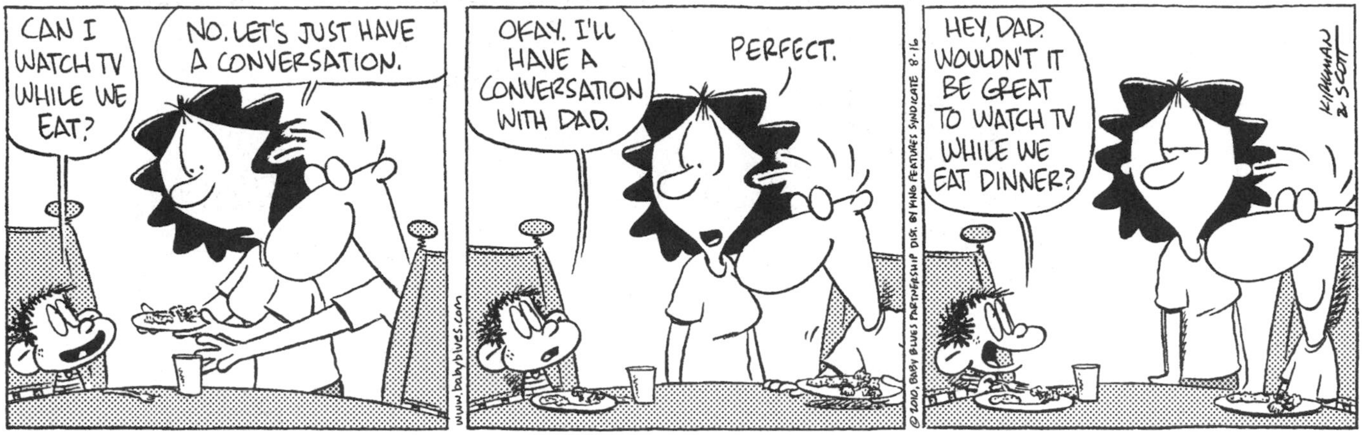
CAN I WATCH TV WHILE WE EAT?
NO. LET'S JUST HAVE A CONVERSATION.
www.babyblues.com
OKAY. I'LL HAVE A CONVERSATION WITH DAD.
PERFECT.
©2010, BABY BLUES PARTNERSHIP DIST. BY KING FEATURES SYNDICATE 8-16
HEY, DAD. WOULDN'T IT BE GREAT TO WATCH TV WHILE WE EAT DINNER?
KIRKMAN & SCOTT

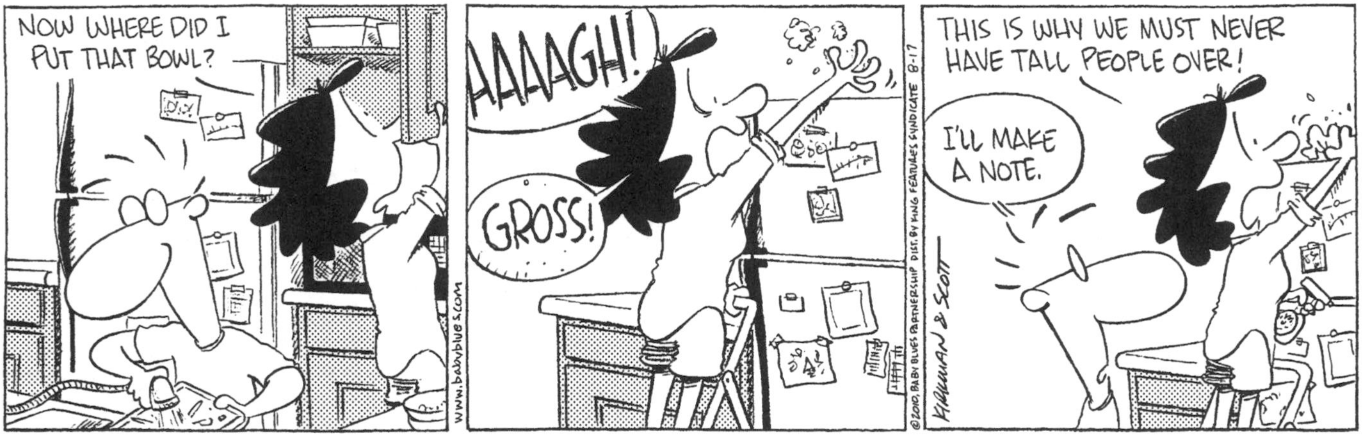
NOW WHERE DID I PUT THAT BOWL?
www.babyblues.com
AAAAGH!
GROSS!
©2010, BABY BLUES PARTNERSHIP DIST. BY KING FEATURES SYNDICATE 8-17
KIRKMAN & SCOTT
THIS IS WHY WE MUST NEVER HAVE TALL PEOPLE OVER!
I'LL MAKE A NOTE.

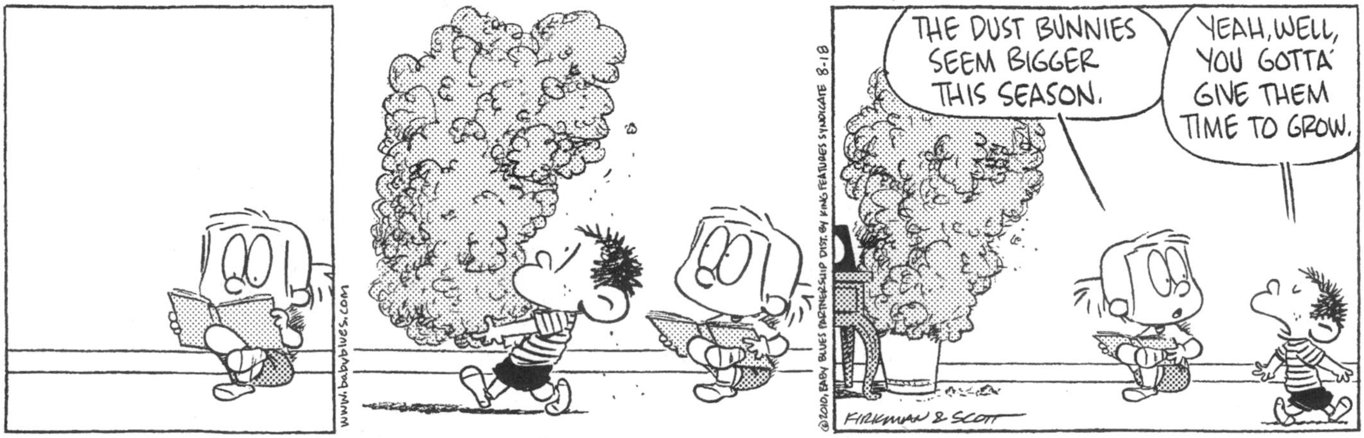
www.babyblues.com
©2010, BABY BLUES PARTNERSHIP DIST. BY KING FEATURES SYNDICATE 8-18
THE DUST BUNNIES SEEM BIGGER THIS SEASON.
YEAH, WELL, YOU GOTTA GIVE THEM TIME TO GROW.
KIRKMAN & SCOTT

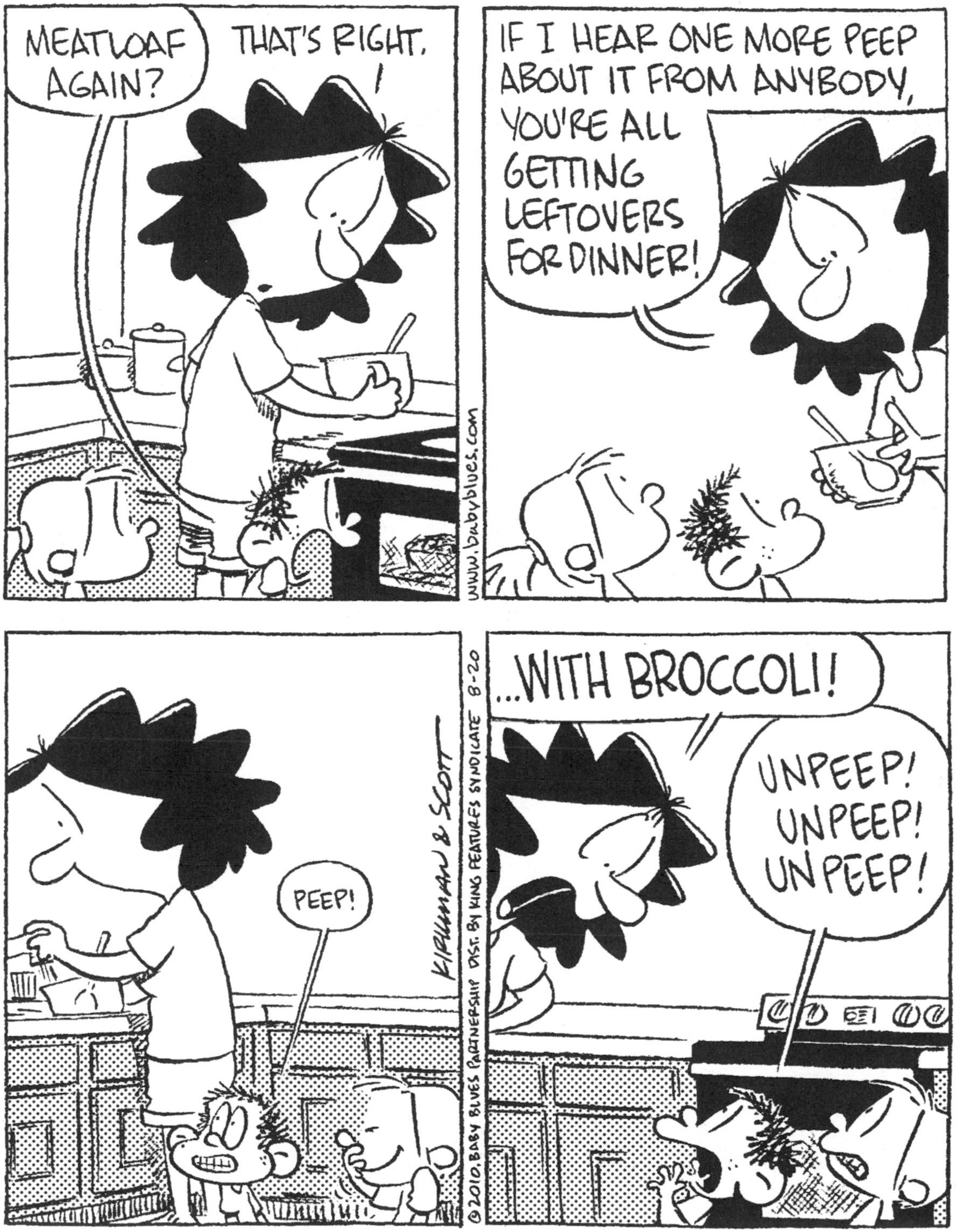
MEATLOAF AGAIN?
THAT'S RIGHT.
IF I HEAR ONE MORE PEEP ABOUT IT FROM ANYBODY,
YOU'RE ALL GETTING LEFTOVERS FOR DINNER!
PEEP!
...WITH BROCCOLI!
UNPEEP! UNPEEP! UNPEEP!
www.babyblues.com
KIRKMAN & SCOTT
©2010, BABY BLUES PARTNERSHIP DIST. BY KING FEATURES SYNDICATE 8-20

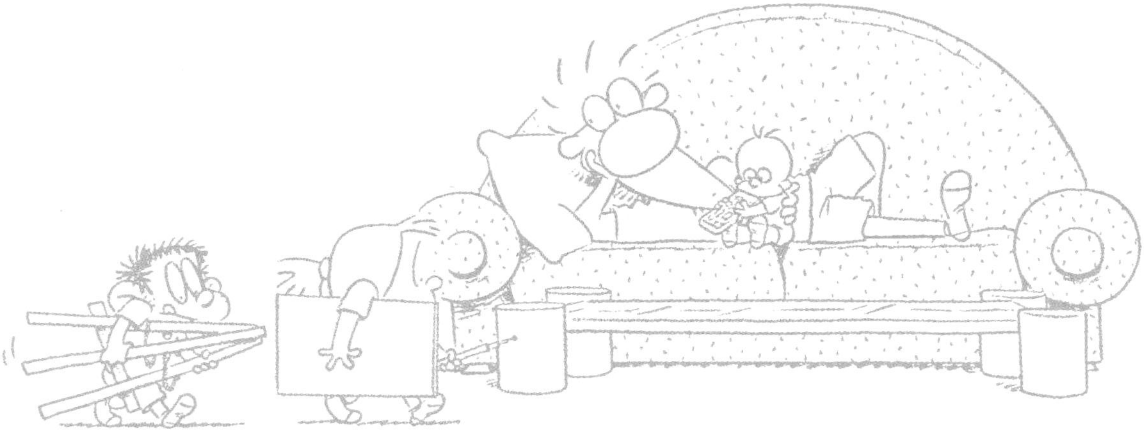

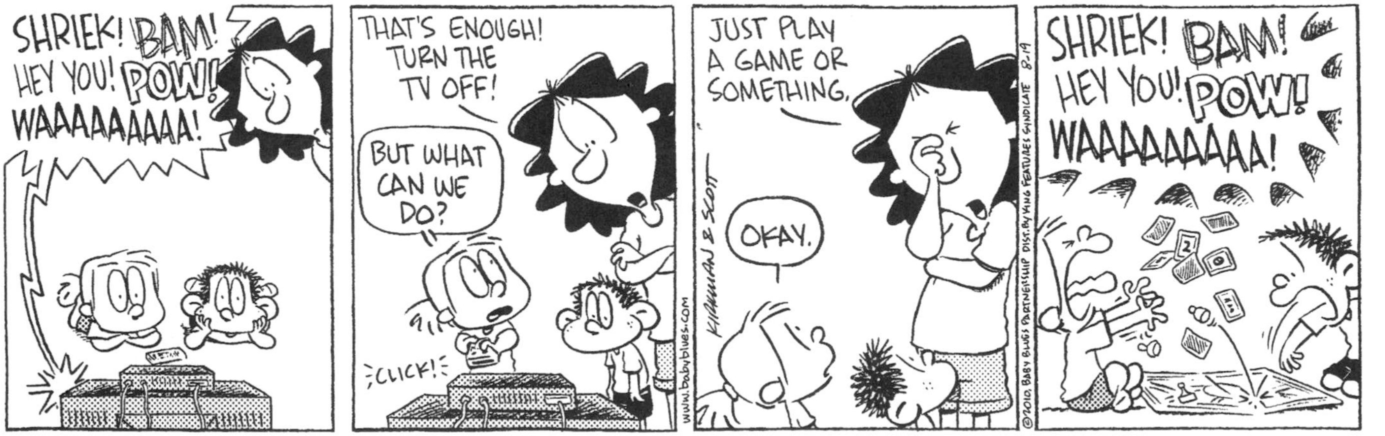
SHRIEK! BAM! HEY YOU! POW! WAAAAAAAAA!
THAT'S ENOUGH! TURN THE TV OFF!
BUT WHAT CAN WE DO?
CLICK!
www.babyblues.com
KIRKMAN & SCOTT
JUST PLAY A GAME OR SOMETHING.
OKAY.
©2010, BABY BLUES PARTNERSHIP DIST. BY KING FEATURES SYNDICATE 8-19
SHRIEK! BAM! HEY YOU! POW! WAAAAAAAAA!

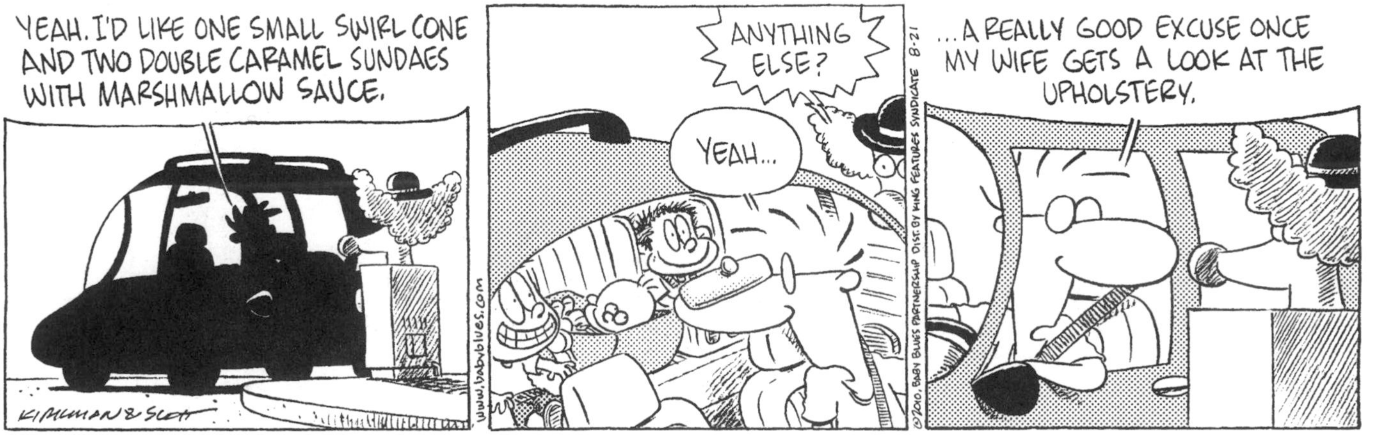
YEAH. I'D LIKE ONE SMALL SWIRL CONE AND TWO DOUBLE CARAMEL SUNDAES WITH MARSHMALLOW SAUCE.
KIRKMAN & SCOTT
www.babyblues.com
ANYTHING ELSE?
YEAH...
©2010, BABY BLUES PARTNERSHIP DIST. BY KING FEATURES SYNDICATE 8-21
...A REALLY GOOD EXCUSE ONCE MY WIFE GETS A LOOK AT THE UPHOLSTERY.

BABY BLUES®
BY RICK KIRKMAN / JERRY SCOTT

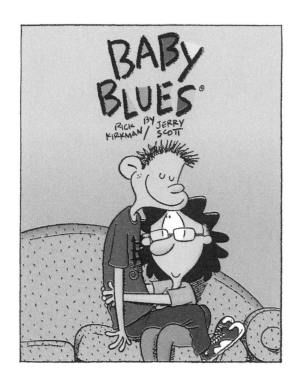

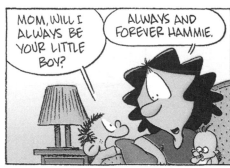

MOM, WILL I ALWAYS BE YOUR LITTLE BOY?
ALWAYS AND FOREVER HAMMIE.
EVEN WHEN I'M IN HIGH SCHOOL?
EVEN WHEN YOU'RE IN HIGH SCHOOL.
EVEN WHEN I'M ALL GROWN UP?
EVEN WHEN YOU'RE ALL GROWN UP.
www.babyblues.com
NO MATTER WHAT HAPPENS?
NO MA–
©2010, BABY BLUES PARTNERSHIP DIST. BY KING FEATURES SYNDICATE
SUDDENLY I DON'T LIKE THE DIRECTION THIS CONVERSATION IS GOING.
HURRY UP! PAINT DRIES IN CARPET REALLY FAST!
KIRKMAN & SCOTT 8-22

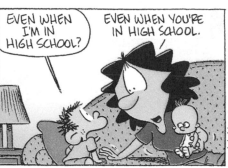

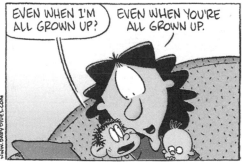

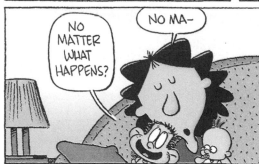

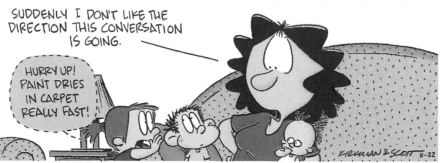

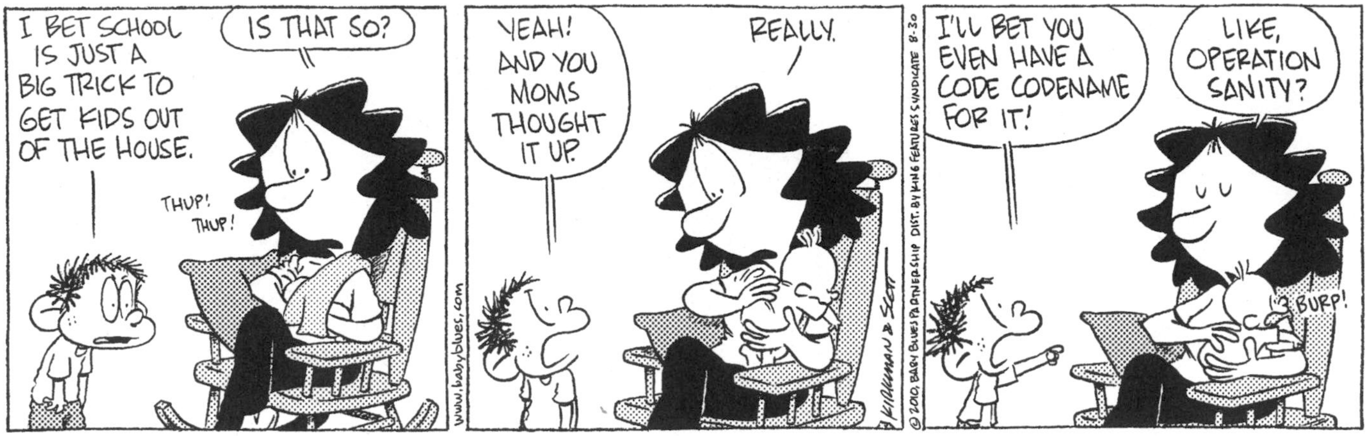
I BET SCHOOL IS JUST A BIG TRICK TO GET KIDS OUT OF THE HOUSE.
IS THAT SO?
THUP! THUP!
www.babyblues.com
YEAH! AND YOU MOMS THOUGHT IT UP.
REALLY.
KIRKMAN & SCOTT
© 2010, BABY BLUES PARTNERSHIP DIST. BY KING FEATURES SYNDICATE 8-30
I'LL BET YOU EVEN HAVE A CODE CODENAME FOR IT!
LIKE, OPERATION SANITY?
BURP!

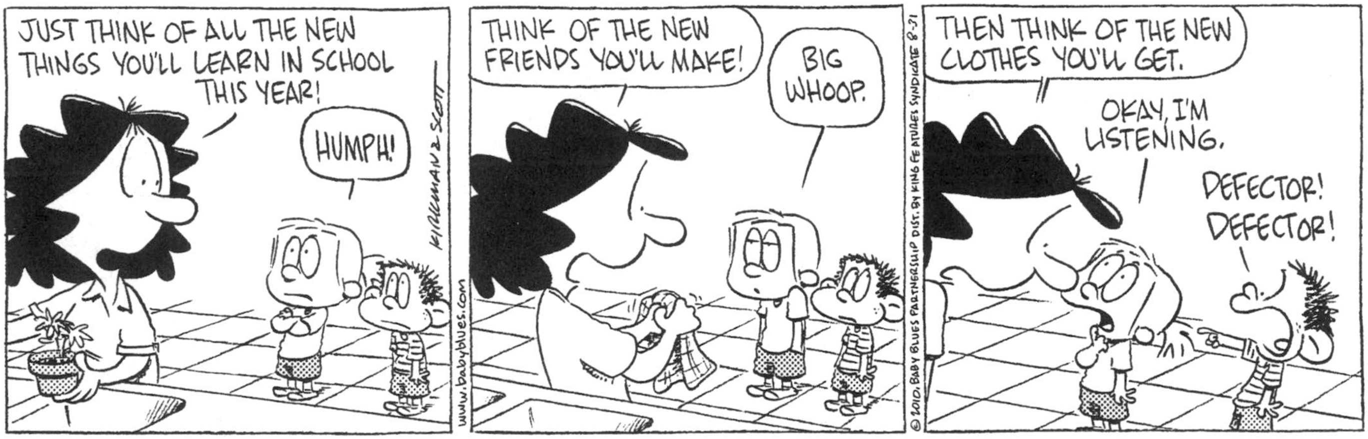
JUST THINK OF ALL THE NEW THINGS YOU'LL LEARN IN SCHOOL THIS YEAR!
HUMPH!
KIRKMAN & SCOTT
www.babyblues.com
THINK OF THE NEW FRIENDS YOU'LL MAKE!
BIG WHOOP.
© 2010, BABY BLUES PARTNERSHIP DIST. BY KING FEATURES SYNDICATE 8-31
THEN THINK OF THE NEW CLOTHES YOU'LL GET.
OKAY, I'M LISTENING.
DEFECTOR! DEFECTOR!

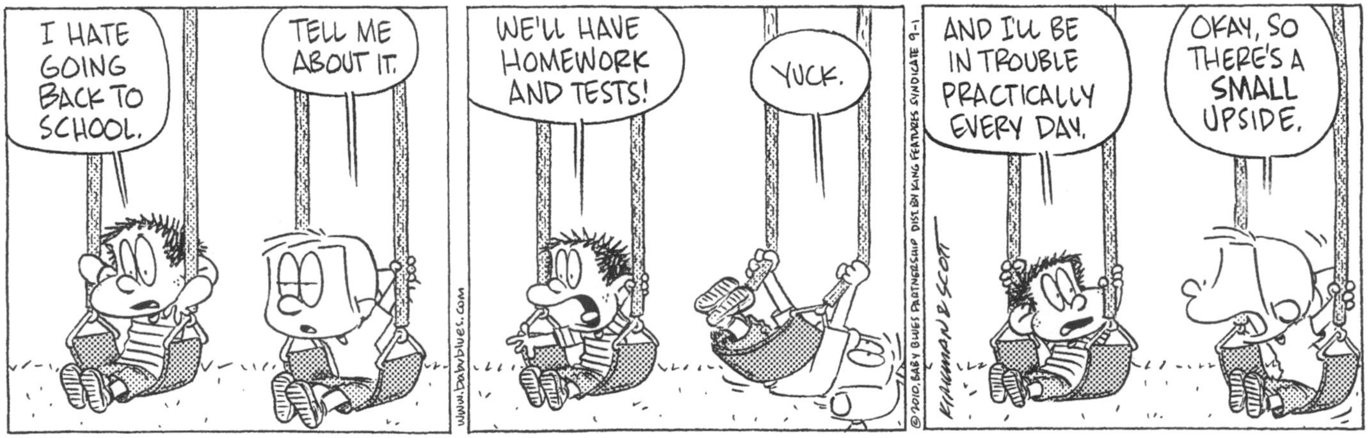
I HATE GOING BACK TO SCHOOL.
TELL ME ABOUT IT.
www.babyblues.com
WE'LL HAVE HOMEWORK AND TESTS!
YUCK.
© 2010, BABY BLUES PARTNERSHIP DIST. BY KING FEATURES SYNDICATE 9-1
KIRKMAN & SCOTT
AND I'LL BE IN TROUBLE PRACTICALLY EVERY DAY.
OKAY, SO THERE'S A SMALL UPSIDE.

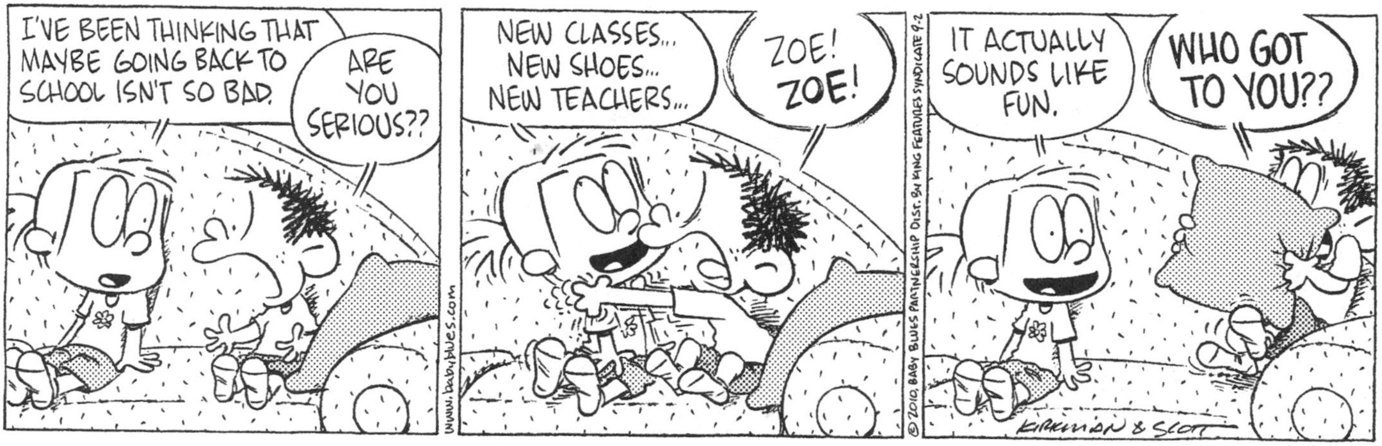
I'VE BEEN THINKING THAT MAYBE GOING BACK TO SCHOOL ISN'T SO BAD.
ARE YOU SERIOUS??
www.babyblues.com
NEW CLASSES... NEW SHOES... NEW TEACHERS...
ZOE! ZOE!
©2010, BABY BLUES PARTNERSHIP DIST. BY KING FEATURES SYNDICATE 9-2
IT ACTUALLY SOUNDS LIKE FUN.
WHO GOT TO YOU??
KIRKMAN & SCOTT

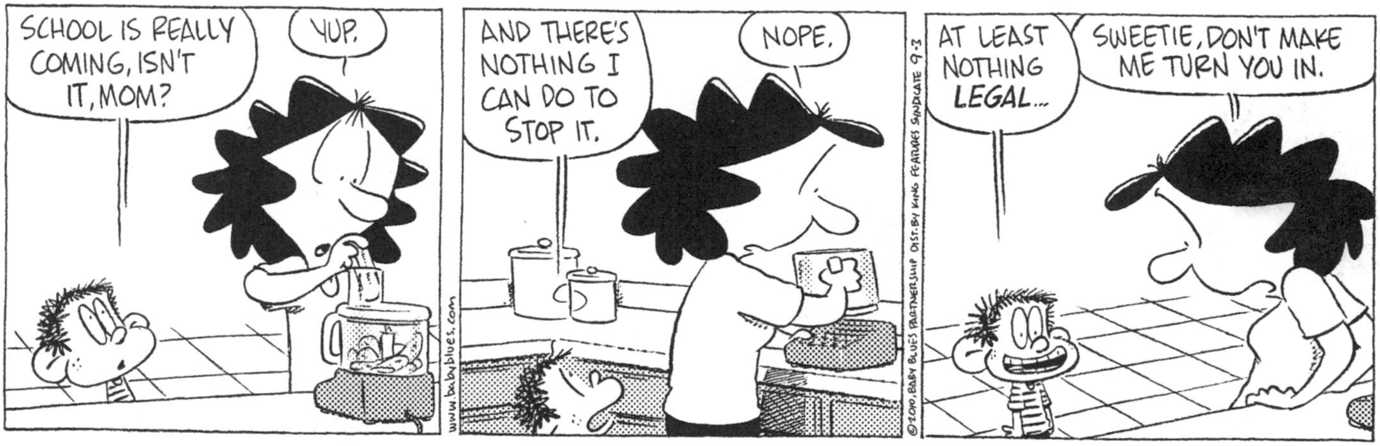
SCHOOL IS REALLY COMING, ISN'T IT, MOM?
YUP.
www.babyblues.com
AND THERE'S NOTHING I CAN DO TO STOP IT.
NOPE.
©2010, BABY BLUES PARTNERSHIP DIST. BY KING FEATURES SYNDICATE 9-3
AT LEAST NOTHING LEGAL...
SWEETIE, DON'T MAKE ME TURN YOU IN.

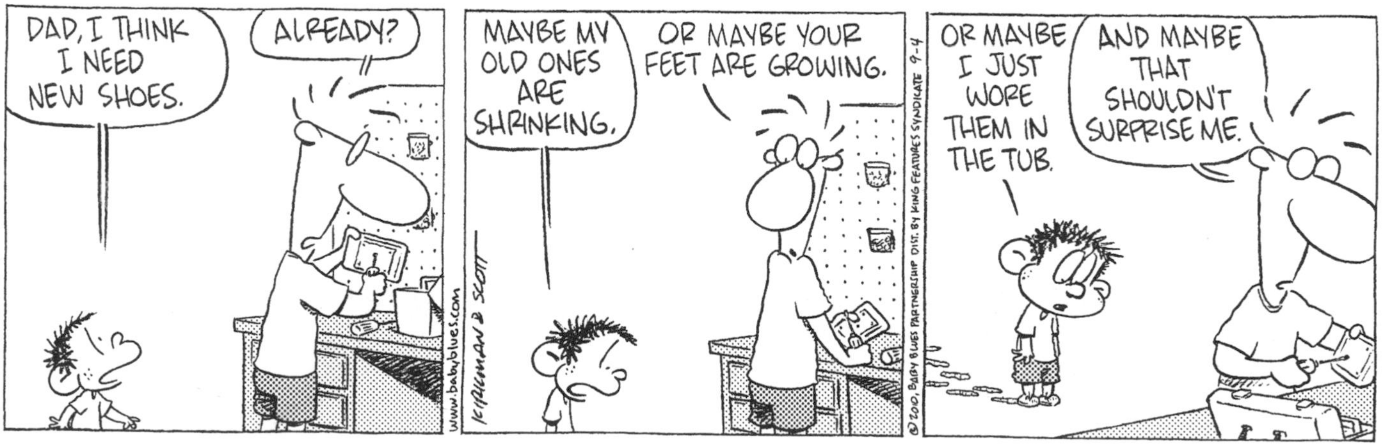
DAD, I THINK I NEED NEW SHOES.
ALREADY?
www.babyblues.com
KIRKMAN & SCOTT
MAYBE MY OLD ONES ARE SHRINKING.
OR MAYBE YOUR FEET ARE GROWING.
©2010, BABY BLUES PARTNERSHIP DIST. BY KING FEATURES SYNDICATE 9-4
OR MAYBE I JUST WORE THEM IN THE TUB.
AND MAYBE THAT SHOULDN'T SURPRISE ME.

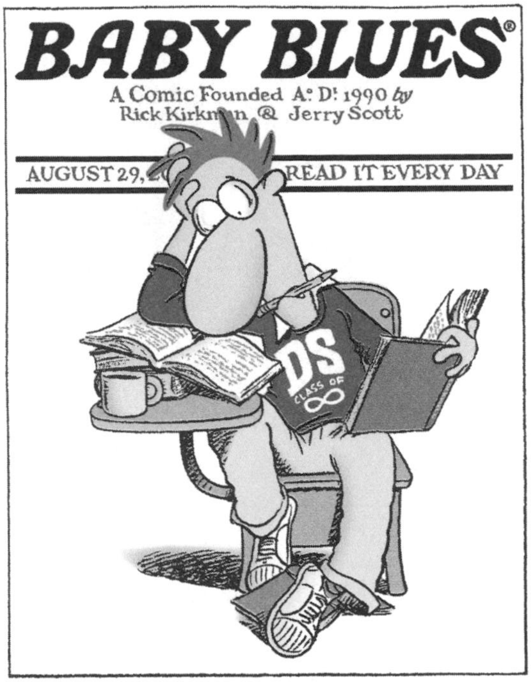
BABY BLUES®
A Comic Founded A° D° 1990 by
Rick Kirkm n & Jerry Scott
AUGUST 29,
READ IT EVERY DAY
DS
CLASS OF ∞

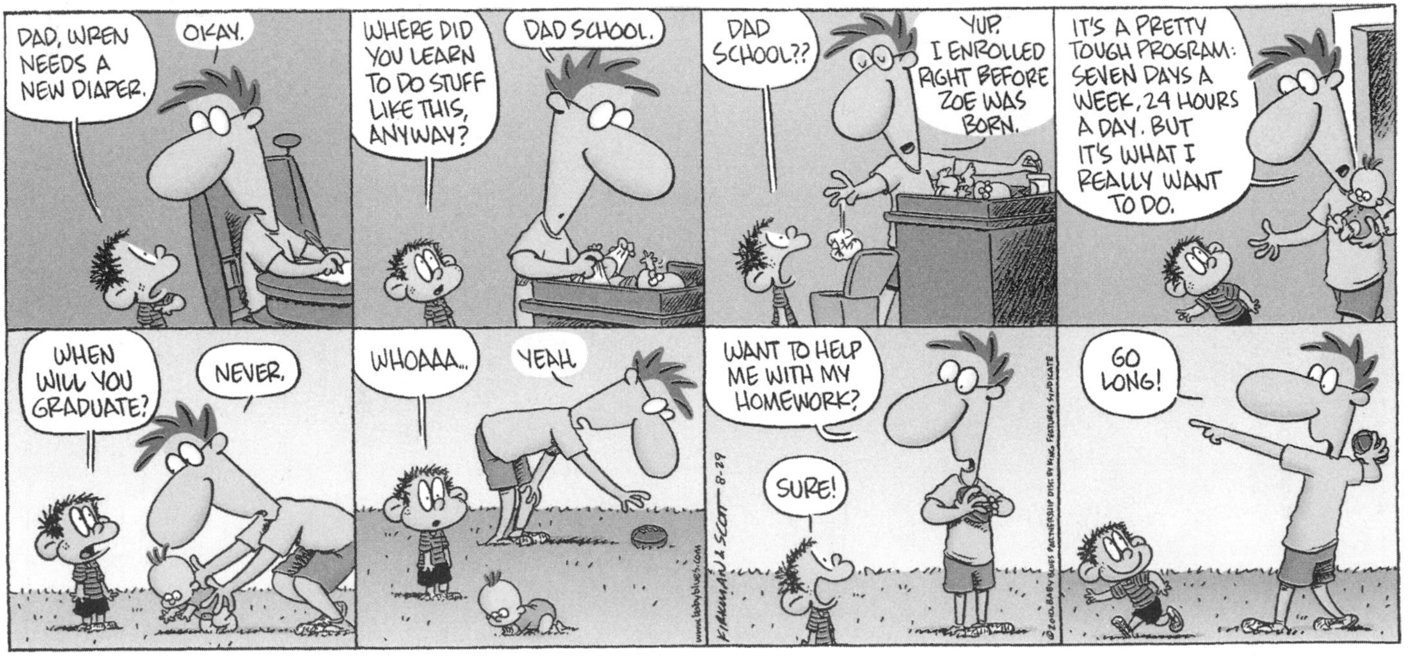
DAD, WREN NEEDS A NEW DIAPER.
OKAY.
WHERE DID YOU LEARN TO DO STUFF LIKE THIS, ANYWAY?
DAD SCHOOL.
DAD SCHOOL??
YUP. I ENROLLED RIGHT BEFORE ZOE WAS BORN.
IT'S A PRETTY TOUGH PROGRAM: SEVEN DAYS A WEEK, 24 HOURS A DAY. BUT IT'S WHAT I REALLY WANT TO DO.
WHEN WILL YOU GRADUATE?
NEVER.
WHOAAA...
YEAH.
WANT TO HELP ME WITH MY HOMEWORK?
SURE!
GO LONG!
www.babyblues.com
KIRKMAN & SCOTT 8-29
©2010 BABY BLUES PARTNERSHIP DIST. BY KING FEATURES SYNDICATE

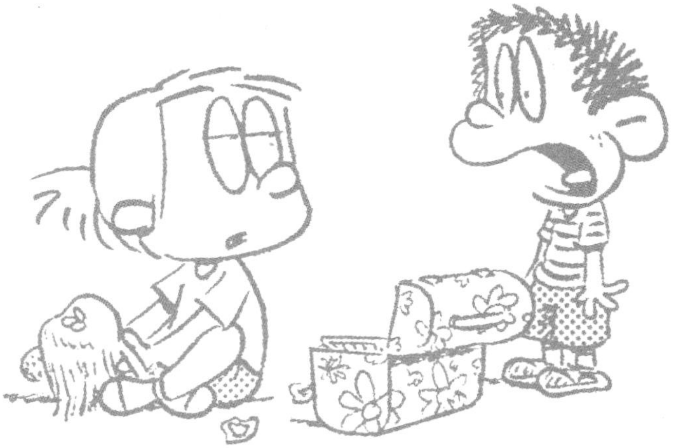

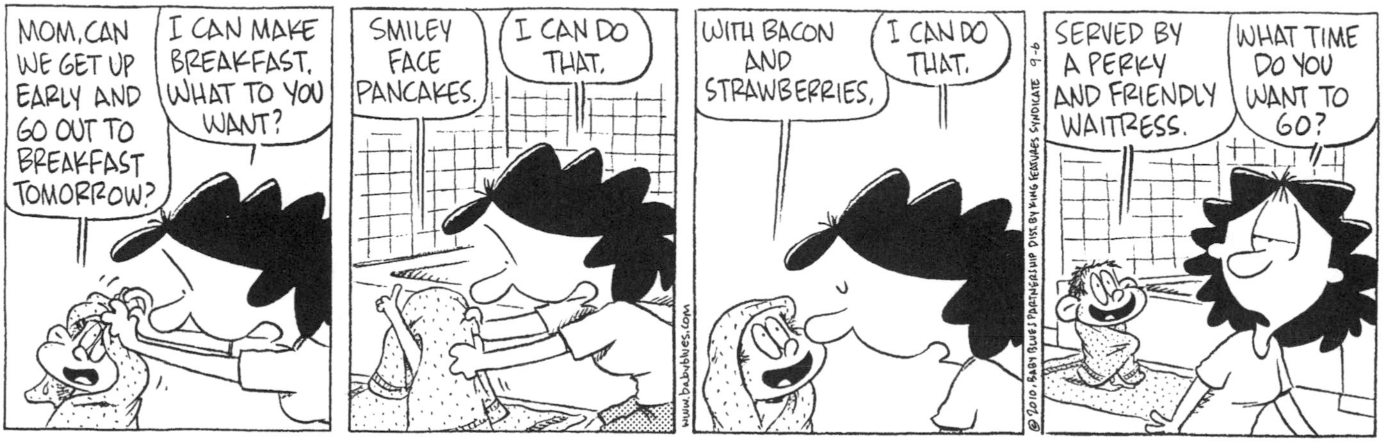
MOM, CAN WE GET UP EARLY AND GO OUT TO BREAKFAST TOMORROW?
I CAN MAKE BREAKFAST. WHAT TO YOU WANT?
SMILEY FACE PANCAKES.
I CAN DO THAT.
WITH BACON AND STRAWBERRIES.
I CAN DO THAT.
SERVED BY A PERKY AND FRIENDLY WAITRESS.
WHAT TIME DO YOU WANT TO GO?
www.babyblues.com
© 2010, BABY BLUES PARTNERSHIP DIST. BY KING FEATURES SYNDICATE 9-6

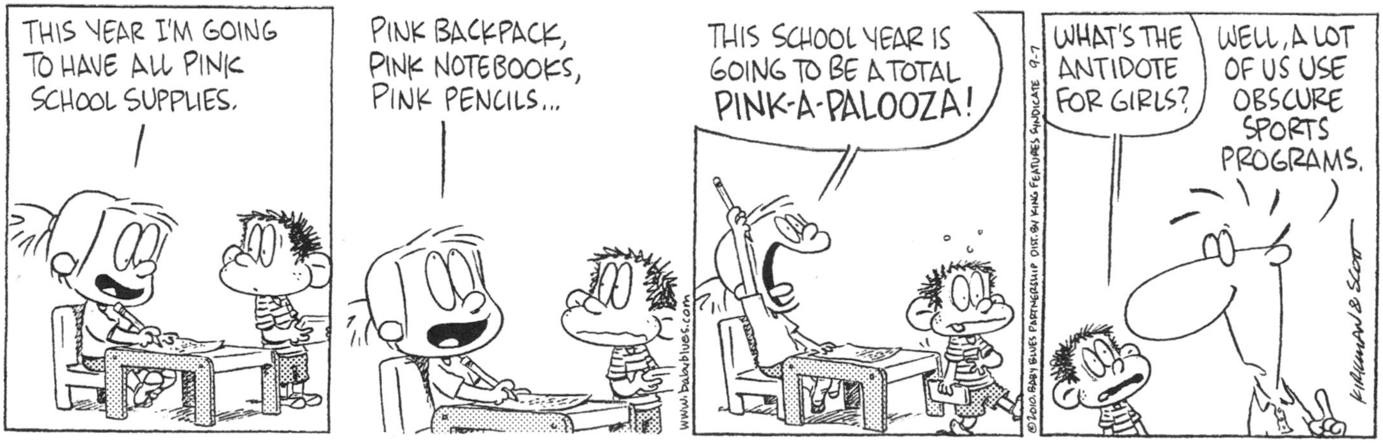
THIS YEAR I'M GOING TO HAVE ALL PINK SCHOOL SUPPLIES.
PINK BACKPACK, PINK NOTEBOOKS, PINK PENCILS...
THIS SCHOOL YEAR IS GOING TO BE A TOTAL PINK-A-PALOOZA!
WHAT'S THE ANTIDOTE FOR GIRLS?
WELL, A LOT OF US USE OBSCURE SPORTS PROGRAMS.
www.babyblues.com
© 2010, BABY BLUES PARTNERSHIP DIST. BY KING FEATURES SYNDICATE 9-7
KIRKMAN & SCOTT

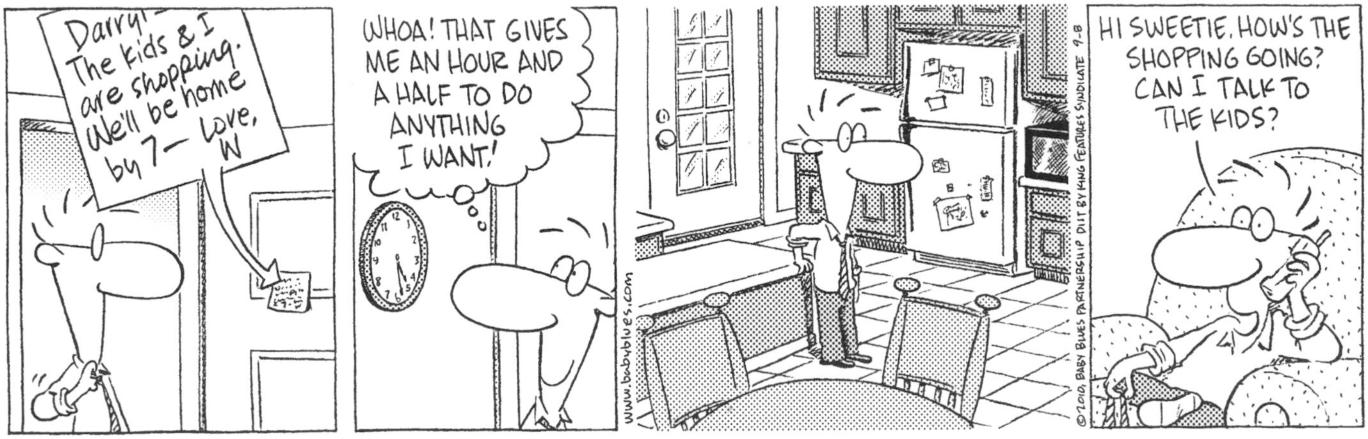
Darryl—
The kids & I are shopping. We'll be home by 7— Love, W
WHOA! THAT GIVES ME AN HOUR AND A HALF TO DO ANYTHING I WANT!
www.babyblues.com
©2010 BABY BLUES PARTNERSHIP DIST BY KING FEATURES SYNDICATE 9-8
HI SWEETIE. HOW'S THE SHOPPING GOING? CAN I TALK TO THE KIDS?

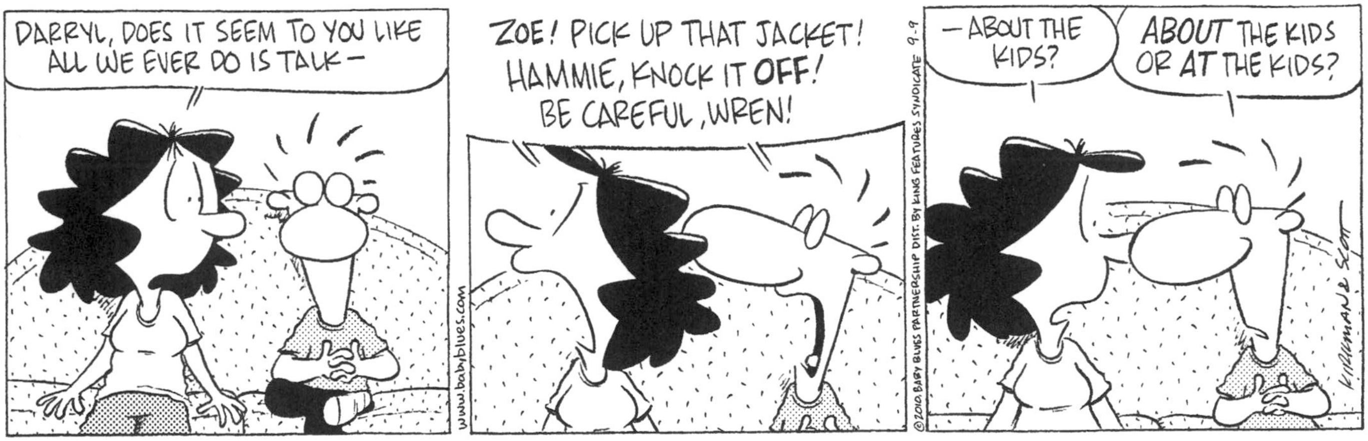
DARRYL, DOES IT SEEM TO YOU LIKE ALL WE EVER DO IS TALK—
www.babyblues.com
ZOE! PICK UP THAT JACKET! HAMMIE, KNOCK IT OFF! BE CAREFUL, WREN!
©2010 BABY BLUES PARTNERSHIP DIST. BY KING FEATURES SYNDICATE 9-9
—ABOUT THE KIDS?
ABOUT THE KIDS OR AT THE KIDS?
KIRKMAN & SCOTT

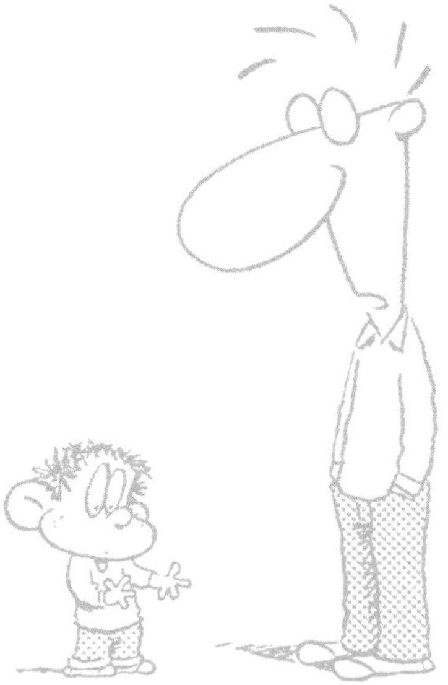

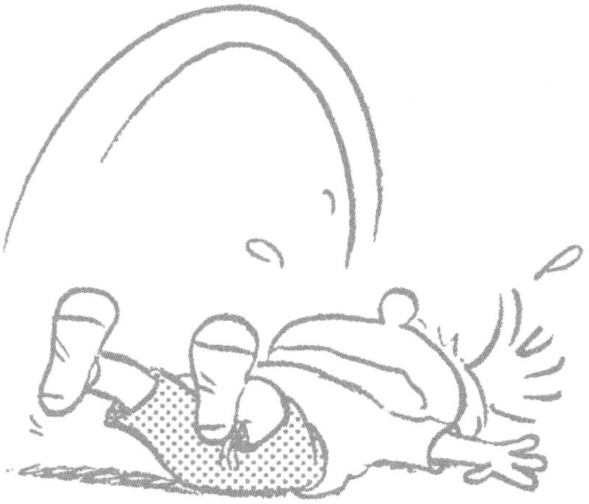

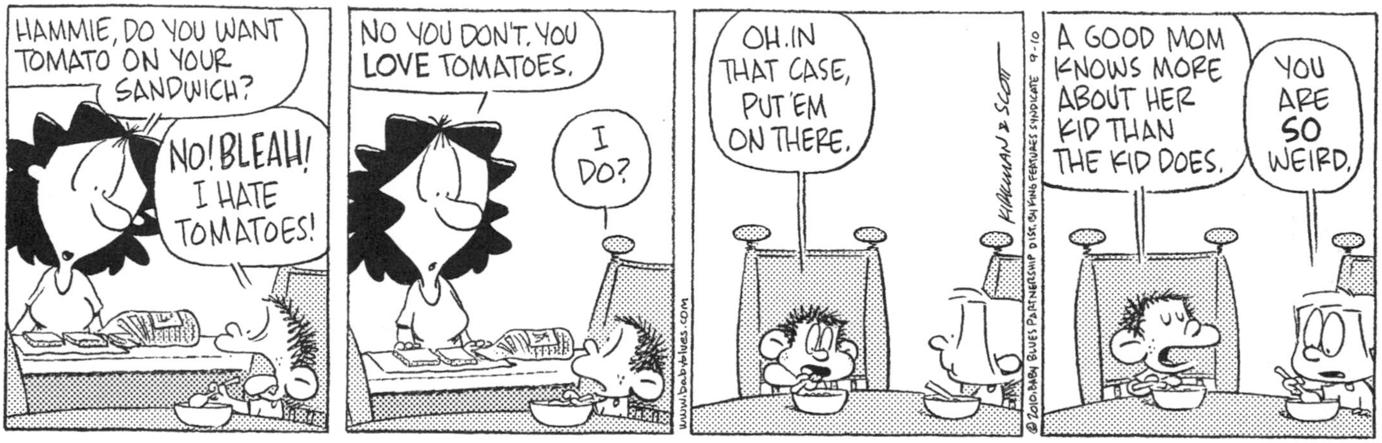
HAMMIE, DO YOU WANT TOMATO ON YOUR SANDWICH?
NO! BLEAH! I HATE TOMATOES!
NO YOU DON'T. YOU LOVE TOMATOES.
I DO?
www.babyblues.com
OH. IN THAT CASE, PUT 'EM ON THERE.
KIRKMAN & SCOTT 9-10
© 2010, BABY BLUES PARTNERSHIP DIST. BY KING FEATURES SYNDICATE
A GOOD MOM KNOWS MORE ABOUT HER KID THAN THE KID DOES.
YOU ARE SO WEIRD.

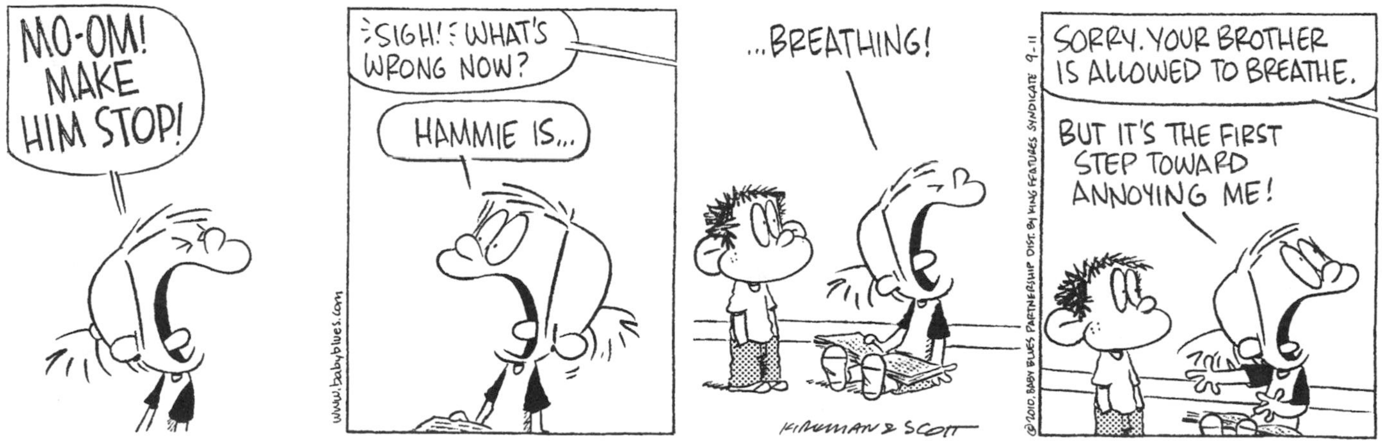
MO-OM! MAKE HIM STOP!
www.babyblues.com
SIGH! WHAT'S WRONG NOW?
HAMMIE IS...
...BREATHING!
KIRKMAN & SCOTT
© 2010, BABY BLUES PARTNERSHIP DIST. BY KING FEATURES SYNDICATE 9-11
SORRY. YOUR BROTHER IS ALLOWED TO BREATHE.
BUT IT'S THE FIRST STEP TOWARD ANNOYING ME!

BABY BLUES®
BY RICK KIRKMAN / JERRY SCOTT
TAP! TAP! TAP! TAP! TAP!

OH! HEY! GUESS WHAT?
WHAT?
I TALKED TO STAN TODAY, AND HE SAID I COULD HAVE THAT FRIDAY OFF NEXT MONTH.
SO WE CAN TAKE THE KIDS TO THE AQUARIUM? THAT'S GREAT! LET'S PUT IT ON THE CALENDAR.
ALREADY ON IT.
TAP! TAP! TAP! TAP! TAP!
YOU CALL THAT A CALENDAR?
September
KIRKMAN & SCOTT 9-12
©2010, BABY BLUES PARTNERSHIP DIST. BY KING FEATURES SYNDICATE www.babyblues.com

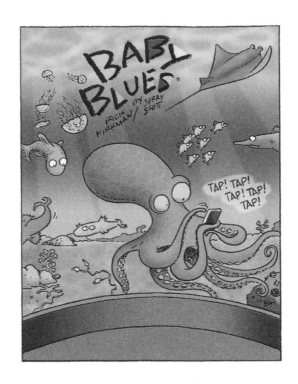

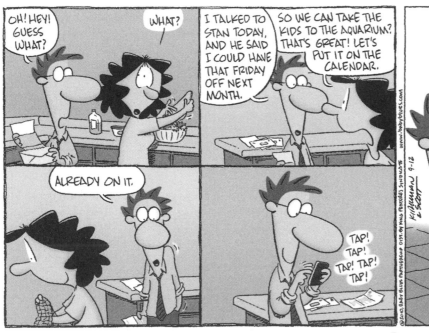

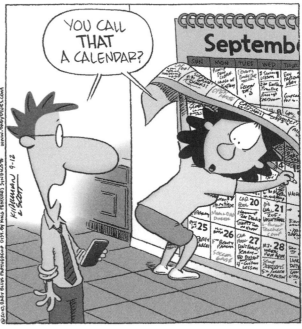

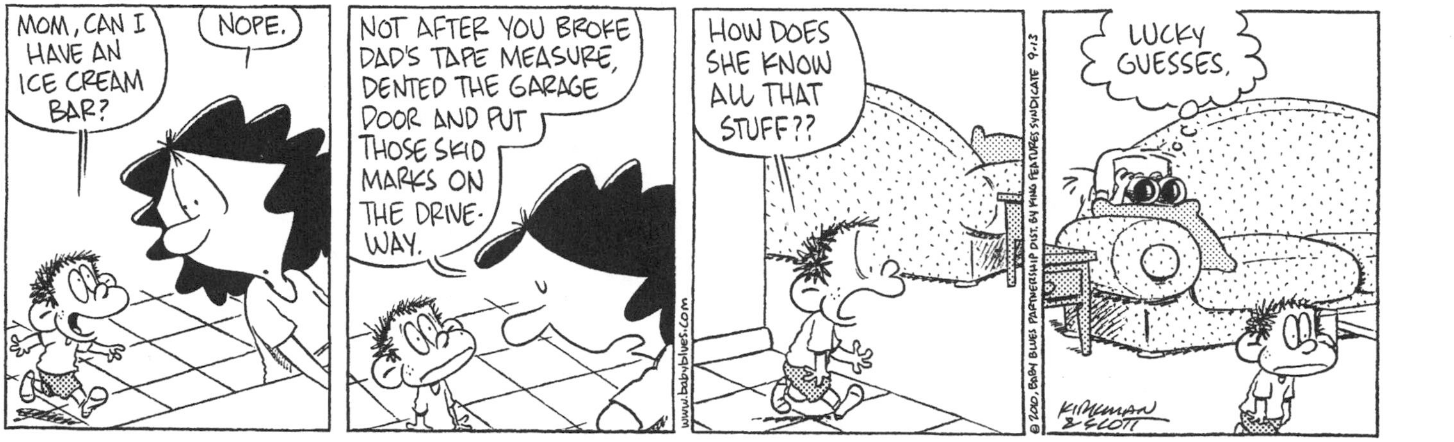
MOM, CAN I HAVE AN ICE CREAM BAR?
NOPE.
NOT AFTER YOU BROKE DAD'S TAPE MEASURE, DENTED THE GARAGE DOOR AND PUT THOSE SKID MARKS ON THE DRIVE-WAY.
www.babyblues.com
HOW DOES SHE KNOW ALL THAT STUFF??
© 2010, BABY BLUES PARTNERSHIP DIST. BY KING FEATURES SYNDICATE 9-13
LUCKY GUESSES.
KIRKMAN & SCOTT

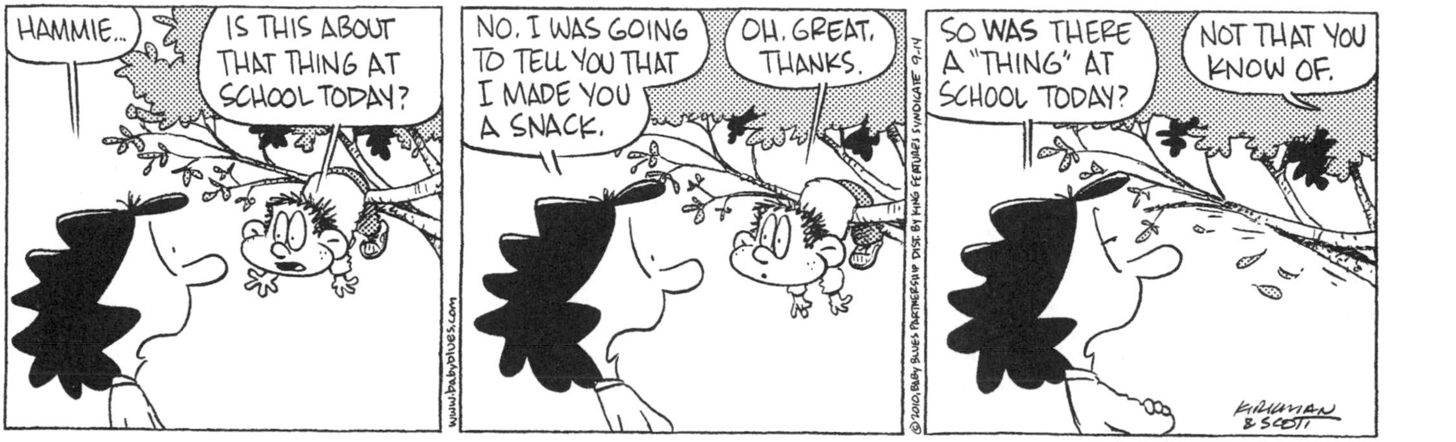
HAMMIE...
IS THIS ABOUT THAT THING AT SCHOOL TODAY?
www.babyblues.com
NO. I WAS GOING TO TELL YOU THAT I MADE YOU A SNACK.
OH. GREAT. THANKS.
© 2010, BABY BLUES PARTNERSHIP DIST. BY KING FEATURES SYNDICATE 9-14
SO WAS THERE A "THING" AT SCHOOL TODAY?
NOT THAT YOU KNOW OF.
KIRKMAN & SCOTT

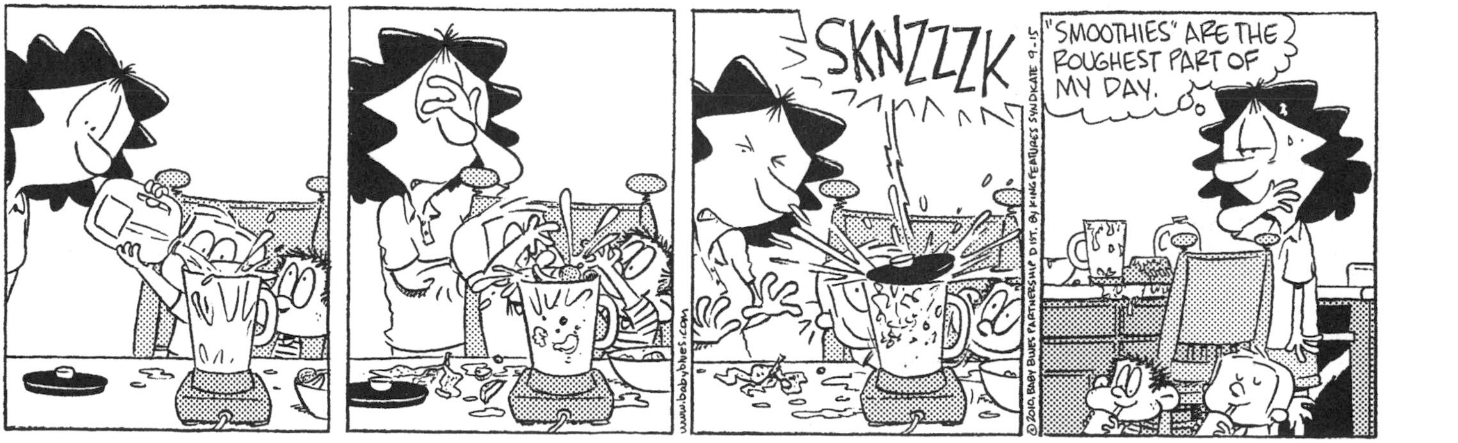
www.babyblues.com
SKNZZZK
© 2010, BABY BLUES PARTNERSHIP DIST. BY KING FEATURES SYNDICATE 9-15
"SMOOTHIES" ARE THE ROUGHEST PART OF MY DAY.

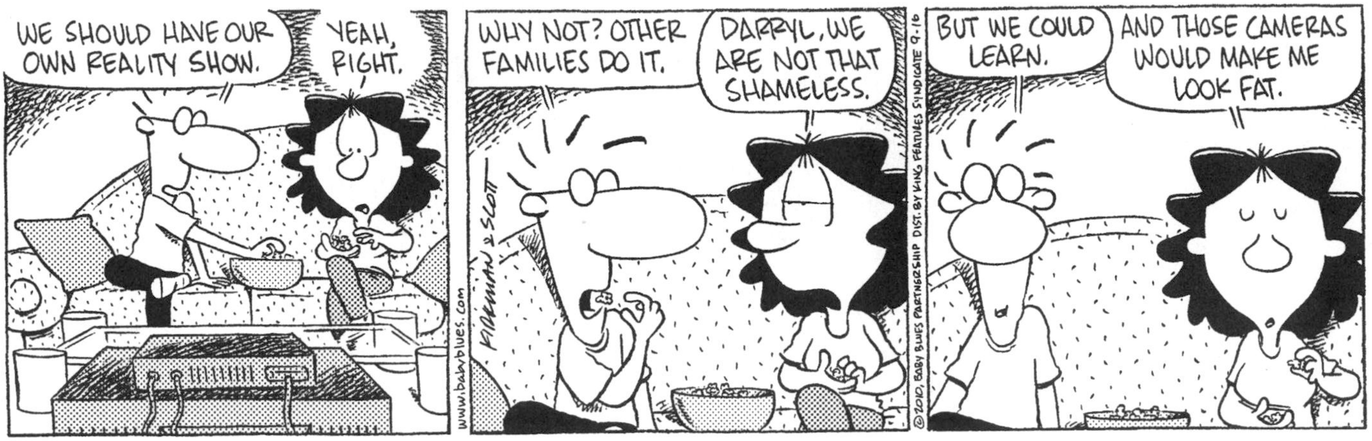
WE SHOULD HAVE OUR OWN REALITY SHOW.
YEAH, RIGHT.
WHY NOT? OTHER FAMILIES DO IT.
DARRYL, WE ARE NOT THAT SHAMELESS.
BUT WE COULD LEARN.
AND THOSE CAMERAS WOULD MAKE ME LOOK FAT.
www.babyblues.com
KIRKMAN & SCOTT
©2010, BABY BLUES PARTNERSHIP DIST. BY KING FEATURES SYNDICATE 9-16

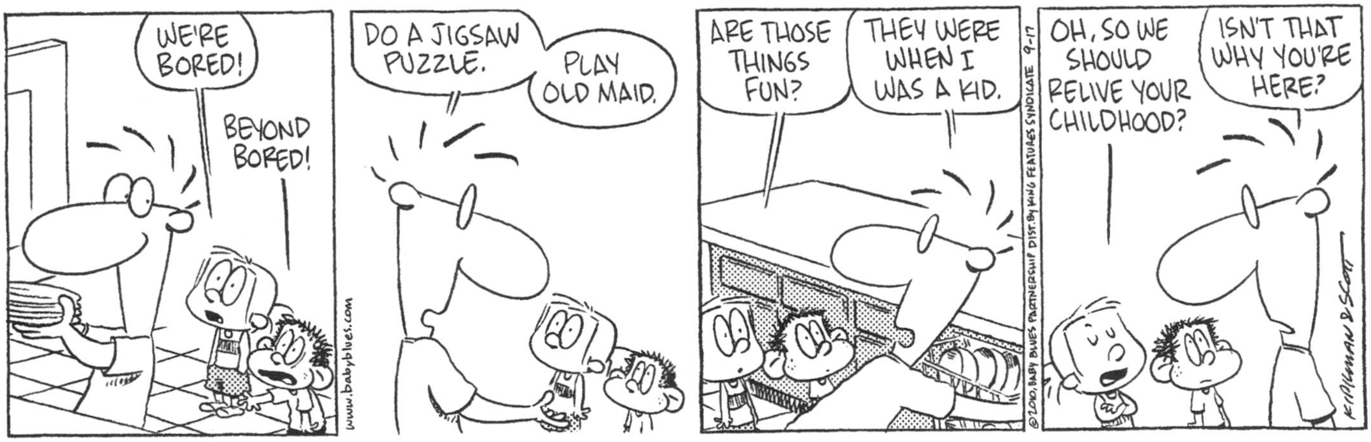
WE'RE BORED!
BEYOND BORED!
DO A JIGSAW PUZZLE.
PLAY OLD MAID.
ARE THOSE THINGS FUN?
THEY WERE WHEN I WAS A KID.
OH, SO WE SHOULD RELIVE YOUR CHILDHOOD?
ISN'T THAT WHY YOU'RE HERE?
www.babyblues.com
©2010, BABY BLUES PARTNERSHIP DIST. BY KING FEATURES SYNDICATE 9-17
KIRKMAN & SCOTT

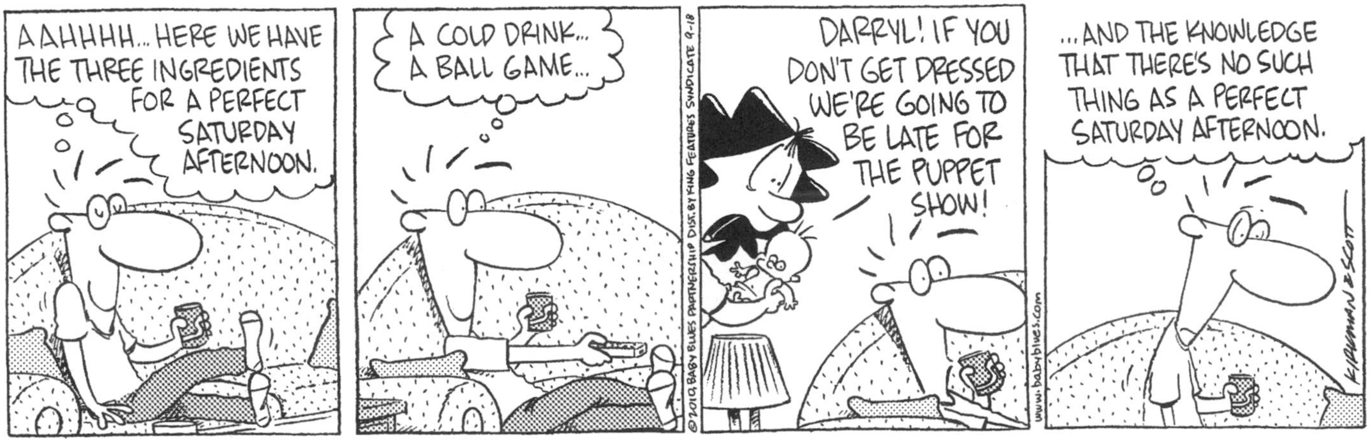
AAHHHH... HERE WE HAVE THE THREE INGREDIENTS FOR A PERFECT SATURDAY AFTERNOON.
A COLD DRINK... A BALL GAME...
DARRYL! IF YOU DON'T GET DRESSED WE'RE GOING TO BE LATE FOR THE PUPPET SHOW!
...AND THE KNOWLEDGE THAT THERE'S NO SUCH THING AS A PERFECT SATURDAY AFTERNOON.
©2010, BABY BLUES PARTNERSHIP DIST. BY KING FEATURES SYNDICATE 9-18
www.babyblues.com
KIRKMAN & SCOTT

BABY BLUES®

SEVEN FEET TALL?? REALLY?
AT LEAST.
OKAY. I GUESS I'LL TRY IT.
YOU'RE GOING TO FEEL LIKE AN NBA PLAYER. GUARANTEED.
WOW! THIS IS AMAZING! I'M—
FLASH!!
—DOOMED!
NOW LET'S TALK ABOUT WHAT IT WILL TAKE FOR THIS PICTURE TO NOT END UP ON MOM'S FACEBOOK PAGE...
KIRKMAN & SCOTT 9-19
©2010, BABY BLUES PARTNERSHIP DIST. BY KING FEATURES SYNDICATE www.babyblues.com

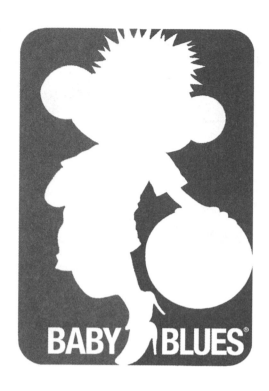

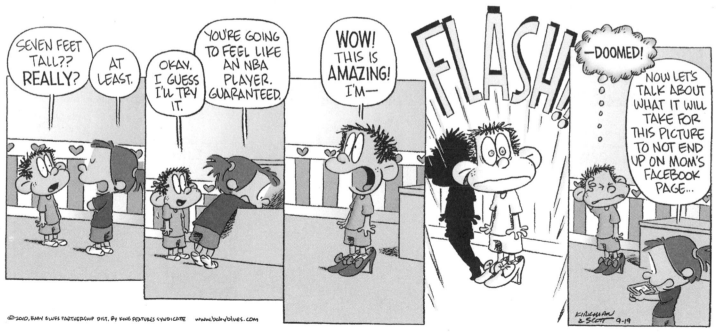

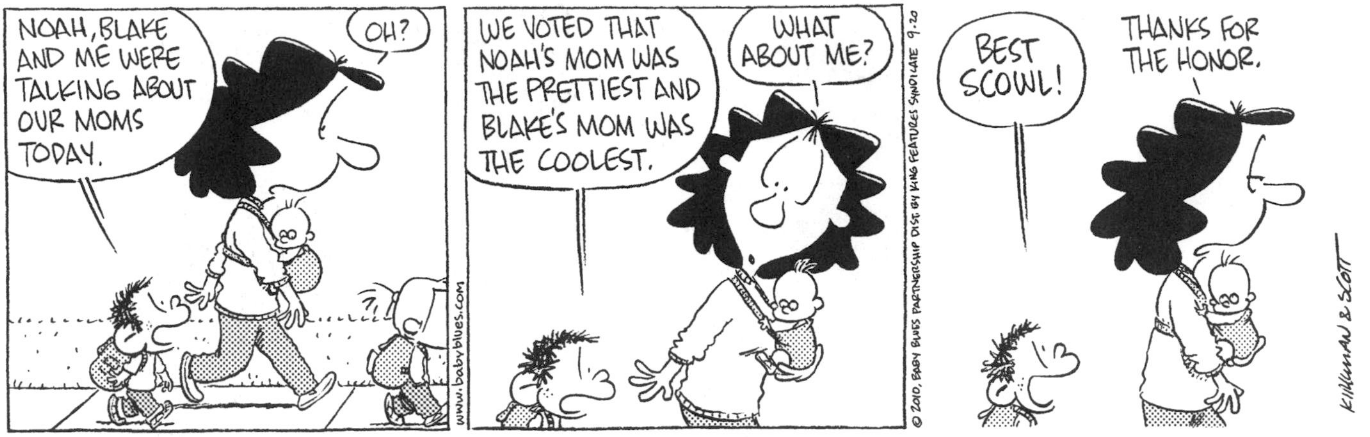
NOAH, BLAKE AND ME WERE TALKING ABOUT OUR MOMS TODAY.
OH?
WE VOTED THAT NOAH'S MOM WAS THE PRETTIEST AND BLAKE'S MOM WAS THE COOLEST.
WHAT ABOUT ME?
BEST SCOWL!
THANKS FOR THE HONOR.
www.babyblues.com
© 2010, BABY BLUES PARTNERSHIP DIST. BY KING FEATURES SYNDICATE 9-20
KIRKMAN & SCOTT

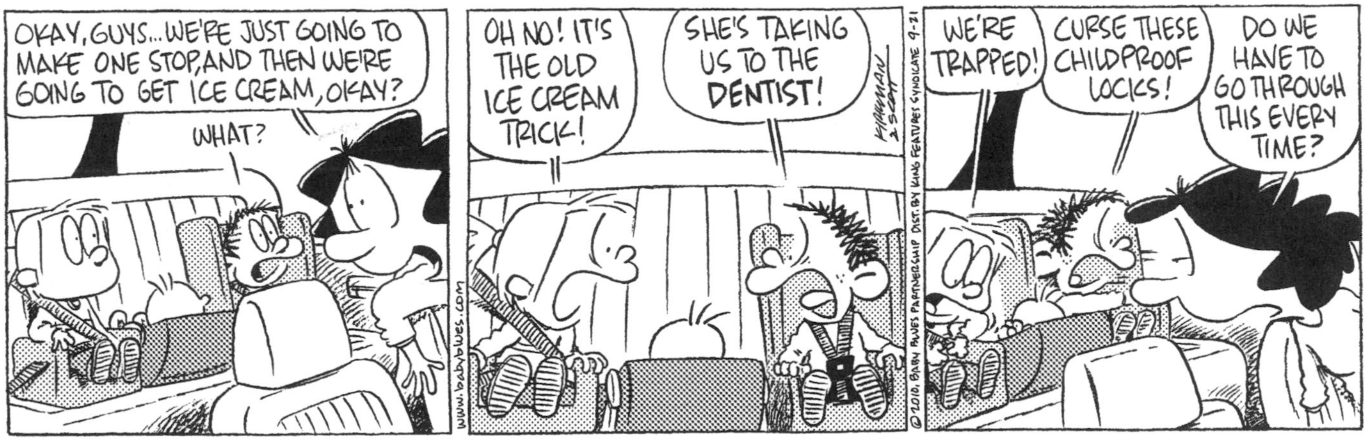
OKAY, GUYS... WE'RE JUST GOING TO MAKE ONE STOP, AND THEN WE'RE GOING TO GET ICE CREAM, OKAY?
WHAT?
OH NO! IT'S THE OLD ICE CREAM TRICK!
SHE'S TAKING US TO THE DENTIST!
WE'RE TRAPPED!
CURSE THESE CHILDPROOF LOCKS!
DO WE HAVE TO GO THROUGH THIS EVERY TIME?
www.babyblues.com
© 2010, BABY BLUES PARTNERSHIP DIST. BY KING FEATURES SYNDICATE 9-21
KIRKMAN & SCOTT

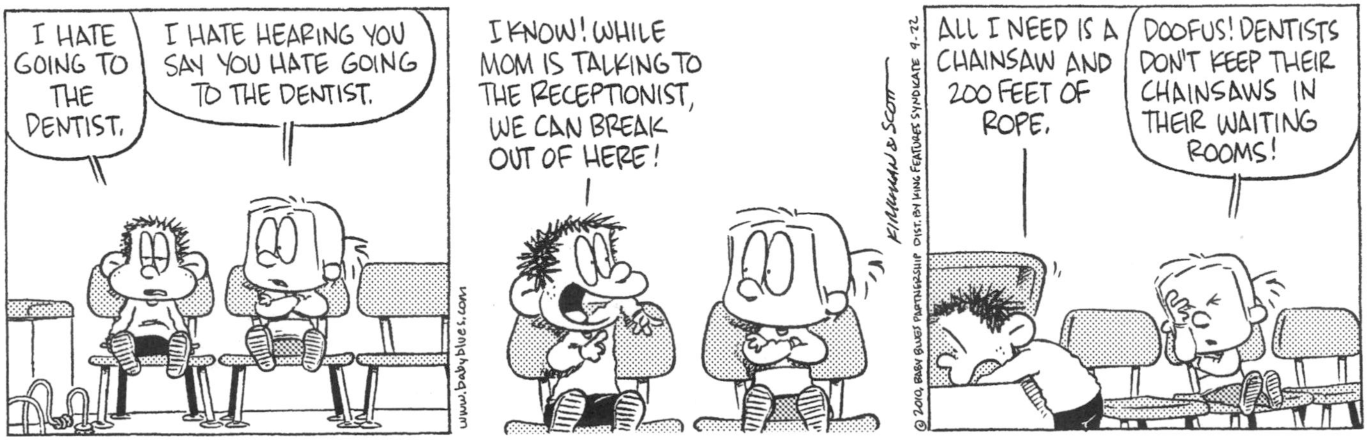
I HATE GOING TO THE DENTIST.
I HATE HEARING YOU SAY YOU HATE GOING TO THE DENTIST.
I KNOW! WHILE MOM IS TALKING TO THE RECEPTIONIST, WE CAN BREAK OUT OF HERE!
ALL I NEED IS A CHAINSAW AND 200 FEET OF ROPE.
DOOFUS! DENTISTS DON'T KEEP THEIR CHAINSAWS IN THEIR WAITING ROOMS!
www.babyblues.com
© 2010, BABY BLUES PARTNERSHIP DIST. BY KING FEATURES SYNDICATE 9-22
KIRKMAN & SCOTT

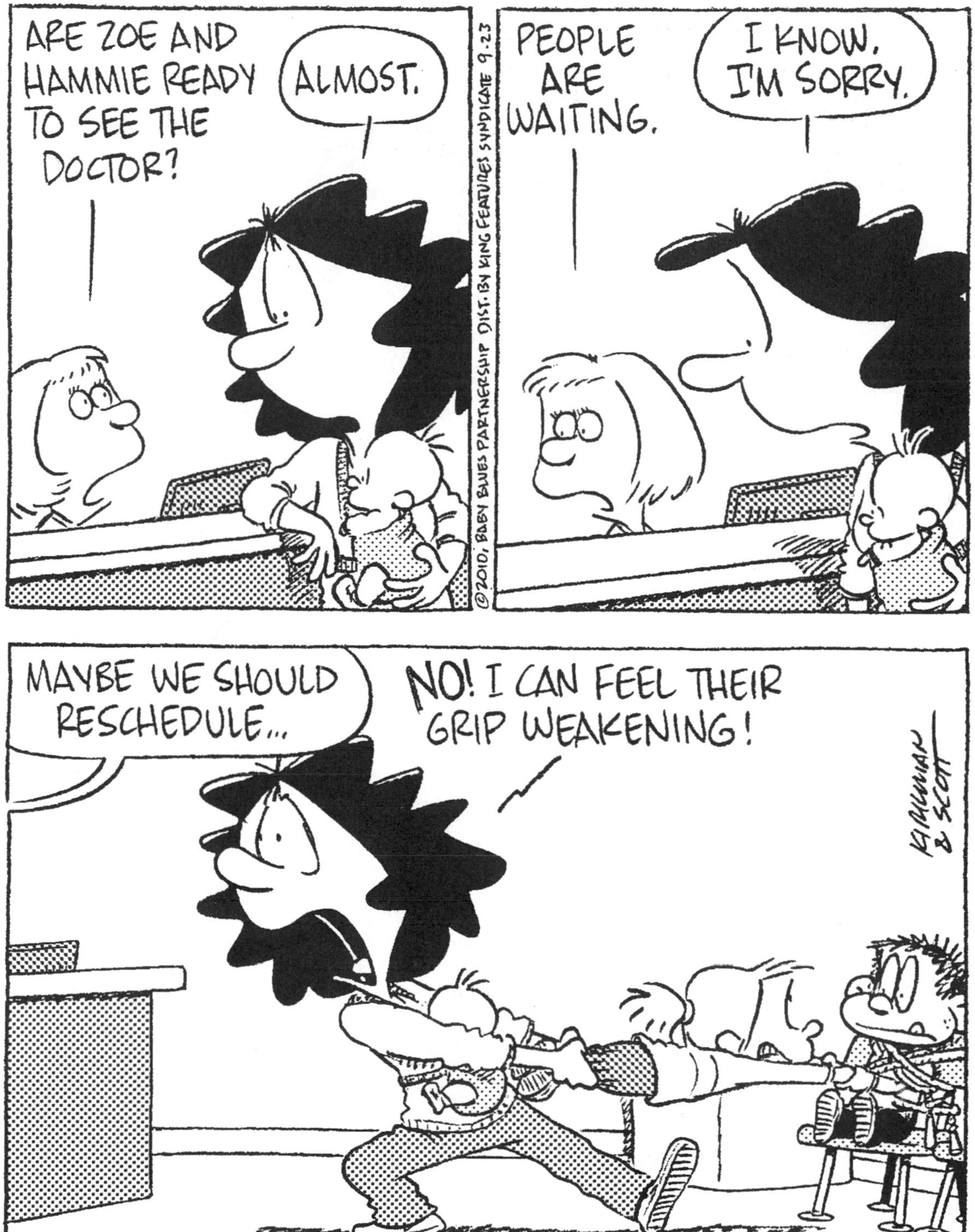
ARE ZOE AND HAMMIE READY TO SEE THE DOCTOR?
ALMOST.
©2010, BABY BLUES PARTNERSHIP DIST. BY KING FEATURES SYNDICATE 9-23
PEOPLE ARE WAITING.
I KNOW. I'M SORRY.
MAYBE WE SHOULD RESCHEDULE...
NO! I CAN FEEL THEIR GRIP WEAKENING!
KIRKMAN & SCOTT

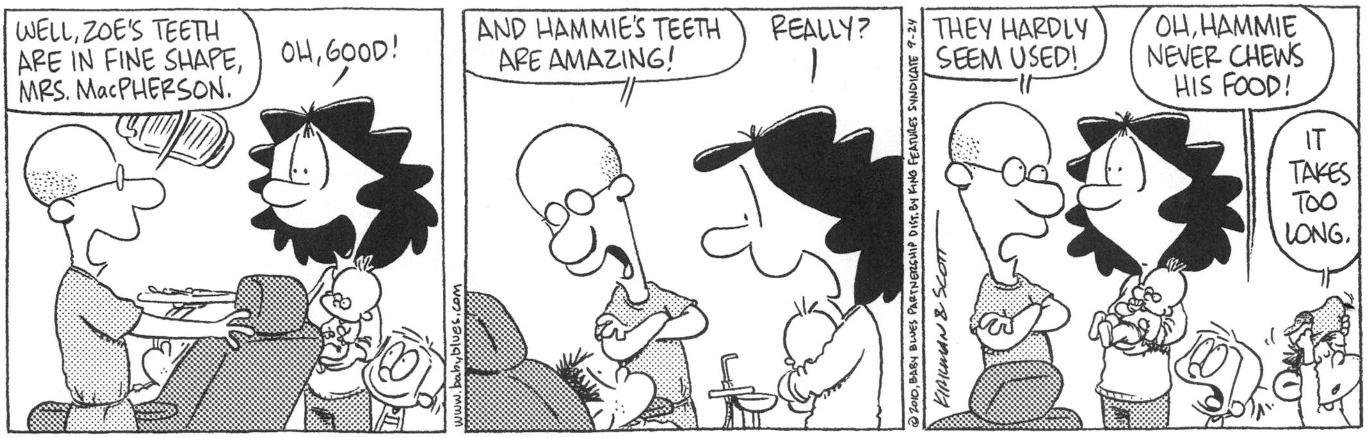
WELL, ZOE'S TEETH ARE IN FINE SHAPE, MRS. MacPHERSON.
OH, GOOD!
www.babyblues.com
AND HAMMIE'S TEETH ARE AMAZING!
REALLY?
© 2010, BABY BLUES PARTNERSHIP DIST. BY KING FEATURES SYNDICATE 9-24
KIRKMAN & SCOTT
THEY HARDLY SEEM USED!
OH, HAMMIE NEVER CHEWS HIS FOOD!
IT TAKES TOO LONG.

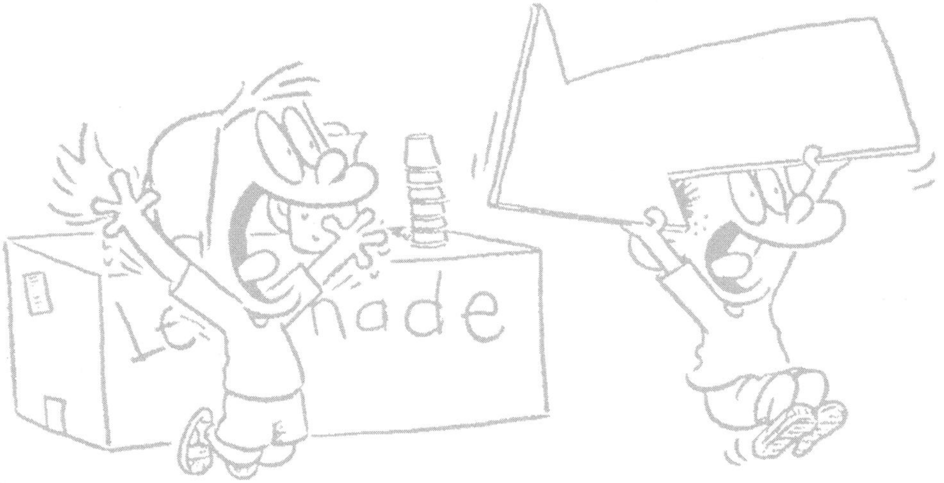

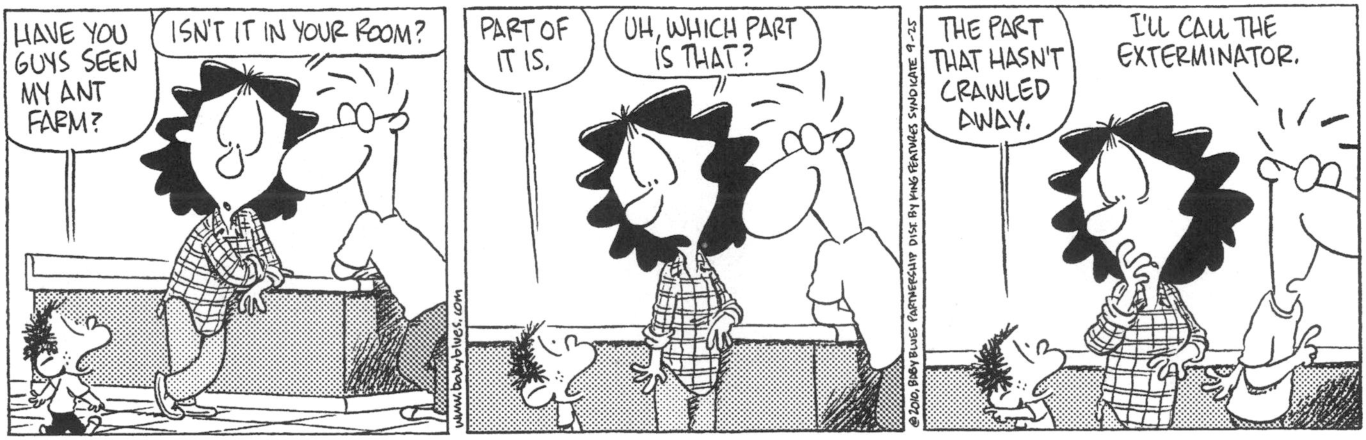
HAVE YOU GUYS SEEN MY ANT FARM?
ISN'T IT IN YOUR ROOM?
www.babyblues.com
PART OF IT IS.
UH, WHICH PART IS THAT?
© 2010, BABY BLUES PARTNERSHIP DIST. BY KING FEATURES SYNDICATE 9-25
THE PART THAT HASN'T CRAWLED AWAY.
I'LL CALL THE EXTERMINATOR.

BABY BLUES

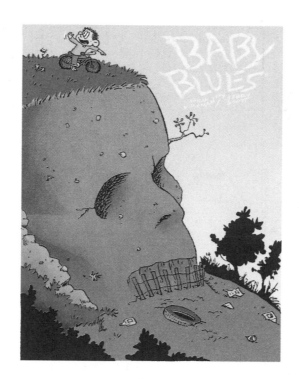

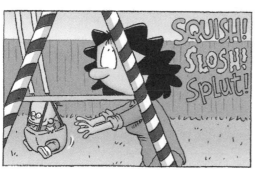

SQUISH!
SLOSH!
SPLUT!
HAMMIE! WHAT HAPPENED??
I CRASHED.
TRENT AND I WERE RIDING OUR BIKES UP DEAD MAN'S HILL.
ALL THE RAIN LAST NIGHT MADE THE PATH REALLY SLIPPERY, AND BEFORE WE KNEW IT, WE WERE SCREAMING DOWN THE HILL BACKWARDS AT ABOUT A MILLION MILES AN HOUR AND LANDING IN A **HUGE** PUDDLE!
OH MY!
www.babyblues.com
YOU NEED TO THINK ABOUT WHAT YOU'RE DOING OUT THERE!
I DID, MOM.
©2010, BABY BLUES PARTNERSHIP DIST. BY KING FEATURES SYNDICATE 9-26
AND YOU **STILL** HAD THIS ACCIDENT?
WHAT ACCIDENT?

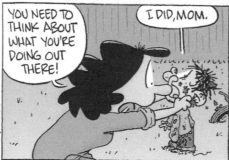

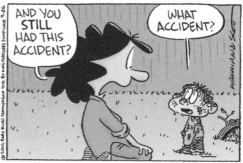

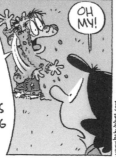

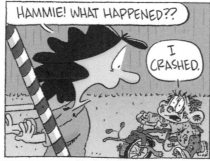

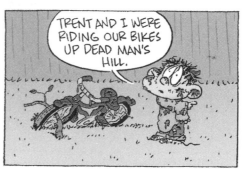

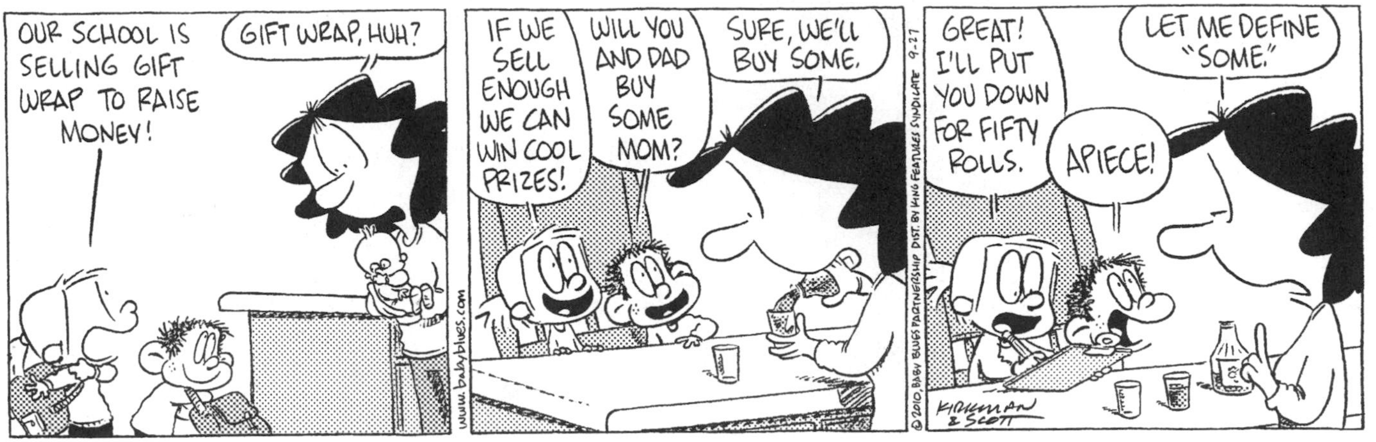
OUR SCHOOL IS SELLING GIFT WRAP TO RAISE MONEY!
GIFT WRAP, HUH?
www.babyblues.com
IF WE SELL ENOUGH WE CAN WIN COOL PRIZES!
WILL YOU AND DAD BUY SOME MOM?
SURE, WE'LL BUY SOME.
© 2010, BABY BLUES PARTNERSHIP DIST. BY KING FEATURES SYNDICATE 9-27
GREAT! I'LL PUT YOU DOWN FOR FIFTY ROLLS.
APIECE!
LET ME DEFINE "SOME."
KIRKMAN & SCOTT

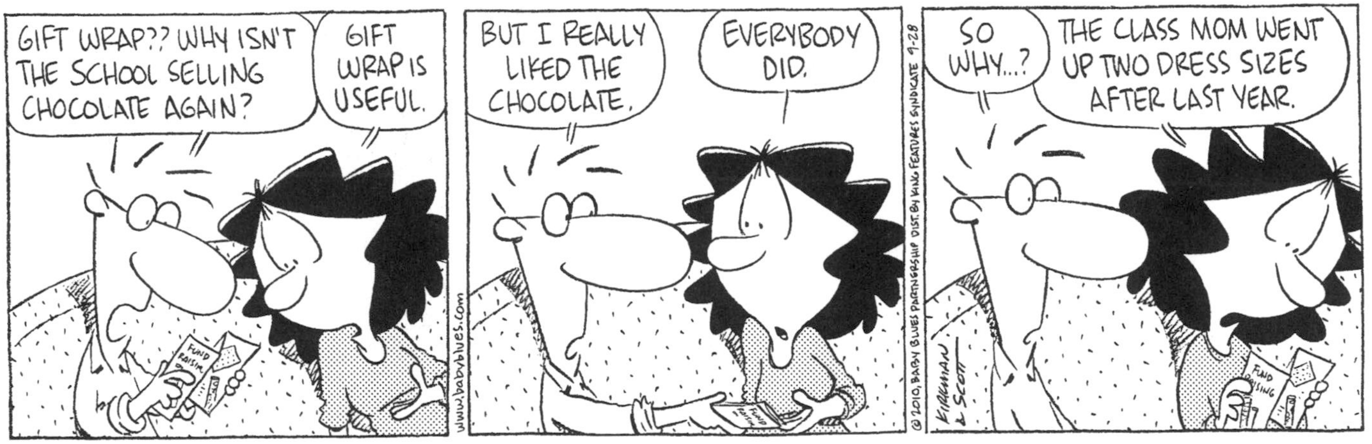
GIFT WRAP?? WHY ISN'T THE SCHOOL SELLING CHOCOLATE AGAIN?
GIFT WRAP IS USEFUL.
www.babyblues.com
BUT I REALLY LIKED THE CHOCOLATE.
EVERYBODY DID.
© 2010, BABY BLUES PARTNERSHIP DIST. BY KING FEATURES SYNDICATE 9-28
SO WHY...?
THE CLASS MOM WENT UP TWO DRESS SIZES AFTER LAST YEAR.
KIRKMAN & SCOTT

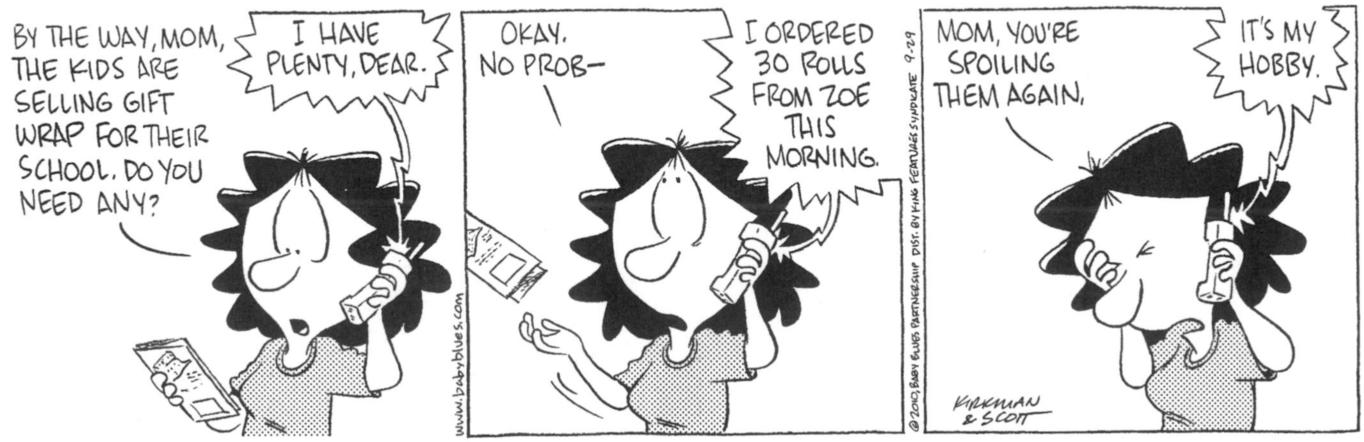
BY THE WAY, MOM, THE KIDS ARE SELLING GIFT WRAP FOR THEIR SCHOOL. DO YOU NEED ANY?
I HAVE PLENTY, DEAR.
www.babyblues.com
OKAY. NO PROB–
I ORDERED 30 ROLLS FROM ZOE THIS MORNING.
© 2010, BABY BLUES PARTNERSHIP DIST. BY KING FEATURES SYNDICATE 9-29
MOM, YOU'RE SPOILING THEM AGAIN.
IT'S MY HOBBY.
KIRKMAN & SCOTT

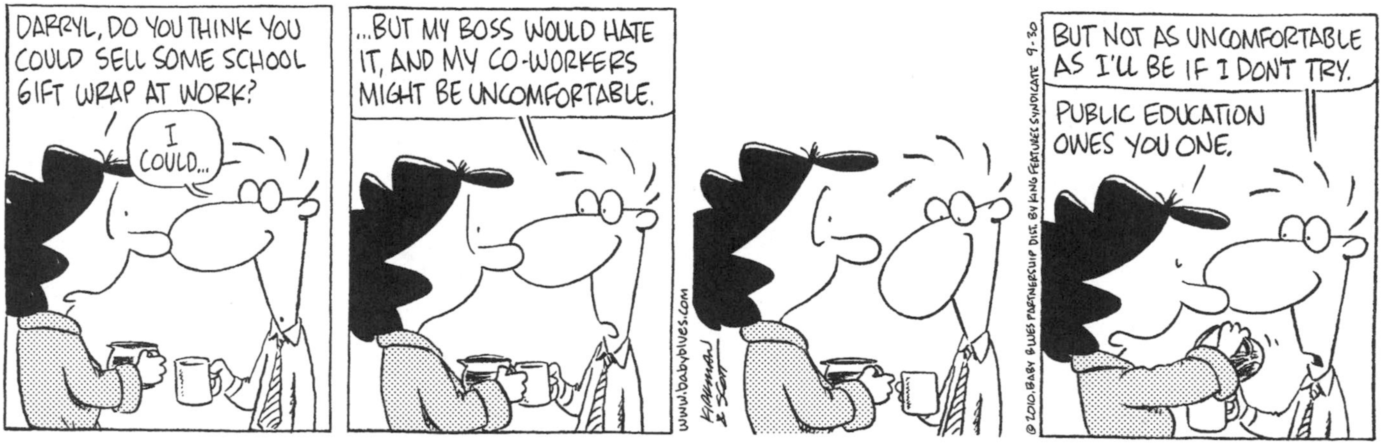
DARRYL, DO YOU THINK YOU COULD SELL SOME SCHOOL GIFT WRAP AT WORK?
I COULD...
...BUT MY BOSS WOULD HATE IT, AND MY CO-WORKERS MIGHT BE UNCOMFORTABLE.
www.babyblues.com
KIRKMAN & SCOTT
© 2010, BABY BLUES PARTNERSHIP DIST. BY KING FEATURES SYNDICATE 9-30
BUT NOT AS UNCOMFORTABLE AS I'LL BE IF I DON'T TRY.
PUBLIC EDUCATION OWES YOU ONE.

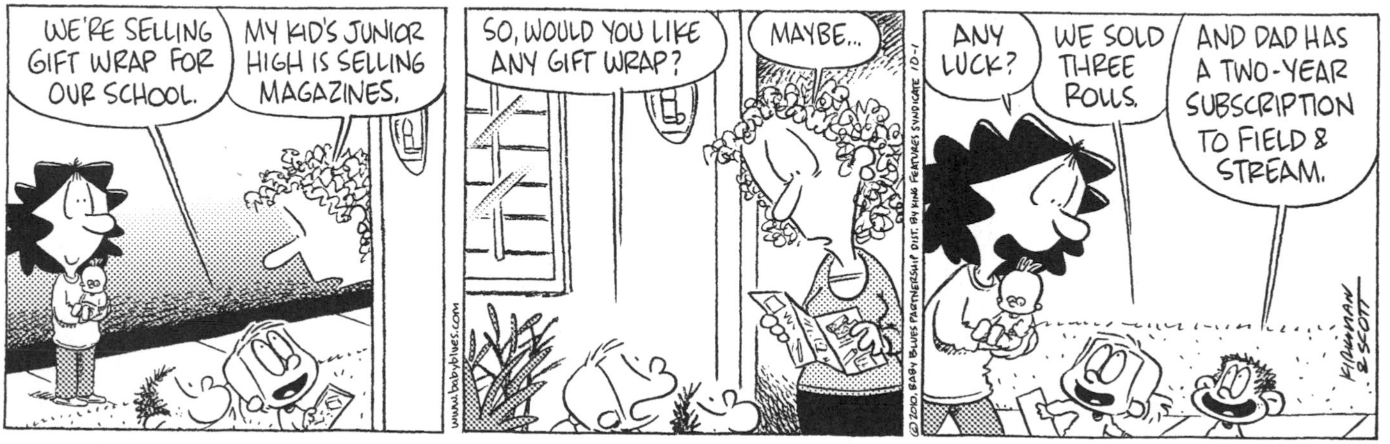
WE'RE SELLING GIFT WRAP FOR OUR SCHOOL.
MY KID'S JUNIOR HIGH IS SELLING MAGAZINES.
www.babyblues.com
SO, WOULD YOU LIKE ANY GIFT WRAP?
MAYBE...
© 2010, BABY BLUES PARTNERSHIP DIST. BY KING FEATURES SYNDICATE 10-1
ANY LUCK?
WE SOLD THREE ROLLS.
AND DAD HAS A TWO-YEAR SUBSCRIPTION TO FIELD & STREAM.
KIRKMAN & SCOTT

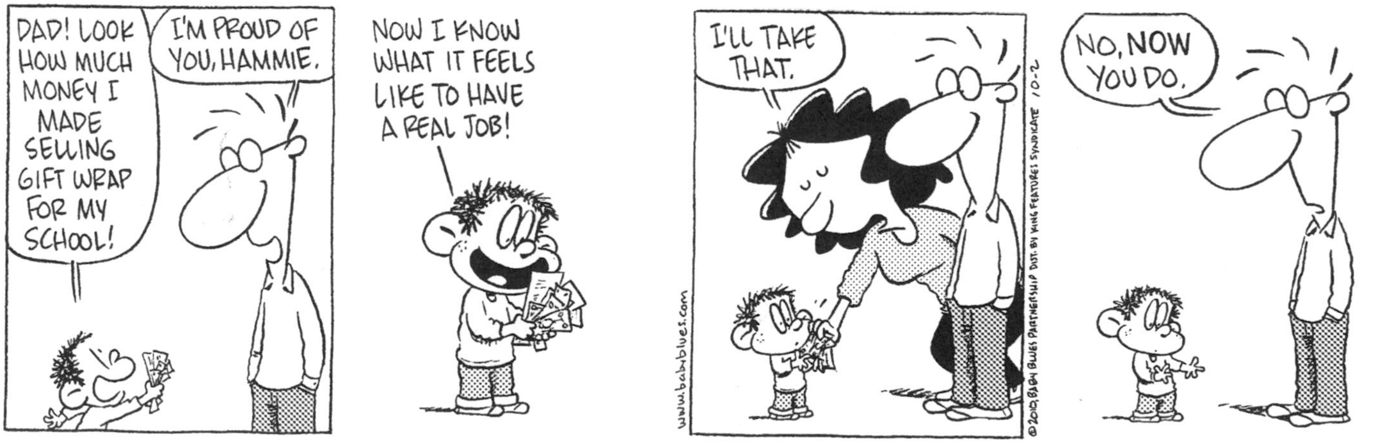
DAD! LOOK HOW MUCH MONEY I MADE SELLING GIFT WRAP FOR MY SCHOOL!
I'M PROUD OF YOU, HAMMIE.
NOW I KNOW WHAT IT FEELS LIKE TO HAVE A REAL JOB!
www.babyblues.com
I'LL TAKE THAT.
© 2010, BABY BLUES PARTNERSHIP DIST. BY KING FEATURES SYNDICATE 10-2
NO, NOW YOU DO.

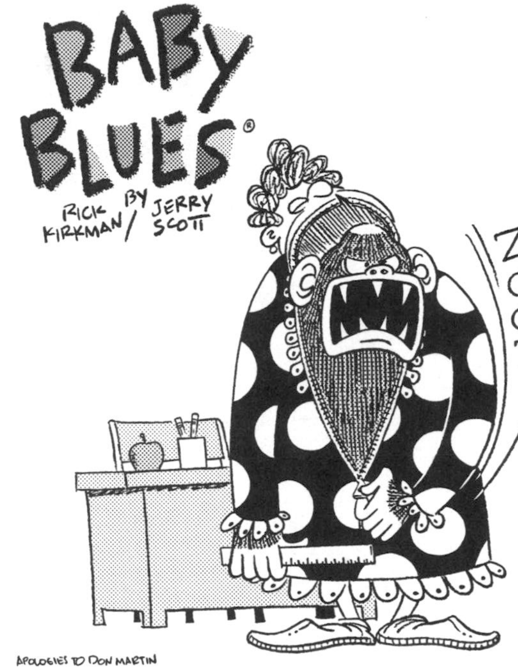
BABY BLUES®
BY RICK KIRKMAN / JERRY SCOTT
ZOOT
APOLOGIES TO DON MARTIN

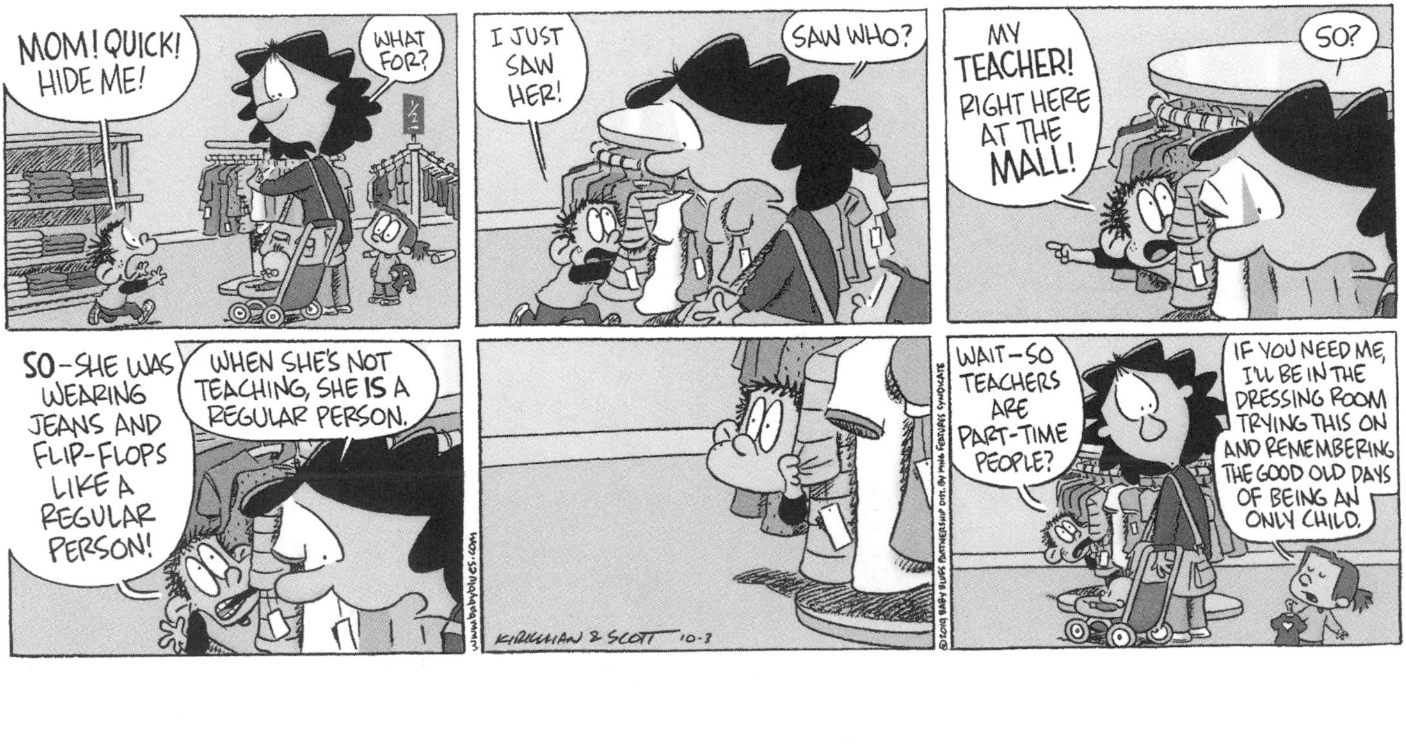
MOM! QUICK! HIDE ME!
WHAT FOR?
I JUST SAW HER!
SAW WHO?
MY TEACHER! RIGHT HERE AT THE MALL!
SO?
SO—SHE WAS WEARING JEANS AND FLIP-FLOPS LIKE A REGULAR PERSON!
WHEN SHE'S NOT TEACHING, SHE IS A REGULAR PERSON.
www.babyblues.com
KIRKMAN & SCOTT 10-3
©2019 BABY BLUES PARTNERSHIP DIST. BY KING FEATURES SYNDICATE
WAIT—SO TEACHERS ARE PART-TIME PEOPLE?
IF YOU NEED ME, I'LL BE IN THE DRESSING ROOM TRYING THIS ON AND REMEMBERING THE GOOD OLD DAYS OF BEING AN ONLY CHILD.

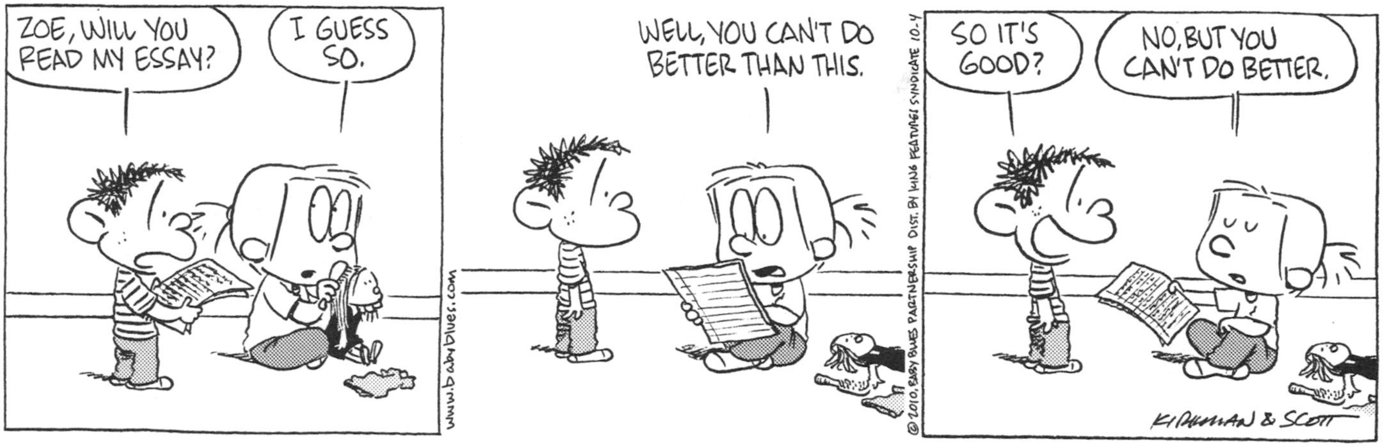
ZOE, WILL YOU READ MY ESSAY?
I GUESS SO.
www.babyblues.com
WELL, YOU CAN'T DO BETTER THAN THIS.
© 2010, BABY BLUES PARTNERSHIP DIST. BY KING FEATURES SYNDICATE 10-4
SO IT'S GOOD?
NO, BUT YOU CAN'T DO BETTER.
KIRKMAN & SCOTT

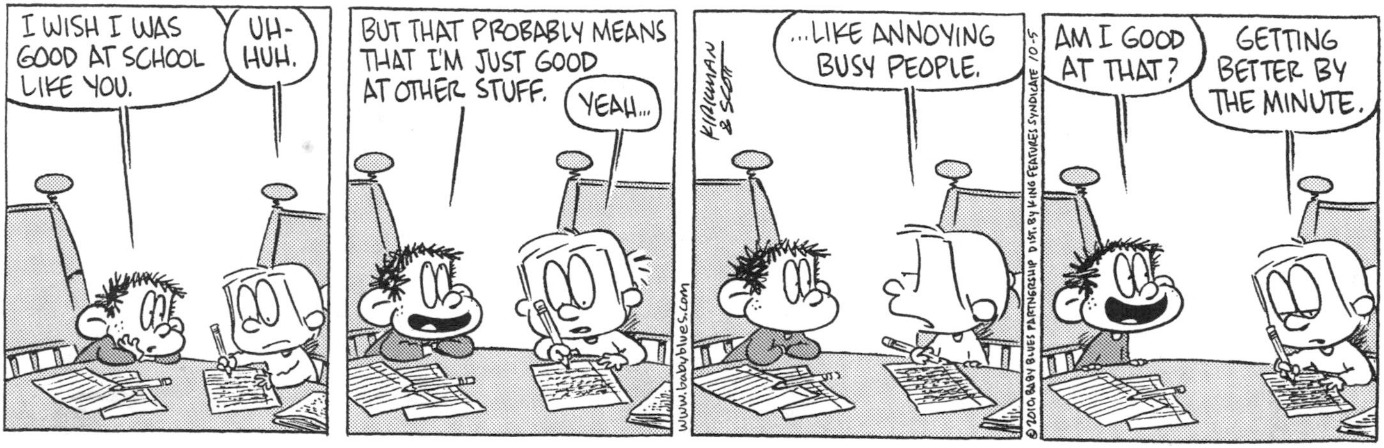
I WISH I WAS GOOD AT SCHOOL LIKE YOU.
UH-HUH.
BUT THAT PROBABLY MEANS THAT I'M JUST GOOD AT OTHER STUFF.
YEAH...
www.babyblues.com
KIRKMAN & SCOTT
...LIKE ANNOYING BUSY PEOPLE.
© 2010, BABY BLUES PARTNERSHIP DIST. BY KING FEATURES SYNDICATE 10-5
AM I GOOD AT THAT?
GETTING BETTER BY THE MINUTE.

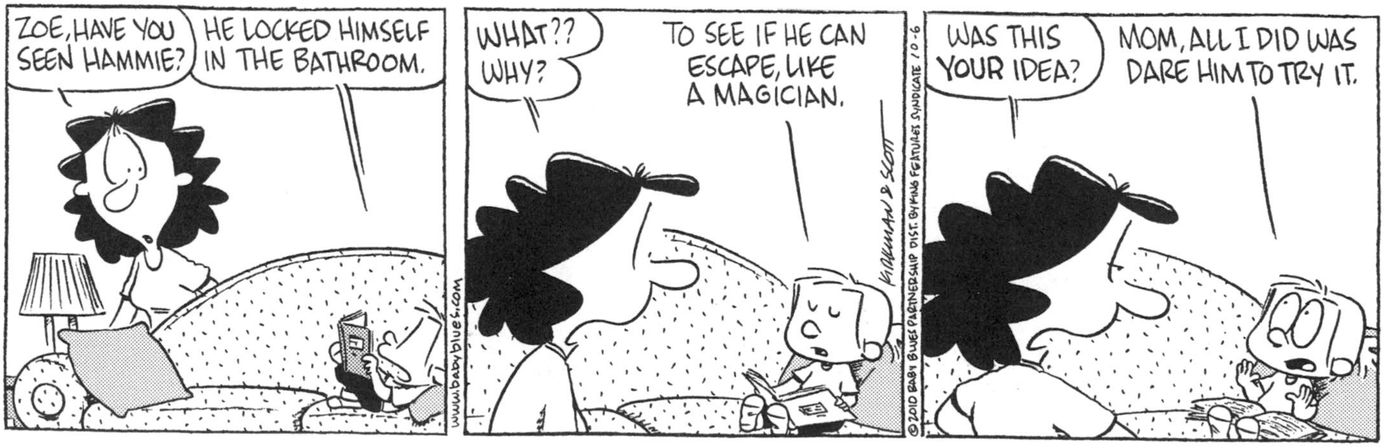
ZOE, HAVE YOU SEEN HAMMIE?
HE LOCKED HIMSELF IN THE BATHROOM.
www.babyblues.com
WHAT?? WHY?
TO SEE IF HE CAN ESCAPE, LIKE A MAGICIAN.
KIRKMAN & SCOTT
© 2010 BABY BLUES PARTNERSHIP DIST. BY KING FEATURES SYNDICATE 10-6
WAS THIS YOUR IDEA?
MOM, ALL I DID WAS DARE HIM TO TRY IT.

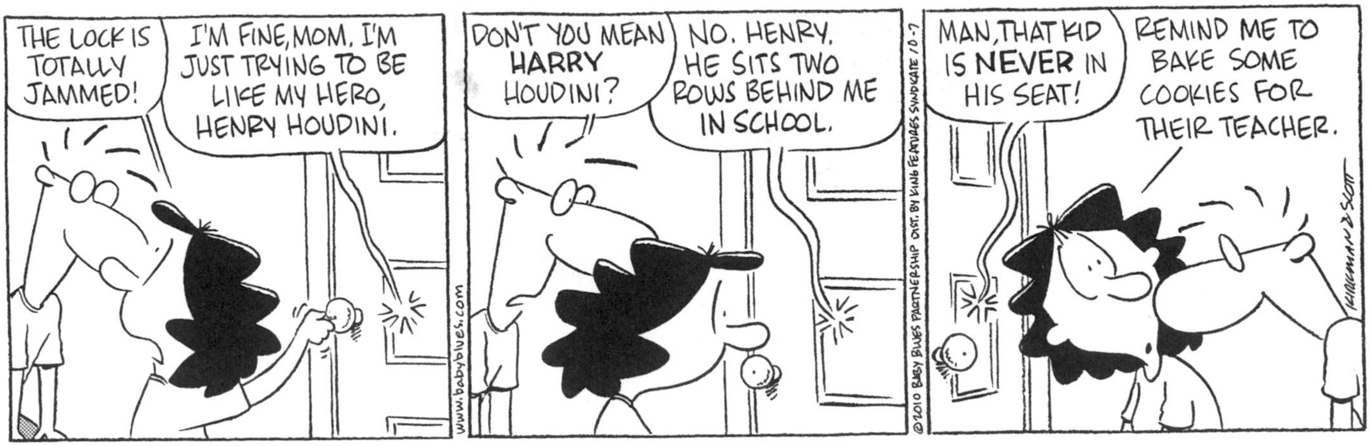
THE LOCK IS TOTALLY JAMMED!
I'M FINE, MOM. I'M JUST TRYING TO BE LIKE MY HERO, HENRY HOUDINI.
www.babyblues.com
DON'T YOU MEAN **HARRY** HOUDINI?
NO. HENRY. HE SITS TWO ROWS BEHIND ME IN SCHOOL.
© 2010 BABY BLUES PARTNERSHIP DIST. BY KING FEATURES SYNDICATE 10-7
MAN, THAT KID IS **NEVER** IN HIS SEAT!
REMIND ME TO BAKE SOME COOKIES FOR THEIR TEACHER.
KIRKMAN & SCOTT

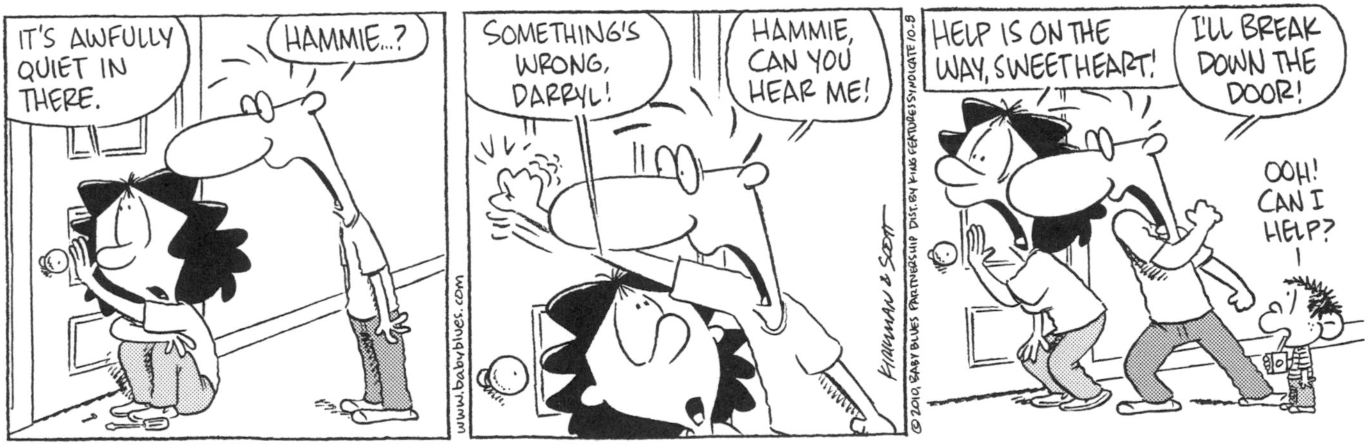
IT'S AWFULLY QUIET IN THERE.
HAMMIE...?
www.babyblues.com
SOMETHING'S WRONG, DARRYL!
HAMMIE, CAN YOU HEAR ME!
KIRKMAN & SCOTT
© 2010, BABY BLUES PARTNERSHIP DIST. BY KING FEATURES SYNDICATE 10-8
HELP IS ON THE WAY, SWEETHEART!
I'LL BREAK DOWN THE DOOR!
OOH! CAN I HELP?

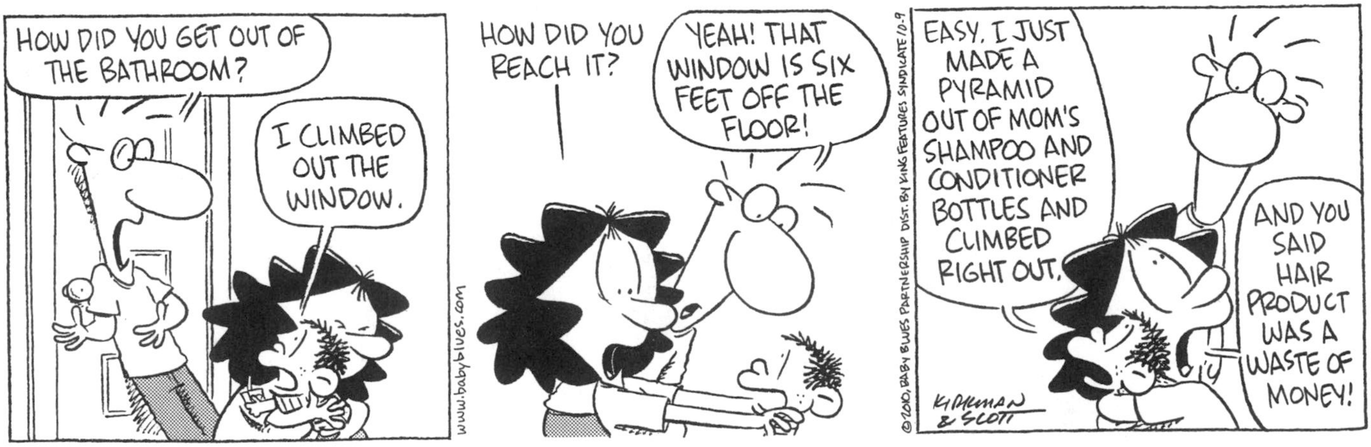
HOW DID YOU GET OUT OF THE BATHROOM?
I CLIMBED OUT THE WINDOW.
www.babyblues.com
HOW DID YOU REACH IT?
YEAH! THAT WINDOW IS SIX FEET OFF THE FLOOR!
© 2010, BABY BLUES PARTNERSHIP DIST. BY KING FEATURES SYNDICATE 10-9
EASY. I JUST MADE A PYRAMID OUT OF MOM'S SHAMPOO AND CONDITIONER BOTTLES AND CLIMBED RIGHT OUT.
AND YOU SAID HAIR PRODUCT WAS A WASTE OF MONEY!
KIRKMAN & SCOTT

WANDA

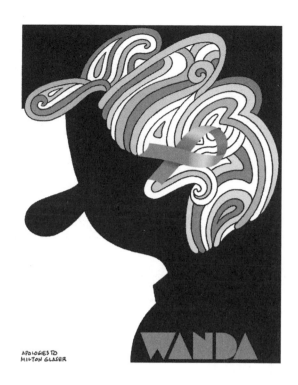

APOLOGIES TO
MILTON GLASER

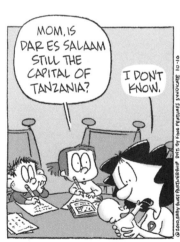

MOM, IS DAR ES SALAAM STILL THE CAPITAL OF TANZANIA?
I DON'T KNOW.
©2010, BABY BLUES PARTNERSHIP DIST. BY KING FEATURES SYNDICATE 10-10
WHAT? I THOUGHT YOU KNEW EVERYTHING!
NO, NOT EVERYTHING...
www.babyblues.com
HONEY, HAVE YOU SEEN MY KEYS?
ON THE DRESSER.
WHAT WAS THE THING I WAS TRYING TO REMEMBER?
PING-PONG BALLS.
WHEN IS THE SCHOOL RECITAL?
TUESDAY NIGHT.
DON'T LET ME FORGET TO...UM...
GO TO THE BANK.
RIGHT. THANKS.
KIRKMAN & SCOTT
...JUST THE IMPORTANT STUFF.

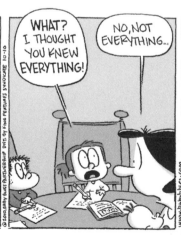

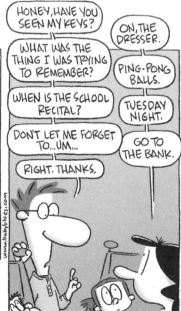

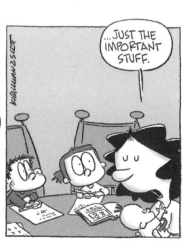

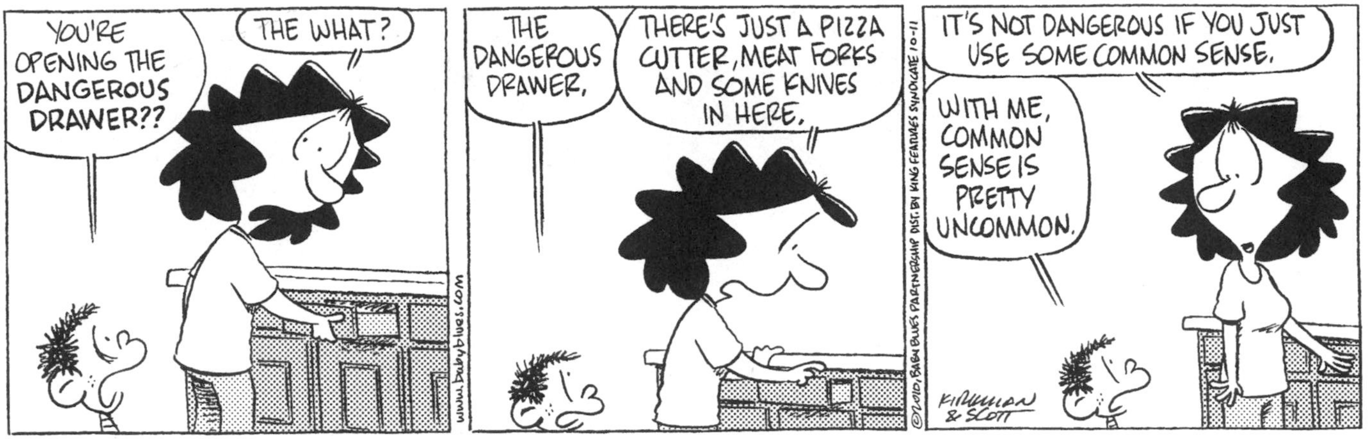
YOU'RE OPENING THE DANGEROUS DRAWER??
THE WHAT?
www.babyblues.com
THE DANGEROUS DRAWER.
THERE'S JUST A PIZZA CUTTER, MEAT FORKS AND SOME KNIVES IN HERE.
©2010, BABY BLUES PARTNERSHIP DIST. BY KING FEATURES SYNDICATE 10-11
IT'S NOT DANGEROUS IF YOU JUST USE SOME COMMON SENSE.
WITH ME, COMMON SENSE IS PRETTY UNCOMMON.
KIRKMAN & SCOTT

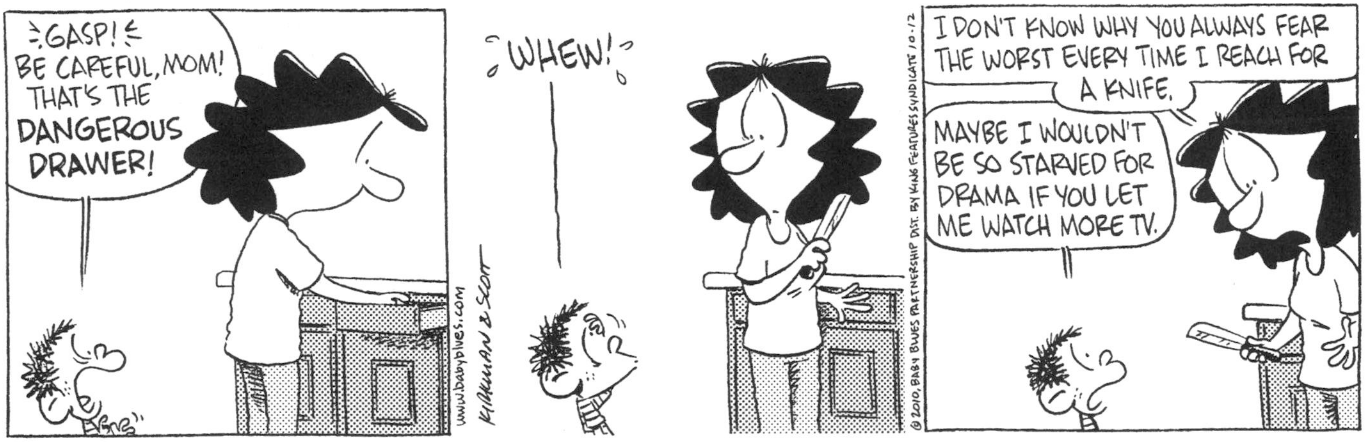
GASP!
BE CAREFUL, MOM! THAT'S THE DANGEROUS DRAWER!
www.babyblues.com
KIRKMAN & SCOTT
WHEW!
©2010, BABY BLUES PARTNERSHIP DIST. BY KING FEATURES SYNDICATE 10-12
I DON'T KNOW WHY YOU ALWAYS FEAR THE WORST EVERY TIME I REACH FOR A KNIFE.
MAYBE I WOULDN'T BE SO STARVED FOR DRAMA IF YOU LET ME WATCH MORE TV.

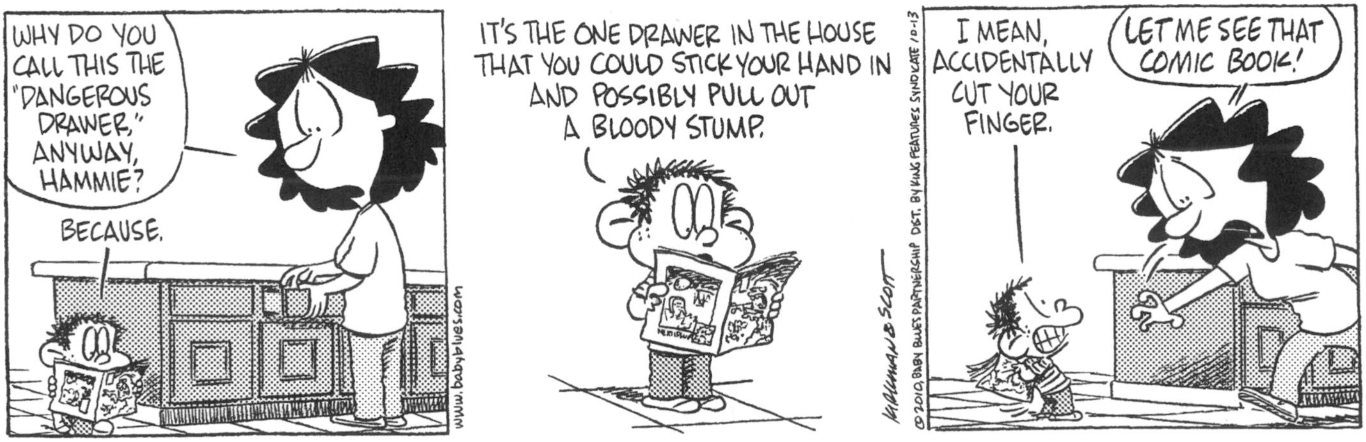
WHY DO YOU CALL THIS THE "DANGEROUS DRAWER," ANYWAY, HAMMIE?
BECAUSE.
www.babyblues.com
IT'S THE ONE DRAWER IN THE HOUSE THAT YOU COULD STICK YOUR HAND IN AND POSSIBLY PULL OUT A BLOODY STUMP.
KIRKMAN & SCOTT
©2010, BABY BLUES PARTNERSHIP DIST. BY KING FEATURES SYNDICATE 10-13
I MEAN, ACCIDENTALLY CUT YOUR FINGER.
LET ME SEE THAT COMIC BOOK!

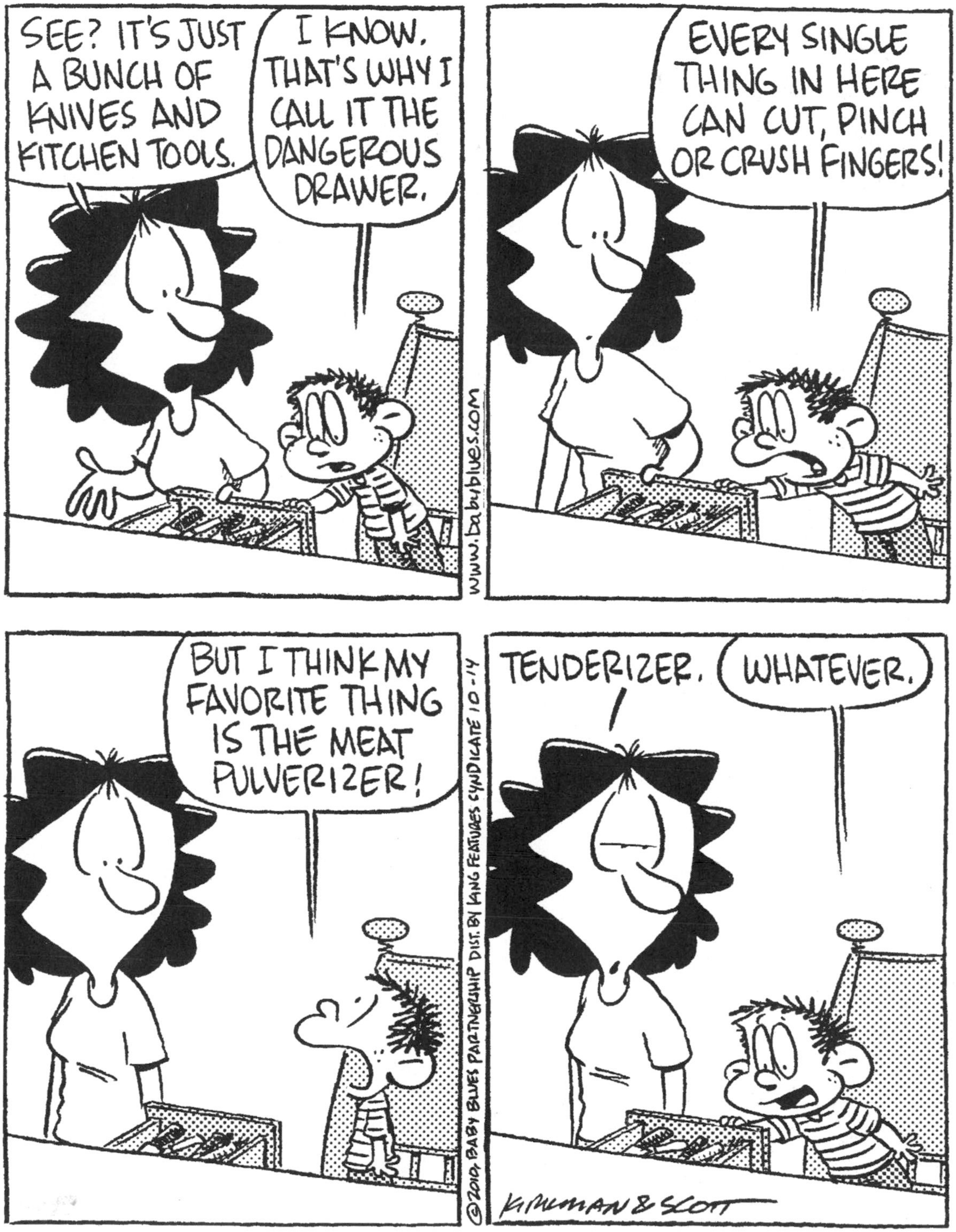
SEE? IT'S JUST A BUNCH OF KNIVES AND KITCHEN TOOLS.
I KNOW. THAT'S WHY I CALL IT THE DANGEROUS DRAWER.
EVERY SINGLE THING IN HERE CAN CUT, PINCH OR CRUSH FINGERS!
BUT I THINK MY FAVORITE THING IS THE MEAT PULVERIZER!
TENDERIZER.
WHATEVER.
www.babyblues.com
©2010, BABY BLUES PARTNERSHIP DIST. BY KING FEATURES SYNDICATE 10-14
KIRKMAN & SCOTT

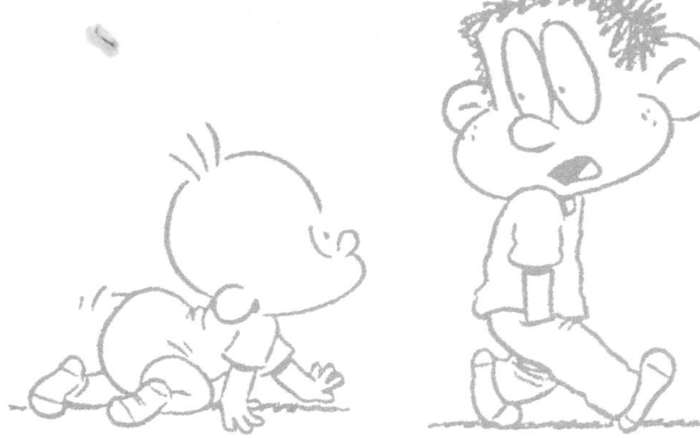

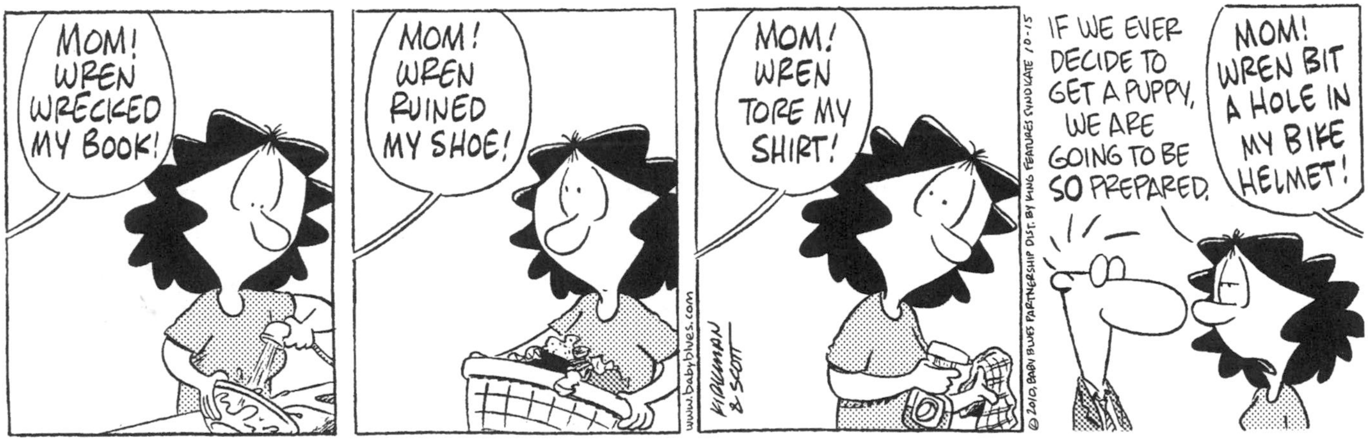
MOM! WREN WRECKED MY BOOK!
MOM! WREN RUINED MY SHOE!
MOM! WREN TORE MY SHIRT!
www.babyblues.com
KIRKMAN & SCOTT
© 2010, BABY BLUES PARTNERSHIP DIST. BY KING FEATURES SYNDICATE 10-15
IF WE EVER DECIDE TO GET A PUPPY, WE ARE GOING TO BE SO PREPARED.
MOM! WREN BIT A HOLE IN MY BIKE HELMET!

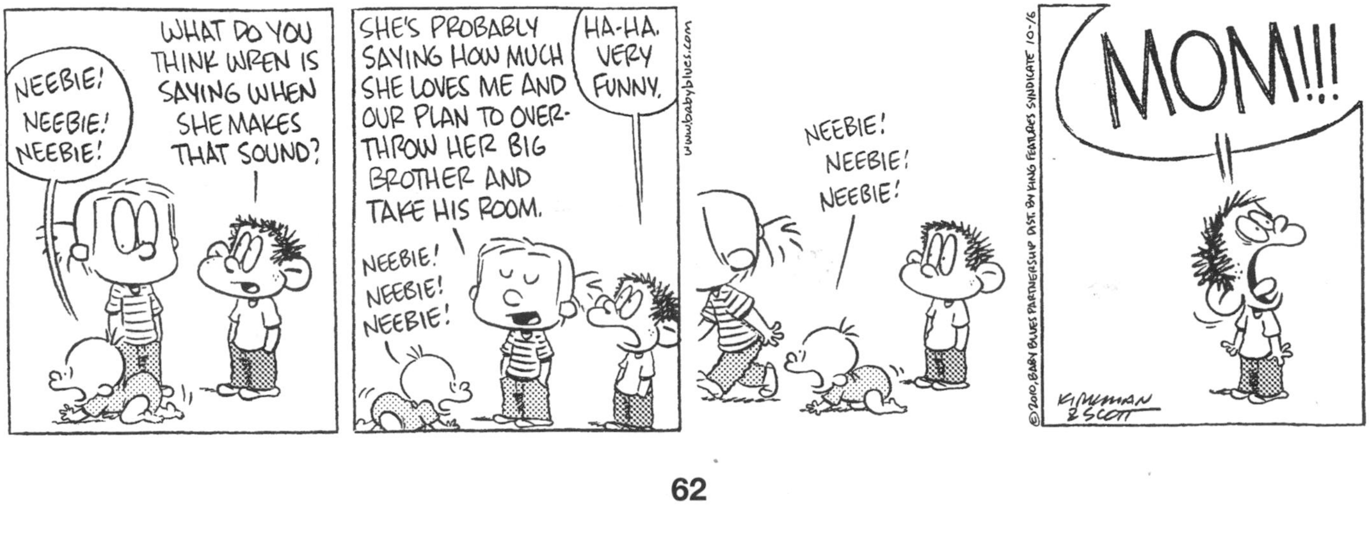
NEEBIE! NEEBIE! NEEBIE!
WHAT DO YOU THINK WREN IS SAYING WHEN SHE MAKES THAT SOUND?
SHE'S PROBABLY SAYING HOW MUCH SHE LOVES ME AND OUR PLAN TO OVER-THROW HER BIG BROTHER AND TAKE HIS ROOM.
HA-HA. VERY FUNNY.
NEEBIE! NEEBIE! NEEBIE!
www.babyblues.com
NEEBIE! NEEBIE! NEEBIE!
© 2010, BABY BLUES PARTNERSHIP DIST. BY KING FEATURES SYNDICATE 10-16
MOM!!!
KIRKMAN & SCOTT

BABY BLUES

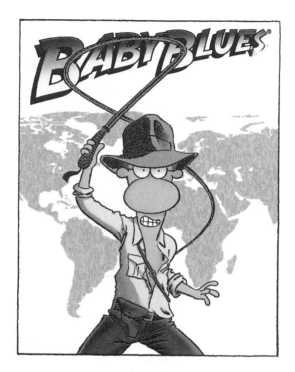

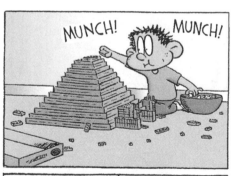

MUNCH!
MUNCH!
UH-OH.
MOM! DAD! I THINK I MIGHT HAVE SWALLOWED A LEGO PIECE!
GASP!
OH NO!
NOW STAY CALM, SON, AND THINK VERY CAREFULLY BEFORE ANSWERING THE QUESTION I'M ABOUT TO ASK YOU.
OKAY.
www.babyblues.com
10-17
IT WASN'T THAT ONE-OF-A-KIND SPECIAL PIECE THAT MAKES THE TOMB OPEN AND THE MUMMY POP OUT, WAS IT?
NO.
KIRKMAN & SCOTT
WE'RE GOING TO BE ALL RIGHT.
THANKS FOR YOUR CONCERN!

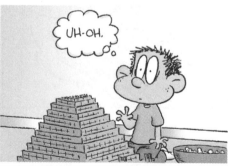

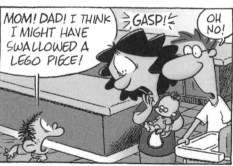

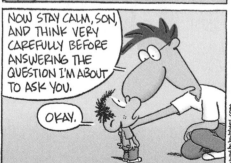

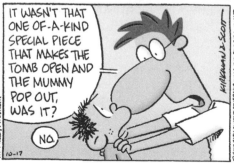

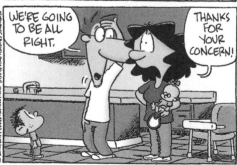

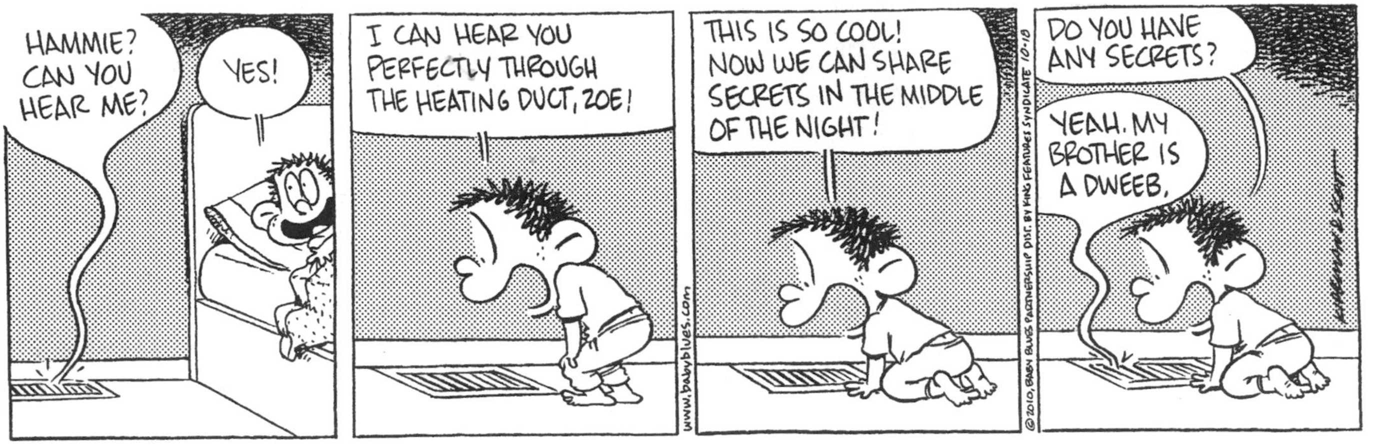
HAMMIE? CAN YOU HEAR ME?
YES!
I CAN HEAR YOU PERFECTLY THROUGH THE HEATING DUCT, ZOE!
www.babyblues.com
THIS IS SO COOL! NOW WE CAN SHARE SECRETS IN THE MIDDLE OF THE NIGHT!
© 2010, BABY BLUES PARTNERSHIP DIST. BY KING FEATURES SYNDICATE 10-18
DO YOU HAVE ANY SECRETS?
YEAH. MY BROTHER IS A DWEEB.

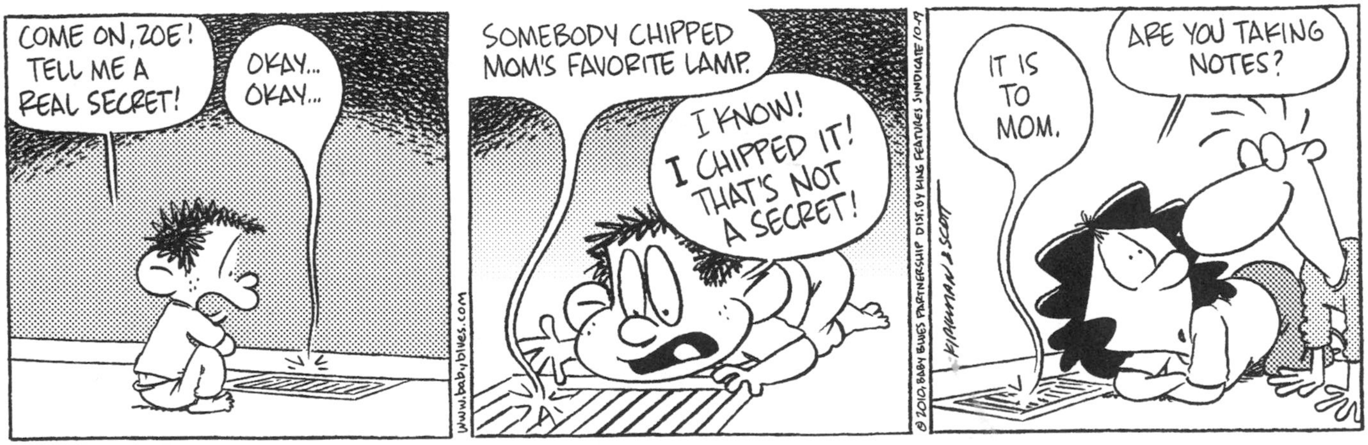
COME ON, ZOE! TELL ME A REAL SECRET!
OKAY... OKAY...
www.babyblues.com
SOMEBODY CHIPPED MOM'S FAVORITE LAMP.
I KNOW! I CHIPPED IT! THAT'S NOT A SECRET!
© 2010, BABY BLUES PARTNERSHIP DIST. BY KING FEATURES SYNDICATE 10-19
KIRKMAN & SCOTT
IT IS TO MOM.
ARE YOU TAKING NOTES?

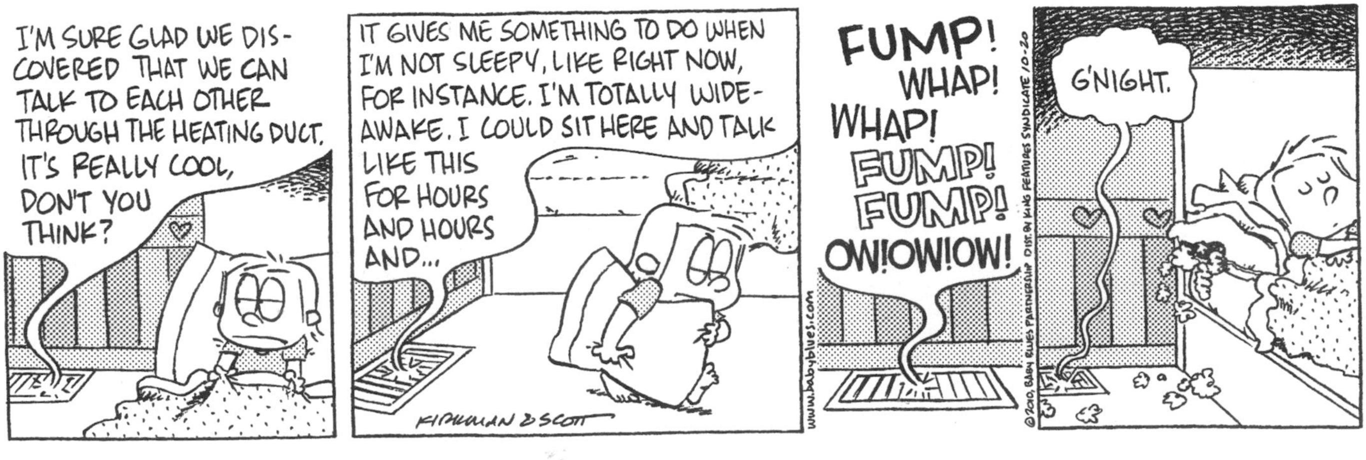
I'M SURE GLAD WE DIS-COVERED THAT WE CAN TALK TO EACH OTHER THROUGH THE HEATING DUCT. IT'S REALLY COOL, DON'T YOU THINK?
IT GIVES ME SOMETHING TO DO WHEN I'M NOT SLEEPY, LIKE RIGHT NOW, FOR INSTANCE. I'M TOTALLY WIDE-AWAKE. I COULD SIT HERE AND TALK LIKE THIS FOR HOURS AND HOURS AND...
KIRKMAN & SCOTT
www.babyblues.com
FUMP! WHAP! WHAP! FUMP! FUMP! OW!OW!OW!
© 2010, BABY BLUES PARTNERSHIP DIST. BY KING FEATURES SYNDICATE 10-20
G'NIGHT.

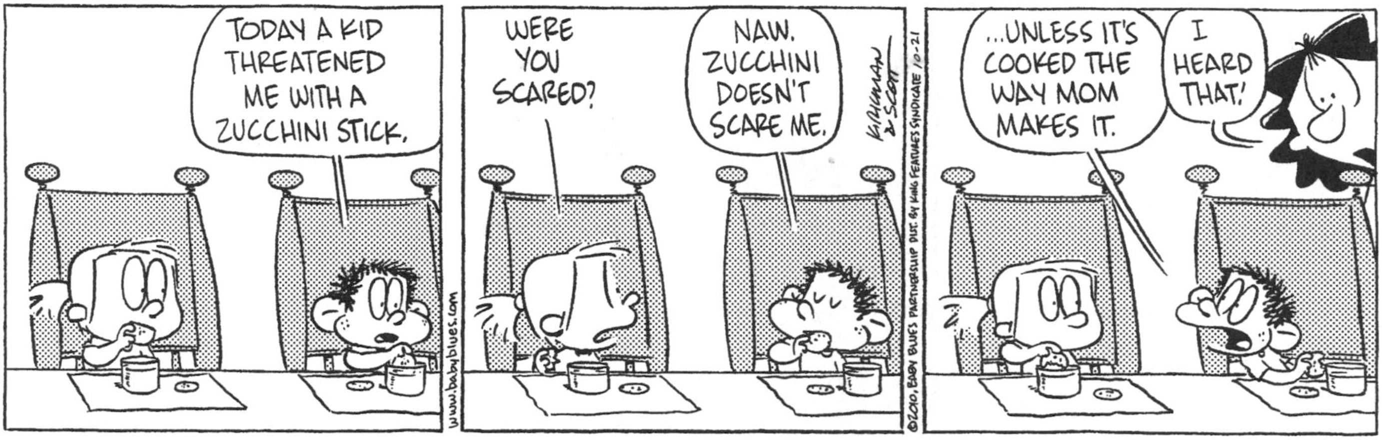
TODAY A KID THREATENED ME WITH A ZUCCHINI STICK.
WERE YOU SCARED?
NAW. ZUCCHINI DOESN'T SCARE ME.
KIRKMAN & SCOTT
...UNLESS IT'S COOKED THE WAY MOM MAKES IT.
I HEARD THAT!
www.babyblues.com
©2010, BABY BLUES PARTNERSHIP DIST. BY KING FEATURES SYNDICATE 10-21

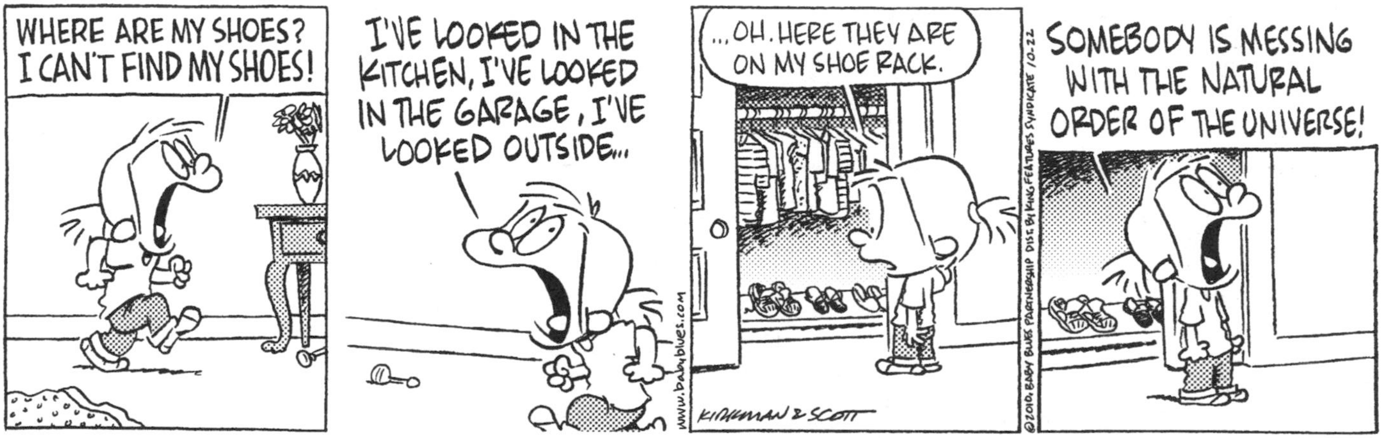
WHERE ARE MY SHOES? I CAN'T FIND MY SHOES!
I'VE LOOKED IN THE KITCHEN, I'VE LOOKED IN THE GARAGE, I'VE LOOKED OUTSIDE...
...OH. HERE THEY ARE ON MY SHOE RACK.
SOMEBODY IS MESSING WITH THE NATURAL ORDER OF THE UNIVERSE!
www.babyblues.com
KIRKMAN & SCOTT
©2010, BABY BLUES PARTNERSHIP DIST. BY KING FEATURES SYNDICATE 10-22

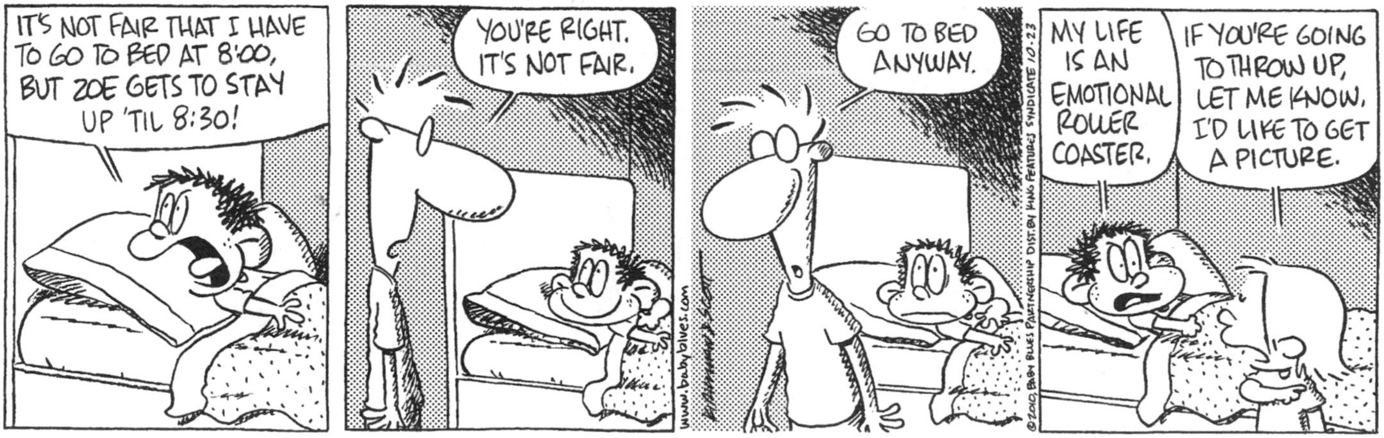
IT'S NOT FAIR THAT I HAVE TO GO TO BED AT 8:00, BUT ZOE GETS TO STAY UP 'TIL 8:30!
YOU'RE RIGHT. IT'S NOT FAIR.
GO TO BED ANYWAY.
MY LIFE IS AN EMOTIONAL ROLLER COASTER.
IF YOU'RE GOING TO THROW UP, LET ME KNOW. I'D LIKE TO GET A PICTURE.
www.babyblues.com
©2010, BABY BLUES PARTNERSHIP DIST. BY KING FEATURES SYNDICATE 10-23

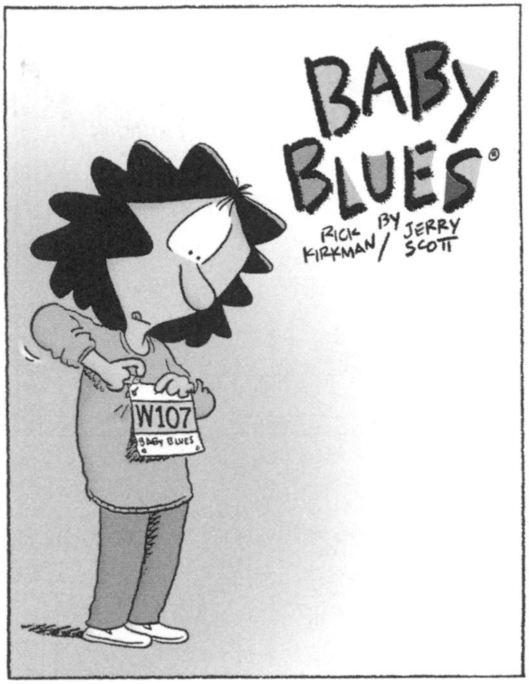
BABY BLUES®
BY RICK KIRKMAN / JERRY SCOTT
W107
BABY BLUES

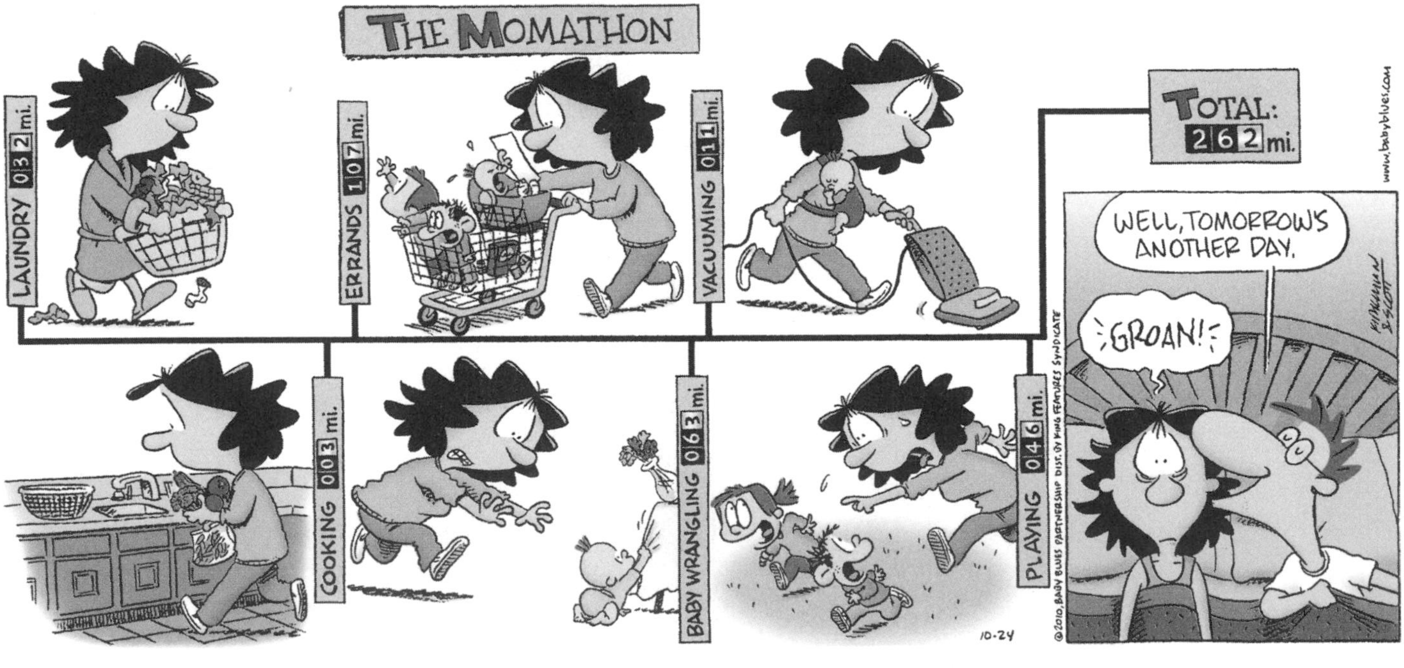
THE MOMATHON
LAUNDRY 0 3 2 mi.
ERRANDS 1 0 7 mi.
VACUUMING 0 1 1 mi.
TOTAL: 2 6 2 mi.
COOKING 0 0 3 mi.
BABY WRANGLING 0 6 3 mi.
PLAYING 0 4 6 mi.
WELL, TOMORROW'S ANOTHER DAY.
GROAN!
KIRKMAN & SCOTT
10-24
©2010, BABY BLUES PARTNERSHIP DIST. BY KING FEATURES SYNDICATE
www.babyblues.com

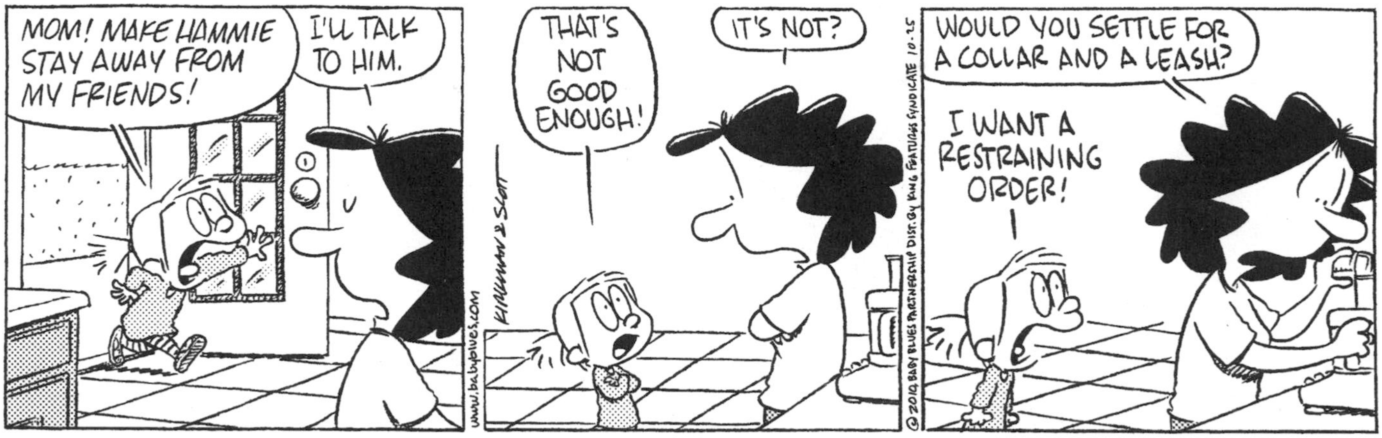
MOM! MAKE HAMMIE STAY AWAY FROM MY FRIENDS!
I'LL TALK TO HIM.
www.babyblues.com
THAT'S NOT GOOD ENOUGH!
KIRKMAN & SCOTT
IT'S NOT?
© 2010 BABY BLUES PARTNERSHIP DIST. BY KING FEATURES SYNDICATE 10-25
WOULD YOU SETTLE FOR A COLLAR AND A LEASH?
I WANT A RESTRAINING ORDER!

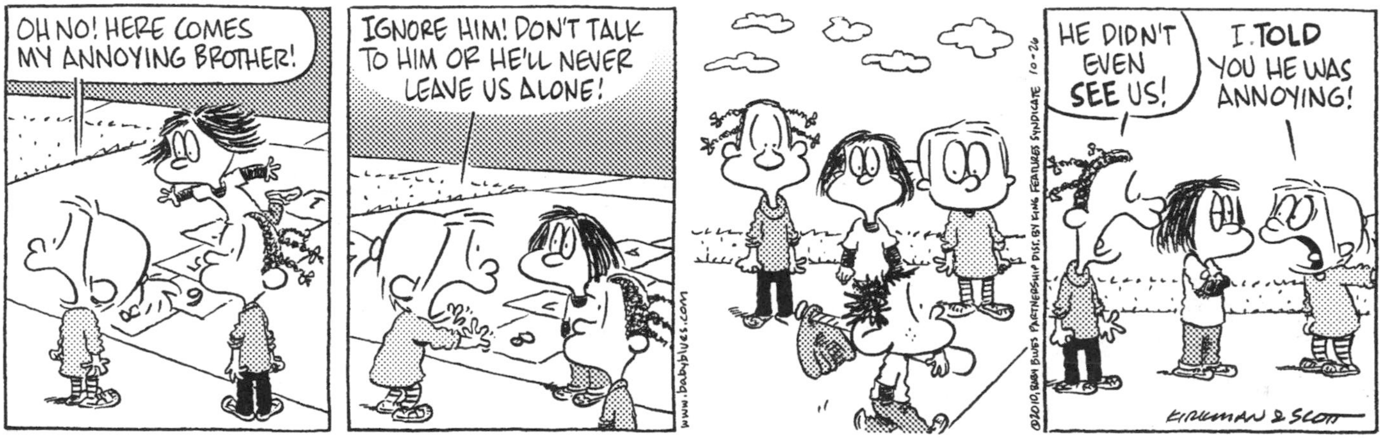
OH NO! HERE COMES MY ANNOYING BROTHER!
IGNORE HIM! DON'T TALK TO HIM OR HE'LL NEVER LEAVE US ALONE!
www.babyblues.com
© 2010, BABY BLUES PARTNERSHIP DIST. BY KING FEATURES SYNDICATE 10-26
HE DIDN'T EVEN SEE US!
I TOLD YOU HE WAS ANNOYING!
KIRKMAN & SCOTT

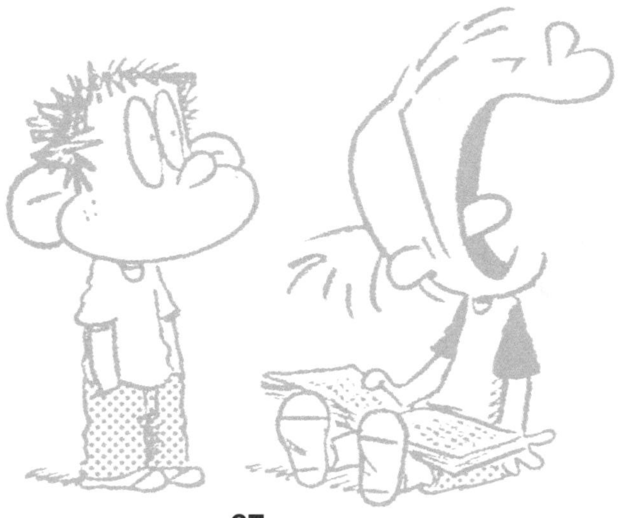

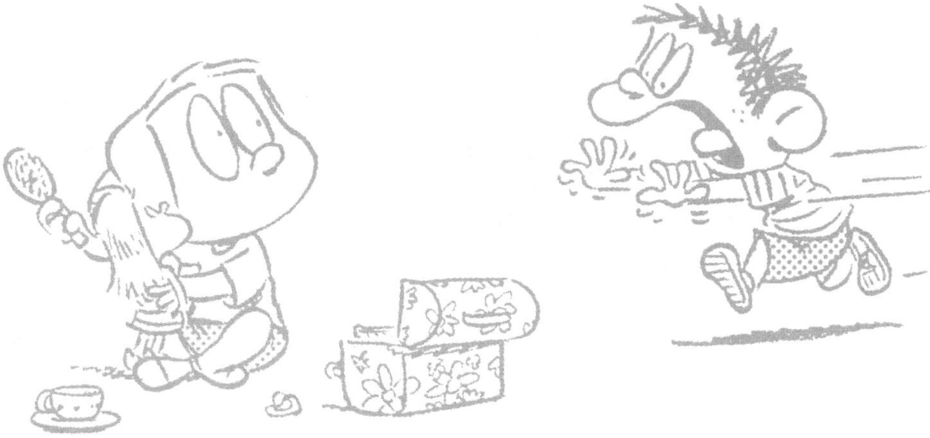

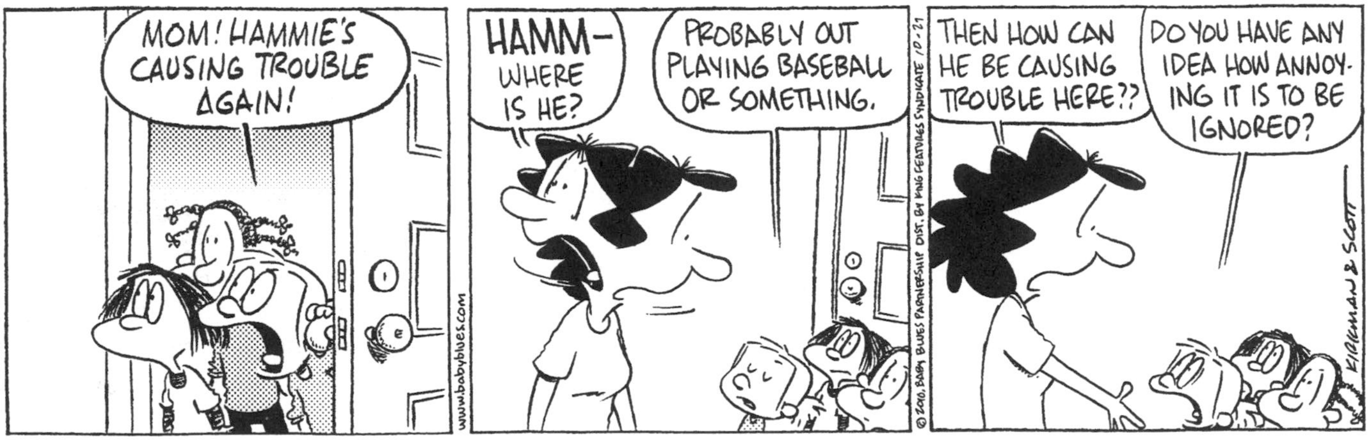
MOM! HAMMIE'S CAUSING TROUBLE AGAIN!
www.babyblues.com
HAMM- WHERE IS HE?
PROBABLY OUT PLAYING BASEBALL OR SOMETHING.
© 2010, BABY BLUES PARTNERSHIP DIST. BY KING FEATURES SYNDICATE 10-21
THEN HOW CAN HE BE CAUSING TROUBLE HERE??
DO YOU HAVE ANY IDEA HOW ANNOYING IT IS TO BE IGNORED?
KIRKMAN & SCOTT

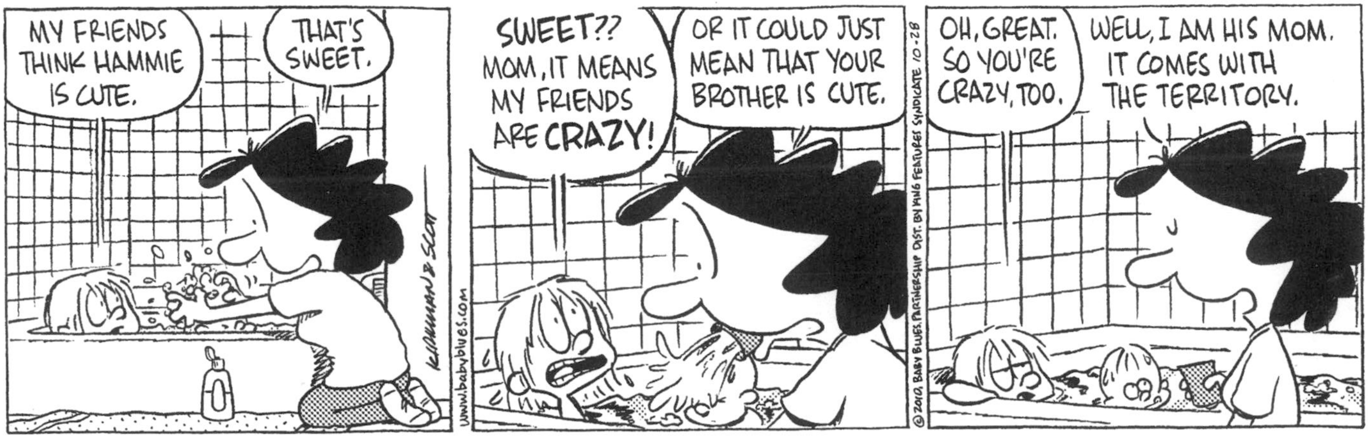
MY FRIENDS THINK HAMMIE IS CUTE.
THAT'S SWEET.
KIRKMAN & SCOTT
www.babyblues.com
SWEET?? MOM, IT MEANS MY FRIENDS ARE CRAZY!
OR IT COULD JUST MEAN THAT YOUR BROTHER IS CUTE.
© 2010, BABY BLUES PARTNERSHIP DIST. BY KING FEATURES SYNDICATE 10-28
OH, GREAT. SO YOU'RE CRAZY, TOO.
WELL, I AM HIS MOM. IT COMES WITH THE TERRITORY.

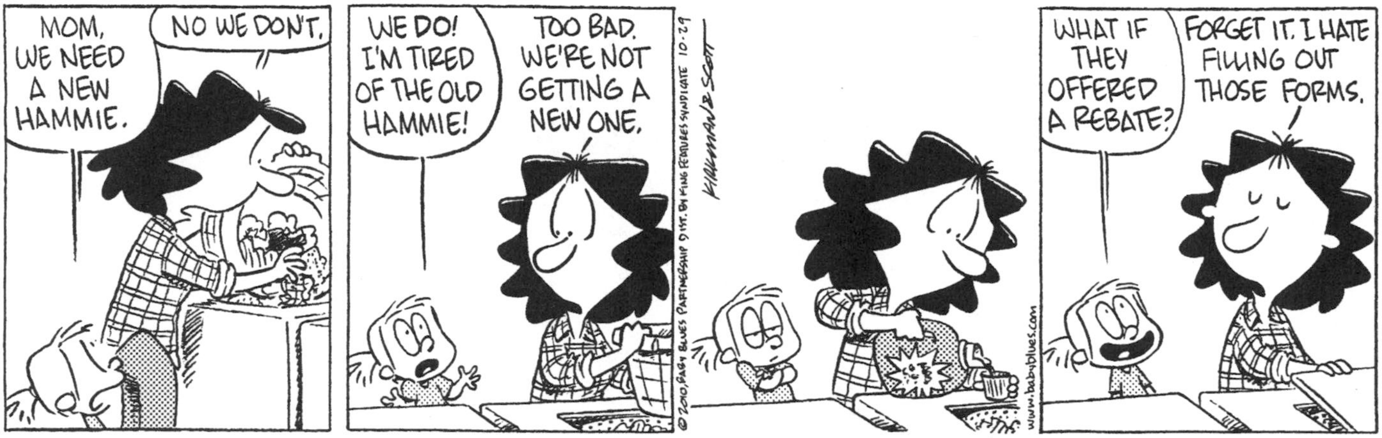
MOM, WE NEED A NEW HAMMIE.
NO WE DON'T.
WE DO! I'M TIRED OF THE OLD HAMMIE!
TOO BAD. WE'RE NOT GETTING A NEW ONE.
WHAT IF THEY OFFERED A REBATE?
FORGET IT. I HATE FILLING OUT THOSE FORMS.
©2010, BABY BLUES PARTNERSHIP DIST. BY KING FEATURES SYNDICATE 10-29
KIRKMAN & SCOTT
www.babyblues.com

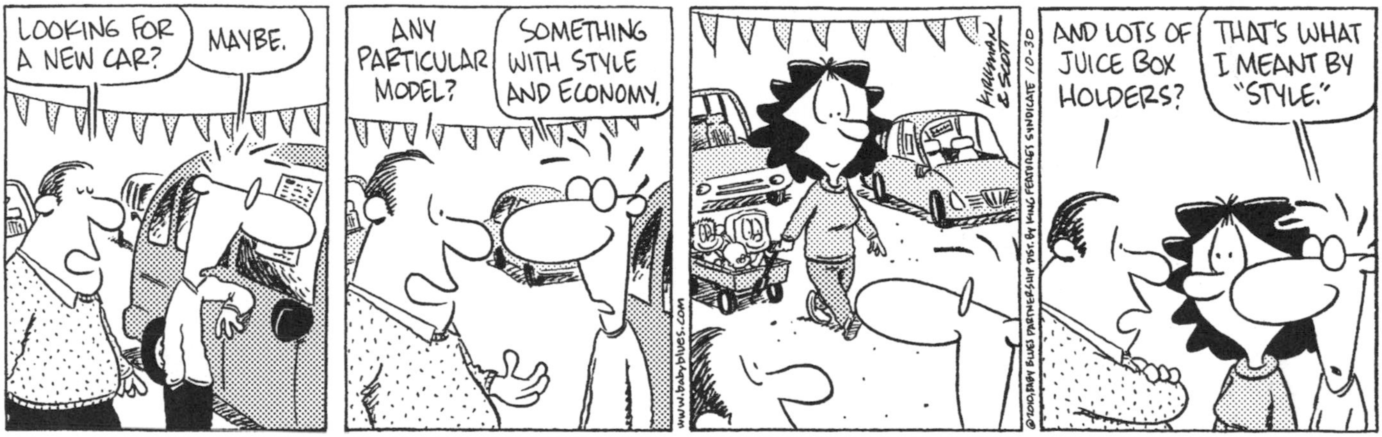
LOOKING FOR A NEW CAR?
MAYBE.
ANY PARTICULAR MODEL?
SOMETHING WITH STYLE AND ECONOMY.
www.babyblues.com
KIRKMAN & SCOTT 10-30
©2010, BABY BLUES PARTNERSHIP DIST. BY KING FEATURES SYNDICATE
AND LOTS OF JUICE BOX HOLDERS?
THAT'S WHAT I MEANT BY "STYLE."

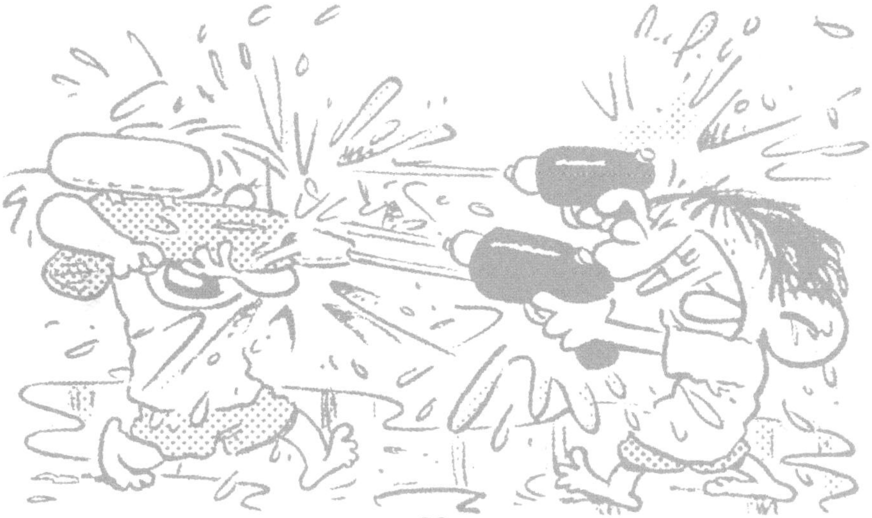

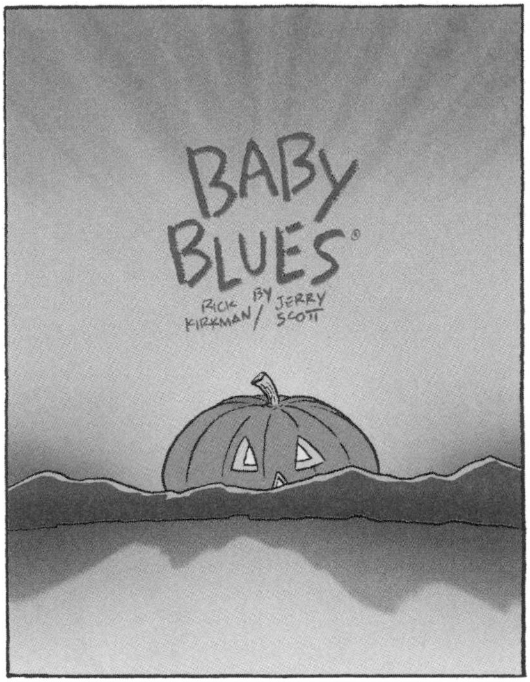
BABY BLUES®
BY RICK KIRKMAN / JERRY SCOTT

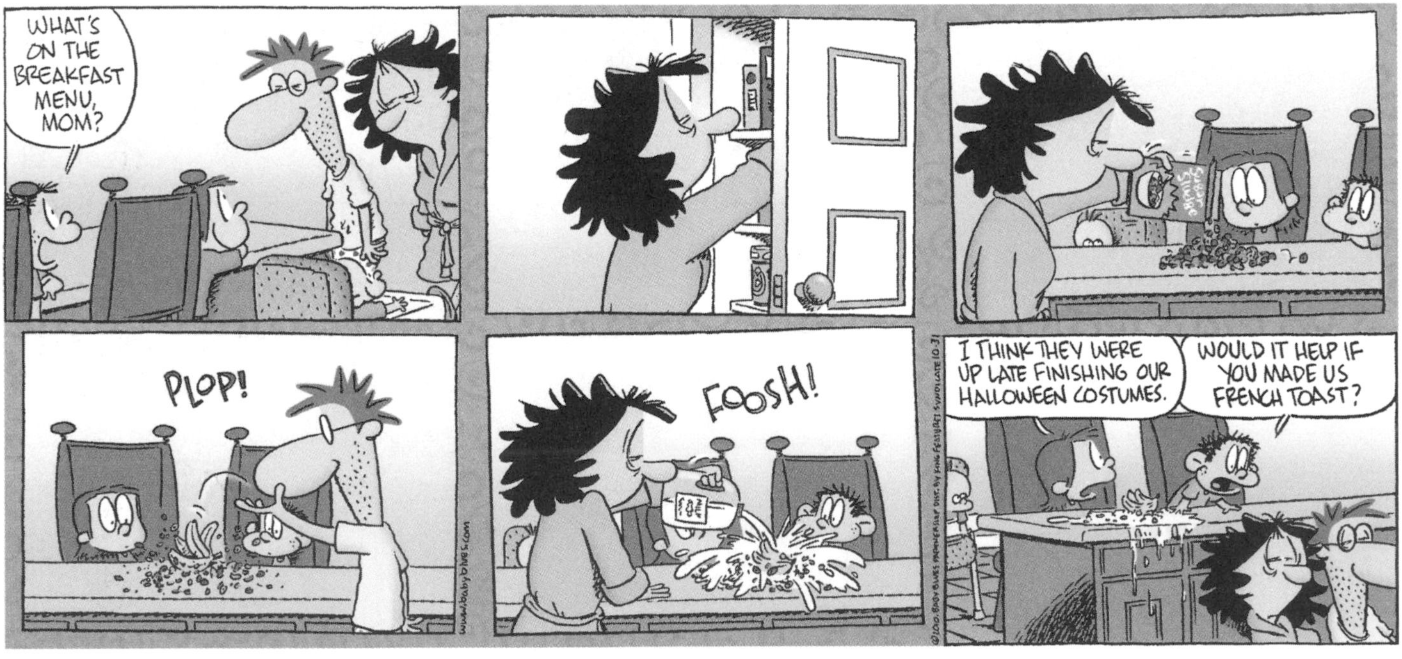
WHAT'S ON THE BREAKFAST MENU, MOM?
PLOP!
www.babyblues.com
FOOSH!
I THINK THEY WERE UP LATE FINISHING OUR HALLOWEEN COSTUMES.
WOULD IT HELP IF YOU MADE US FRENCH TOAST?

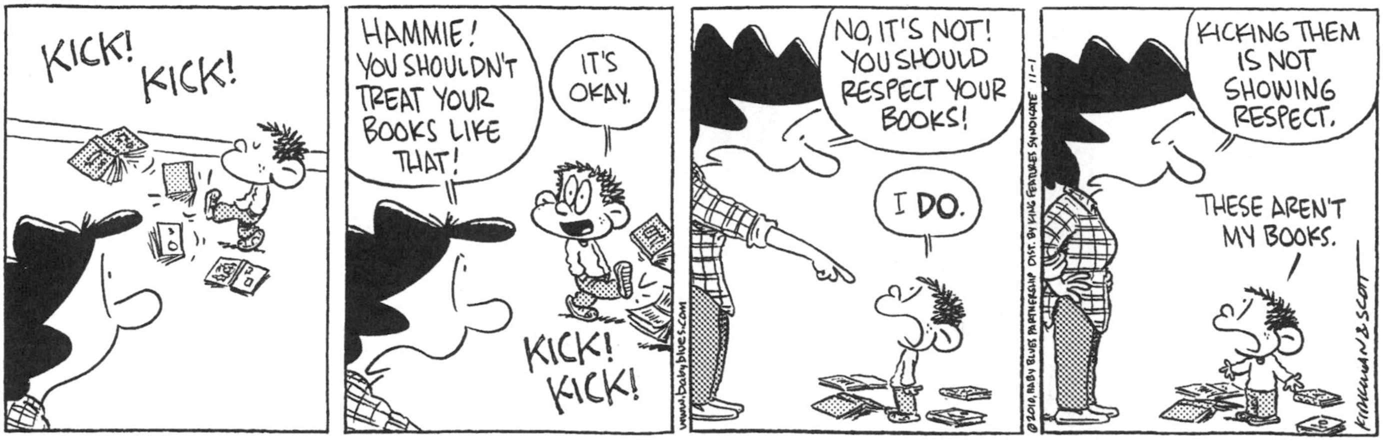
KICK! KICK!
HAMMIE! YOU SHOULDN'T TREAT YOUR BOOKS LIKE THAT!
IT'S OKAY.
KICK! KICK!
www.babyblues.com
NO, IT'S NOT! YOU SHOULD RESPECT YOUR BOOKS!
I DO.
© 2010, BABY BLUES PARTNERSHIP DIST. BY KING FEATURES SYNDICATE 11-1
KICKING THEM IS NOT SHOWING RESPECT.
THESE AREN'T MY BOOKS.
KIRKMAN & SCOTT

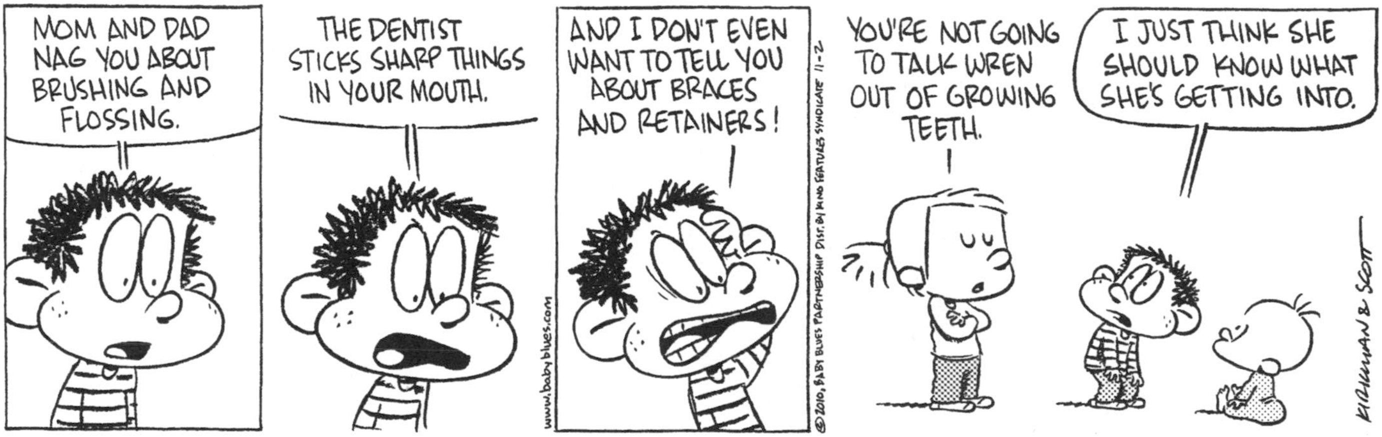
MOM AND DAD NAG YOU ABOUT BRUSHING AND FLOSSING.
THE DENTIST STICKS SHARP THINGS IN YOUR MOUTH.
www.babyblues.com
AND I DON'T EVEN WANT TO TELL YOU ABOUT BRACES AND RETAINERS!
© 2010, BABY BLUES PARTNERSHIP DIST. BY KING FEATURES SYNDICATE 11-2
YOU'RE NOT GOING TO TALK WREN OUT OF GROWING TEETH.
I JUST THINK SHE SHOULD KNOW WHAT SHE'S GETTING INTO.
KIRKMAN & SCOTT

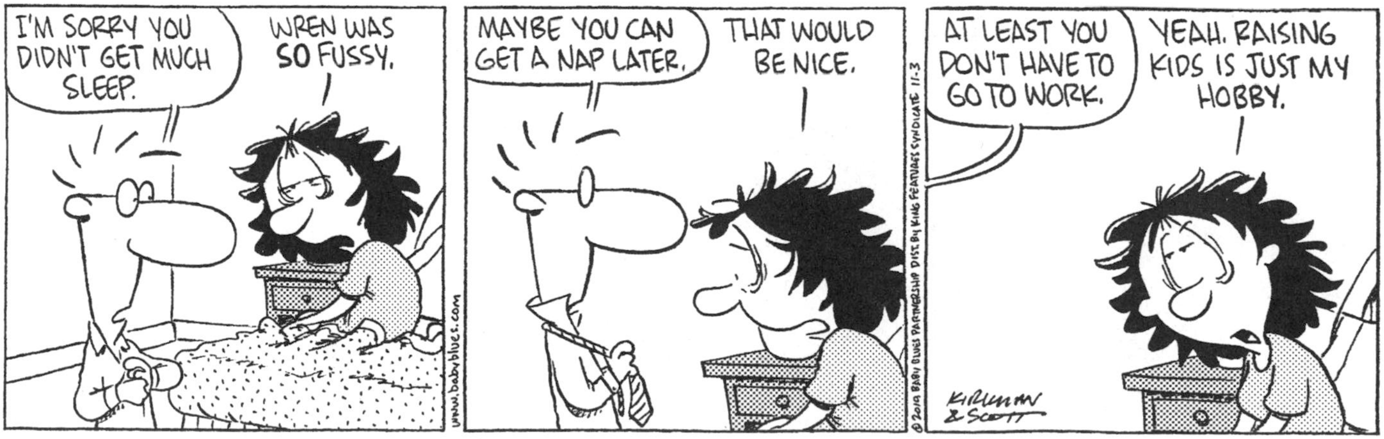
I'M SORRY YOU DIDN'T GET MUCH SLEEP.
WREN WAS SO FUSSY.
www.babyblues.com
MAYBE YOU CAN GET A NAP LATER.
THAT WOULD BE NICE.
© 2010 BABY BLUES PARTNERSHIP DIST. BY KING FEATURES SYNDICATE 11-3
KIRKMAN & SCOTT
AT LEAST YOU DON'T HAVE TO GO TO WORK.
YEAH. RAISING KIDS IS JUST MY HOBBY.

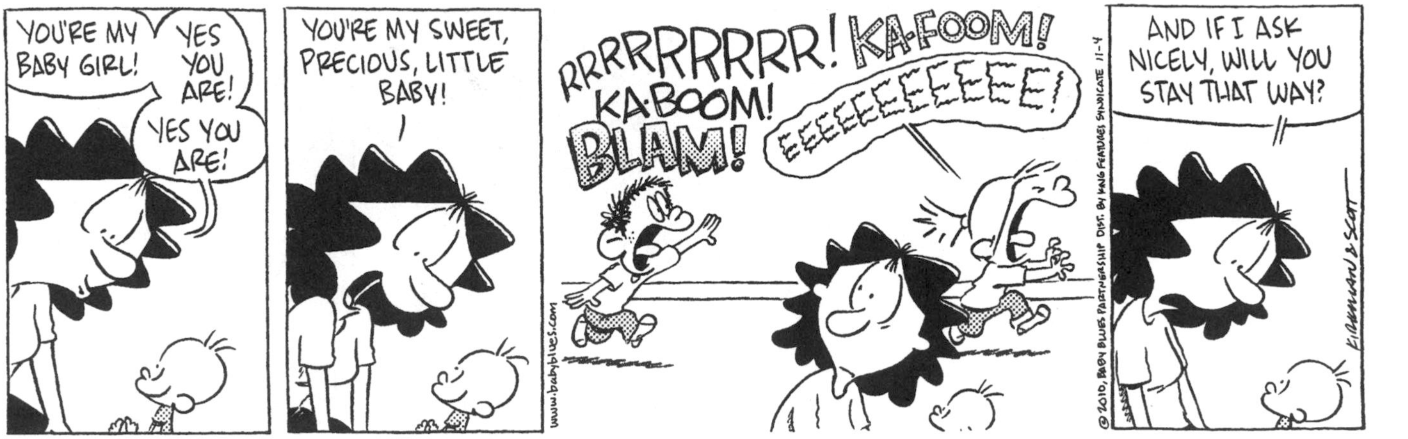
YOU'RE MY BABY GIRL!
YES YOU ARE!
YES YOU ARE!
YOU'RE MY SWEET, PRECIOUS, LITTLE BABY!
RRRRRRRRRR! KA-FOOM!
KA-BOOM!
BLAM!
EEEEEEEEEEE!
www.babyblues.com
© 2010, BABY BLUES PARTNERSHIP DIST. BY KING FEATURES SYNDICATE 11-4
AND IF I ASK NICELY, WILL YOU STAY THAT WAY?
KIRKMAN & SCOTT

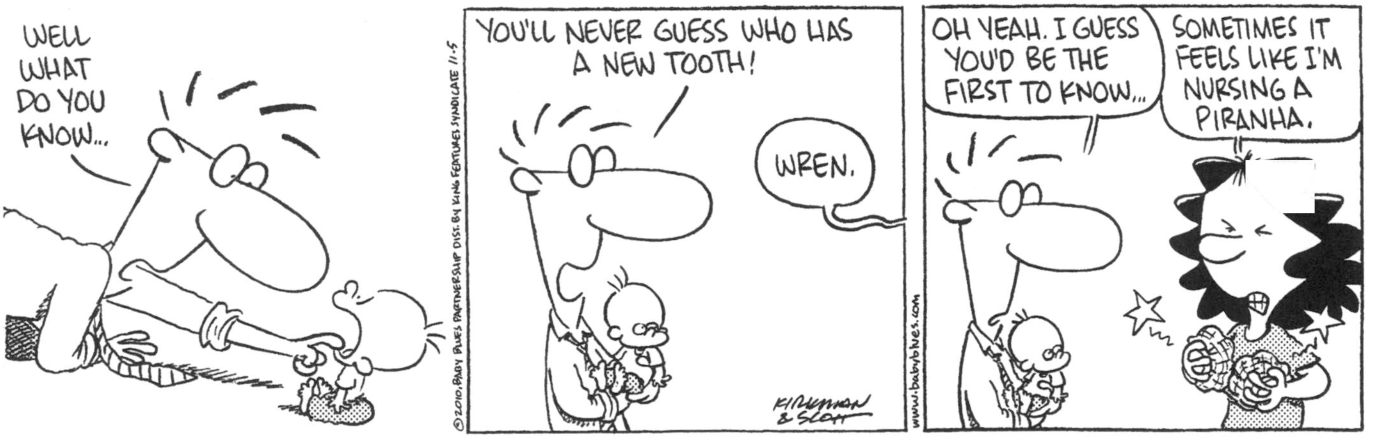
WELL WHAT DO YOU KNOW...
© 2010, BABY BLUES PARTNERSHIP DIST. BY KING FEATURES SYNDICATE 11-5
YOU'LL NEVER GUESS WHO HAS A NEW TOOTH!
WREN.
KIRKMAN & SCOTT
www.babyblues.com
OH YEAH. I GUESS YOU'D BE THE FIRST TO KNOW...
SOMETIMES IT FEELS LIKE I'M NURSING A PIRANHA.

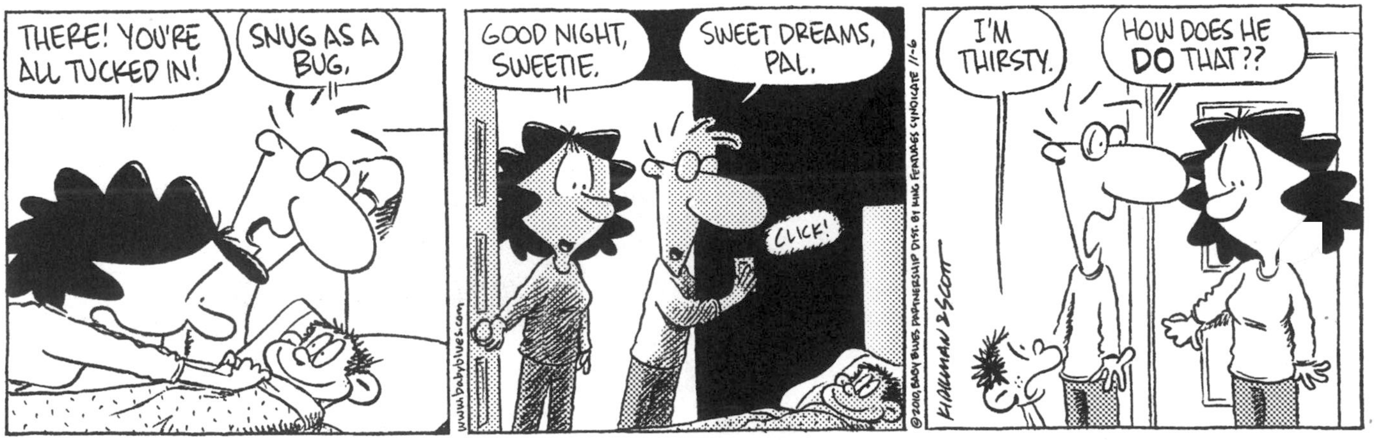
THERE! YOU'RE ALL TUCKED IN!
SNUG AS A BUG.
www.babyblues.com
GOOD NIGHT, SWEETIE.
SWEET DREAMS, PAL.
CLICK!
© 2010, BABY BLUES PARTNERSHIP DIST. BY KING FEATURES SYNDICATE 11-6
KIRKMAN & SCOTT
I'M THIRSTY.
HOW DOES HE DO THAT??

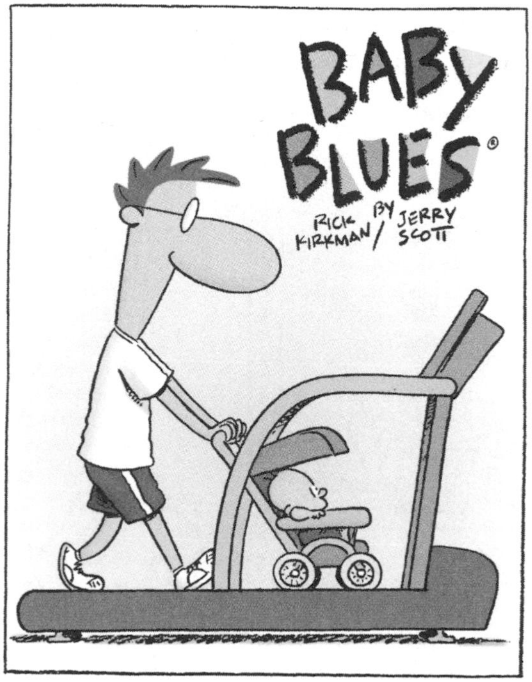
BABY BLUES®
BY RICK KIRKMAN/ JERRY SCOTT

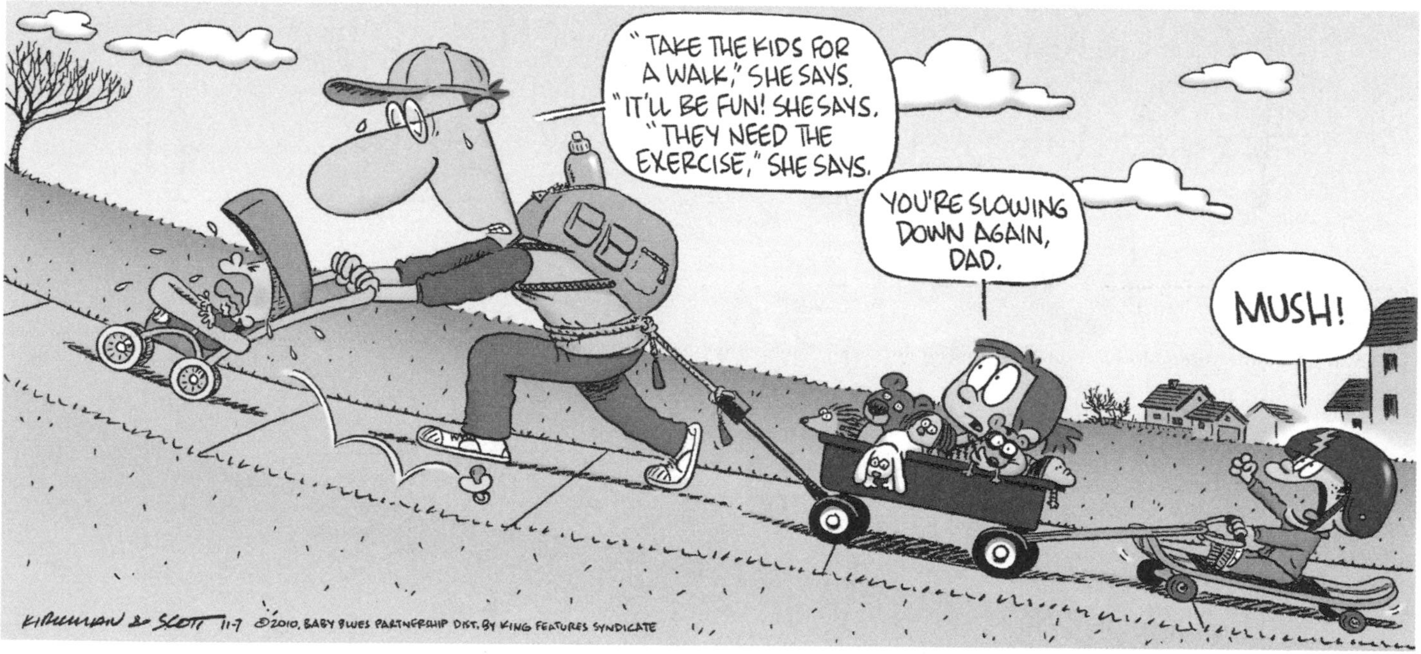
"TAKE THE KIDS FOR A WALK," SHE SAYS. "IT'LL BE FUN! SHE SAYS. "THEY NEED THE EXERCISE," SHE SAYS.
YOU'RE SLOWING DOWN AGAIN, DAD.
MUSH!
KIRKMAN & SCOTT 11-7 ©2010, BABY BLUES PARTNERSHIP DIST. BY KING FEATURES SYNDICATE

MOM, WAS I A CUTE AND FUNNY BABY?
YOU SURE WERE.
© 2010, BABY BLUES PARTNERSHIP DIST. BY KING FEATURES SYNDICATE 11-11
AND DID I MAKE YOU AND DAD HAPPY?
ABSOLUTELY.
THEN WHY DID YOU HAVE HIM?
WELL, YOUR DAD REALLY NEEDED AN EXCUSE TO PLAY WITH LITTLE METAL CARS AGAIN.
KIRKMAN & SCOTT

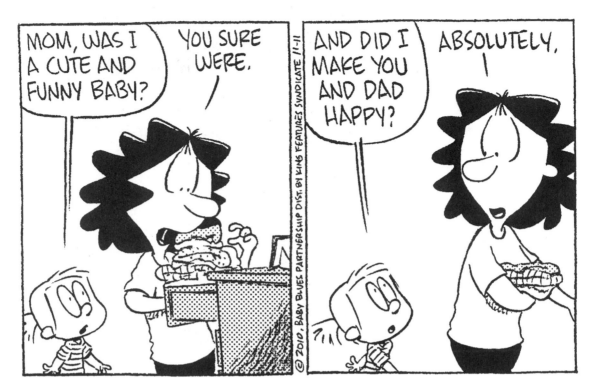

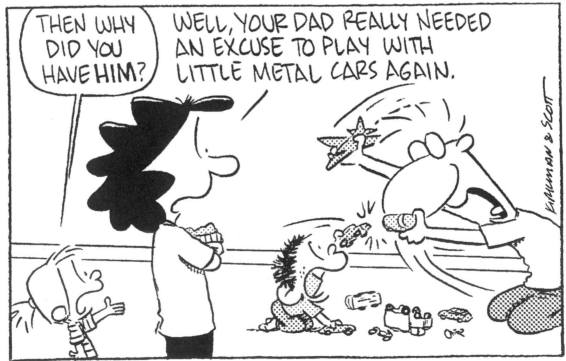

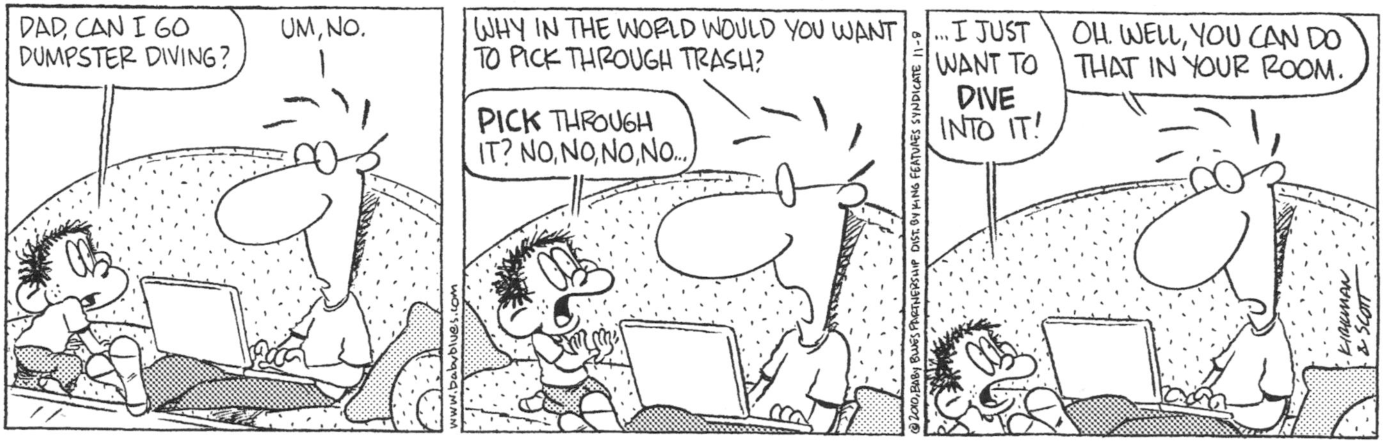
DAD, CAN I GO DUMPSTER DIVING?
UM, NO.
www.babyblues.com
WHY IN THE WORLD WOULD YOU WANT TO PICK THROUGH TRASH?
PICK THROUGH IT? NO, NO, NO, NO...
©2010, BABY BLUES PARTNERSHIP DIST. BY KING FEATURES SYNDICATE 11-9
...I JUST WANT TO DIVE INTO IT!
OH. WELL, YOU CAN DO THAT IN YOUR ROOM.
KIRKMAN & SCOTT

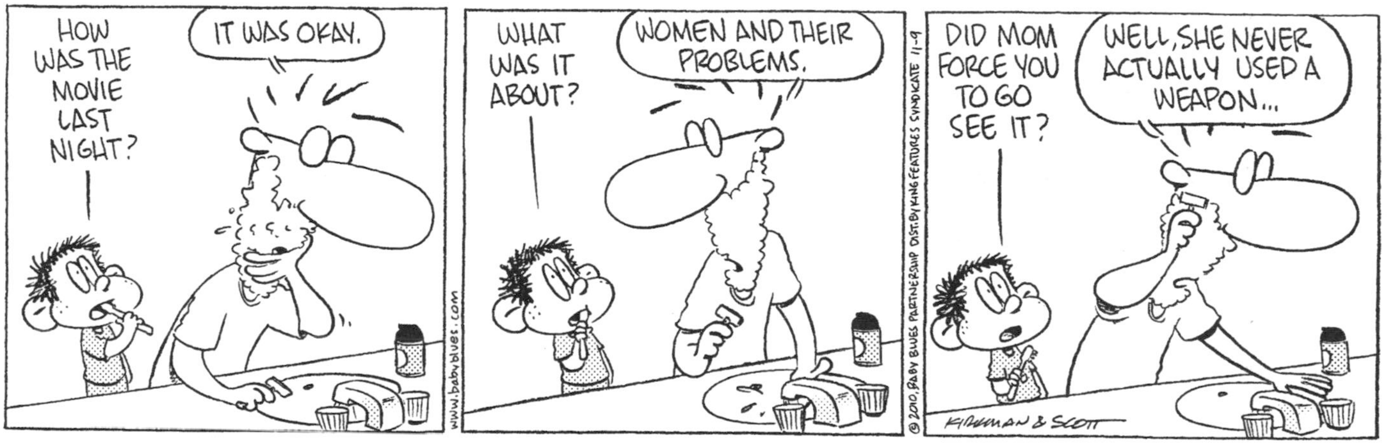
HOW WAS THE MOVIE LAST NIGHT?
IT WAS OKAY.
www.babyblues.com
WHAT WAS IT ABOUT?
WOMEN AND THEIR PROBLEMS.
©2010, BABY BLUES PARTNERSHIP DIST. BY KING FEATURES SYNDICATE 11-9
DID MOM FORCE YOU TO GO SEE IT?
WELL, SHE NEVER ACTUALLY USED A WEAPON...
KIRKMAN & SCOTT

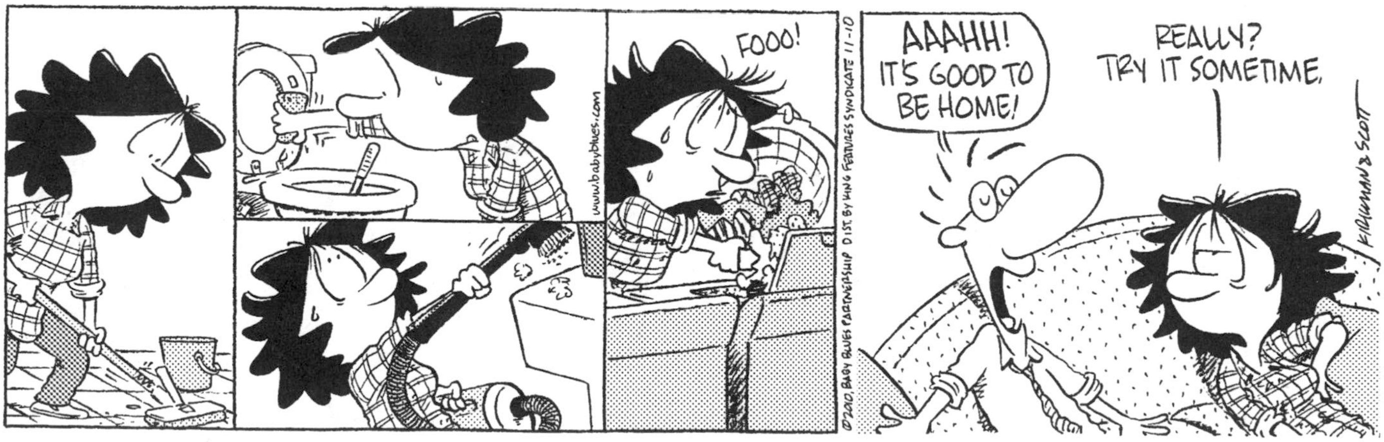
www.babyblues.com
FOOO!
©2010, BABY BLUES PARTNERSHIP DIST. BY KING FEATURES SYNDICATE 11-10
AAAHH! IT'S GOOD TO BE HOME!
REALLY? TRY IT SOMETIME.
KIRKMAN & SCOTT

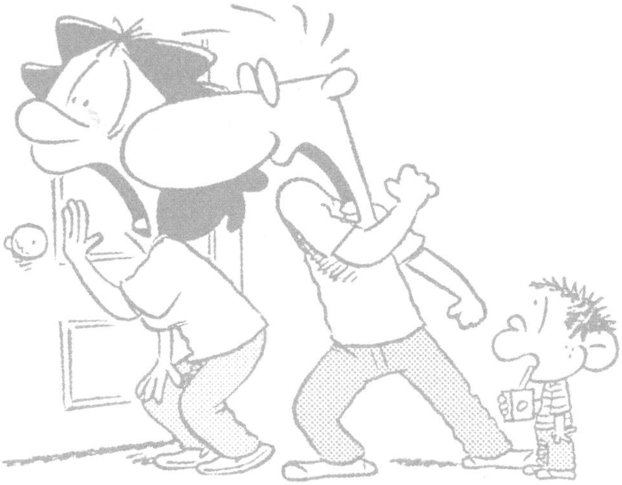

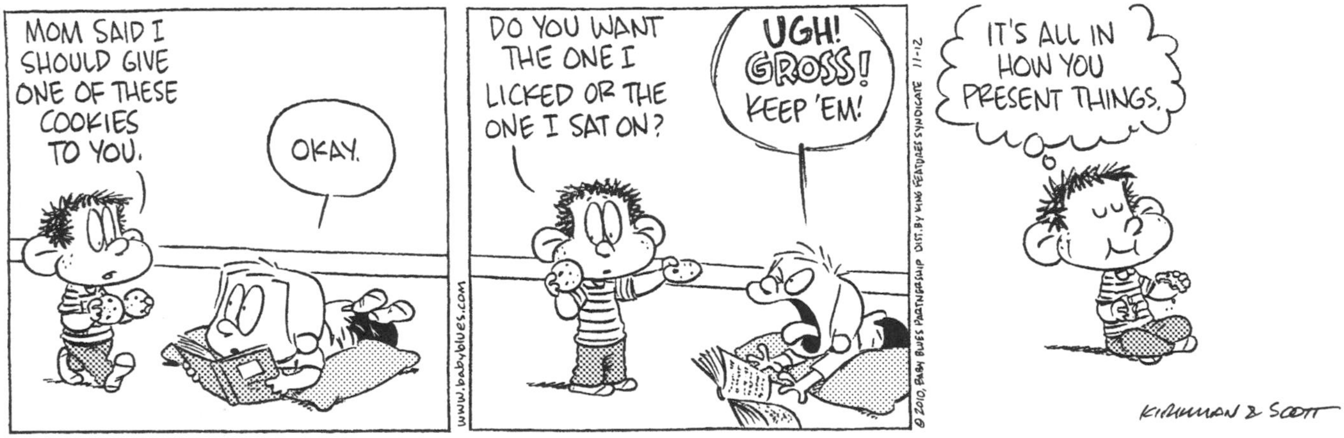

MOM SAID I SHOULD GIVE ONE OF THESE COOKIES TO YOU.
OKAY.
www.babyblues.com
DO YOU WANT THE ONE I LICKED OR THE ONE I SAT ON?
UGH! GROSS! KEEP 'EM!
© 2010, BABY BLUES PARTNERSHIP DIST. BY KING FEATURES SYNDICATE 11-12
IT'S ALL IN HOW YOU PRESENT THINGS.
KIRKMAN & SCOTT

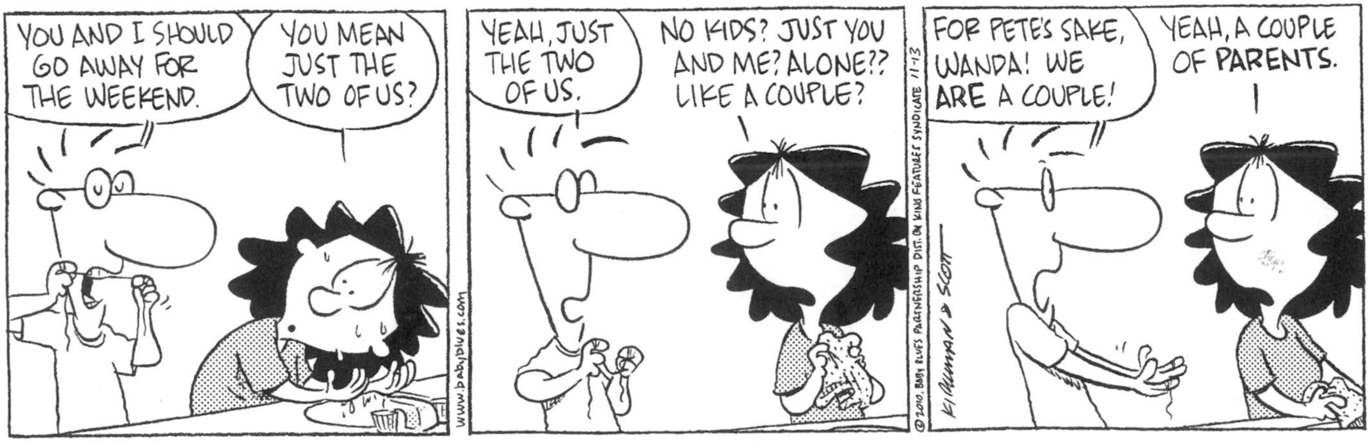

YOU AND I SHOULD GO AWAY FOR THE WEEKEND.
YOU MEAN JUST THE TWO OF US?
www.babyblues.com
YEAH, JUST THE TWO OF US.
NO KIDS? JUST YOU AND ME? ALONE?? LIKE A COUPLE?
© 2010, BABY BLUES PARTNERSHIP DIST. BY KING FEATURES SYNDICATE 11-13
KIRKMAN & SCOTT
FOR PETE'S SAKE, WANDA! WE **ARE** A COUPLE!
YEAH, A COUPLE OF **PARENTS**.

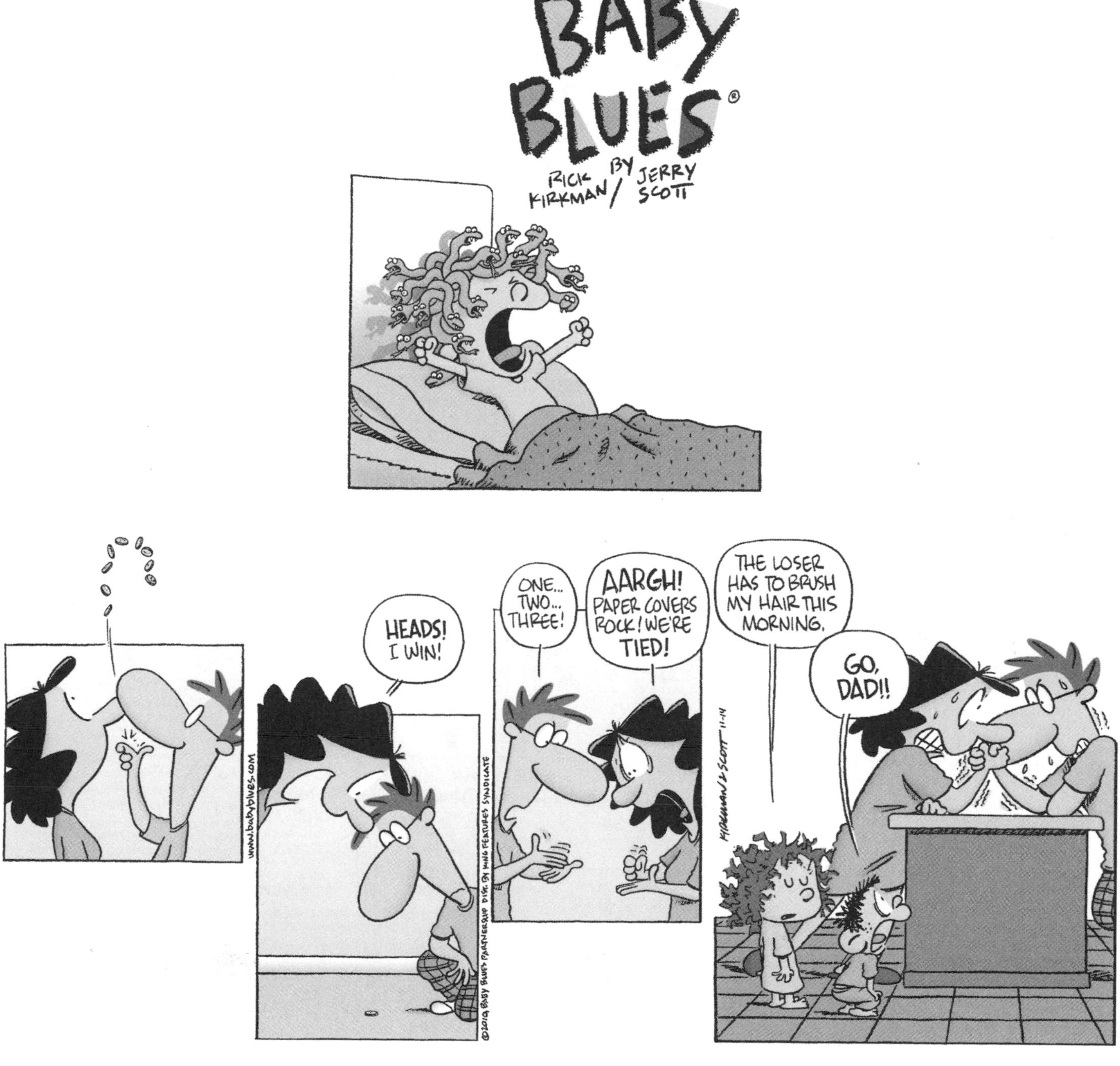
BABY BLUES®
BY RICK KIRKMAN / JERRY SCOTT
www.babyblues.com
HEADS! I WIN!
©2019 BABY BLUES PARTNERSHIP DIST. BY KING FEATURES SYNDICATE
ONE... TWO... THREE!
AARGH! PAPER COVERS ROCK! WE'RE TIED!
KIRKMAN & SCOTT 11-14
THE LOSER HAS TO BRUSH MY HAIR THIS MORNING.
GO, DAD!!

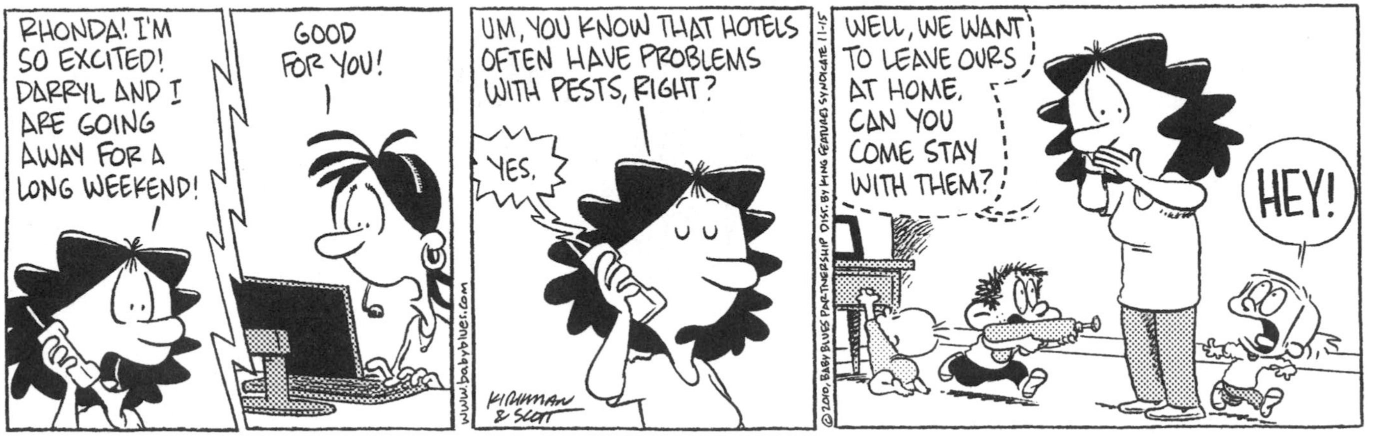
RHONDA! I'M SO EXCITED! DARRYL AND I ARE GOING AWAY FOR A LONG WEEKEND!
GOOD FOR YOU!
www.babyblues.com
UM, YOU KNOW THAT HOTELS OFTEN HAVE PROBLEMS WITH PESTS, RIGHT?
YES.
KIRKMAN & SCOTT
©2010, BABY BLUES PARTNERSHIP DIST. BY KING FEATURES SYNDICATE 11-15
WELL, WE WANT TO LEAVE OURS AT HOME. CAN YOU COME STAY WITH THEM?
HEY!

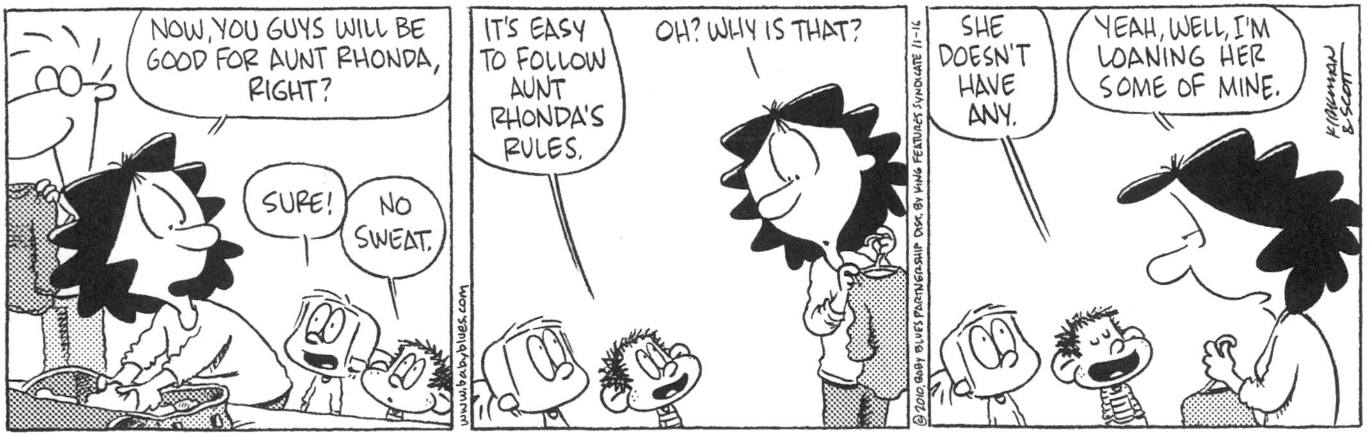
NOW, YOU GUYS WILL BE GOOD FOR AUNT RHONDA, RIGHT?
SURE!
NO SWEAT.
www.babyblues.com
IT'S EASY TO FOLLOW AUNT RHONDA'S RULES.
OH? WHY IS THAT?
©2010, BABY BLUES PARTNERSHIP DIST. BY KING FEATURES SYNDICATE 11-16
SHE DOESN'T HAVE ANY.
YEAH, WELL, I'M LOANING HER SOME OF MINE.
KIRKMAN & SCOTT

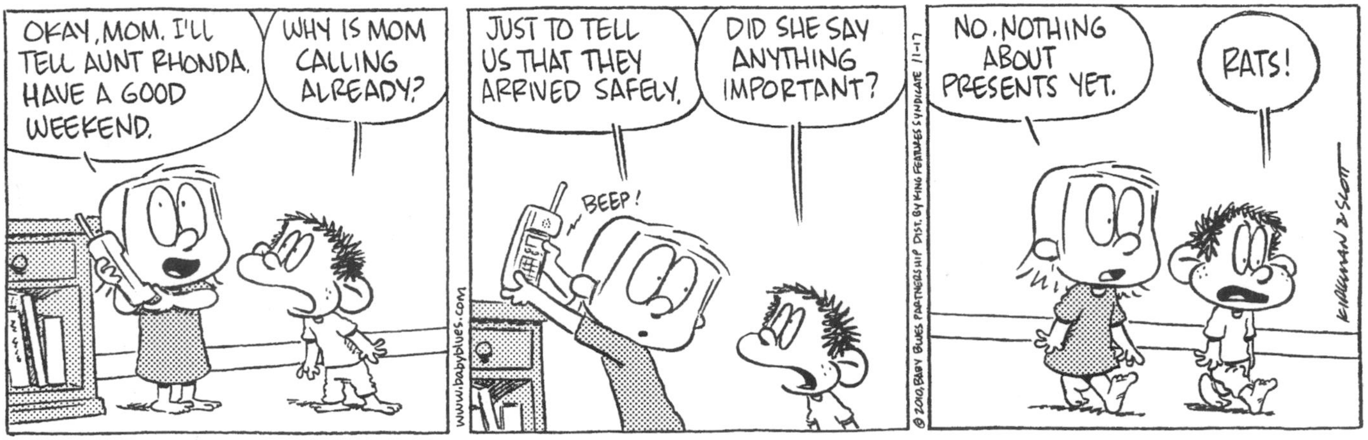
OKAY, MOM. I'LL TELL AUNT RHONDA. HAVE A GOOD WEEKEND.
WHY IS MOM CALLING ALREADY?
www.babyblues.com
BEEP!
JUST TO TELL US THAT THEY ARRIVED SAFELY.
DID SHE SAY ANYTHING IMPORTANT?
©2010, BABY BLUES PARTNERSHIP DIST. BY KING FEATURES SYNDICATE 11-17
NO. NOTHING ABOUT PRESENTS YET.
RATS!
KIRKMAN & SCOTT

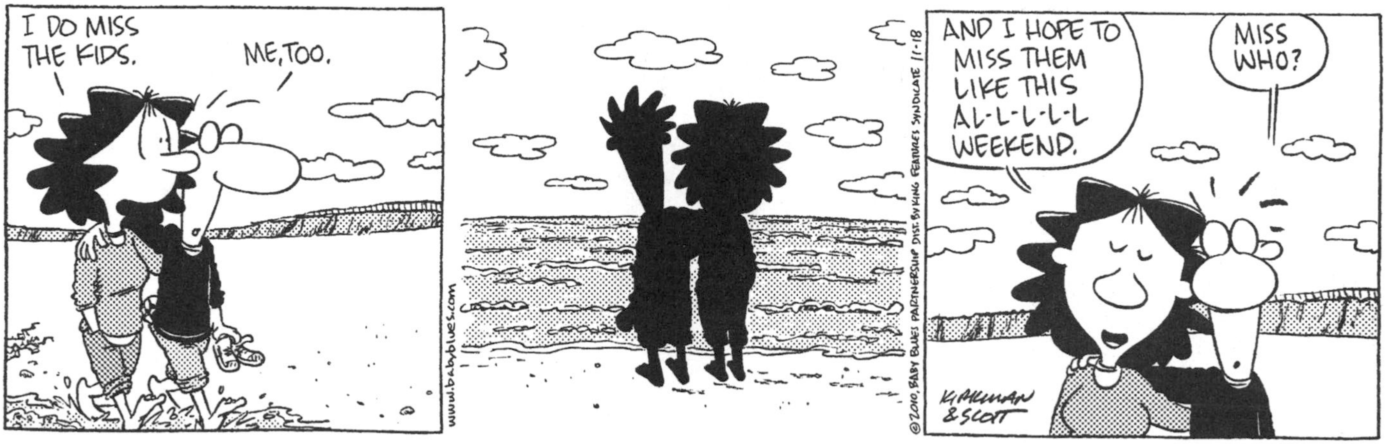
I DO MISS THE KIDS.
ME, TOO.
www.babyblues.com
©2010, BABY BLUES PARTNERSHIP DIST. BY KING FEATURES SYNDICATE 11-18
AND I HOPE TO MISS THEM LIKE THIS AL-L-L-L-L WEEKEND.
MISS WHO?
KIRKMAN & SCOTT

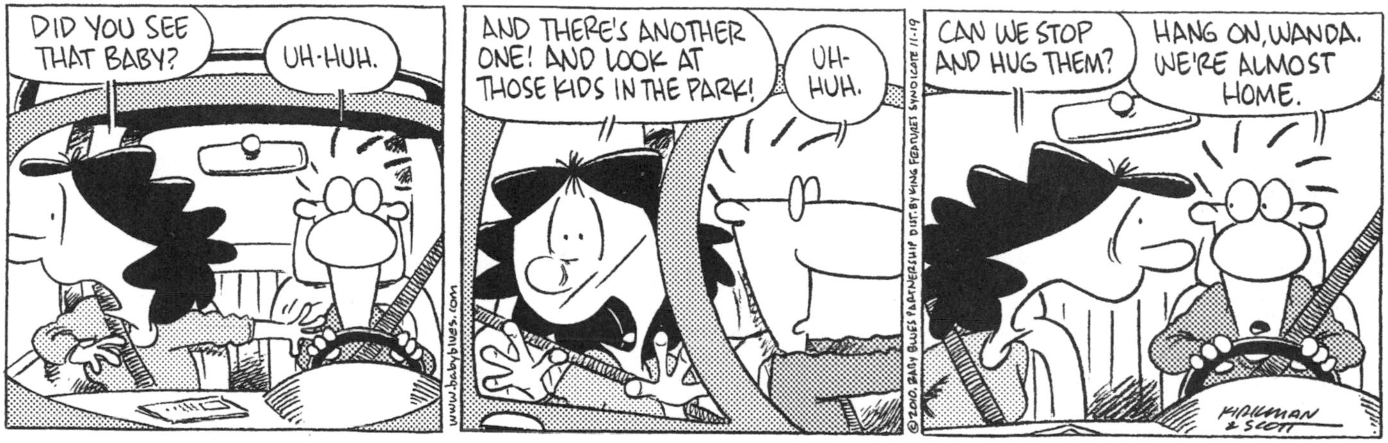
DID YOU SEE THAT BABY?
UH-HUH.
www.babyblues.com
AND THERE'S ANOTHER ONE! AND LOOK AT THOSE KIDS IN THE PARK!
UH-HUH.
©2010, BABY BLUES PARTNERSHIP DIST. BY KING FEATURES SYNDICATE 11-19
CAN WE STOP AND HUG THEM?
HANG ON, WANDA. WE'RE ALMOST HOME.
KIRKMAN & SCOTT

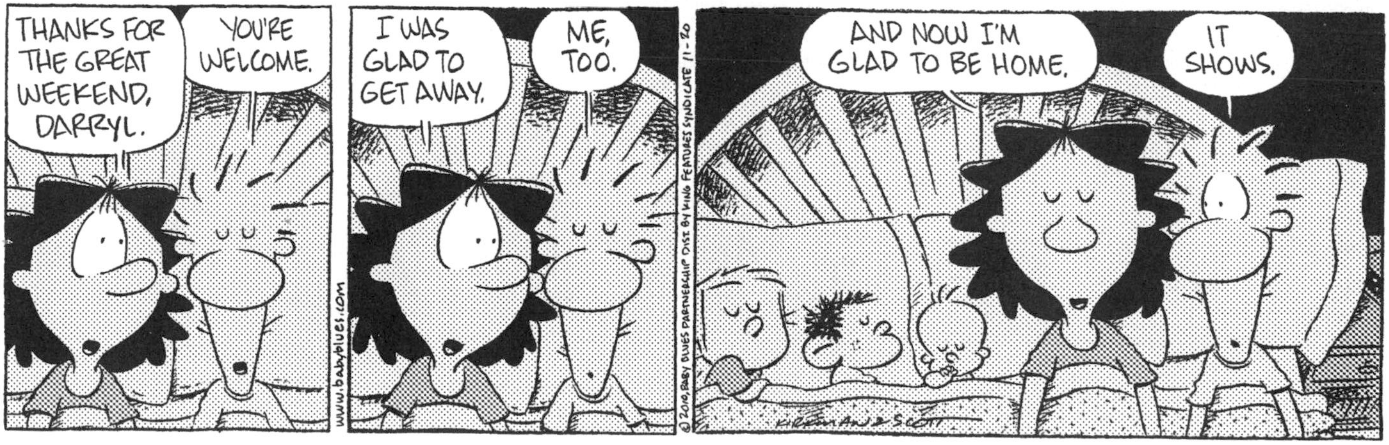
THANKS FOR THE GREAT WEEKEND, DARRYL.
YOU'RE WELCOME.
www.babyblues.com
I WAS GLAD TO GET AWAY.
ME, TOO.
©2010 BABY BLUES PARTNERSHIP DIST. BY KING FEATURES SYNDICATE 11-20
AND NOW I'M GLAD TO BE HOME.
IT SHOWS.
KIRKMAN & SCOTT

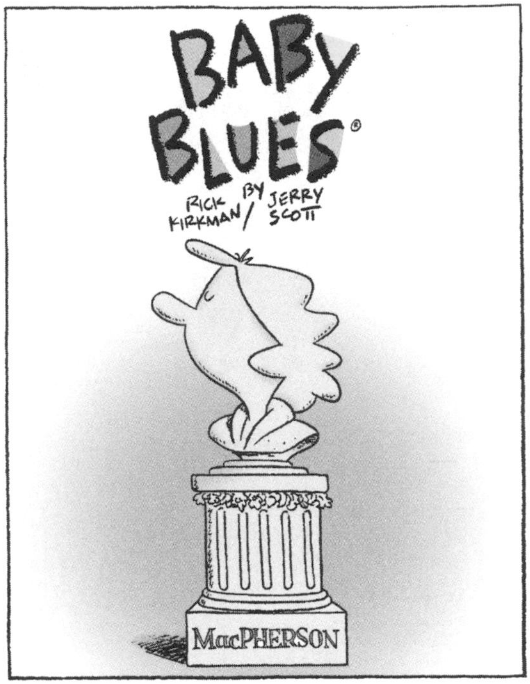
BABY BLUES®
BY RICK KIRKMAN / JERRY SCOTT
MacPHERSON

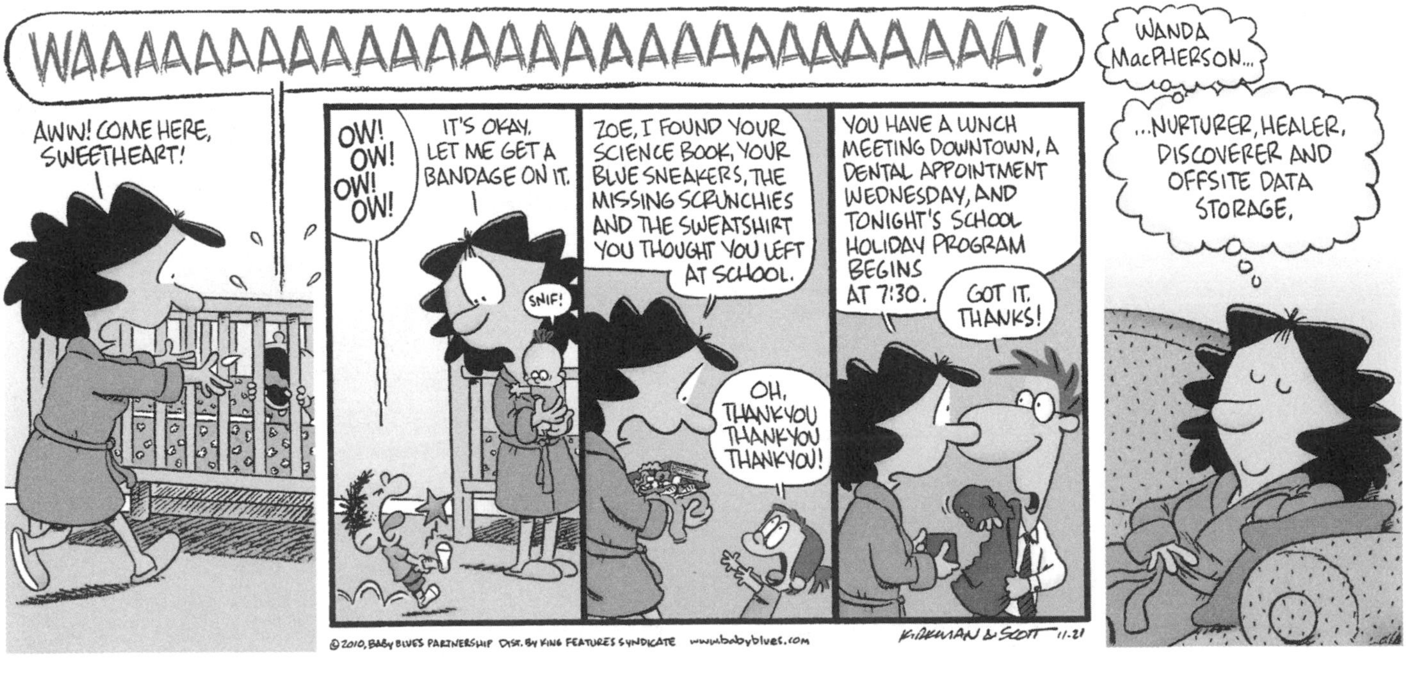
WAAAAAAAAAAAAAAAAAAAAAAAAAAAA!
AWW! COME HERE, SWEETHEART!
OW! OW! OW! OW!
IT'S OKAY. LET ME GET A BANDAGE ON IT.
SNIF!
ZOE, I FOUND YOUR SCIENCE BOOK, YOUR BLUE SNEAKERS, THE MISSING SCRUNCHIES AND THE SWEATSHIRT YOU THOUGHT YOU LEFT AT SCHOOL.
OH, THANKYOU THANKYOU THANKYOU!
YOU HAVE A LUNCH MEETING DOWNTOWN, A DENTAL APPOINTMENT WEDNESDAY, AND TONIGHT'S SCHOOL HOLIDAY PROGRAM BEGINS AT 7:30.
GOT IT. THANKS!
WANDA MacPHERSON...
...NURTURER, HEALER, DISCOVERER AND OFFSITE DATA STORAGE.
©2010, BABY BLUES PARTNERSHIP DIST. BY KING FEATURES SYNDICATE www.babyblues.com
KIRKMAN & SCOTT 11-21

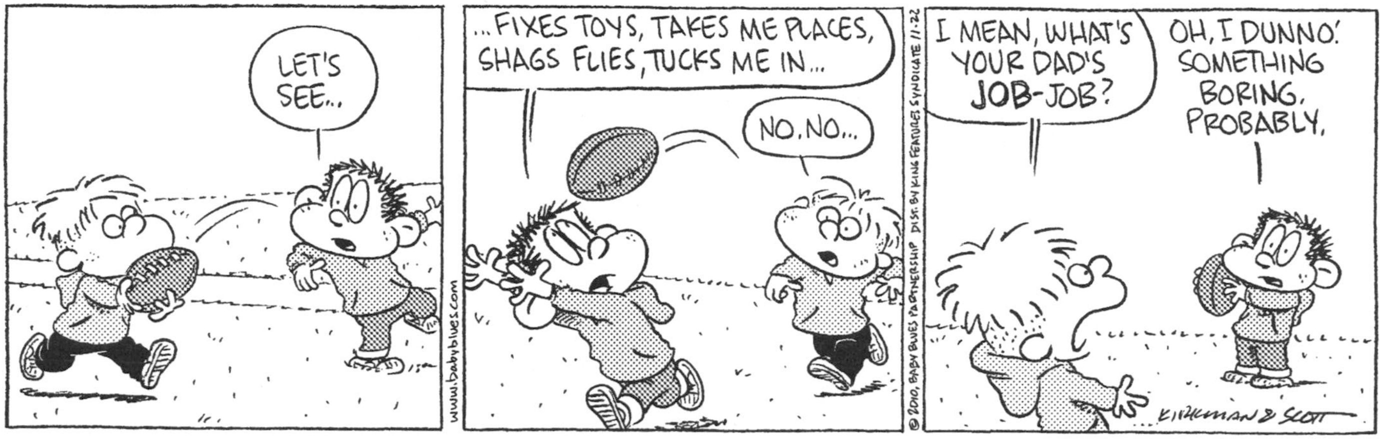
LET'S SEE...
...FIXES TOYS, TAKES ME PLACES, SHAGS FLIES, TUCKS ME IN...
NO, NO...
I MEAN, WHAT'S YOUR DAD'S JOB-JOB?
OH, I DUNNO! SOMETHING BORING, PROBABLY.
www.babyblues.com
© 2010, BABY BLUES PARTNERSHIP DIST. BY KING FEATURES SYNDICATE 11-22
KIRKMAN & SCOTT

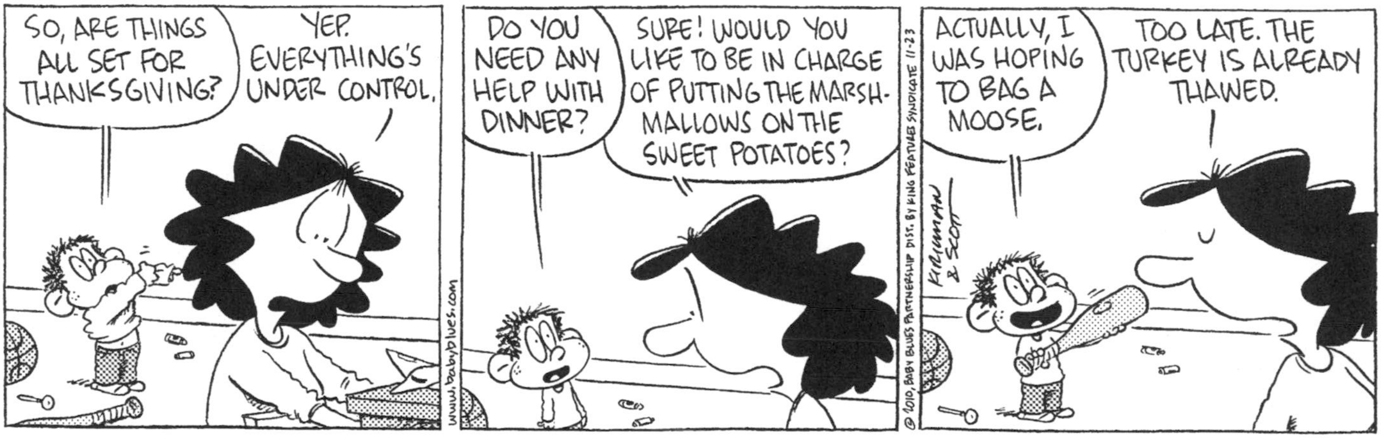
SO, ARE THINGS ALL SET FOR THANKSGIVING?
YEP. EVERYTHING'S UNDER CONTROL.
DO YOU NEED ANY HELP WITH DINNER?
SURE! WOULD YOU LIKE TO BE IN CHARGE OF PUTTING THE MARSH-MALLOWS ON THE SWEET POTATOES?
ACTUALLY, I WAS HOPING TO BAG A MOOSE.
TOO LATE. THE TURKEY IS ALREADY THAWED.
www.babyblues.com
© 2010, BABY BLUES PARTNERSHIP DIST. BY KING FEATURES SYNDICATE 11-23
KIRKMAN & SCOTT

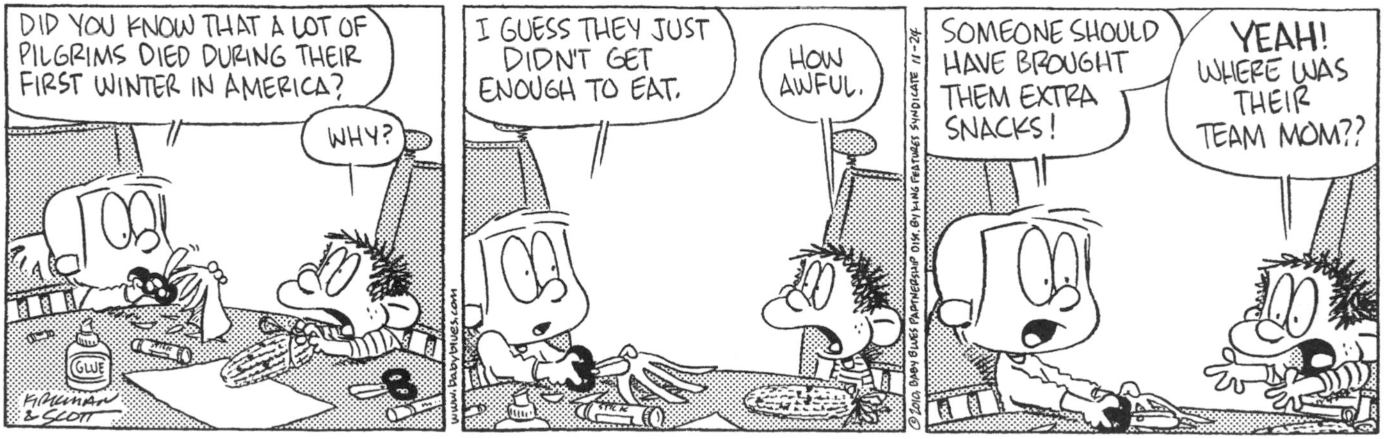
DID YOU KNOW THAT A LOT OF PILGRIMS DIED DURING THEIR FIRST WINTER IN AMERICA?
WHY?
GLUE
KIRKMAN & SCOTT
I GUESS THEY JUST DIDN'T GET ENOUGH TO EAT.
HOW AWFUL.
www.babyblues.com
© 2010, BABY BLUES PARTNERSHIP DIST. BY KING FEATURES SYNDICATE 11-24
SOMEONE SHOULD HAVE BROUGHT THEM EXTRA SNACKS!
YEAH! WHERE WAS THEIR TEAM MOM??

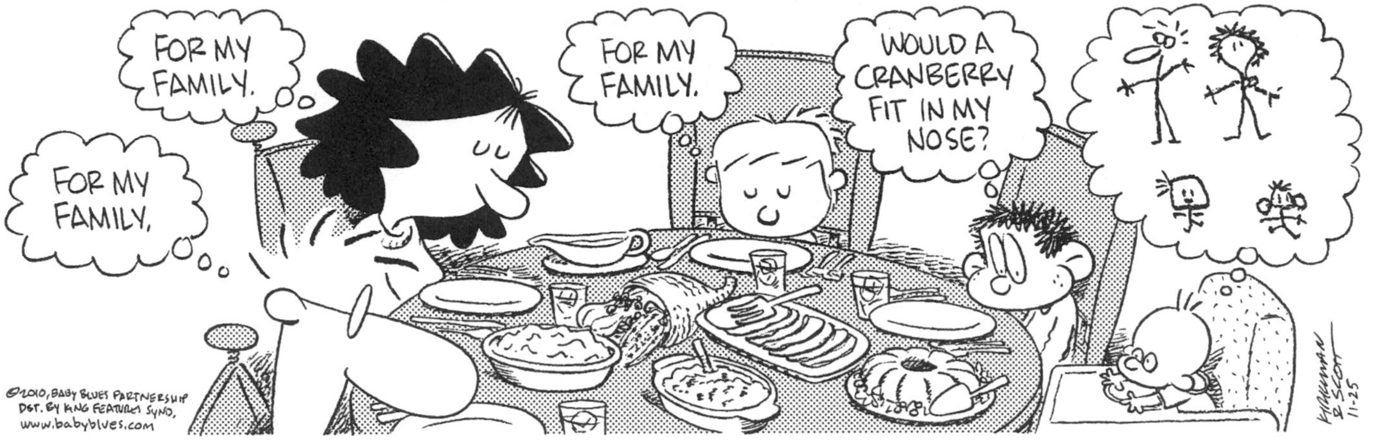
FOR MY FAMILY.
FOR MY FAMILY.
FOR MY FAMILY.
WOULD A CRANBERRY FIT IN MY NOSE?
©2010, BABY BLUES PARTNERSHIP DST. BY KING FEATURES SYND. www.babyblues.com
KIRKMAN & SCOTT 11-25

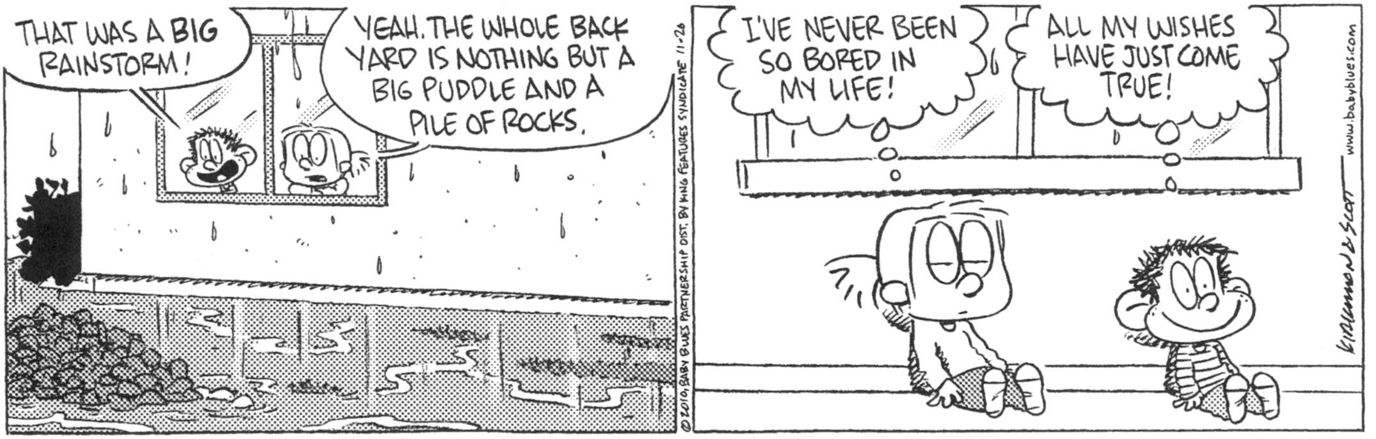
THAT WAS A BIG RAINSTORM!
YEAH. THE WHOLE BACK YARD IS NOTHING BUT A BIG PUDDLE AND A PILE OF ROCKS.
©2010, BABY BLUES PARTNERSHIP DIST. BY KING FEATURES SYNDICATE 11-26
I'VE NEVER BEEN SO BORED IN MY LIFE!
ALL MY WISHES HAVE JUST COME TRUE!
KIRKMAN & SCOTT
www.babyblues.com

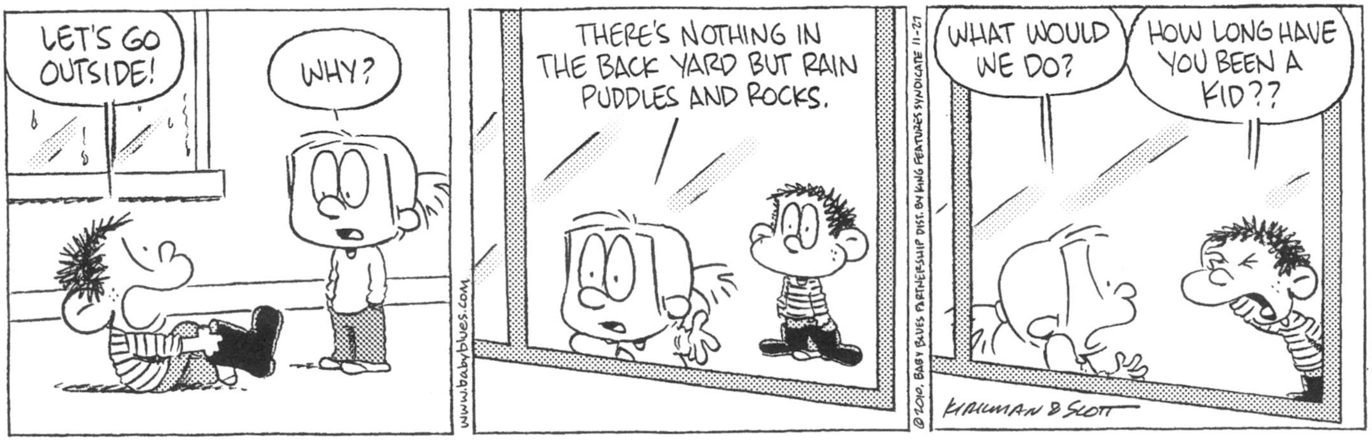
LET'S GO OUTSIDE!
WHY?
www.babyblues.com
THERE'S NOTHING IN THE BACK YARD BUT RAIN PUDDLES AND ROCKS.
©2010, BABY BLUES PARTNERSHIP DIST. BY KING FEATURES SYNDICATE 11-27
WHAT WOULD WE DO?
HOW LONG HAVE YOU BEEN A KID??
KIRKMAN & SCOTT

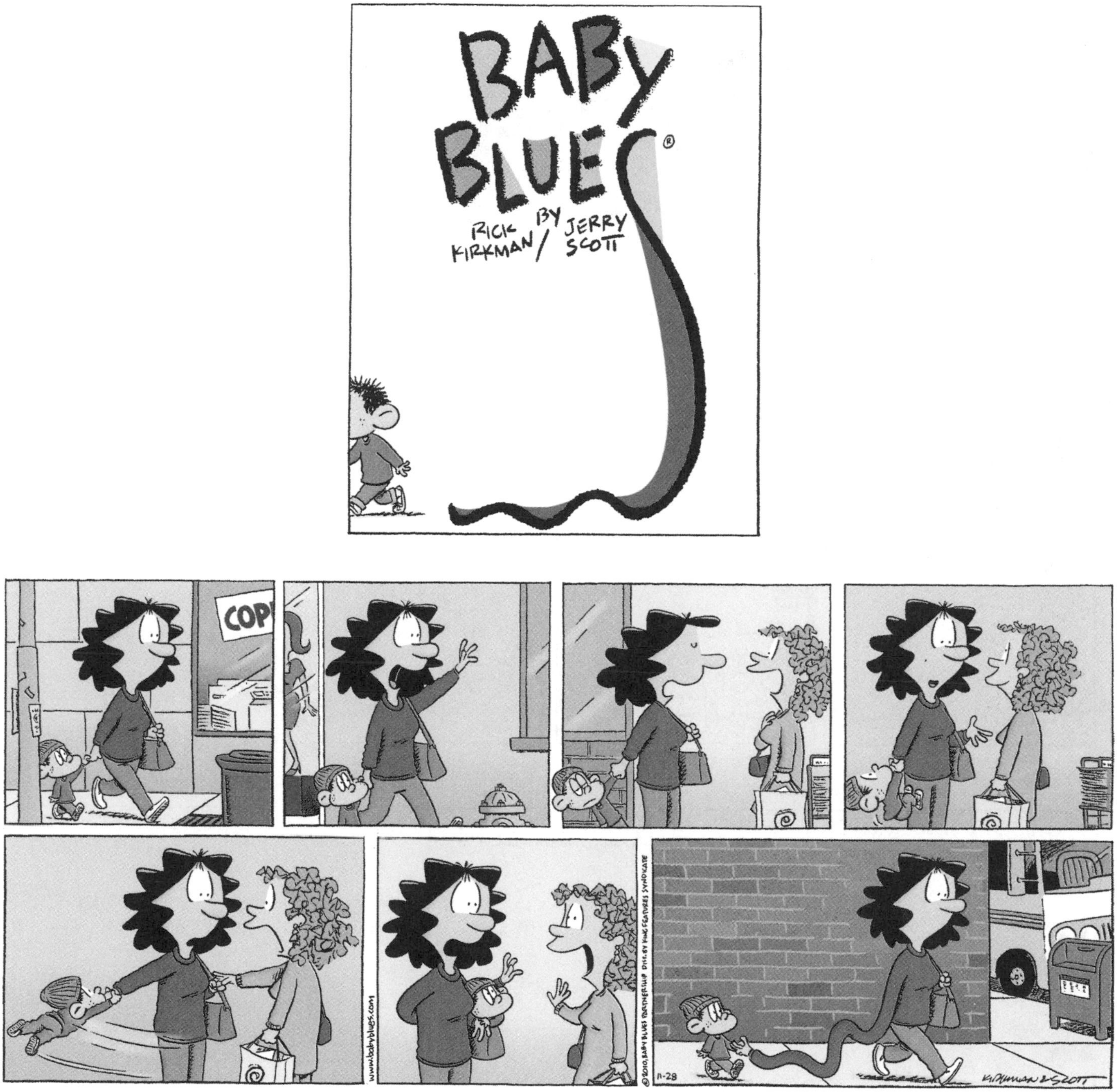
BABY BLUES®
BY RICK KIRKMAN / JERRY SCOTT
COP
www.babyblues.com
©2010, BABY BLUES PARTNERSHIP DIST. BY KING FEATURES SYNDICATE
11-28
KIRKMAN & SCOTT

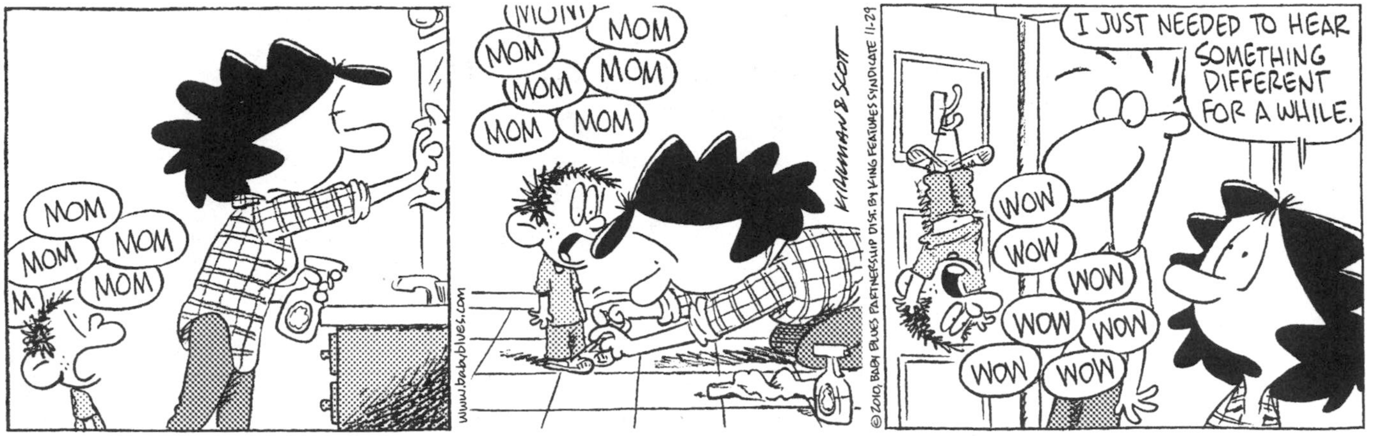
MOM
MOM
MOM
MOM
M
www.babyblues.com
MOM
MOM
MOM
MOM
MOM
MOM
KIRKMAN & SCOTT
©2010, BABY BLUES PARTNERSHIP DIST. BY KING FEATURES SYNDICATE 11-29
I JUST NEEDED TO HEAR SOMETHING DIFFERENT FOR A WHILE.
WOW
WOW
WOW
WOW
WOW
WOW
WOW

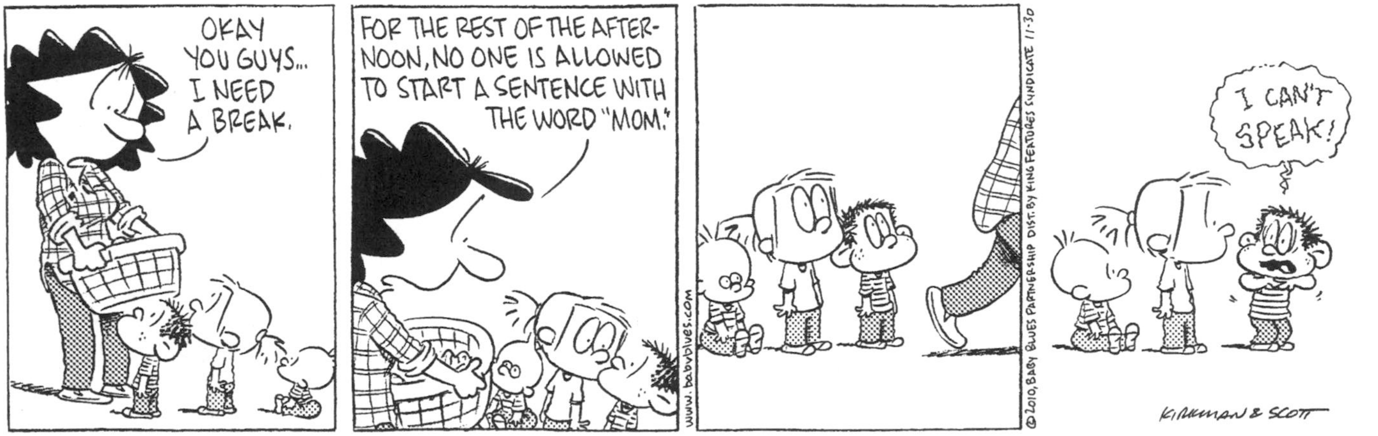
OKAY YOU GUYS... I NEED A BREAK.
FOR THE REST OF THE AFTER-NOON, NO ONE IS ALLOWED TO START A SENTENCE WITH THE WORD "MOM."
www.babyblues.com
©2010, BABY BLUES PARTNERSHIP DIST. BY KING FEATURES SYNDICATE 11-30
I CAN'T SPEAK!
KIRKMAN & SCOTT

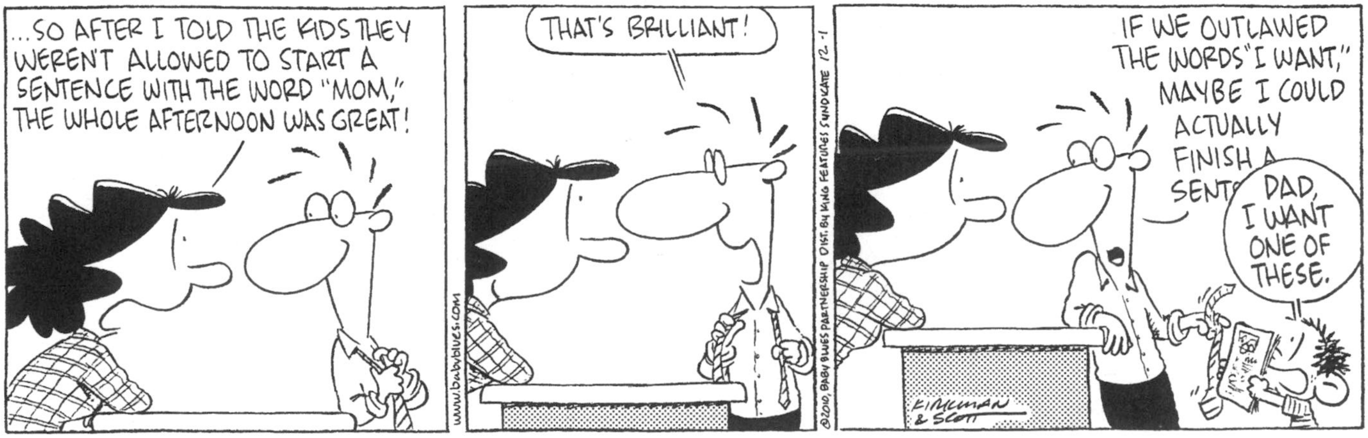
...SO AFTER I TOLD THE KIDS THEY WEREN'T ALLOWED TO START A SENTENCE WITH THE WORD "MOM," THE WHOLE AFTERNOON WAS GREAT!
www.babyblues.com
THAT'S BRILLIANT!
©2010, BABY BLUES PARTNERSHIP DIST. BY KING FEATURES SYNDICATE 12-1
IF WE OUTLAWED THE WORDS "I WANT," MAYBE I COULD ACTUALLY FINISH A SENT
DAD, I WANT ONE OF THESE.
KIRKMAN & SCOTT

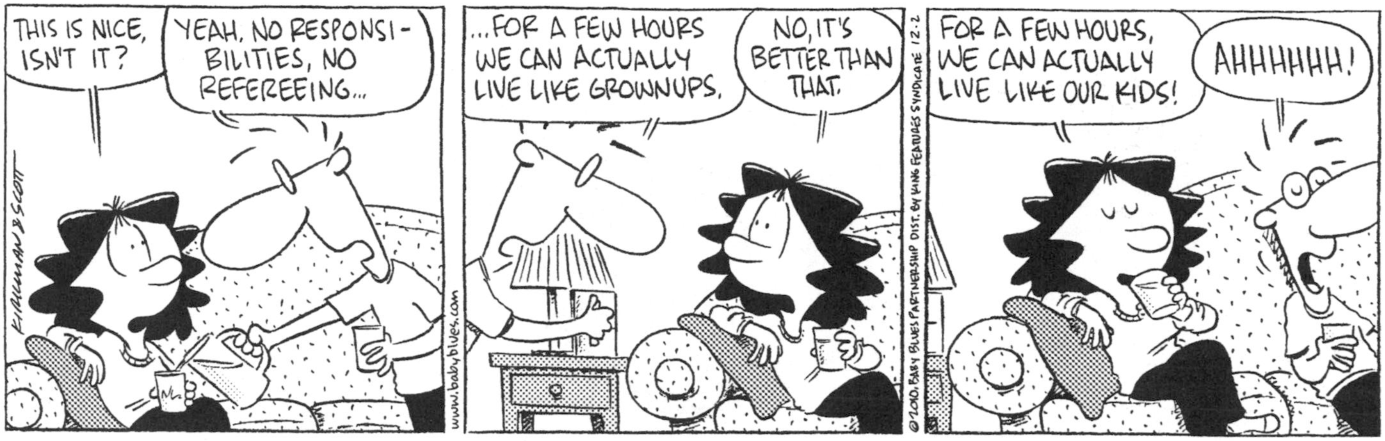
THIS IS NICE, ISN'T IT?
YEAH, NO RESPONSIBILITIES, NO REFEREEING...
...FOR A FEW HOURS WE CAN ACTUALLY LIVE LIKE GROWNUPS.
NO, IT'S BETTER THAN THAT.
FOR A FEW HOURS, WE CAN ACTUALLY LIVE LIKE OUR KIDS!
AHHHHHH!
KIRKMAN & SCOTT
www.babyblues.com
© 2010, BABY BLUES PARTNERSHIP DIST. BY KING FEATURES SYNDICATE 12-2

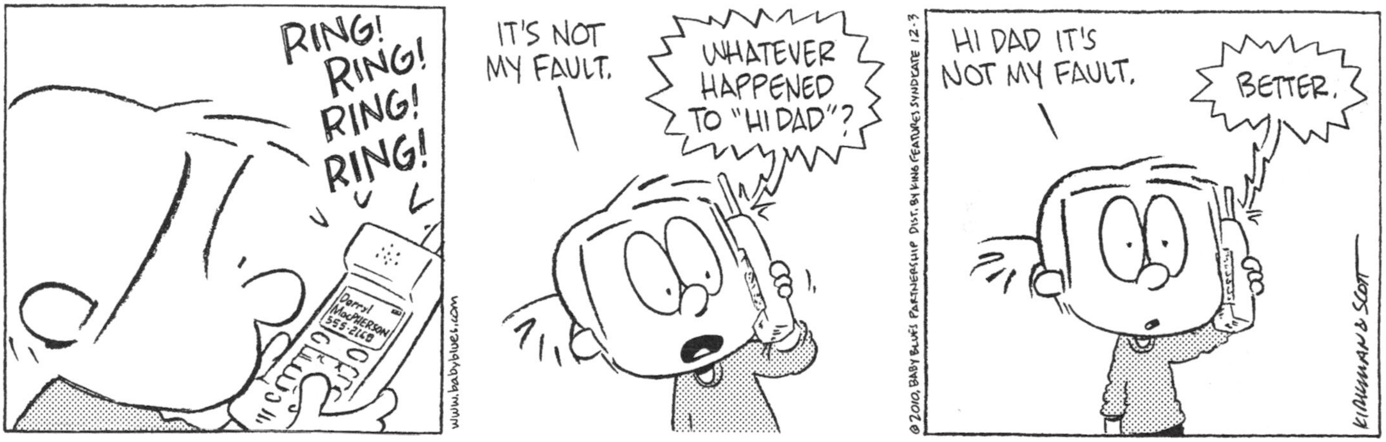
RING! RING! RING! RING!
Darryl MacPherson 555-2168
www.babyblues.com
IT'S NOT MY FAULT.
WHATEVER HAPPENED TO "HI DAD"?
© 2010, BABY BLUES PARTNERSHIP DIST. BY KING FEATURES SYNDICATE 12-3
HI DAD IT'S NOT MY FAULT.
BETTER.
KIRKMAN & SCOTT

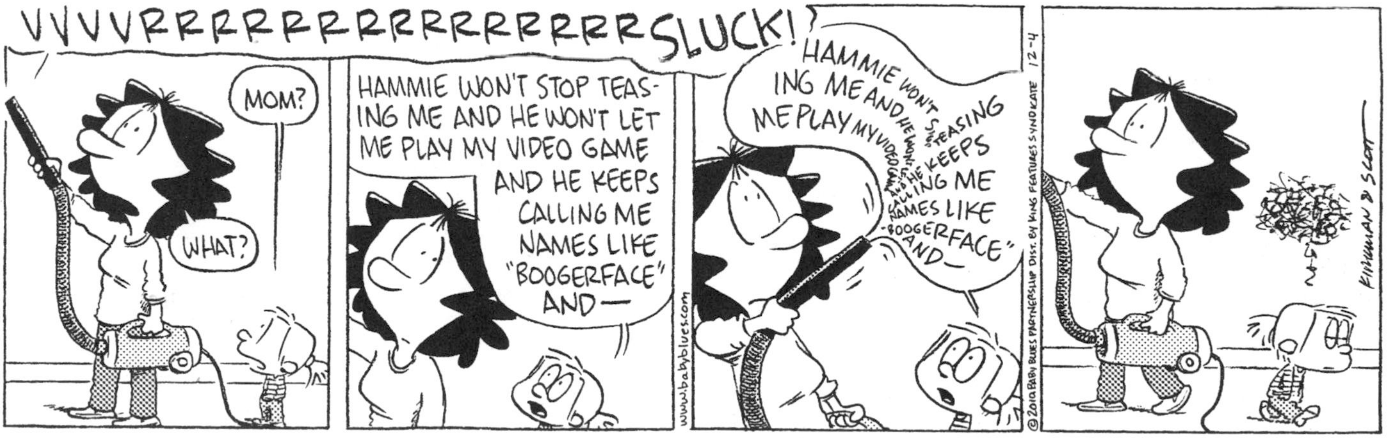
VVVVRRRRRRRRRRRRRRRRRSLUCK!
MOM?
WHAT?
HAMMIE WON'T STOP TEASING ME AND HE WON'T LET ME PLAY MY VIDEO GAME AND HE KEEPS CALLING ME NAMES LIKE "BOOGERFACE" AND—
www.babyblues.com
HAMMIE WON'T ... ING ME AND HE ... ME PLAY MY VIDEO ... TEASING ... AND HE KEEPS CALLING ME NAMES LIKE "BOOGERFACE" AND—
© 2010 BABY BLUES PARTNERSHIP DIST. BY KING FEATURES SYNDICATE 12-4
KIRKMAN & SCOTT

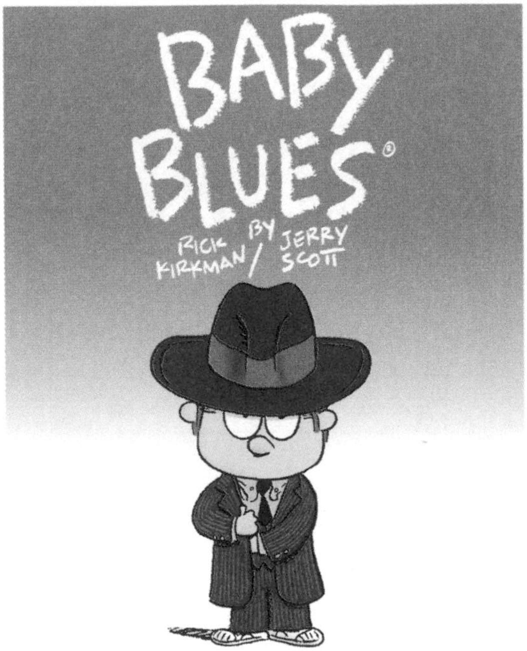
BABY BLUES®
BY RICK KIRKMAN / JERRY SCOTT

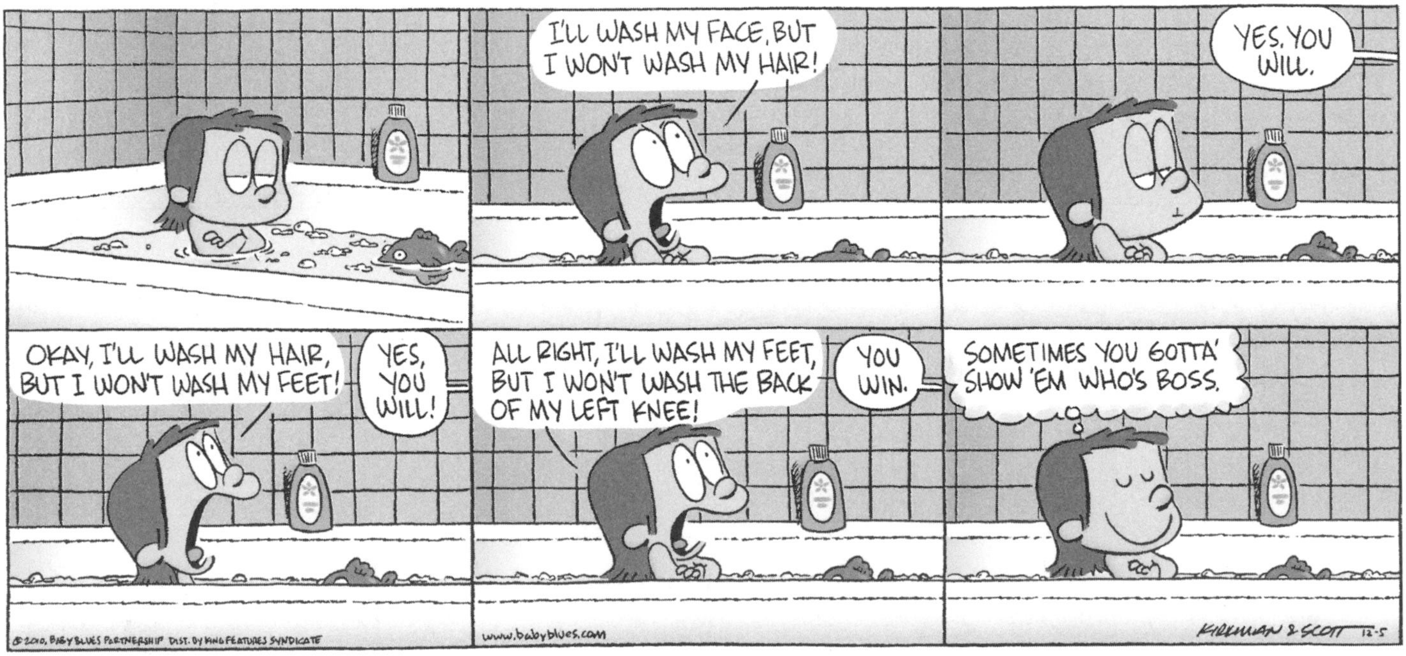
I'LL WASH MY FACE, BUT I WON'T WASH MY HAIR!
YES, YOU WILL.
OKAY, I'LL WASH MY HAIR, BUT I WON'T WASH MY FEET!
YES, YOU WILL!
ALL RIGHT, I'LL WASH MY FEET, BUT I WON'T WASH THE BACK OF MY LEFT KNEE!
YOU WIN.
SOMETIMES YOU GOTTA' SHOW 'EM WHO'S BOSS.
© 2010, BABY BLUES PARTNERSHIP DIST. BY KING FEATURES SYNDICATE
www.babyblues.com
KIRKMAN & SCOTT 12-5

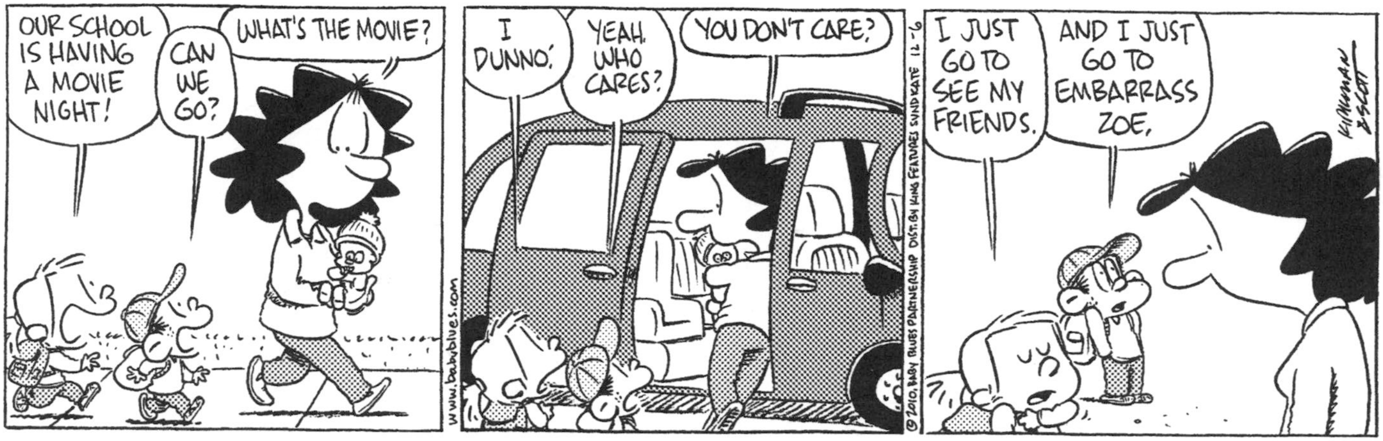
OUR SCHOOL IS HAVING A MOVIE NIGHT!
CAN WE GO?
WHAT'S THE MOVIE?
I DUNNO.
YEAH. WHO CARES?
YOU DON'T CARE?
I JUST GO TO SEE MY FRIENDS.
AND I JUST GO TO EMBARRASS ZOE.
www.babyblues.com
© 2010, BABY BLUES PARTNERSHIP DIST. BY KING FEATURES SYNDICATE 12-6
KIRKMAN & SCOTT

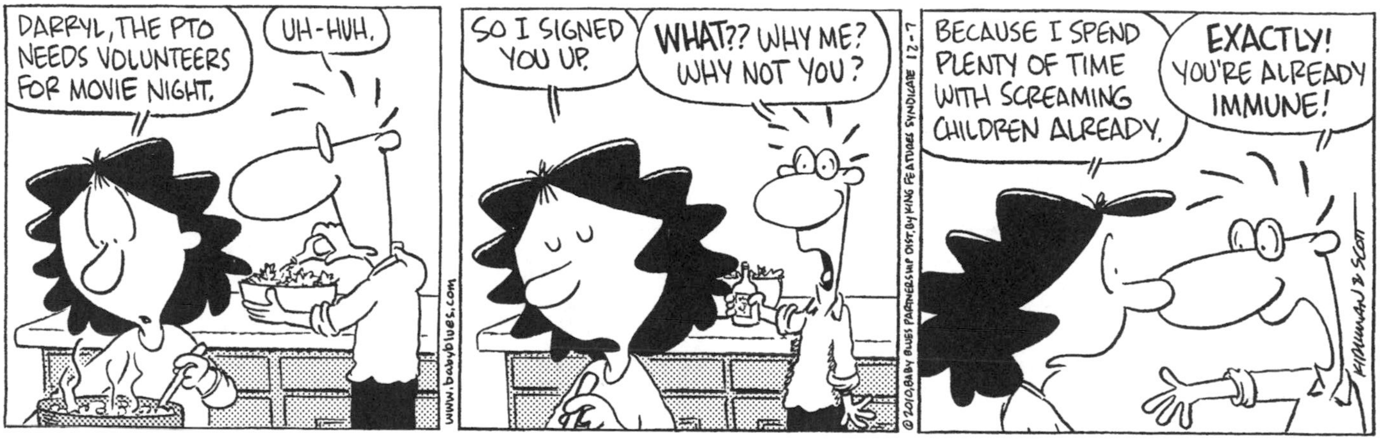
DARRYL, THE PTO NEEDS VOLUNTEERS FOR MOVIE NIGHT.
UH-HUH.
SO I SIGNED YOU UP.
WHAT?? WHY ME? WHY NOT YOU?
BECAUSE I SPEND PLENTY OF TIME WITH SCREAMING CHILDREN ALREADY.
EXACTLY! YOU'RE ALREADY IMMUNE!
www.babyblues.com
© 2010, BABY BLUES PARTNERSHIP DIST. BY KING FEATURES SYNDICATE 12-7
KIRKMAN & SCOTT

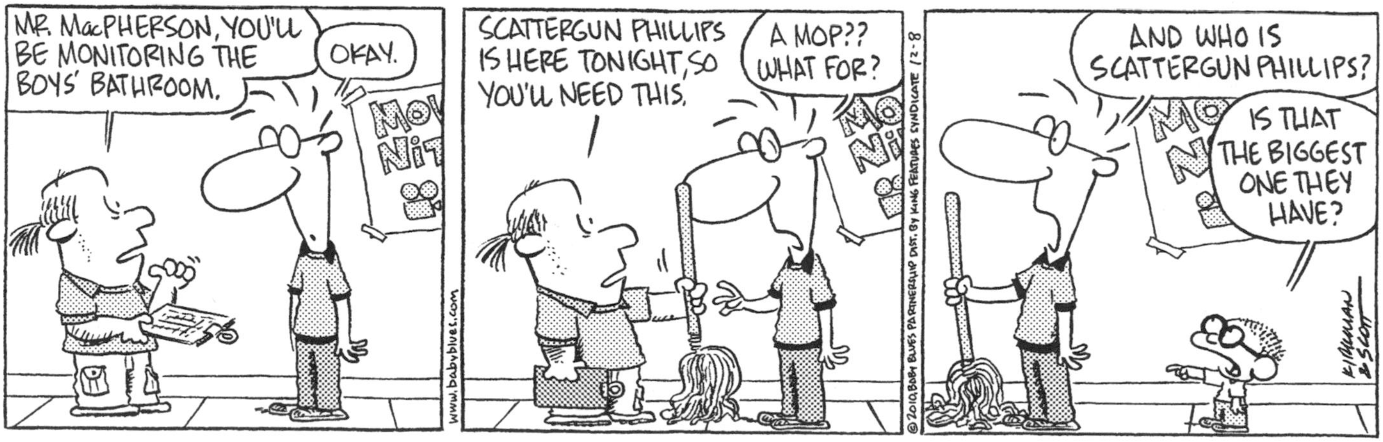
MR. MacPHERSON, YOU'LL BE MONITORING THE BOYS' BATHROOM.
OKAY.
SCATTERGUN PHILLIPS IS HERE TONIGHT, SO YOU'LL NEED THIS.
A MOP?? WHAT FOR?
AND WHO IS SCATTERGUN PHILLIPS?
IS THAT THE BIGGEST ONE THEY HAVE?
www.babyblues.com
© 2010, BABY BLUES PARTNERSHIP DIST. BY KING FEATURES SYNDICATE 12-8
KIRKMAN & SCOTT

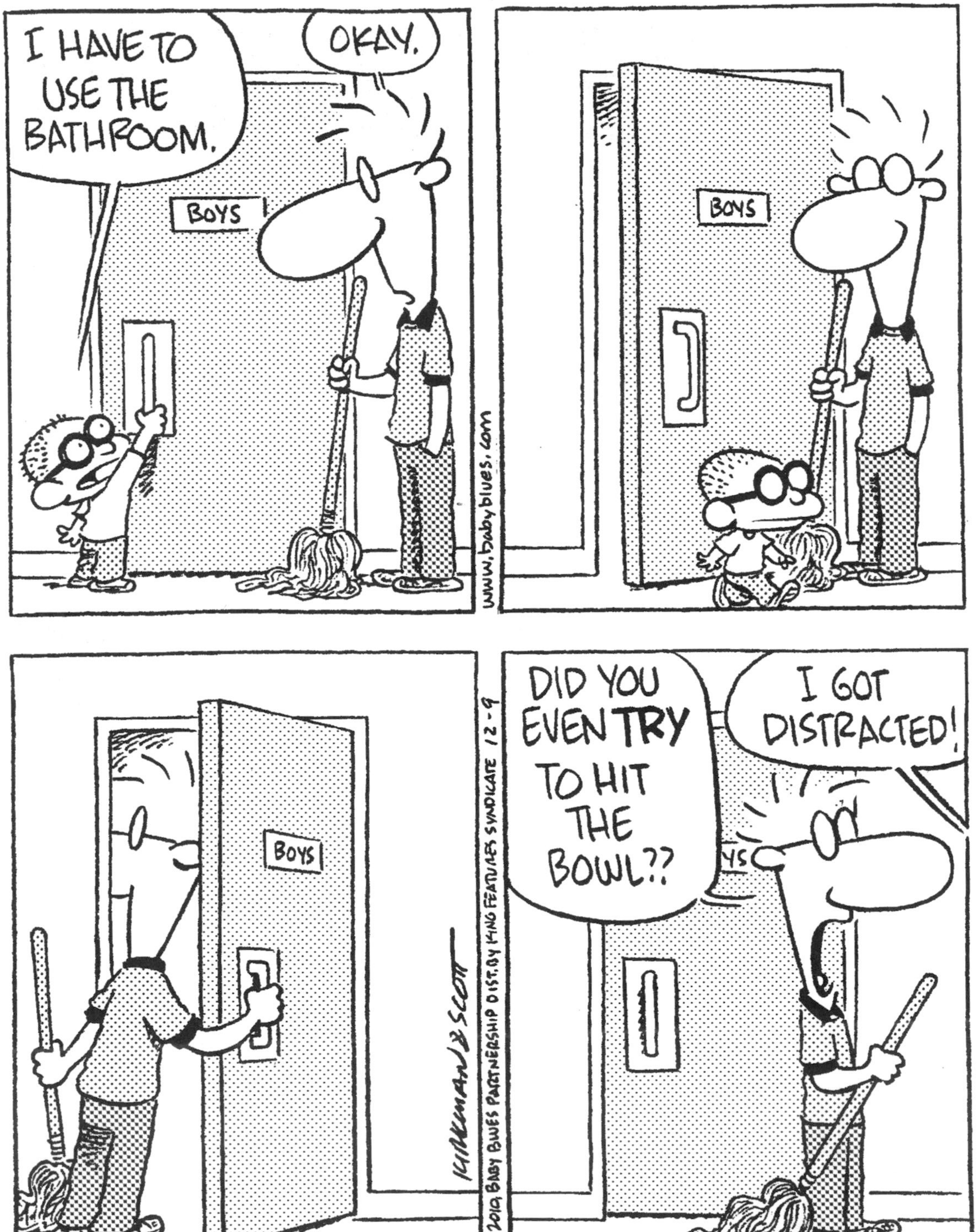
I HAVE TO USE THE BATHROOM.
OKAY.
BOYS
www.babyblues.com
BOYS
BOYS
© 2010 BABY BLUES PARTNERSHIP DIST. BY KING FEATURES SYNDICATE 12-9
KIRKMAN & SCOTT
DID YOU EVEN TRY TO HIT THE BOWL??
I GOT DISTRACTED!

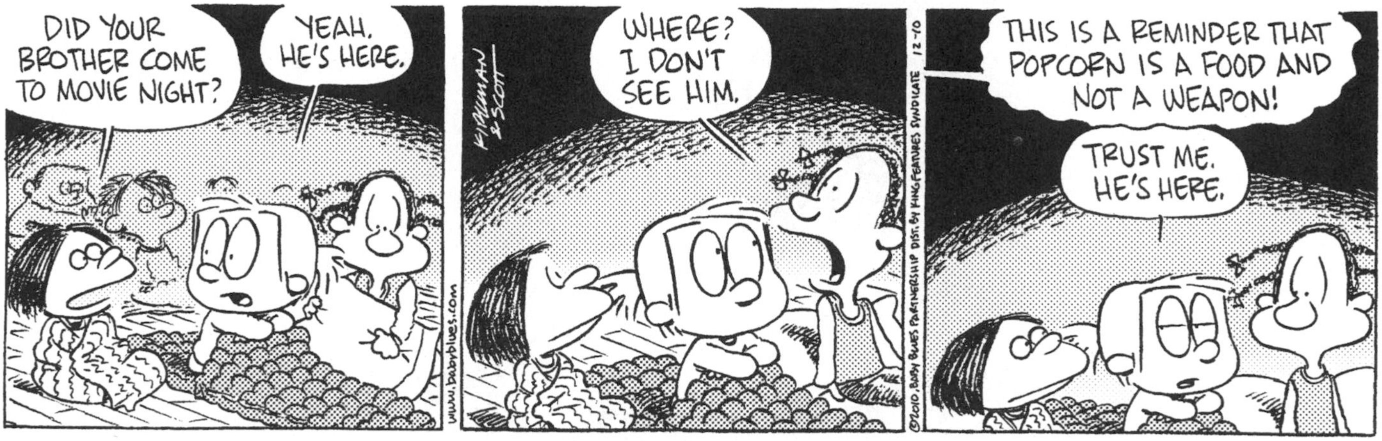
DID YOUR BROTHER COME TO MOVIE NIGHT?
YEAH. HE'S HERE.
KIRKMAN & SCOTT
www.babyblues.com
WHERE? I DON'T SEE HIM.
12-10
©2010, BABY BLUES PARTNERSHIP DIST. BY KING FEATURES SYNDICATE
THIS IS A REMINDER THAT POPCORN IS A FOOD AND NOT A WEAPON!
TRUST ME. HE'S HERE.

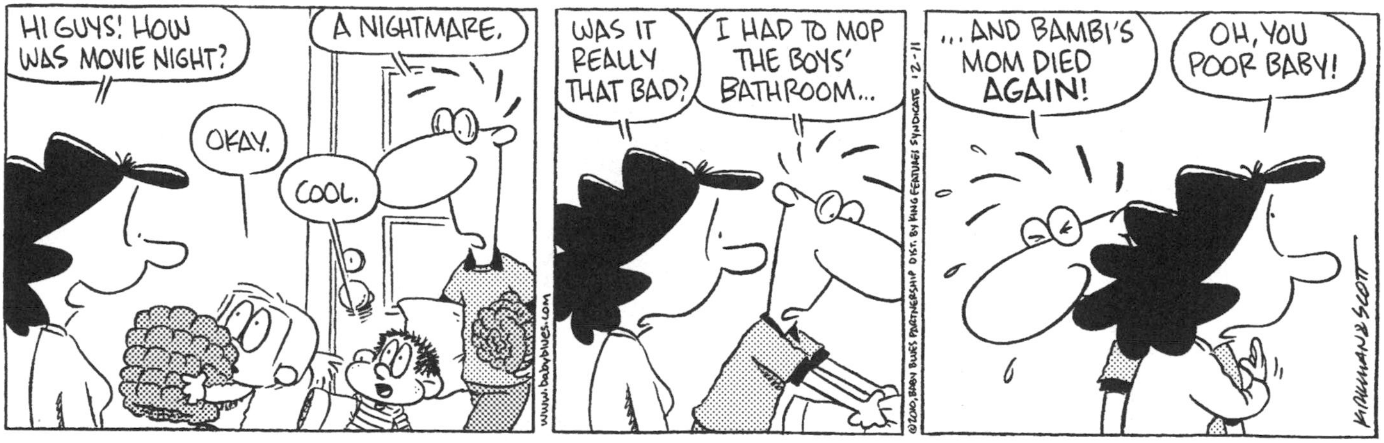
HI GUYS! HOW WAS MOVIE NIGHT?
A NIGHTMARE.
OKAY.
COOL.
www.babyblues.com
WAS IT REALLY THAT BAD?
I HAD TO MOP THE BOYS' BATHROOM...
12-11
©2010, BABY BLUES PARTNERSHIP DIST. BY KING FEATURES SYNDICATE
...AND BAMBI'S MOM DIED AGAIN!
OH, YOU POOR BABY!
KIRKMAN & SCOTT

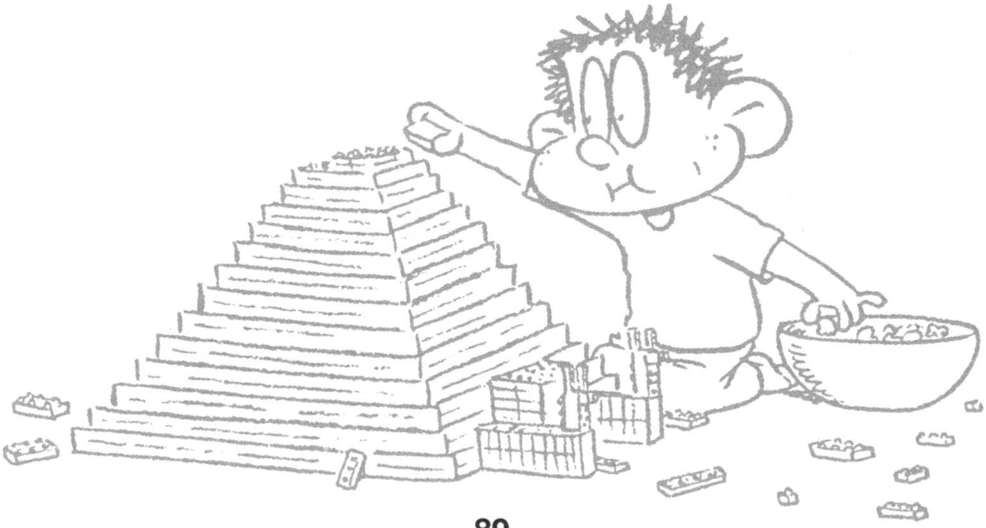

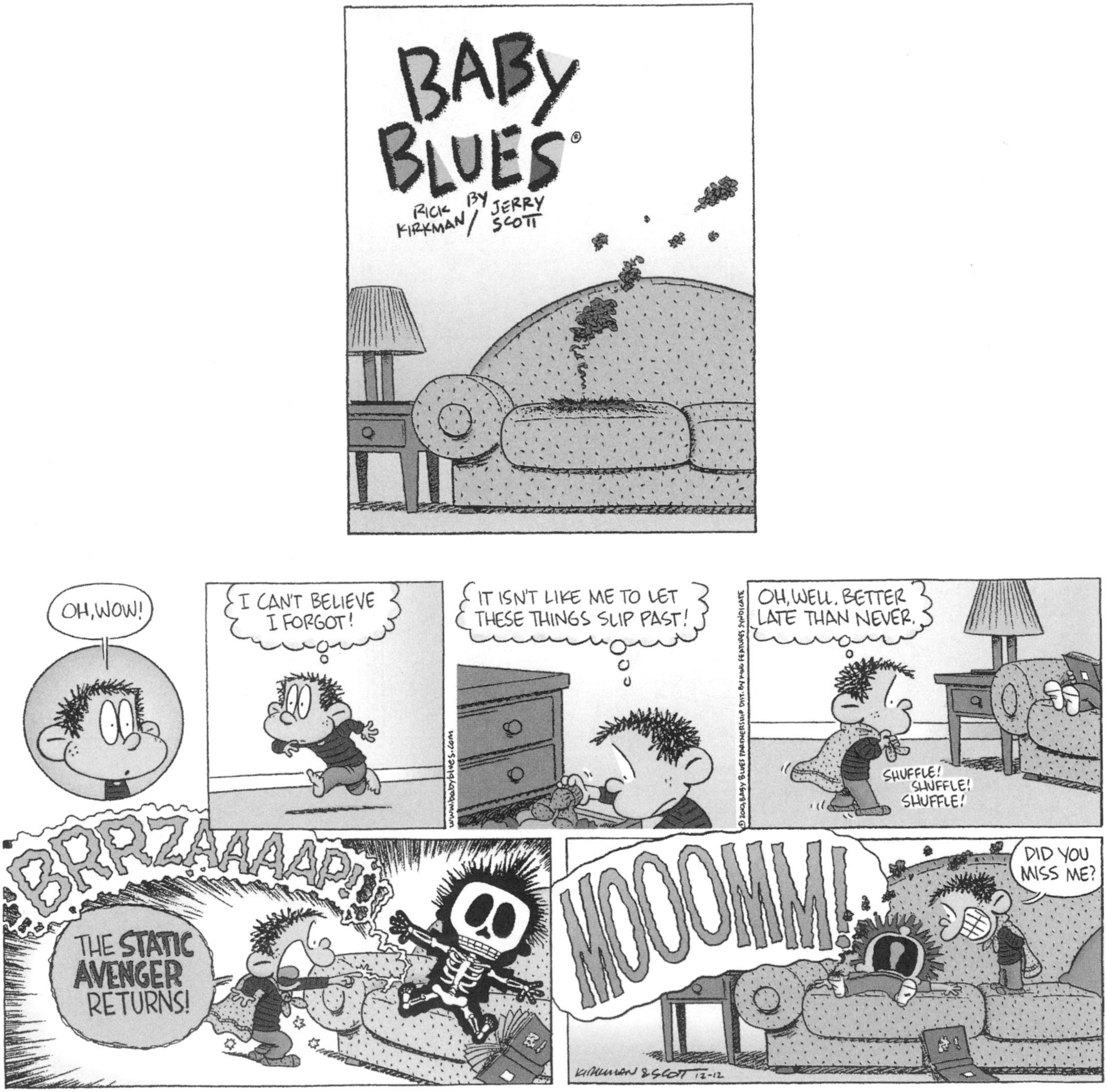
BABY BLUES®
BY RICK KIRKMAN / JERRY SCOTT
OH, WOW!
I CAN'T BELIEVE I FORGOT!
www.babyblues.com
IT ISN'T LIKE ME TO LET THESE THINGS SLIP PAST!
© 2000, BABY BLUES PARTNERSHIP DIST. BY KING FEATURES SYNDICATE
OH, WELL. BETTER LATE THAN NEVER.
SHUFFLE! SHUFFLE! SHUFFLE!
BRRZAAAAP!
THE STATIC AVENGER RETURNS!
MOOOMM!
DID YOU MISS ME?
KIRKMAN & SCOTT 12-12

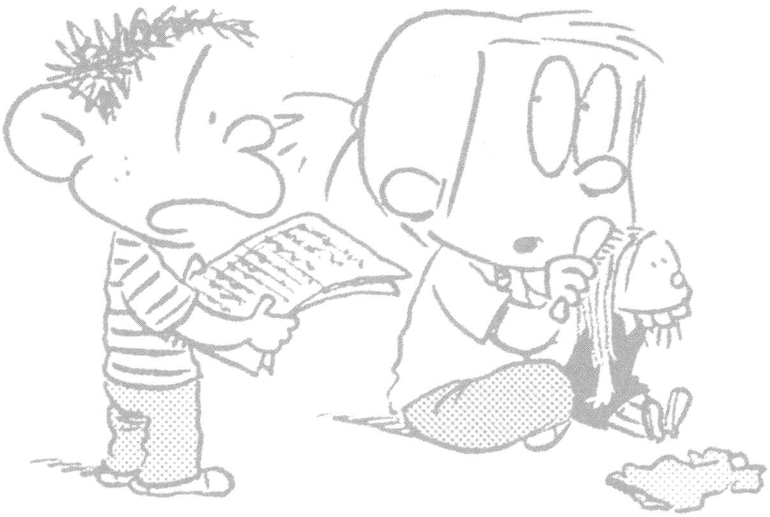

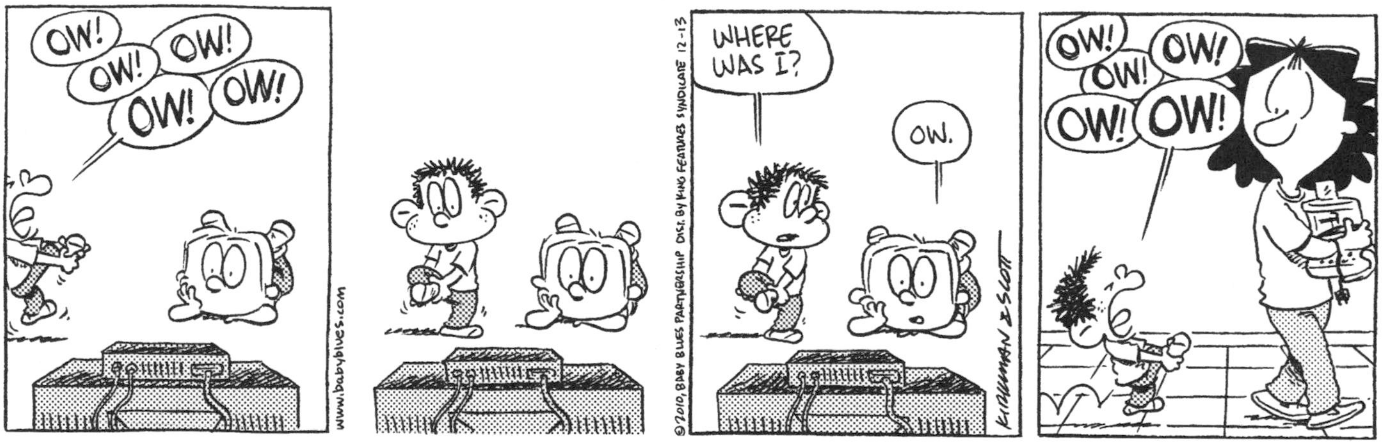
OW! OW! OW! OW! OW!
www.babyblues.com
WHERE WAS I?
OW.
©2010, BABY BLUES PARTNERSHIP DIST. BY KING FEATURES SYNDICATE 12-13
KIRKMAN & SCOTT
OW! OW! OW! OW! OW!

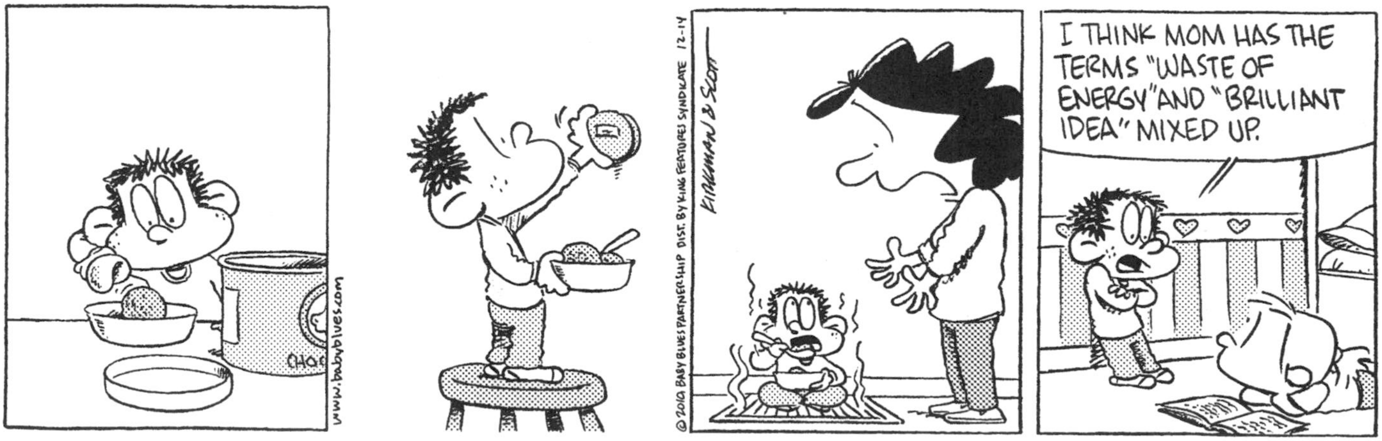
www.babyblues.com
©2010 BABY BLUES PARTNERSHIP DIST. BY KING FEATURES SYNDICATE 12-14
KIRKMAN & SCOTT
I THINK MOM HAS THE TERMS "WASTE OF ENERGY" AND "BRILLIANT IDEA" MIXED UP.

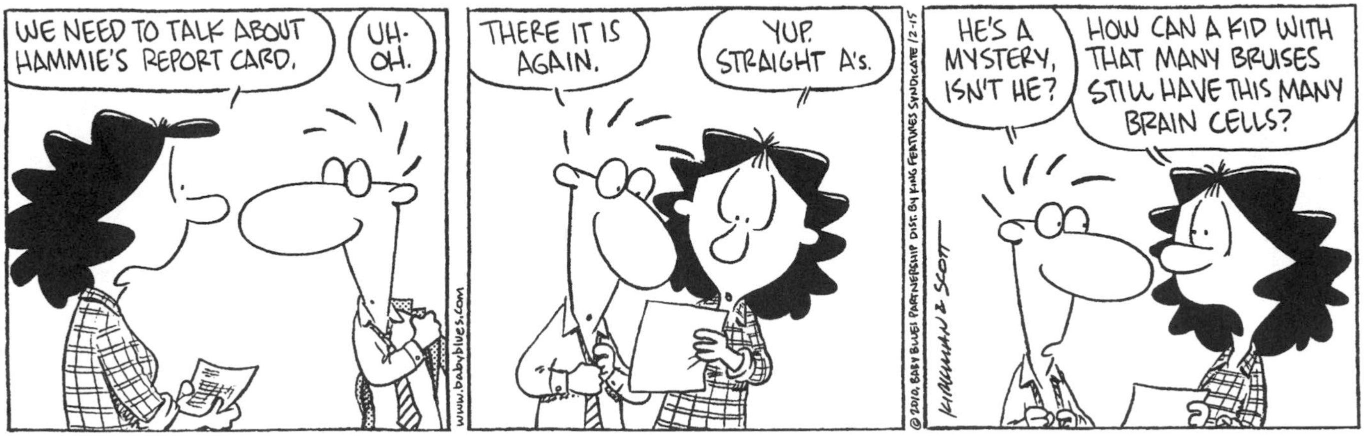
WE NEED TO TALK ABOUT HAMMIE'S REPORT CARD.
UH-OH.
www.babyblues.com
THERE IT IS AGAIN.
YUP. STRAIGHT A's.
© 2010, BABY BLUES PARTNERSHIP DIST. BY KING FEATURES SYNDICATE 12-15
KIRKMAN & SCOTT
HE'S A MYSTERY, ISN'T HE?
HOW CAN A KID WITH THAT MANY BRUISES STILL HAVE THIS MANY BRAIN CELLS?

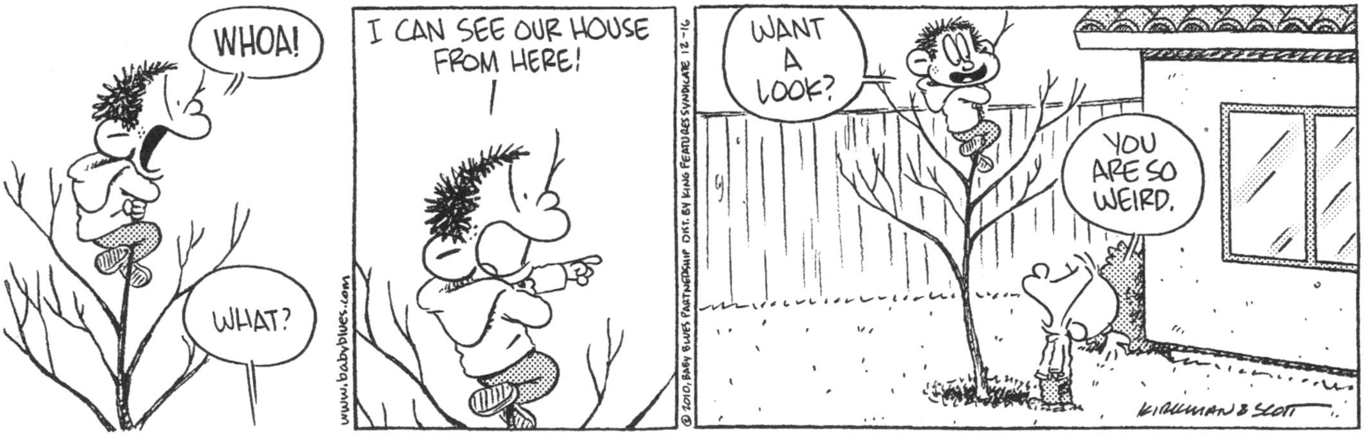
WHOA!
WHAT?
www.babyblues.com
I CAN SEE OUR HOUSE FROM HERE!
© 2010, BABY BLUES PARTNERSHIP DIST. BY KING FEATURES SYNDICATE 12-16
WANT A LOOK?
YOU ARE SO WEIRD.
KIRKMAN & SCOTT

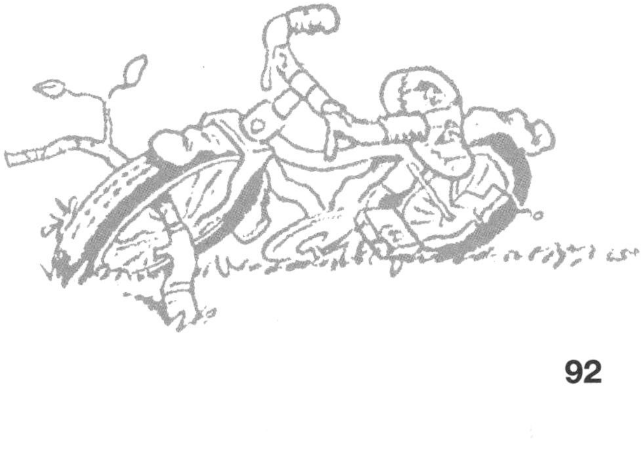

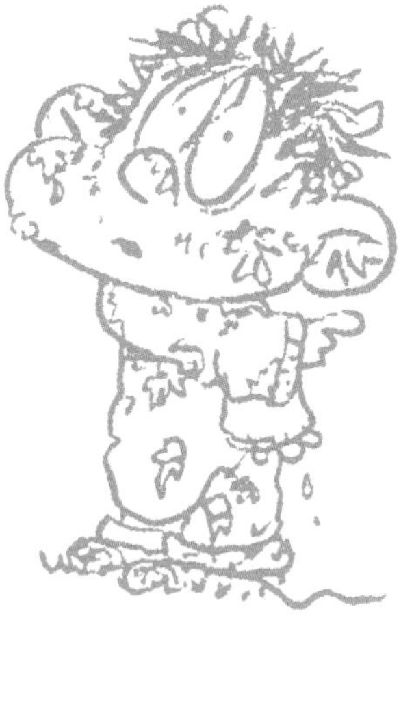

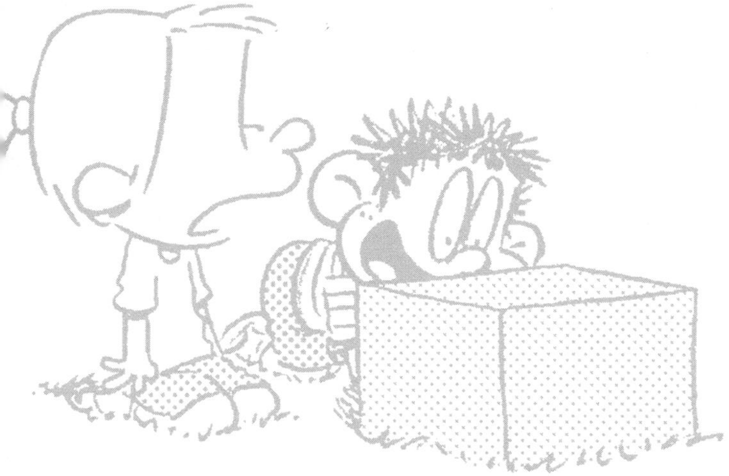

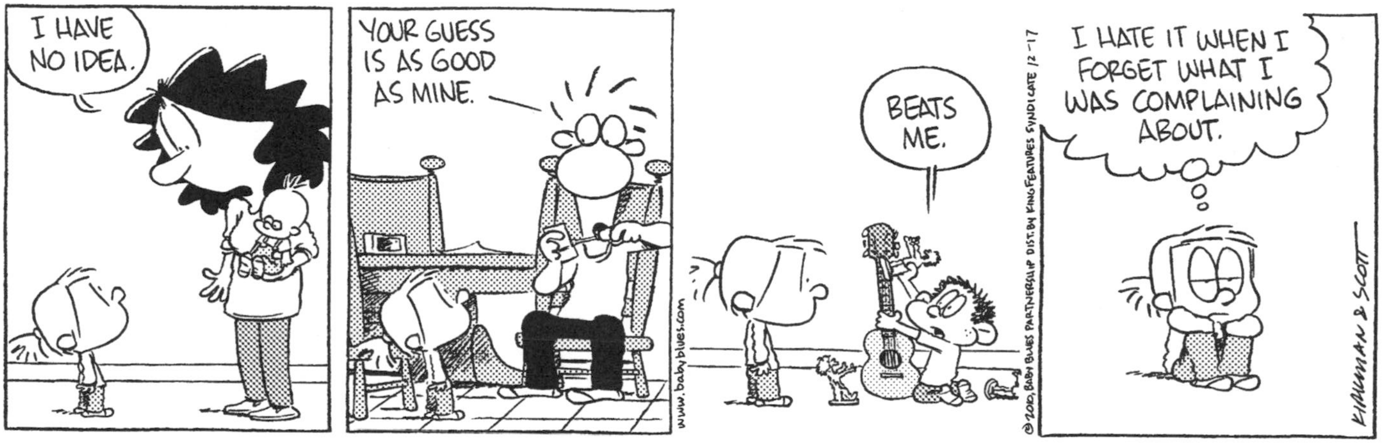
I HAVE NO IDEA.
YOUR GUESS IS AS GOOD AS MINE.
www.babyblues.com
BEATS ME.
© 2010, BABY BLUES PARTNERSHIP DIST. BY KING FEATURES SYNDICATE 12-17
I HATE IT WHEN I FORGET WHAT I WAS COMPLAINING ABOUT.
KIRKMAN & SCOTT

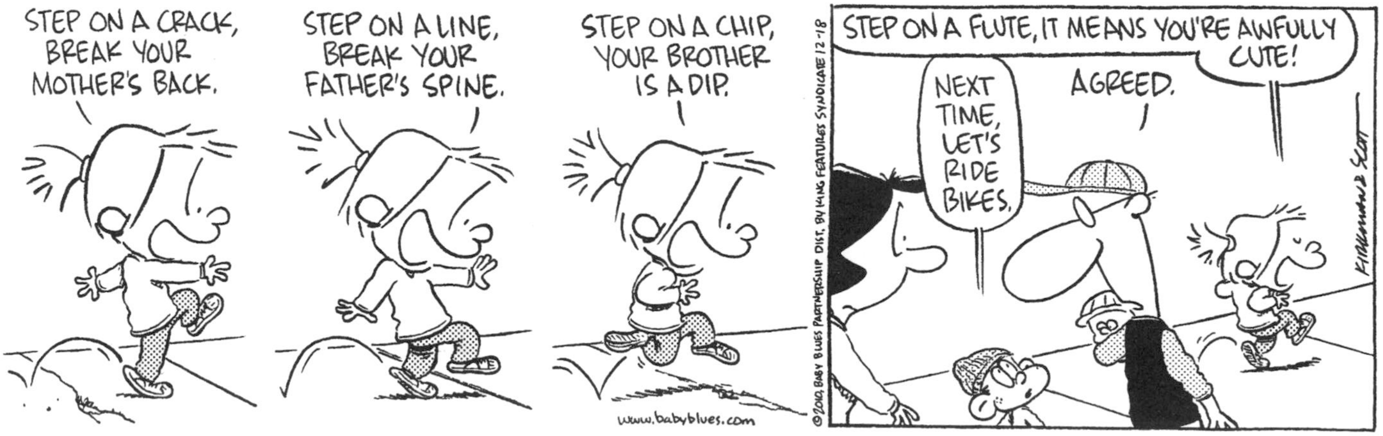
STEP ON A CRACK, BREAK YOUR MOTHER'S BACK.
STEP ON A LINE, BREAK YOUR FATHER'S SPINE.
STEP ON A CHIP, YOUR BROTHER IS A DIP.
www.babyblues.com
© 2010, BABY BLUES PARTNERSHIP DIST. BY KING FEATURES SYNDICATE 12-18
STEP ON A FLUTE, IT MEANS YOU'RE AWFULLY CUTE!
NEXT TIME, LET'S RIDE BIKES.
AGREED.
KIRKMAN & SCOTT

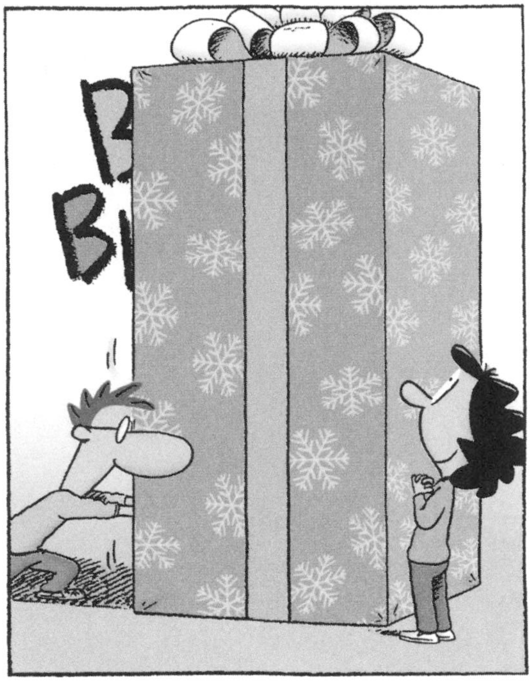

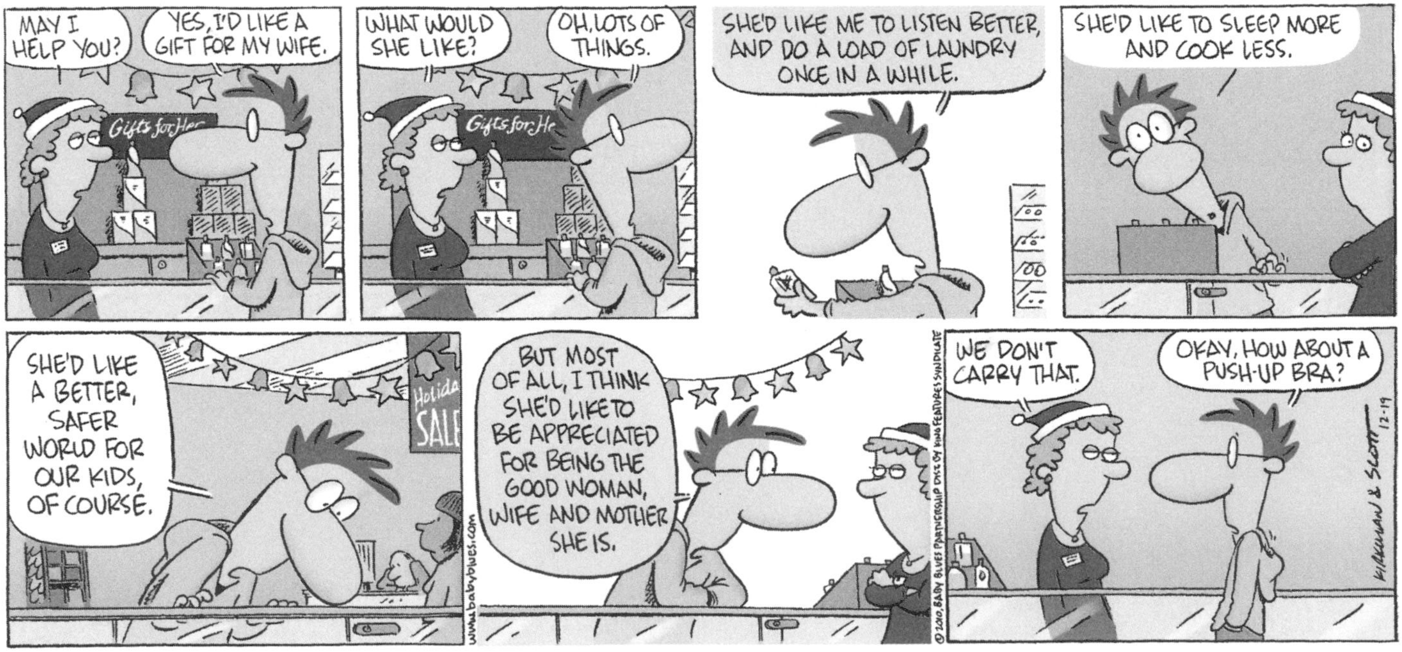

MAY I HELP YOU?
YES, I'D LIKE A GIFT FOR MY WIFE.
Gifts for Her
WHAT WOULD SHE LIKE?
OH, LOTS OF THINGS.
SHE'D LIKE ME TO LISTEN BETTER, AND DO A LOAD OF LAUNDRY ONCE IN A WHILE.
SHE'D LIKE TO SLEEP MORE AND COOK LESS.
SHE'D LIKE A BETTER, SAFER WORLD FOR OUR KIDS, OF COURSE.
BUT MOST OF ALL, I THINK SHE'D LIKE TO BE APPRECIATED FOR BEING THE GOOD WOMAN, WIFE AND MOTHER SHE IS.
WE DON'T CARRY THAT.
OKAY, HOW ABOUT A PUSH-UP BRA?
www.babyblues.com
© 2010, BABY BLUES PARTNERSHIP DIST. BY KING FEATURES SYNDICATE
KIRKMAN & SCOTT 12-19

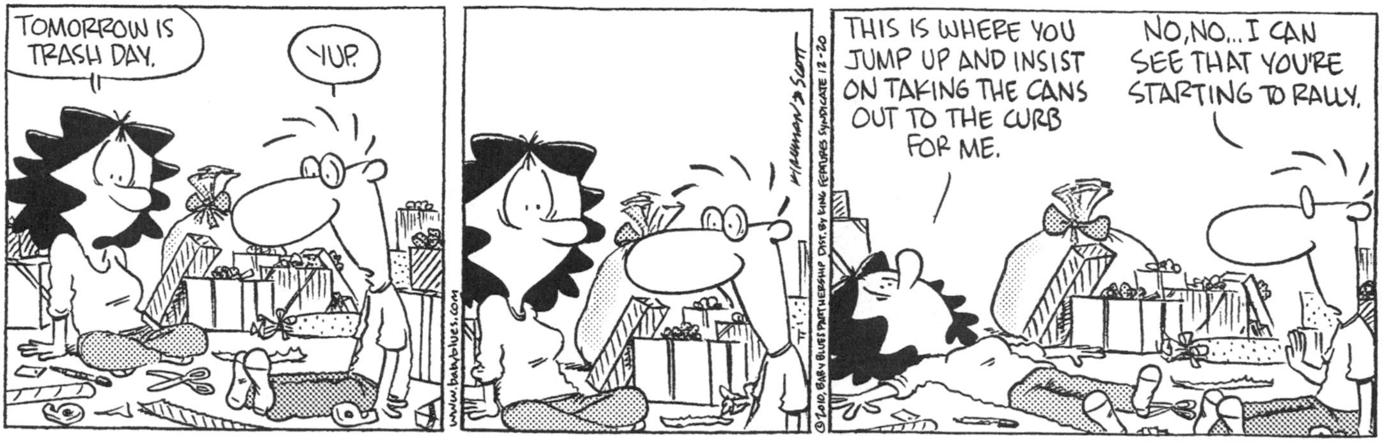
TOMORROW IS TRASH DAY.
YUP.
KIRKMAN & SCOTT
© 2010 BABY BLUES PARTNERSHIP DIST. BY KING FEATURES SYNDICATE 12-20
www.babyblues.com
THIS IS WHERE YOU JUMP UP AND INSIST ON TAKING THE CANS OUT TO THE CURB FOR ME.
NO, NO... I CAN SEE THAT YOU'RE STARTING TO RALLY.

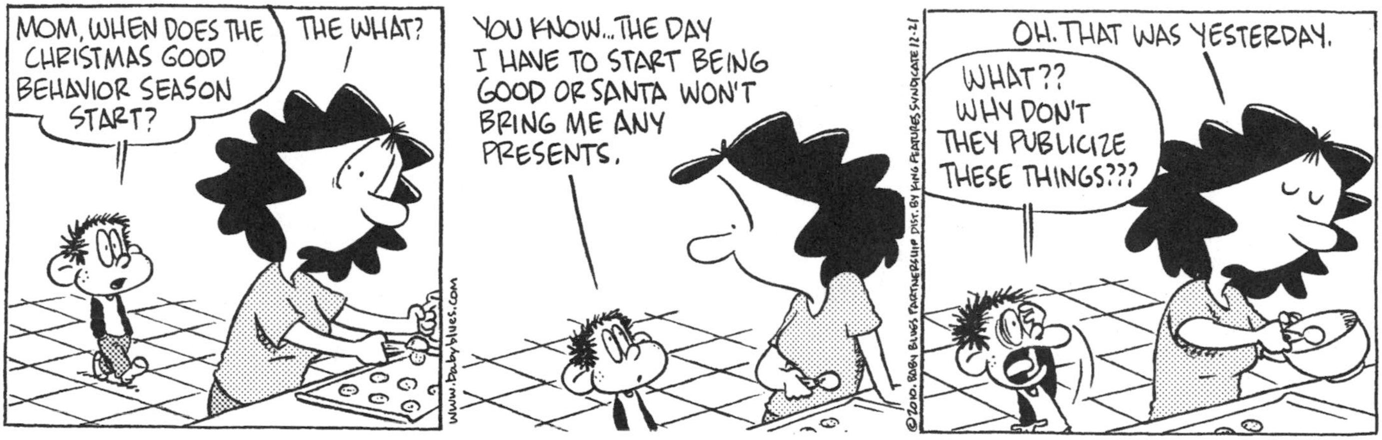
MOM, WHEN DOES THE CHRISTMAS GOOD BEHAVIOR SEASON START?
THE WHAT?
www.babyblues.com
YOU KNOW... THE DAY I HAVE TO START BEING GOOD OR SANTA WON'T BRING ME ANY PRESENTS.
© 2010 BABY BLUES PARTNERSHIP DIST. BY KING FEATURES SYNDICATE 12-21
OH. THAT WAS YESTERDAY.
WHAT?? WHY DON'T THEY PUBLICIZE THESE THINGS???

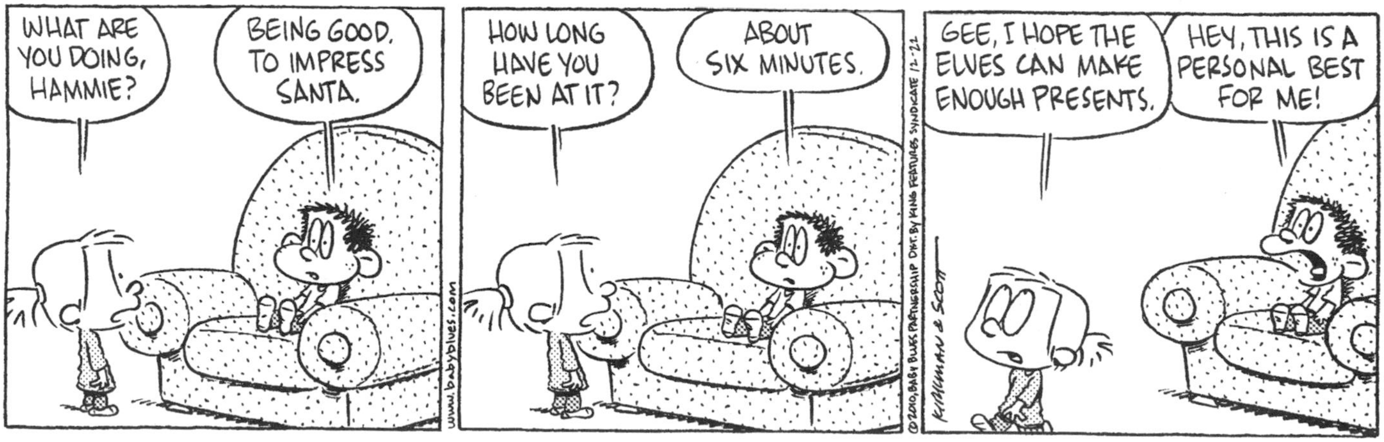
WHAT ARE YOU DOING, HAMMIE?
BEING GOOD. TO IMPRESS SANTA.
www.babyblues.com
HOW LONG HAVE YOU BEEN AT IT?
ABOUT SIX MINUTES.
© 2010 BABY BLUES PARTNERSHIP DIST. BY KING FEATURES SYNDICATE 12-22
KIRKMAN & SCOTT
GEE, I HOPE THE ELVES CAN MAKE ENOUGH PRESENTS.
HEY, THIS IS A PERSONAL BEST FOR ME!

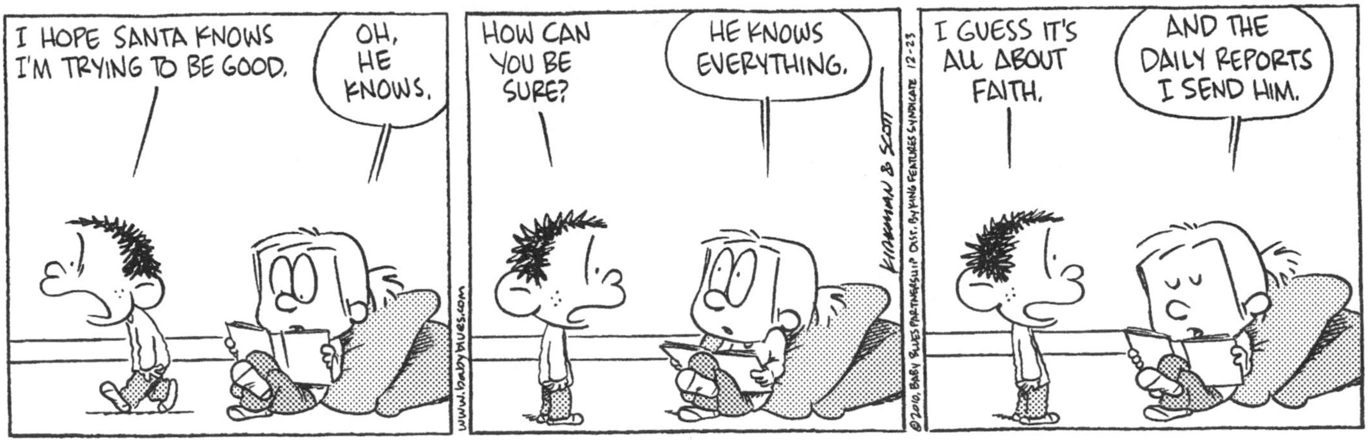
I HOPE SANTA KNOWS I'M TRYING TO BE GOOD.
OH, HE KNOWS.
www.babyblues.com
HOW CAN YOU BE SURE?
HE KNOWS EVERYTHING.
KIRKMAN & SCOTT
©2010, BABY BLUES PARTNERSHIP DIST. BY KING FEATURES SYNDICATE 12-23
I GUESS IT'S ALL ABOUT FAITH.
AND THE DAILY REPORTS I SEND HIM.

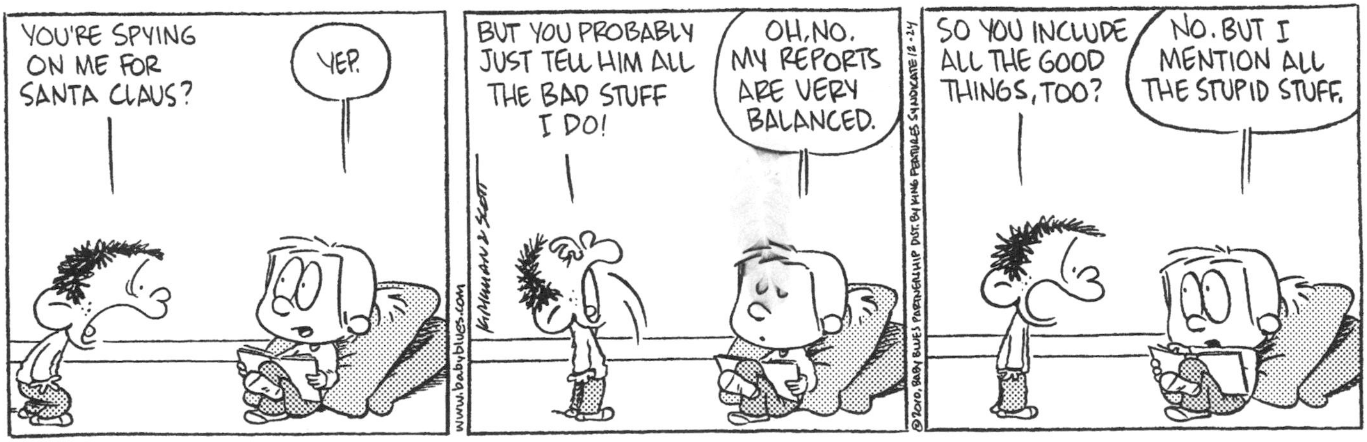
YOU'RE SPYING ON ME FOR SANTA CLAUS?
YEP.
www.babyblues.com
BUT YOU PROBABLY JUST TELL HIM ALL THE BAD STUFF I DO!
KIRKMAN & SCOTT
OH, NO. MY REPORTS ARE VERY BALANCED.
©2010, BABY BLUES PARTNERSHIP DIST. BY KING FEATURES SYNDICATE 12-24
SO YOU INCLUDE ALL THE GOOD THINGS, TOO?
NO. BUT I MENTION ALL THE STUPID STUFF.

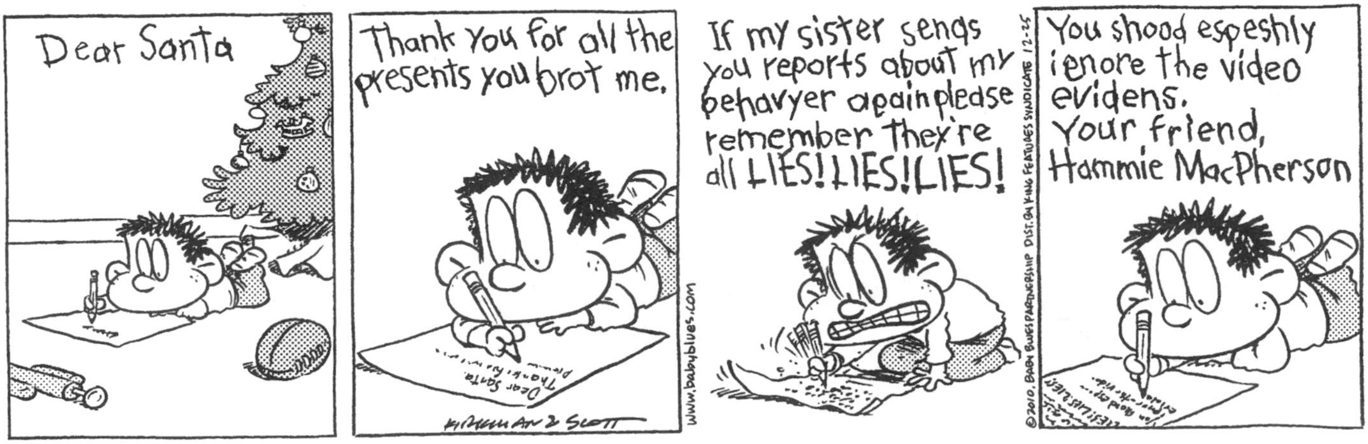
Dear Santa
Thank you for all the presents you brot me.
KIRKMAN & SCOTT
www.babyblues.com
If my sister sends you reports about my behavyer again please remember they're all LIES! LIES! LIES!
©2010, BABY BLUES PARTNERSHIP DIST. BY KING FEATURES SYNDICATE 12-25
You shood espeshly ignore the video evidens.
Your friend,
Hammie MacPherson

ZOE! HAMMIE!

I NEED ONE OF YOU TO SET THE TABLE FOR DINNER!

≈GROAN!≈   ≈GROAN!≈

WHOSE TURN IS IT?

I DON'T KNOW. WHY DON'T WE FLIP A COIN?

THAT'S A GREAT IDEA.

HEADS, YOU DO IT. TAILS, I TELL MOM THAT YOU AND TRENT USED HER GOOD JEWELRY TO PLAY PIRATES.

www.babyblues.com

TWICE.

© 2010, BABY BLUES PARTNERSHIP DIST. BY KING FEATURES SYNDICATE

NEVER GAMBLE WITH YOUR SISTER.

KIRKMAN & SCOTT 12-26

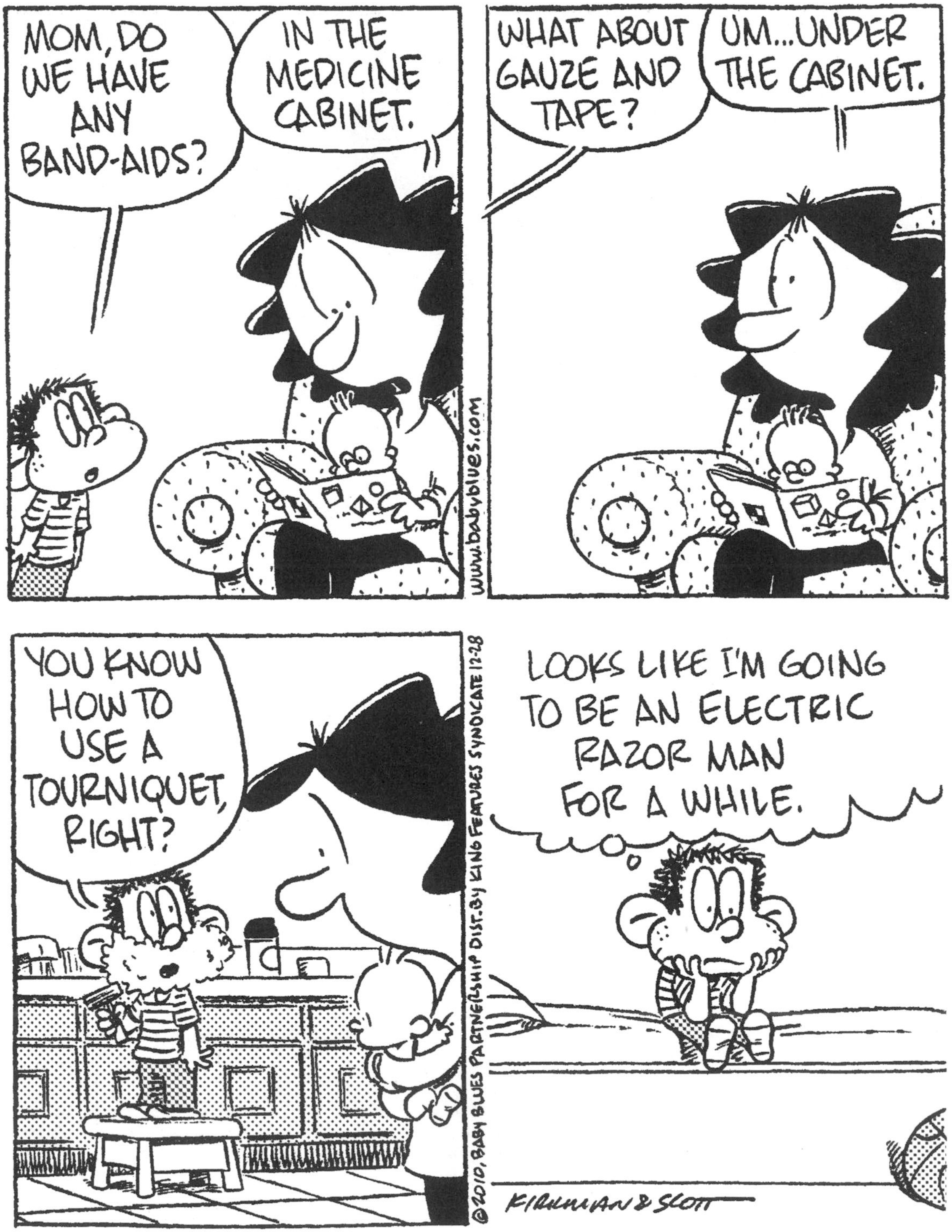
MOM, DO WE HAVE ANY BAND-AIDS?
IN THE MEDICINE CABINET.
WHAT ABOUT GAUZE AND TAPE?
UM...UNDER THE CABINET.
YOU KNOW HOW TO USE A TOURNIQUET, RIGHT?
LOOKS LIKE I'M GOING TO BE AN ELECTRIC RAZOR MAN FOR A WHILE.
WWW.BABYBLUES.COM
©2010, BABY BLUES PARTNERSHIP DIST. BY KING FEATURES SYNDICATE 12-28
KIRKMAN & SCOTT

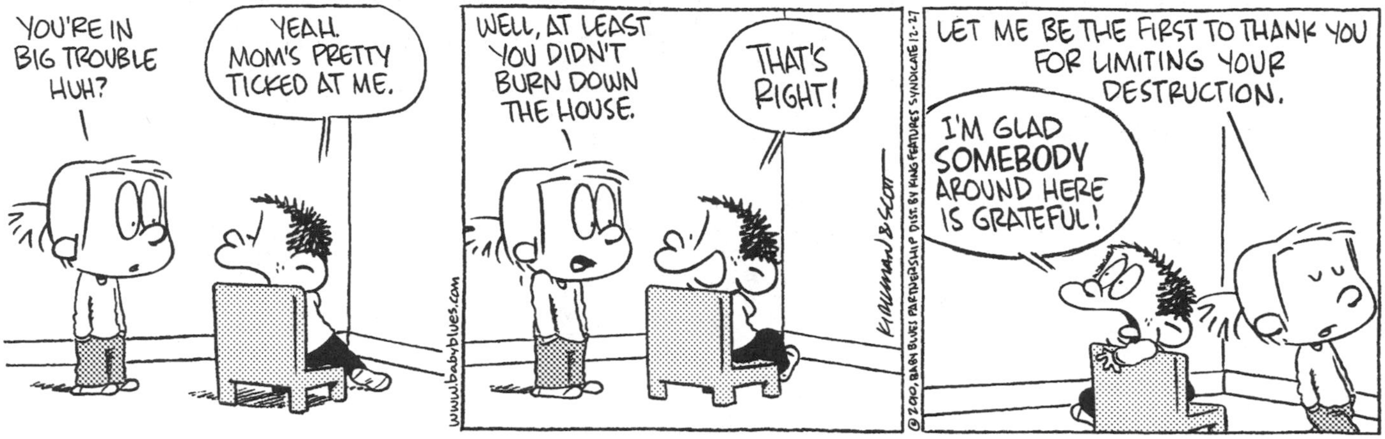
YOU'RE IN BIG TROUBLE HUH?
YEAH. MOM'S PRETTY TICKED AT ME.
www.babyblues.com
WELL, AT LEAST YOU DIDN'T BURN DOWN THE HOUSE.
THAT'S RIGHT!
KIRKMAN & SCOTT
©2010, BABY BLUES PARTNERSHIP DIST. BY KING FEATURES SYNDICATE 12-27
LET ME BE THE FIRST TO THANK YOU FOR LIMITING YOUR DESTRUCTION.
I'M GLAD SOMEBODY AROUND HERE IS GRATEFUL!

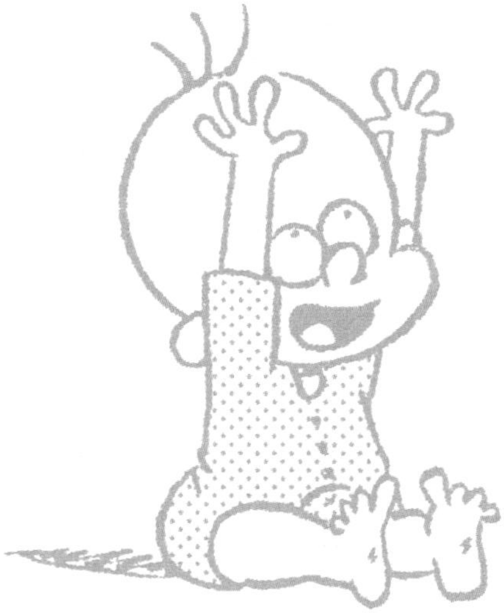

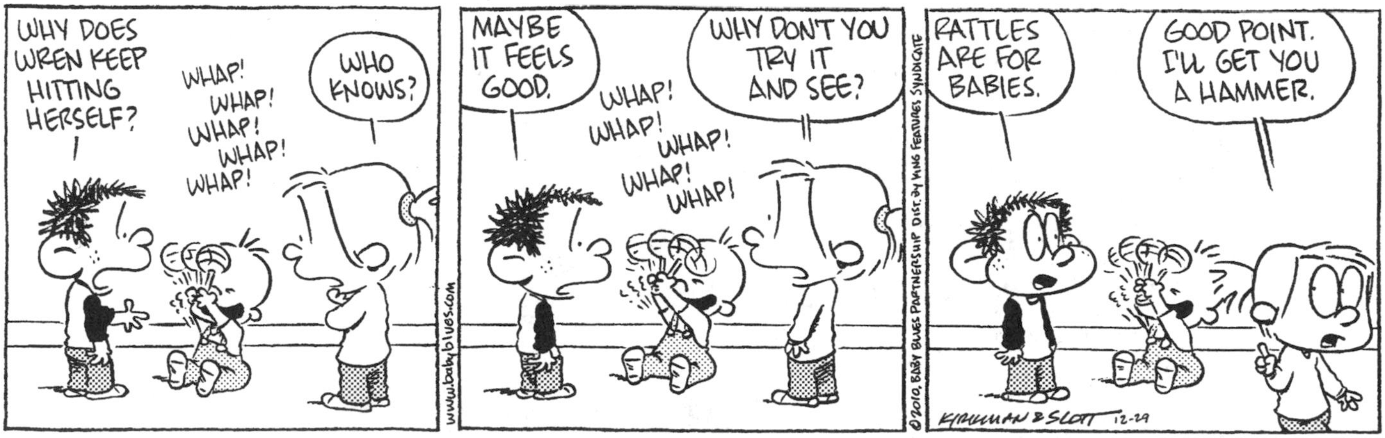
WHY DOES WREN KEEP HITTING HERSELF?
WHAP! WHAP! WHAP! WHAP! WHAP!
WHO KNOWS?
www.babyblues.com
MAYBE IT FEELS GOOD.
WHAP! WHAP! WHAP! WHAP! WHAP!
WHY DON'T YOU TRY IT AND SEE?
©2010, BABY BLUES PARTNERSHIP DIST. BY KING FEATURES SYNDICATE
RATTLES ARE FOR BABIES.
GOOD POINT. I'LL GET YOU A HAMMER.
KIRKMAN & SCOTT 12-29

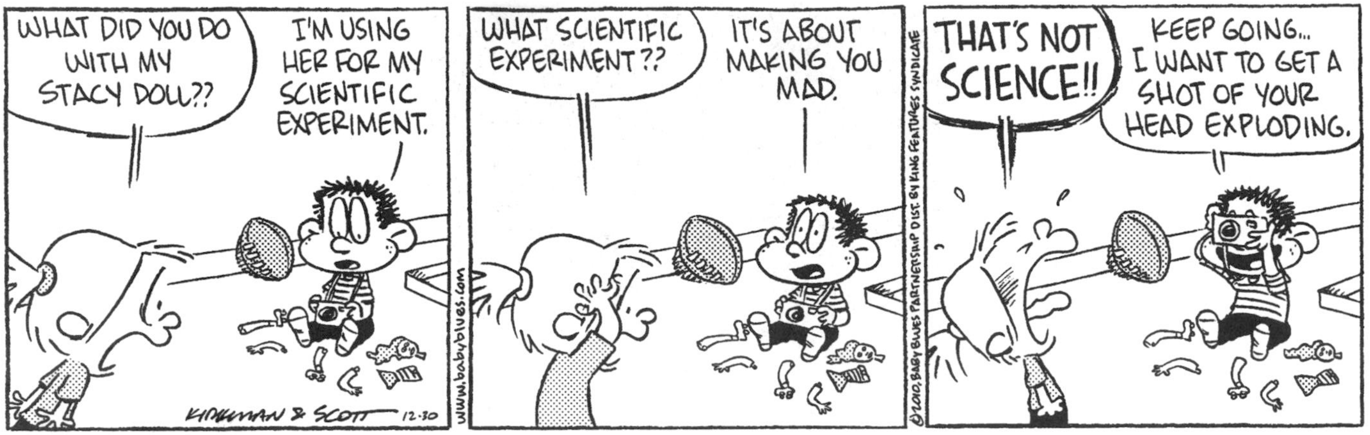
WHAT DID YOU DO WITH MY STACY DOLL??
I'M USING HER FOR MY SCIENTIFIC EXPERIMENT.
KIRKMAN & SCOTT 12-30
www.babyblues.com
WHAT SCIENTIFIC EXPERIMENT??
IT'S ABOUT MAKING YOU MAD.
© 2010, BABY BLUES PARTNERSHIP DIST. BY KING FEATURES SYNDICATE
THAT'S NOT SCIENCE!!
KEEP GOING... I WANT TO GET A SHOT OF YOUR HEAD EXPLODING.

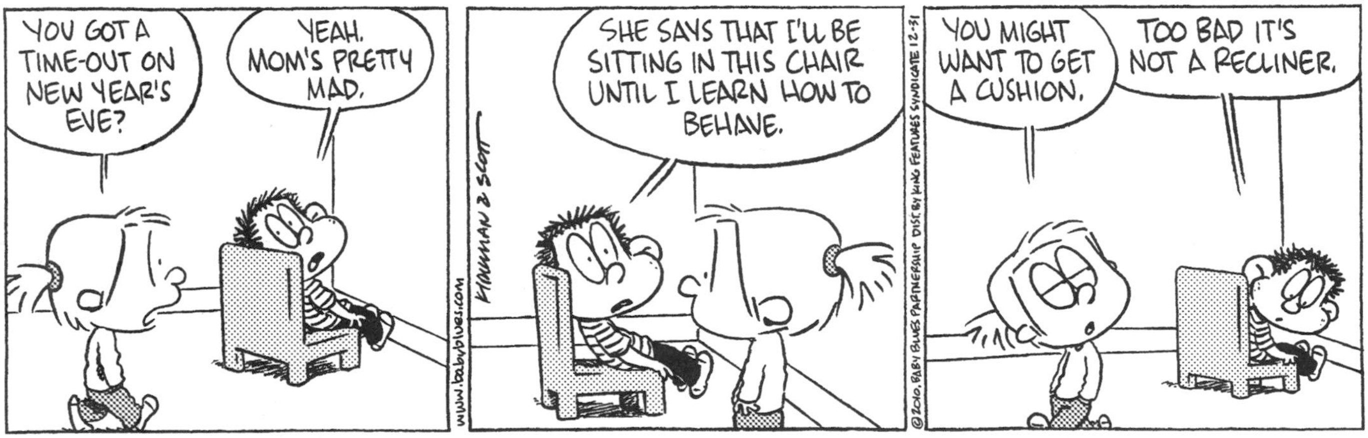
YOU GOT A TIME-OUT ON NEW YEAR'S EVE?
YEAH. MOM'S PRETTY MAD.
www.babyblues.com
KIRKMAN & SCOTT
SHE SAYS THAT I'LL BE SITTING IN THIS CHAIR UNTIL I LEARN HOW TO BEHAVE.
© 2010, BABY BLUES PARTNERSHIP DIST. BY KING FEATURES SYNDICATE 12-31
YOU MIGHT WANT TO GET A CUSHION.
TOO BAD IT'S NOT A RECLINER.

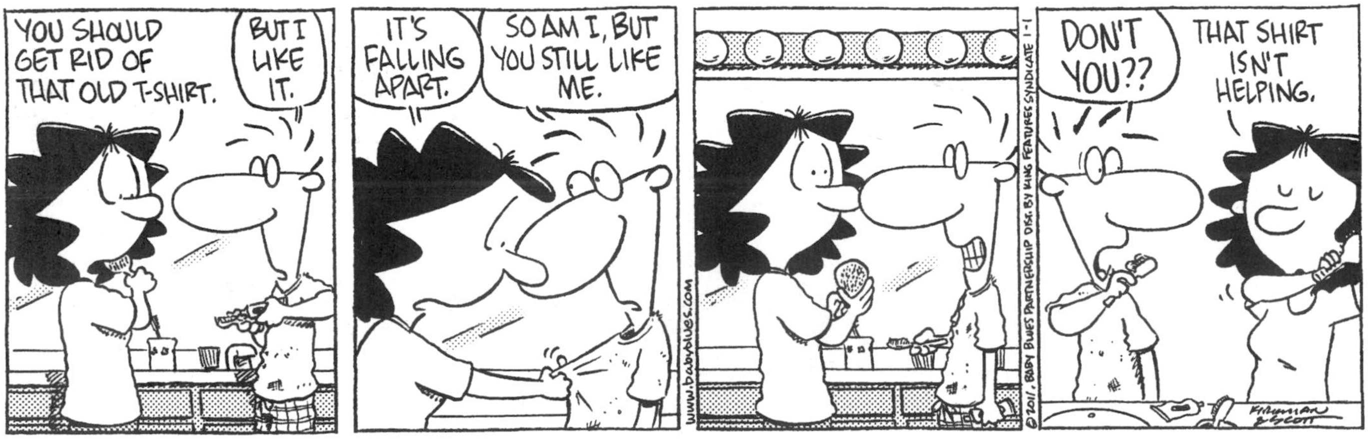
YOU SHOULD GET RID OF THAT OLD T-SHIRT.
BUT I LIKE IT.
IT'S FALLING APART.
SO AM I, BUT YOU STILL LIKE ME.
www.babyblues.com
© 2011, BABY BLUES PARTNERSHIP DIST. BY KING FEATURES SYNDICATE 1-1
DON'T YOU??
THAT SHIRT ISN'T HELPING.
KIRKMAN & SCOTT

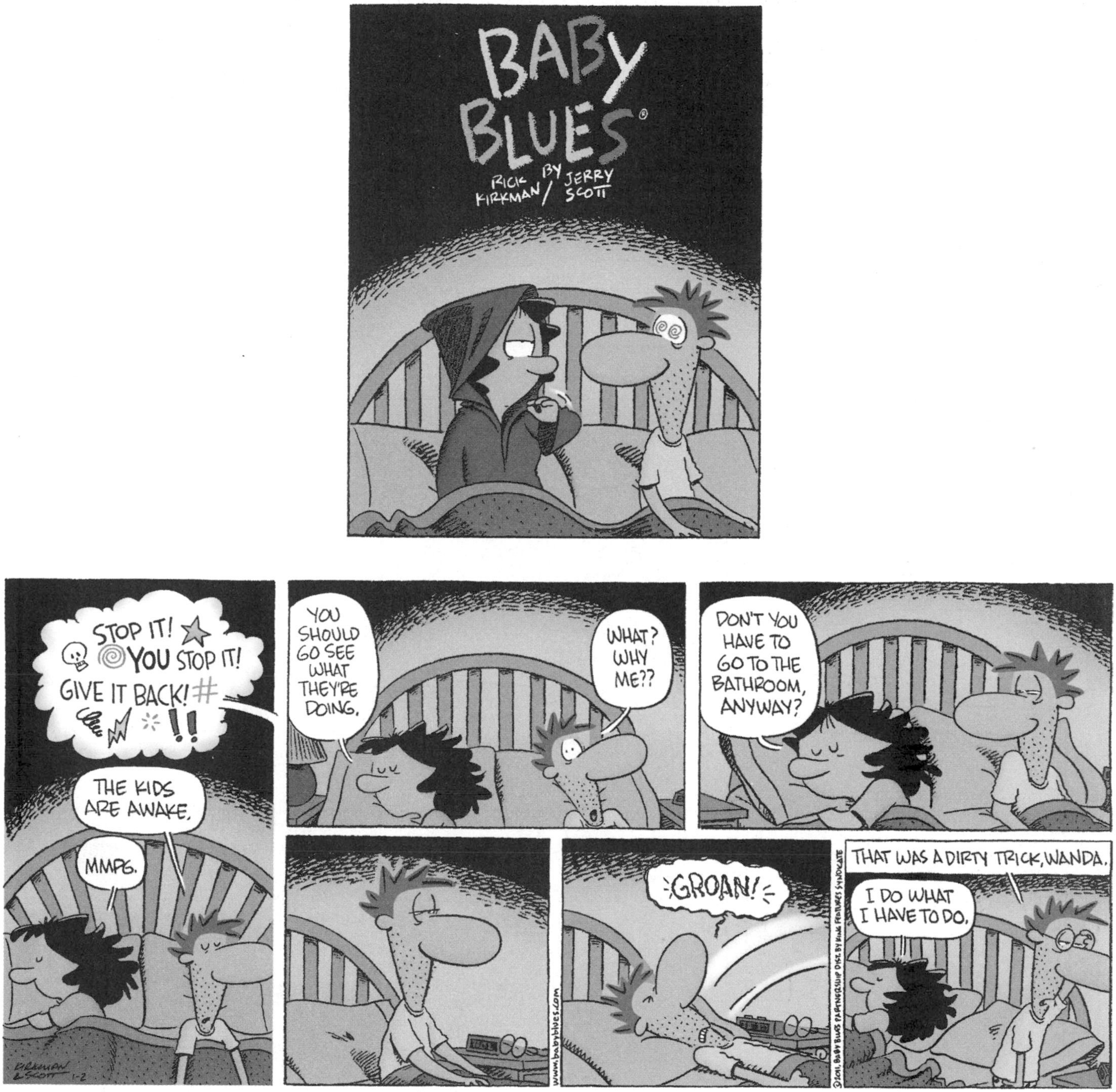
BABY BLUES®
BY RICK KIRKMAN / JERRY SCOTT
STOP IT! YOU STOP IT! GIVE IT BACK! # !!
THE KIDS ARE AWAKE.
MMPG.
KIRKMAN & SCOTT 1-2
YOU SHOULD GO SEE WHAT THEY'RE DOING.
WHAT? WHY ME??
DON'T YOU HAVE TO GO TO THE BATHROOM, ANYWAY?
www.babyblues.com
GROAN!
THAT WAS A DIRTY TRICK, WANDA.
I DO WHAT I HAVE TO DO.

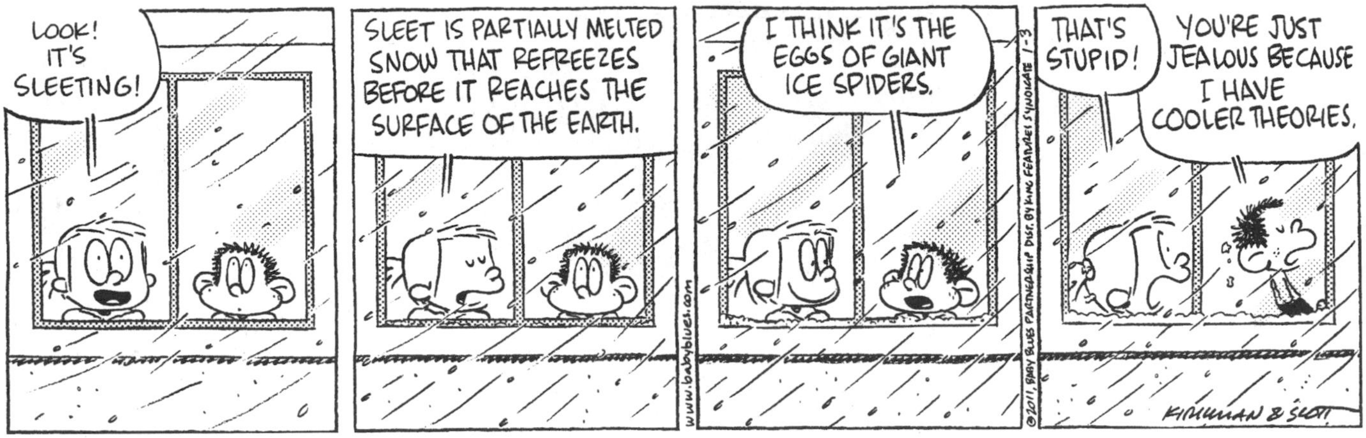
LOOK! IT'S SLEETING!
SLEET IS PARTIALLY MELTED SNOW THAT REFREEZES BEFORE IT REACHES THE SURFACE OF THE EARTH.
www.babyblues.com
I THINK IT'S THE EGGS OF GIANT ICE SPIDERS.
©2011, BABY BLUES PARTNERSHIP DIST. BY KING FEATURES SYNDICATE 1-3
THAT'S STUPID!
YOU'RE JUST JEALOUS BECAUSE I HAVE COOLER THEORIES.
KIRKMAN & SCOTT

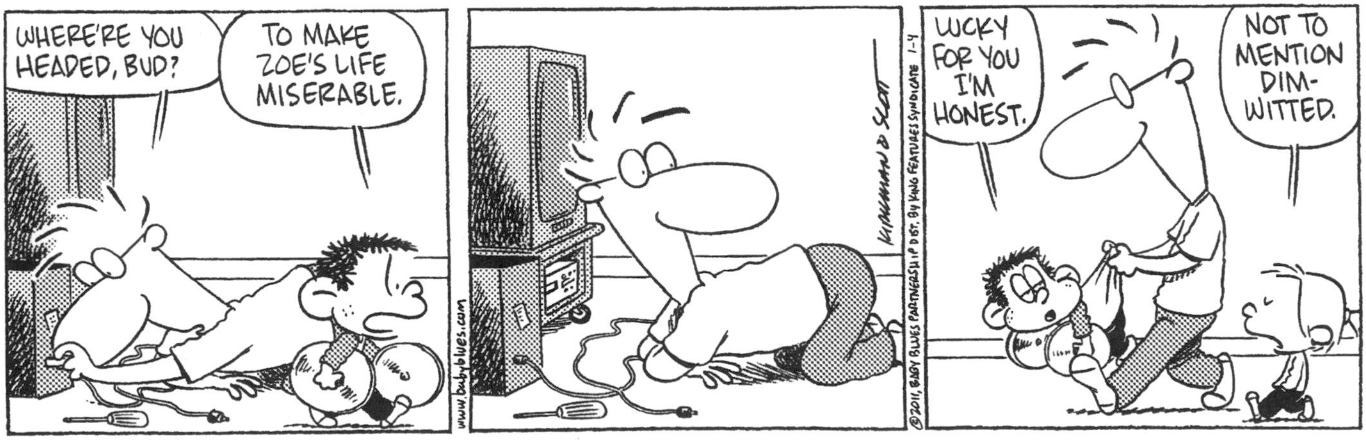
WHERE'RE YOU HEADED, BUD?
TO MAKE ZOE'S LIFE MISERABLE.
www.babyblues.com
KIRKMAN & SCOTT 1-4
©2011, BABY BLUES PARTNERSHIP DIST. BY KING FEATURES SYNDICATE
LUCKY FOR YOU I'M HONEST.
NOT TO MENTION DIM-WITTED.

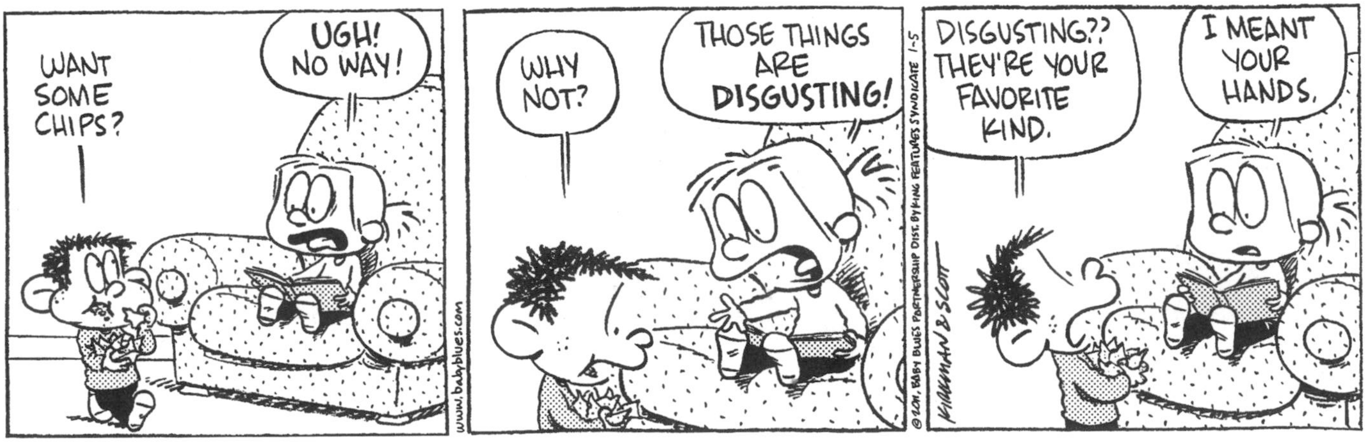
WANT SOME CHIPS?
UGH! NO WAY!
www.babyblues.com
WHY NOT?
THOSE THINGS ARE **DISGUSTING!**
©2011, BABY BLUES PARTNERSHIP DIST. BY KING FEATURES SYNDICATE 1-5
KIRKMAN & SCOTT
DISGUSTING?? THEY'RE YOUR FAVORITE KIND.
I MEANT YOUR HANDS.

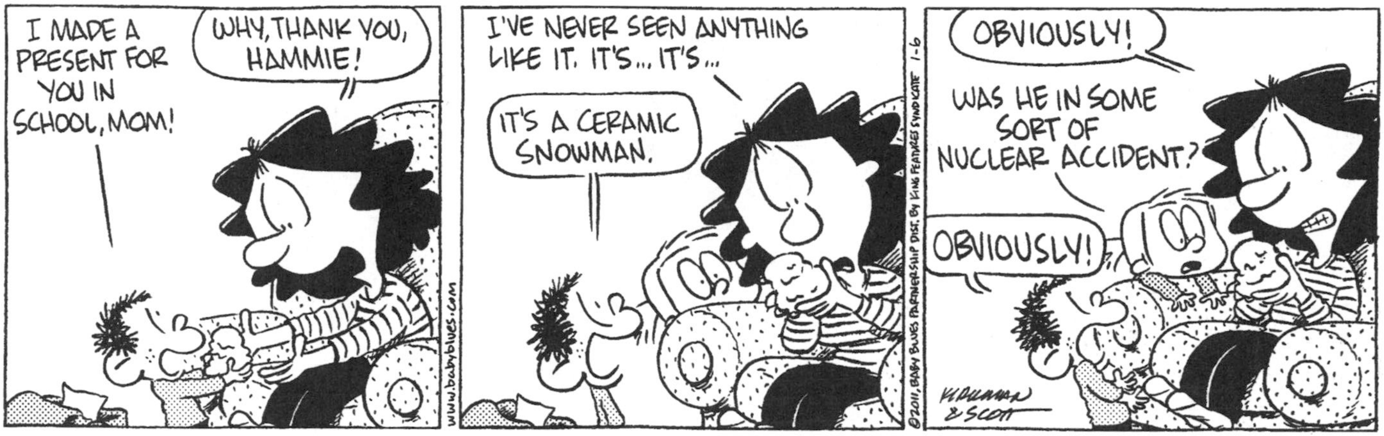
I MADE A PRESENT FOR YOU IN SCHOOL, MOM!
WHY, THANK YOU, HAMMIE!
www.babyblues.com
I'VE NEVER SEEN ANYTHING LIKE IT. IT'S... IT'S...
IT'S A CERAMIC SNOWMAN.
© 2011, BABY BLUES PARTNERSHIP DIST. BY KING FEATURES SYNDICATE 1-6
OBVIOUSLY!
WAS HE IN SOME SORT OF NUCLEAR ACCIDENT?
OBVIOUSLY!
KIRKMAN & SCOTT

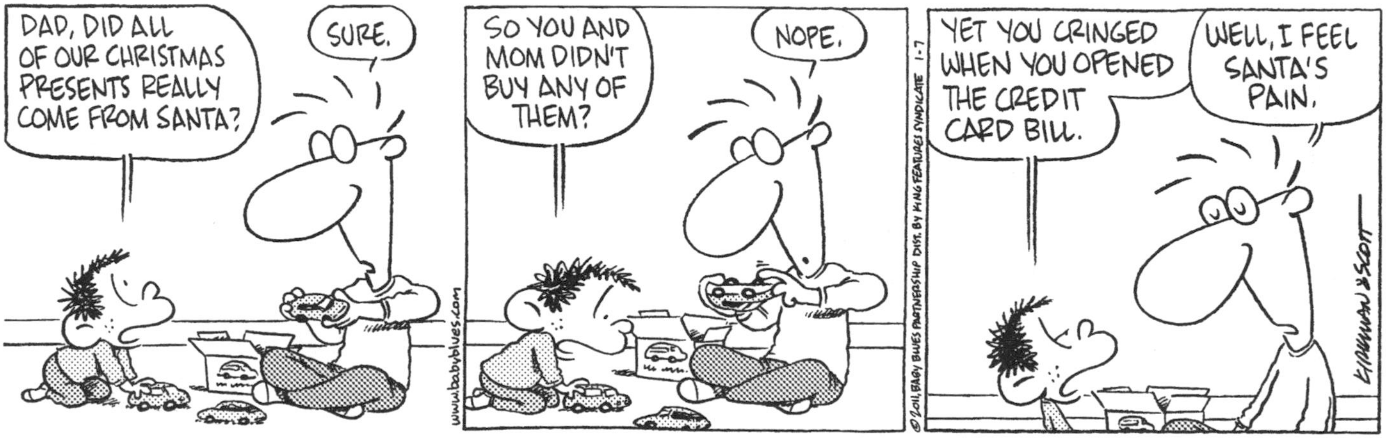
DAD, DID ALL OF OUR CHRISTMAS PRESENTS REALLY COME FROM SANTA?
SURE.
www.babyblues.com
SO YOU AND MOM DIDN'T BUY ANY OF THEM?
NOPE.
© 2011 BABY BLUES PARTNERSHIP DIST. BY KING FEATURES SYNDICATE 1-7
YET YOU CRINGED WHEN YOU OPENED THE CREDIT CARD BILL.
WELL, I FEEL SANTA'S PAIN.
KIRKMAN & SCOTT

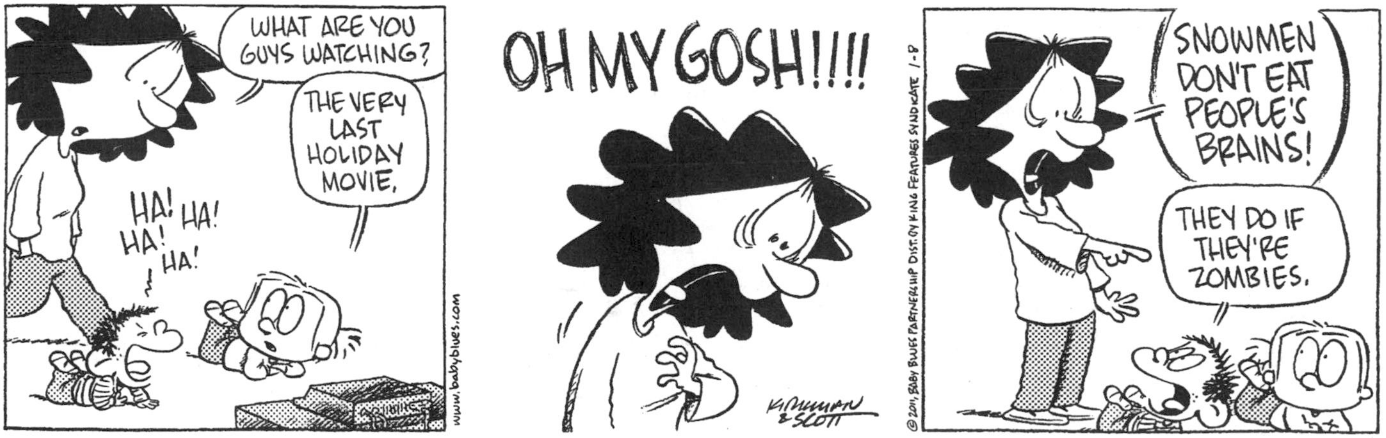
WHAT ARE YOU GUYS WATCHING?
THE VERY LAST HOLIDAY MOVIE.
HA! HA! HA! HA!
www.babyblues.com
OH MY GOSH!!!!
KIRKMAN & SCOTT
© 2011, BABY BLUES PARTNERSHIP DIST. BY KING FEATURES SYNDICATE 1-8
SNOWMEN DON'T EAT PEOPLE'S BRAINS!
THEY DO IF THEY'RE ZOMBIES.

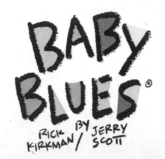

BABY BLUES®
BY
RICK KIRKMAN / JERRY SCOTT

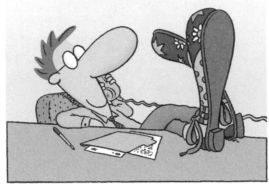

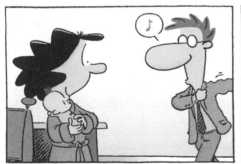

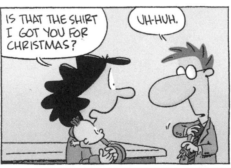

♪
IS THAT THE SHIRT I GOT YOU FOR CHRISTMAS?
UH-HUH.
AND THE TIE, TOO... RIGHT?
YUP.
AND YOU GOT ME THESE SLACKS FOR MY BIRTHDAY, THE JACKET WAS AN ANNIVERSARY GIFT, AND I BELIEVE THE SOCKS AND UNDERWEAR WERE MY BIG FATHER'S DAY SURPRISE.
www.babyblues.com
WOW. YOU'RE RESPONSIBLE FOR EVERYTHING I WEAR, AREN'T YOU?
DON'T BE SILLY...
© 2011, BABY BLUES PARTNERSHIP DIST. BY KING FEATURES SYNDICATE
...SOMETIMES I LET YOU PICK OUT YOUR OWN SHOES.
OBVIOUSLY.
KIRKMAN & SCOTT 1-9

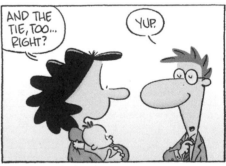

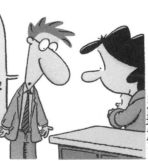

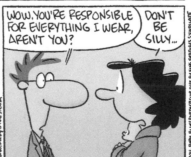

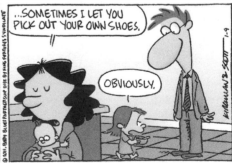

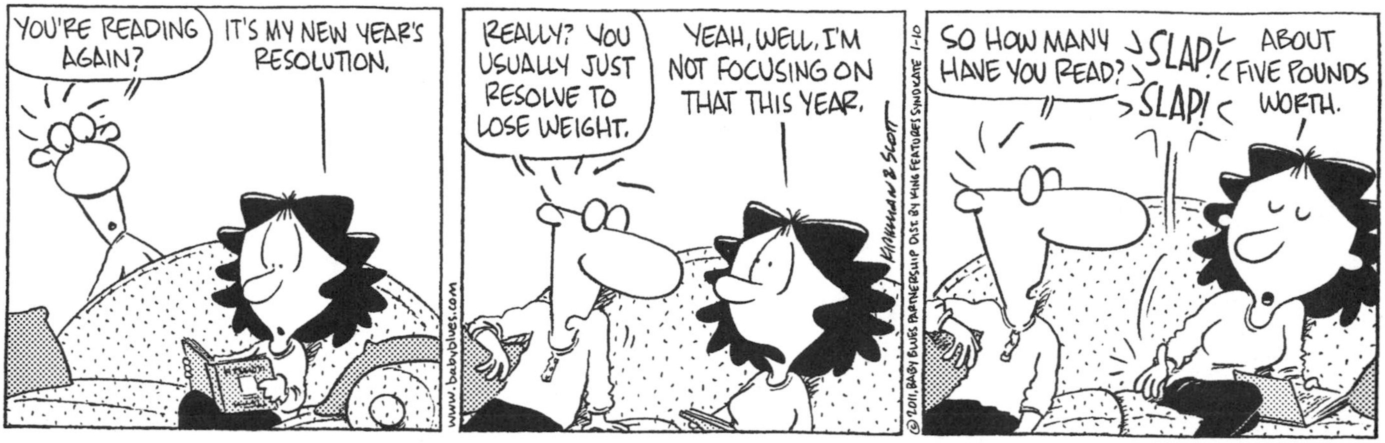
YOU'RE READING AGAIN?
IT'S MY NEW YEAR'S RESOLUTION.
www.babyblues.com
REALLY? YOU USUALLY JUST RESOLVE TO LOSE WEIGHT.
YEAH, WELL, I'M NOT FOCUSING ON THAT THIS YEAR.
KIRKMAN & SCOTT
©2011, BABY BLUES PARTNERSHIP DIST. BY KING FEATURES SYNDICATE 1-10
SO HOW MANY HAVE YOU READ?
SLAP!
SLAP!
ABOUT FIVE POUNDS WORTH.

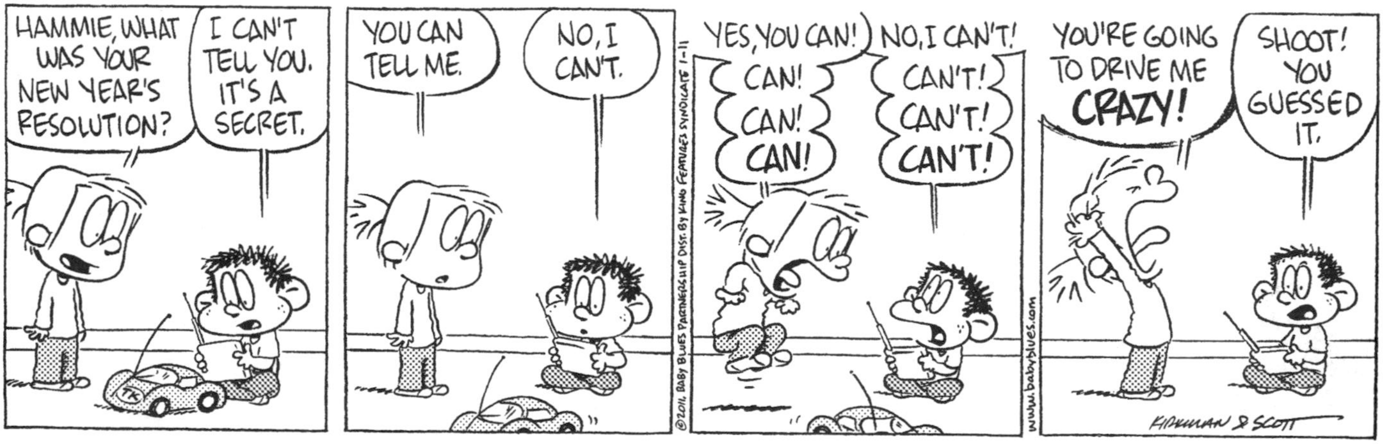
HAMMIE, WHAT WAS YOUR NEW YEAR'S RESOLUTION?
I CAN'T TELL YOU. IT'S A SECRET.
YOU CAN TELL ME.
NO, I CAN'T.
©2011, BABY BLUES PARTNERSHIP DIST. BY KING FEATURES SYNDICATE 1-11
YES, YOU CAN! CAN! CAN! CAN!
NO, I CAN'T! CAN'T! CAN'T! CAN'T!
www.babyblues.com
YOU'RE GOING TO DRIVE ME CRAZY!
SHOOT! YOU GUESSED IT.
KIRKMAN & SCOTT

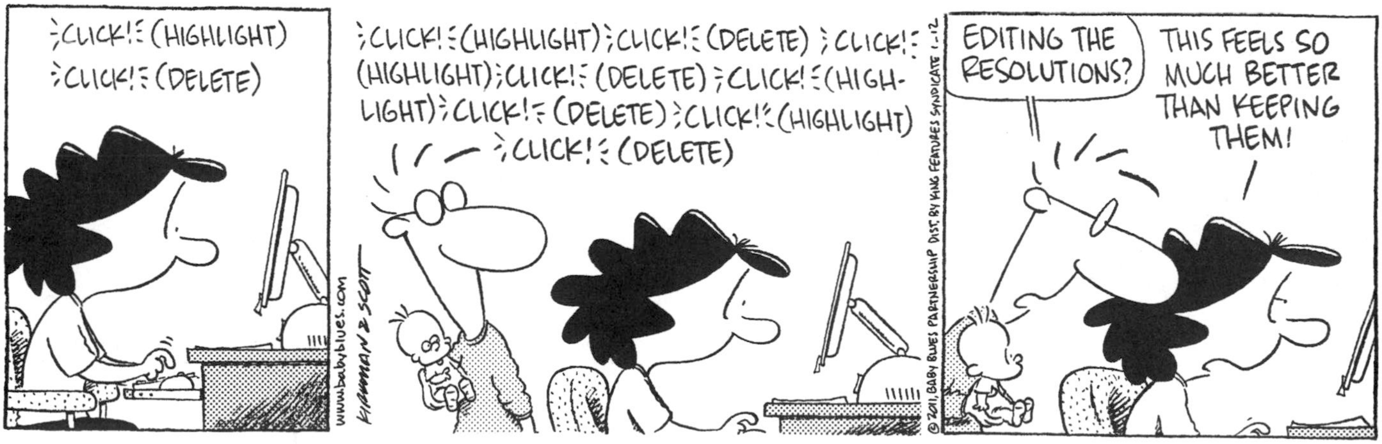
CLICK! (HIGHLIGHT)
CLICK! (DELETE)
www.babyblues.com
KIRKMAN & SCOTT
CLICK! (HIGHLIGHT) CLICK! (DELETE) CLICK! (HIGHLIGHT) CLICK! (DELETE) CLICK! (HIGHLIGHT) CLICK! (DELETE) CLICK! (HIGHLIGHT) CLICK! (DELETE)
©2011, BABY BLUES PARTNERSHIP DIST. BY KING FEATURES SYNDICATE 1-12
EDITING THE RESOLUTIONS?
THIS FEELS SO MUCH BETTER THAN KEEPING THEM!

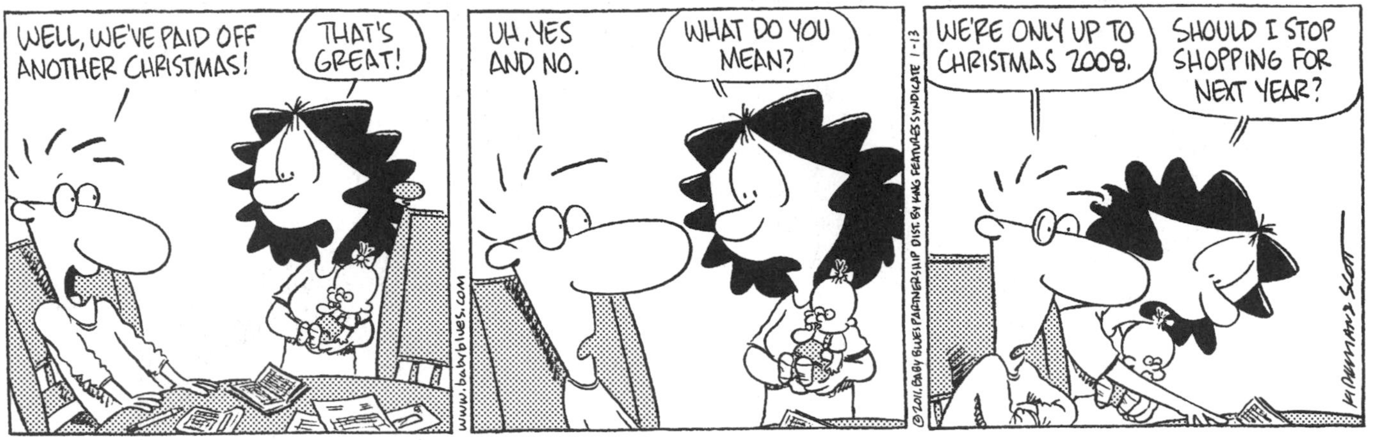
WELL, WE'VE PAID OFF ANOTHER CHRISTMAS!
THAT'S GREAT!
www.babyblues.com
UH, YES AND NO.
WHAT DO YOU MEAN?
©2011, BABY BLUES PARTNERSHIP DIST. BY KING FEATURES SYNDICATE 1-13
WE'RE ONLY UP TO CHRISTMAS 2008.
SHOULD I STOP SHOPPING FOR NEXT YEAR?
KIRKMAN & SCOTT

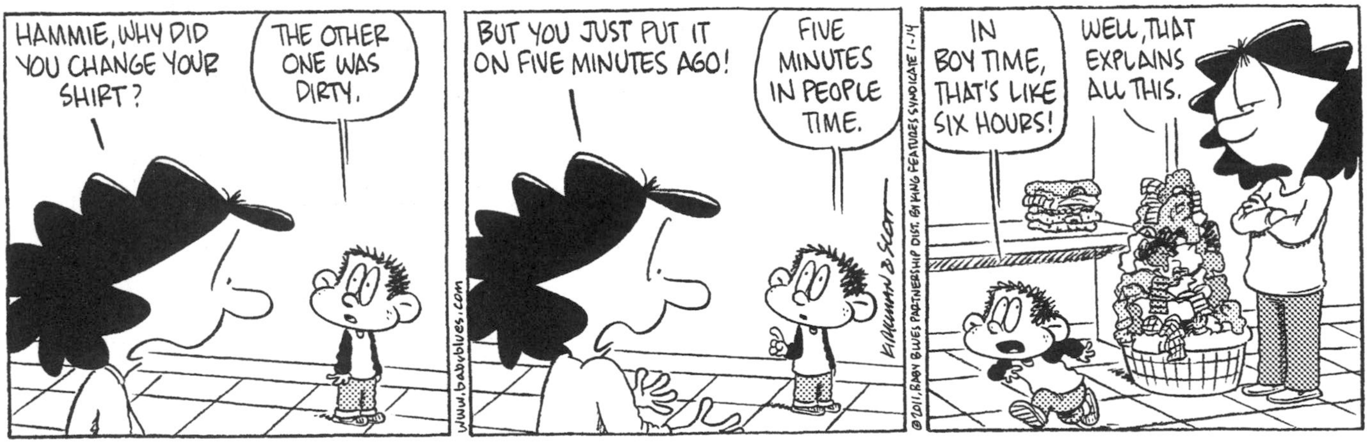
HAMMIE, WHY DID YOU CHANGE YOUR SHIRT?
THE OTHER ONE WAS DIRTY.
www.babyblues.com
BUT YOU JUST PUT IT ON FIVE MINUTES AGO!
FIVE MINUTES IN PEOPLE TIME.
KIRKMAN & SCOTT
©2011, BABY BLUES PARTNERSHIP DIST. BY KING FEATURES SYNDICATE 1-14
IN BOY TIME, THAT'S LIKE SIX HOURS!
WELL, THAT EXPLAINS ALL THIS.

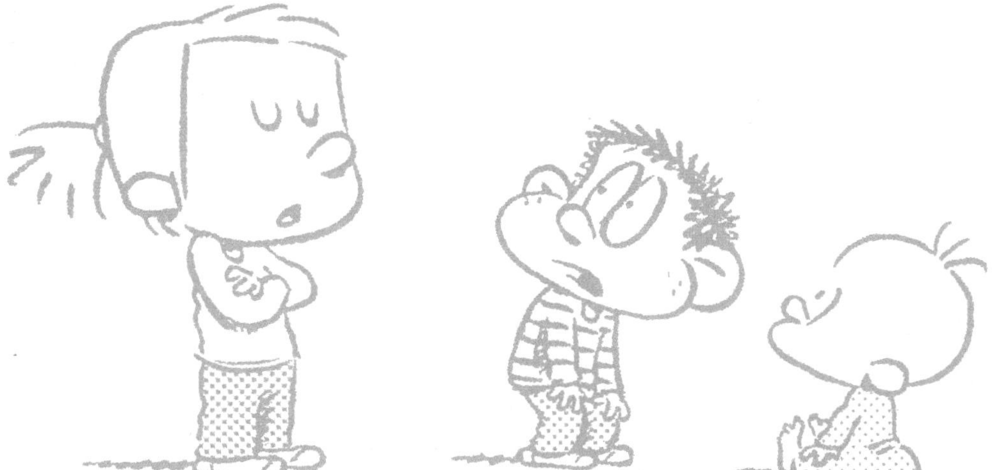

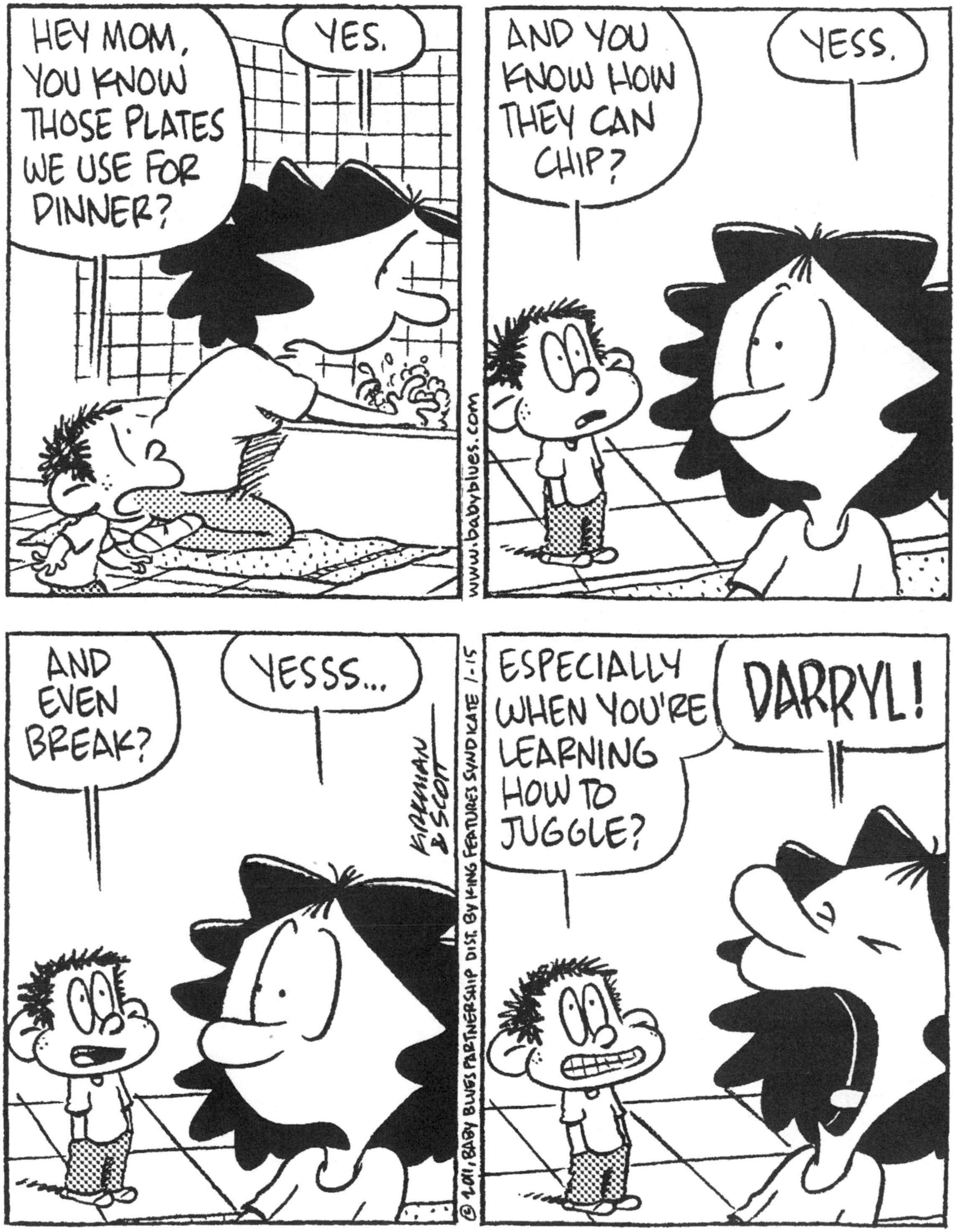
HEY MOM, YOU KNOW THOSE PLATES WE USE FOR DINNER?
YES.
AND YOU KNOW HOW THEY CAN CHIP?
YESS.
AND EVEN BREAK?
YESSS...
ESPECIALLY WHEN YOU'RE LEARNING HOW TO JUGGLE?
DARRYL!
www.babyblues.com
KIRKMAN & SCOTT
© 2011, BABY BLUES PARTNERSHIP DIST. BY KING FEATURES SYNDICATE 1-15

BABY BLUES®
BY RICK KIRKMAN / JERRY SCOTT

OH, WOW!
WHAT?
IT SAYS HERE THAT MARRIED PEOPLE ACTUALLY LIVE LONGER THAN SINGLE PEOPLE.
WOOF! WOOF!
AAAIEEEEEEE!
HEY!
RIP!
STOP!
BAM!
SPANG!
CRASH!
WAS THAT WITH OR WITHOUT KIDS?
KIRKMAN & SCOTT 1-16
© 2011, BABY BLUES PARTNERSHIP DIST. BY KING FEATURES SYNDICATE www.babyblues.com

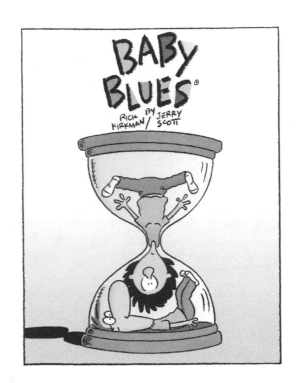

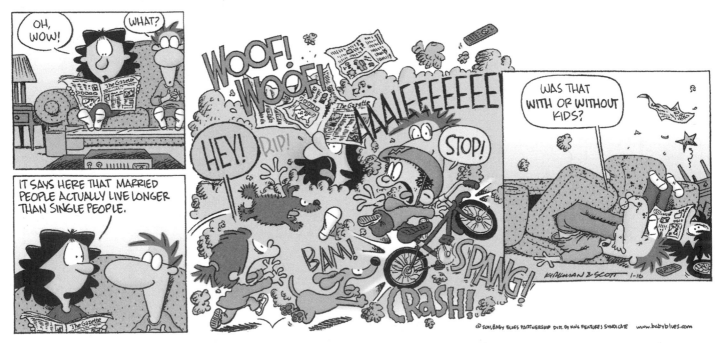

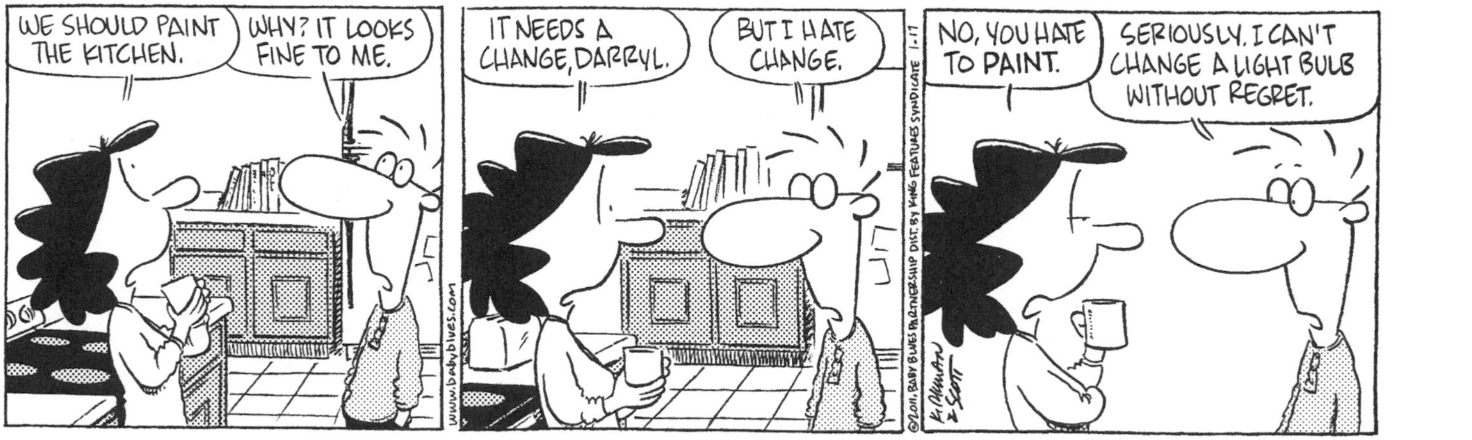
WE SHOULD PAINT THE KITCHEN.
WHY? IT LOOKS FINE TO ME.
www.babyblues.com
IT NEEDS A CHANGE, DARRYL.
BUT I HATE CHANGE.
© 2011, BABY BLUES PARTNERSHIP DIST. BY KING FEATURES SYNDICATE 1-17
KIRKMAN & SCOTT
NO, YOU HATE TO PAINT.
SERIOUSLY. I CAN'T CHANGE A LIGHT BULB WITHOUT REGRET.

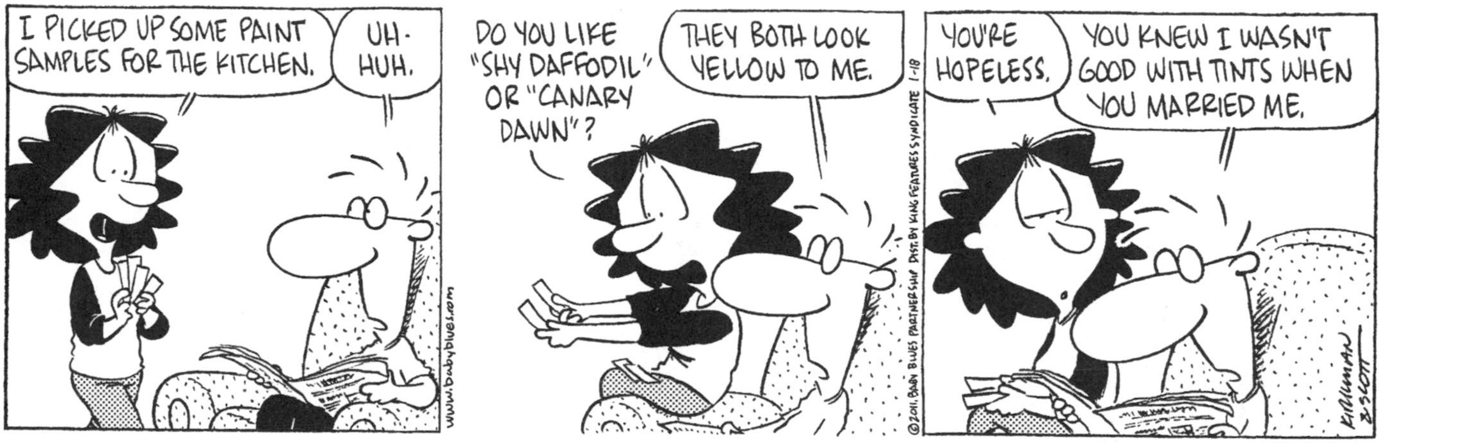
I PICKED UP SOME PAINT SAMPLES FOR THE KITCHEN.
UH-HUH.
www.babyblues.com
DO YOU LIKE "SHY DAFFODIL" OR "CANARY DAWN"?
THEY BOTH LOOK YELLOW TO ME.
© 2011, BABY BLUES PARTNERSHIP DIST. BY KING FEATURES SYNDICATE 1-18
YOU'RE HOPELESS.
YOU KNEW I WASN'T GOOD WITH TINTS WHEN YOU MARRIED ME.
KIRKMAN & SCOTT

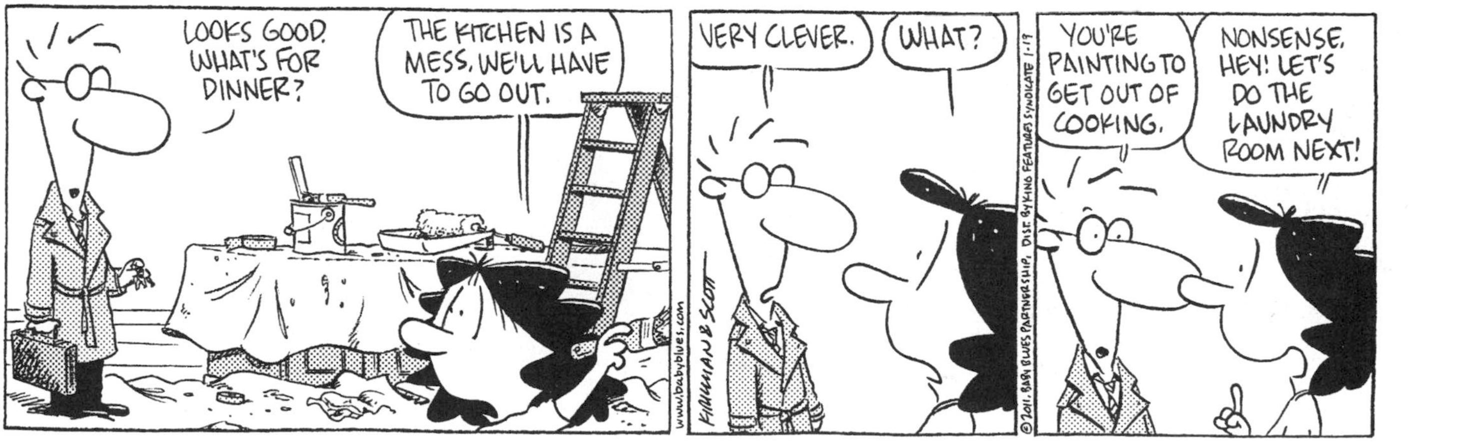
LOOKS GOOD. WHAT'S FOR DINNER?
THE KITCHEN IS A MESS. WE'LL HAVE TO GO OUT.
www.babyblues.com
KIRKMAN & SCOTT
VERY CLEVER.
WHAT?
© 2011, BABY BLUES PARTNERSHIP. DIST. BY KING FEATURES SYNDICATE 1-19
YOU'RE PAINTING TO GET OUT OF COOKING.
NONSENSE. HEY! LET'S DO THE LAUNDRY ROOM NEXT!

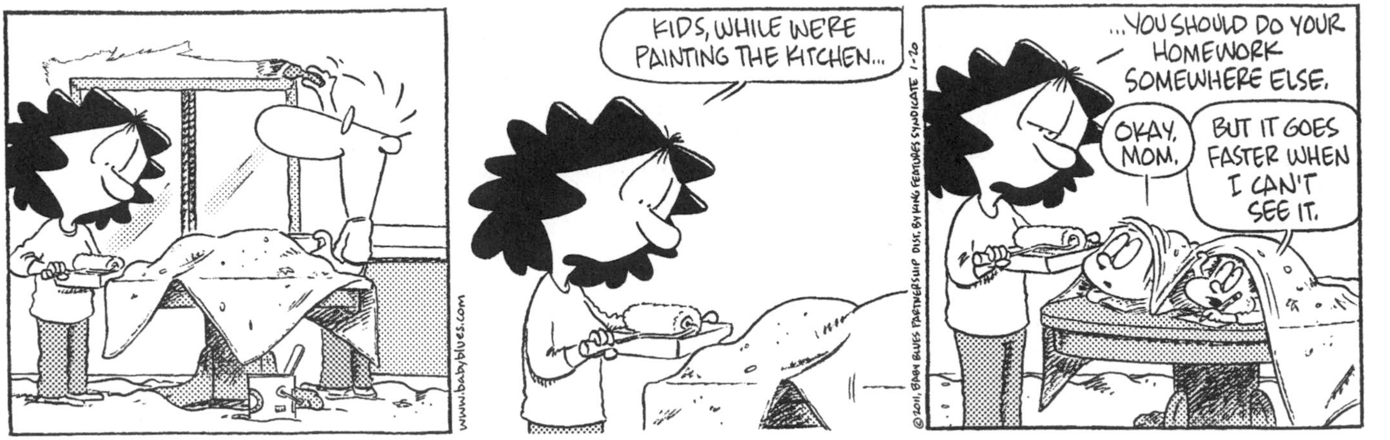
www.babyblues.com
KIDS, WHILE WE'RE PAINTING THE KITCHEN...
© 2011, BABY BLUES PARTNERSHIP DIST. BY KING FEATURES SYNDICATE 1-20
...YOU SHOULD DO YOUR HOMEWORK SOMEWHERE ELSE.
OKAY, MOM.
BUT IT GOES FASTER WHEN I CAN'T SEE IT.

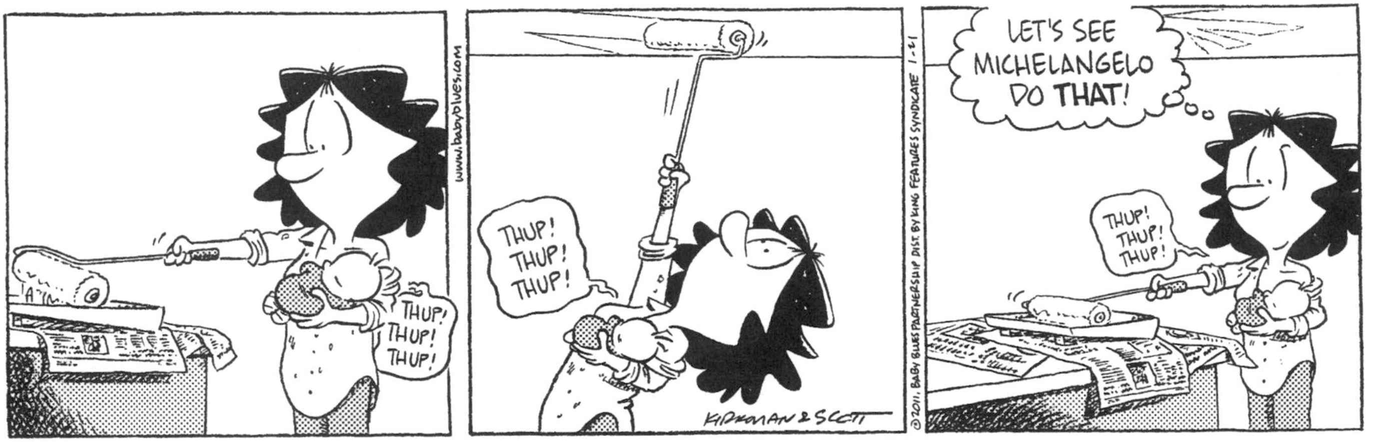
www.babyblues.com
THUP! THUP! THUP!
THUP! THUP! THUP!
KIRKMAN & SCOTT
© 2011, BABY BLUES PARTNERSHIP DIST. BY KING FEATURES SYNDICATE 1-21
LET'S SEE MICHELANGELO DO THAT!
THUP! THUP! THUP!

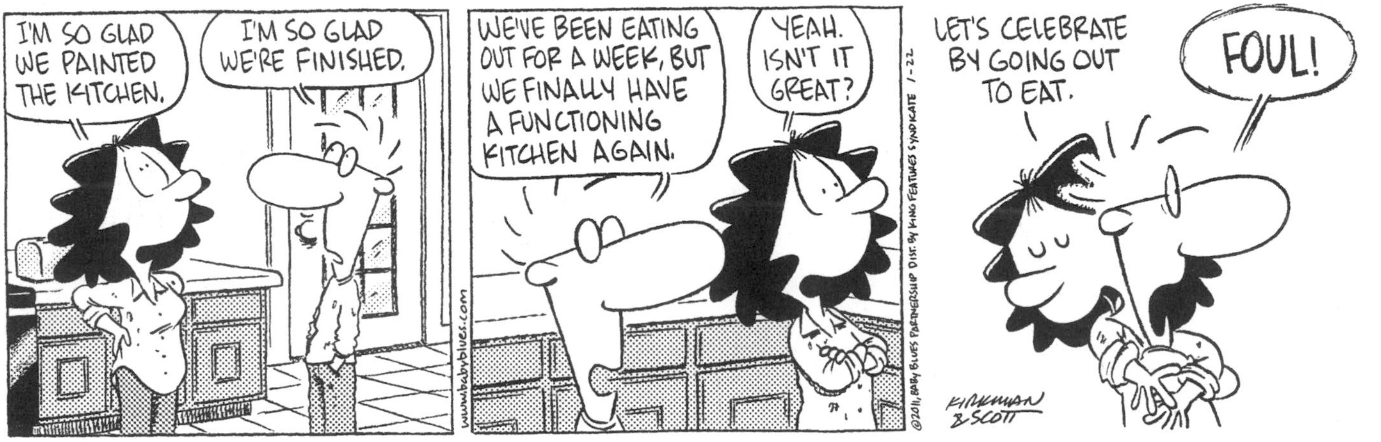
I'M SO GLAD WE PAINTED THE KITCHEN.
I'M SO GLAD WE'RE FINISHED.
www.babyblues.com
WE'VE BEEN EATING OUT FOR A WEEK, BUT WE FINALLY HAVE A FUNCTIONING KITCHEN AGAIN.
YEAH. ISN'T IT GREAT?
© 2011, BABY BLUES PARTNERSHIP DIST. BY KING FEATURES SYNDICATE 1-22
LET'S CELEBRATE BY GOING OUT TO EAT.
FOUL!
KIRKMAN & SCOTT

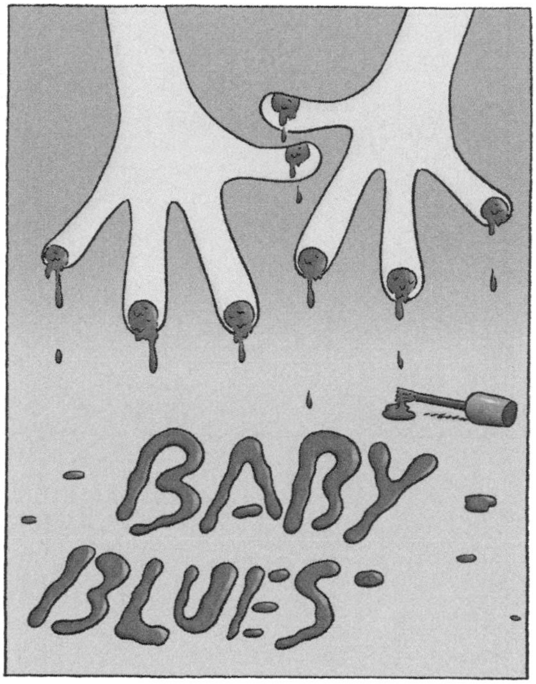
BABY
BLUES

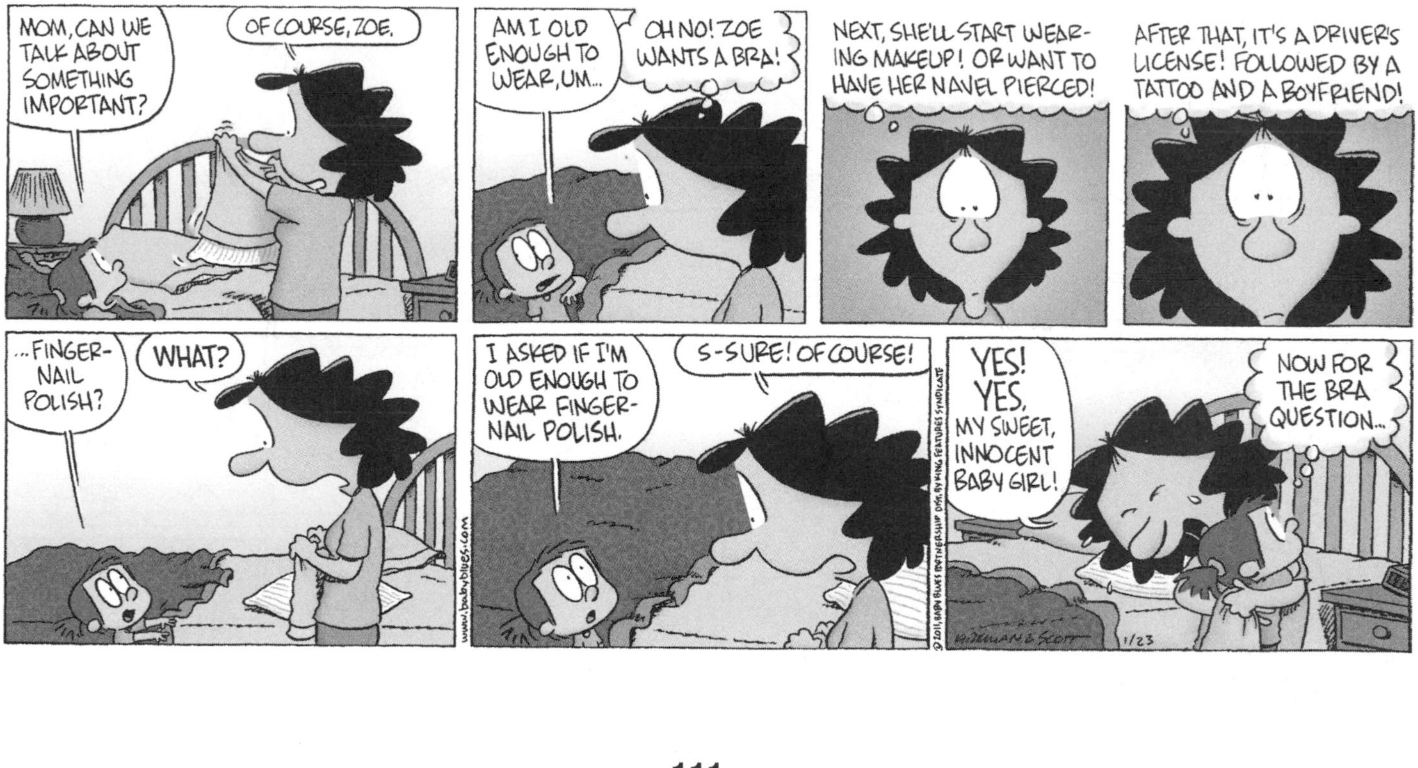
MOM, CAN WE TALK ABOUT SOMETHING IMPORTANT?
OF COURSE, ZOE.
AM I OLD ENOUGH TO WEAR, UM...
OH NO! ZOE WANTS A BRA!
NEXT, SHE'LL START WEARING MAKEUP! OR WANT TO HAVE HER NAVEL PIERCED!
AFTER THAT, IT'S A DRIVER'S LICENSE! FOLLOWED BY A TATTOO AND A BOYFRIEND!
...FINGER-NAIL POLISH?
WHAT?
www.babyblues.com
I ASKED IF I'M OLD ENOUGH TO WEAR FINGER-NAIL POLISH.
S-SURE! OF COURSE!
YES! YES, MY SWEET, INNOCENT BABY GIRL!
NOW FOR THE BRA QUESTION...
1/23

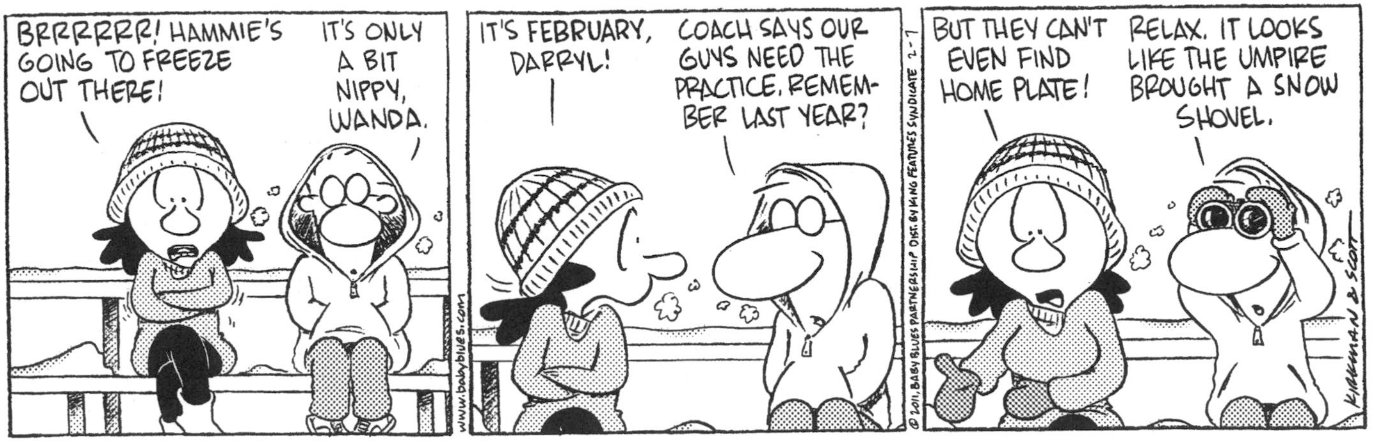
BRRRRRR! HAMMIE'S GOING TO FREEZE OUT THERE!
IT'S ONLY A BIT NIPPY, WANDA.
IT'S FEBRUARY, DARRYL!
COACH SAYS OUR GUYS NEED THE PRACTICE. REMEMBER LAST YEAR?
BUT THEY CAN'T EVEN FIND HOME PLATE!
RELAX. IT LOOKS LIKE THE UMPIRE BROUGHT A SNOW SHOVEL.
www.babyblues.com
© 2011, BABY BLUES PARTNERSHIP DIST. BY KING FEATURES SYNDICATE 2-7
KIRKMAN & SCOTT

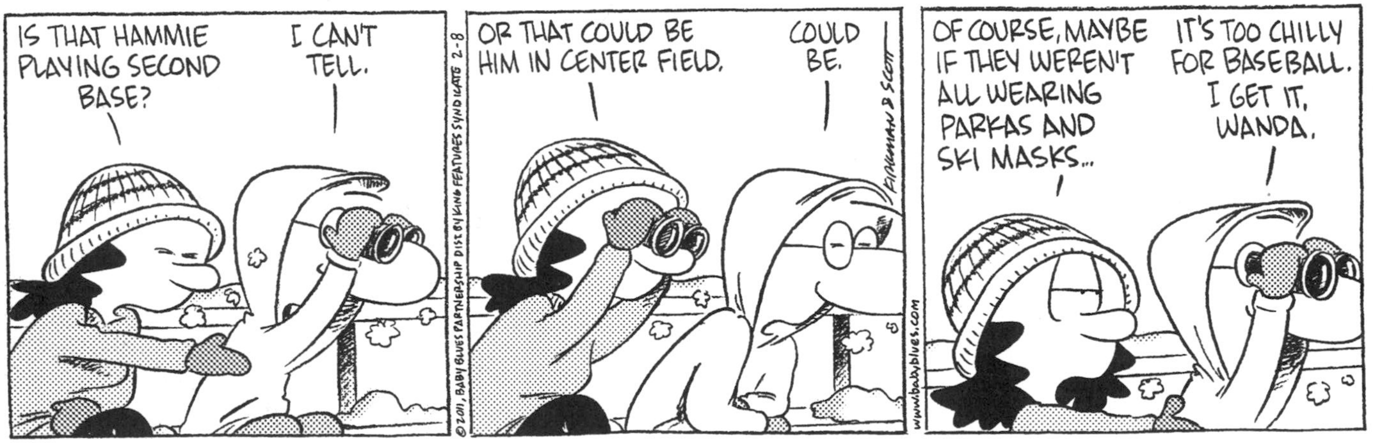
IS THAT HAMMIE PLAYING SECOND BASE?
I CAN'T TELL.
OR THAT COULD BE HIM IN CENTER FIELD.
COULD BE.
OF COURSE, MAYBE IF THEY WEREN'T ALL WEARING PARKAS AND SKI MASKS...
IT'S TOO CHILLY FOR BASEBALL. I GET IT, WANDA.
© 2011, BABY BLUES PARTNERSHIP DIST. BY KING FEATURES SYNDICATE 2-8
KIRKMAN & SCOTT
www.babyblues.com

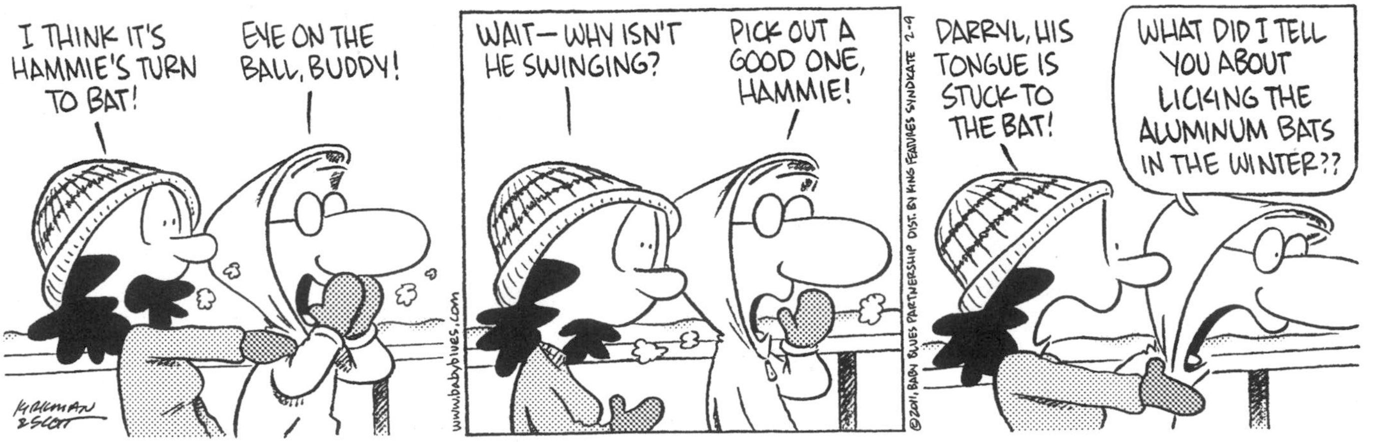
I THINK IT'S HAMMIE'S TURN TO BAT!
EYE ON THE BALL, BUDDY!
WAIT— WHY ISN'T HE SWINGING?
PICK OUT A GOOD ONE, HAMMIE!
DARRYL, HIS TONGUE IS STUCK TO THE BAT!
WHAT DID I TELL YOU ABOUT LICKING THE ALUMINUM BATS IN THE WINTER??
KIRKMAN & SCOTT
www.babyblues.com
© 2011, BABY BLUES PARTNERSHIP DIST. BY KING FEATURES SYNDICATE 2-9

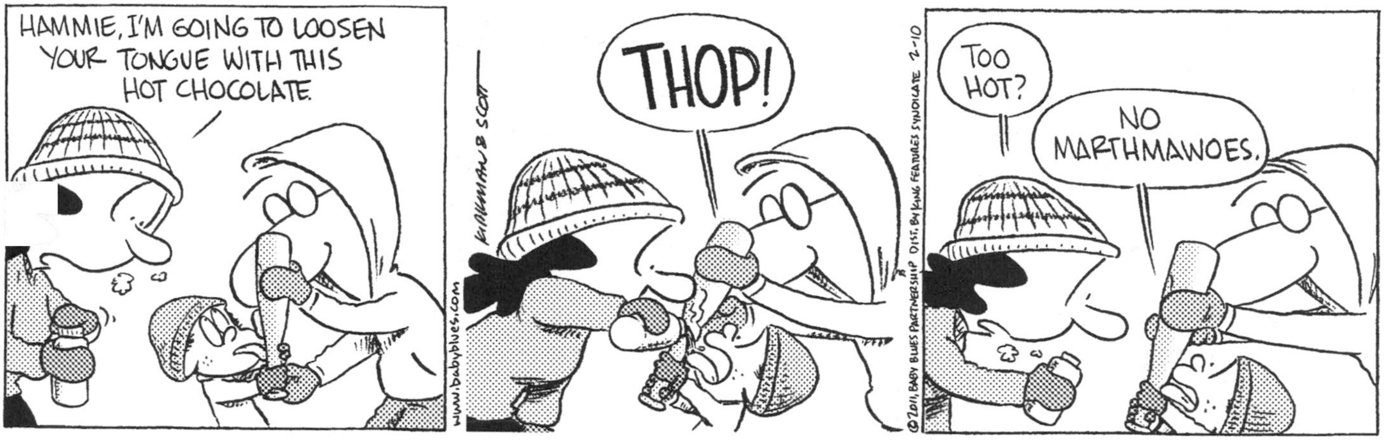
HAMMIE, I'M GOING TO LOOSEN YOUR TONGUE WITH THIS HOT CHOCOLATE.
www.babyblues.com
KIRKMAN & SCOTT
THOP!
© 2011, BABY BLUES PARTNERSHIP DIST. BY KING FEATURES SYNDICATE 2-10
TOO HOT?
NO MARTHMAWOES.

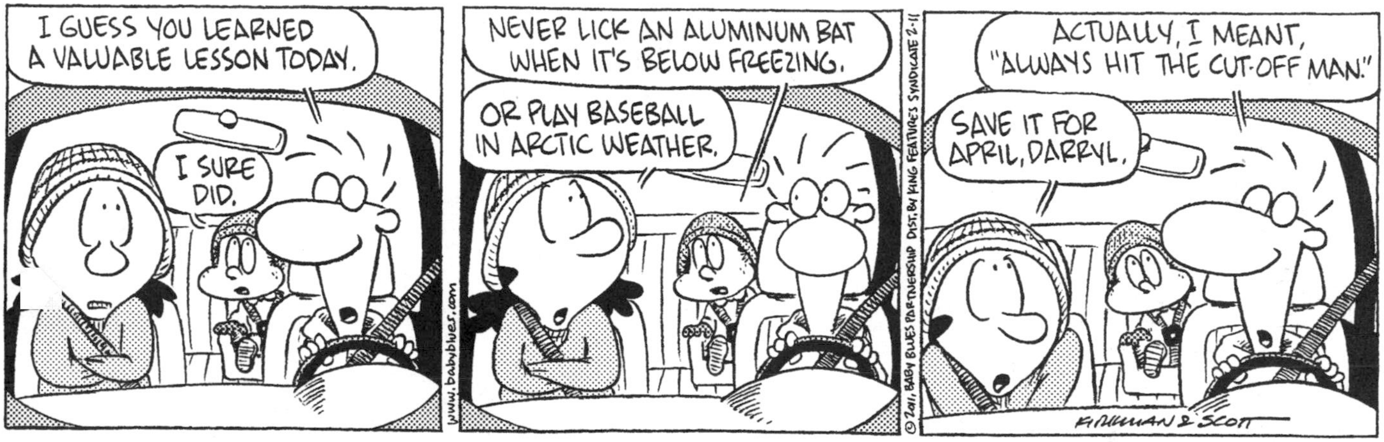
I GUESS YOU LEARNED A VALUABLE LESSON TODAY.
I SURE DID.
www.babyblues.com
NEVER LICK AN ALUMINUM BAT WHEN IT'S BELOW FREEZING.
OR PLAY BASEBALL IN ARCTIC WEATHER.
© 2011, BABY BLUES PARTNERSHIP DIST. BY KING FEATURES SYNDICATE 2-11
ACTUALLY, I MEANT, "ALWAYS HIT THE CUT-OFF MAN."
SAVE IT FOR APRIL, DARRYL.
KIRKMAN & SCOTT

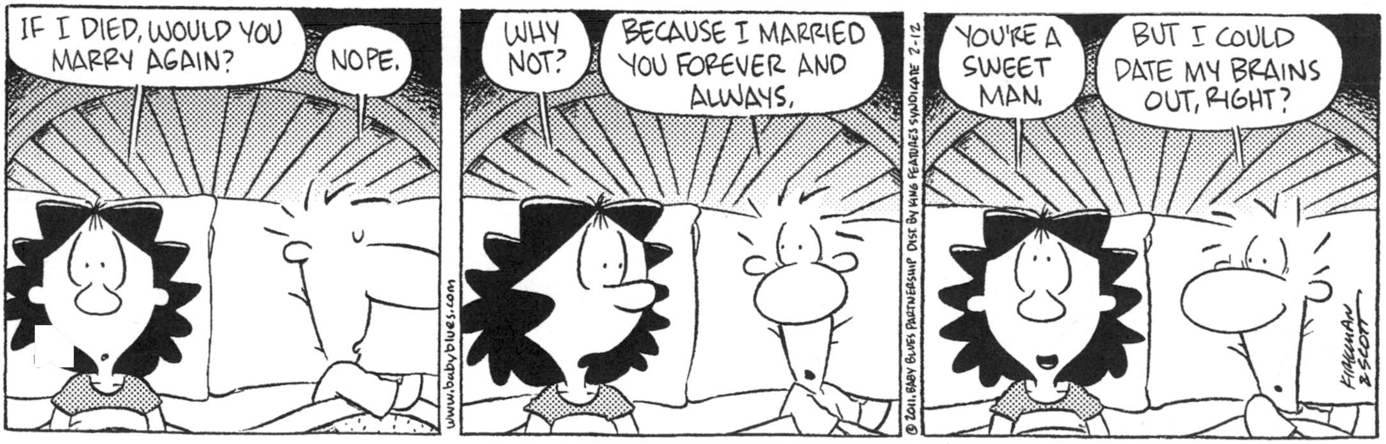
IF I DIED, WOULD YOU MARRY AGAIN?
NOPE.
www.babyblues.com
WHY NOT?
BECAUSE I MARRIED YOU FOREVER AND ALWAYS.
© 2011, BABY BLUES PARTNERSHIP DIST. BY KING FEATURES SYNDICATE 2-12
YOU'RE A SWEET MAN.
BUT I COULD DATE MY BRAINS OUT, RIGHT?
KIRKMAN & SCOTT

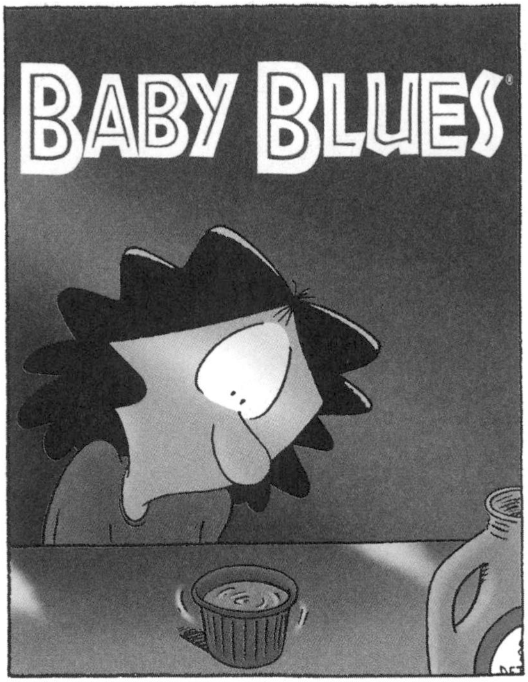
BABY BLUES®

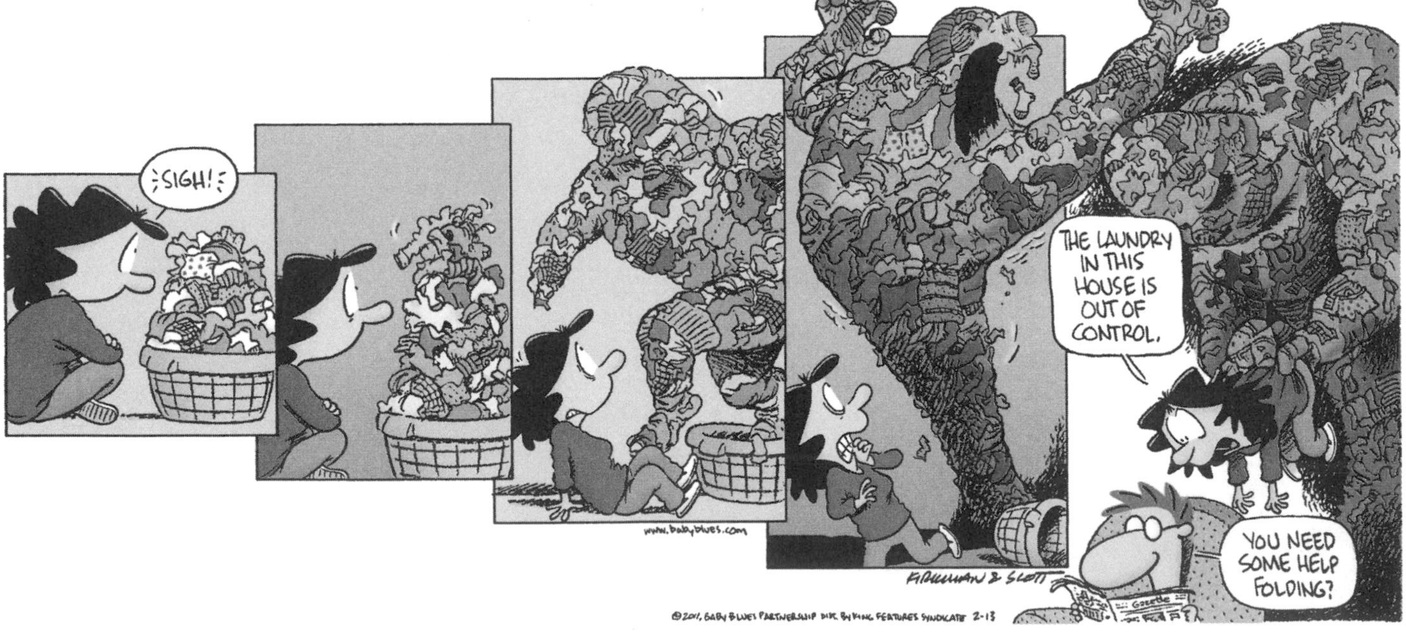
SIGH!
THE LAUNDRY IN THIS HOUSE IS OUT OF CONTROL.
YOU NEED SOME HELP FOLDING?
www.babyblues.com
KIRKMAN & SCOTT
©2011, BABY BLUES PARTNERSHIP DIST. BY KING FEATURES SYNDICATE 2-13

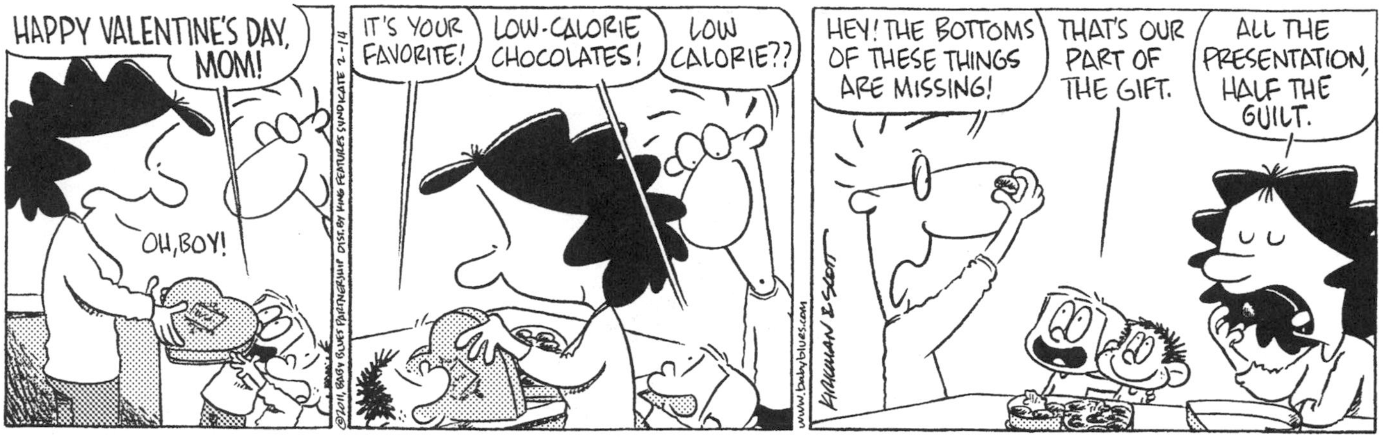
HAPPY VALENTINE'S DAY, MOM!
OH, BOY!
©2011, BABY BLUES PARTNERSHIP DIST. BY KING FEATURES SYNDICATE 2-14
IT'S YOUR FAVORITE!
LOW-CALORIE CHOCOLATES!
LOW CALORIE??
www.babyblues.com
KIRKMAN & SCOTT
HEY! THE BOTTOMS OF THESE THINGS ARE MISSING!
THAT'S OUR PART OF THE GIFT.
ALL THE PRESENTATION, HALF THE GUILT.

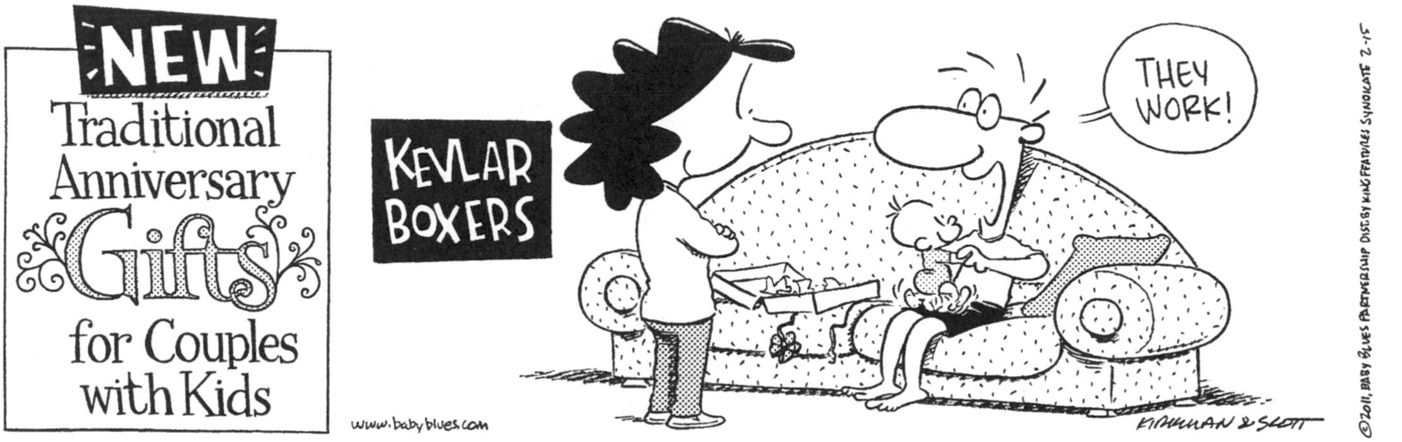
NEW
Traditional Anniversary Gifts for Couples with Kids
KEVLAR BOXERS
THEY WORK!
www.babyblues.com
KIRKMAN & SCOTT
©2011, BABY BLUES PARTNERSHIP DIST. BY KING FEATURES SYNDICATE 2-15

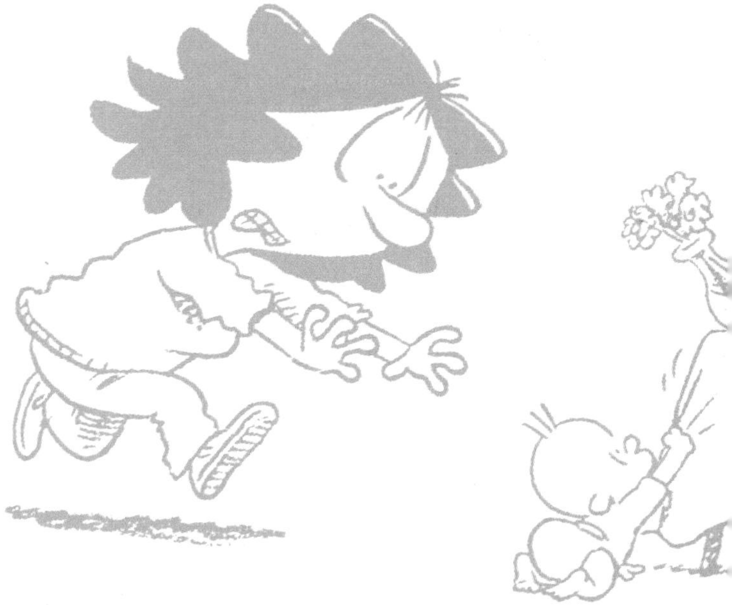

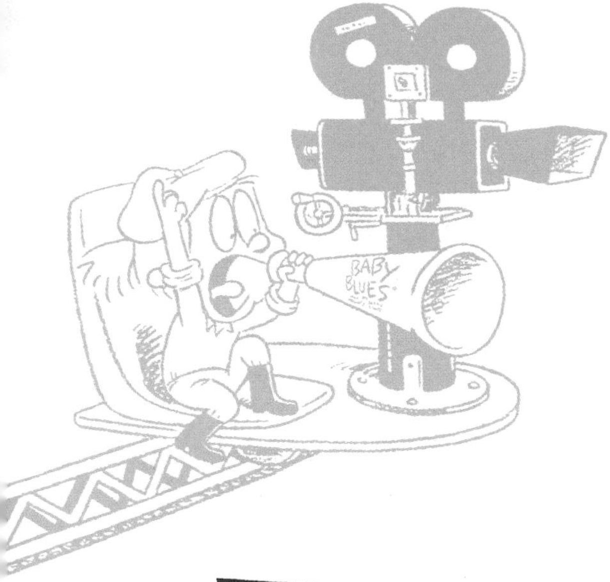
BABY BLUES

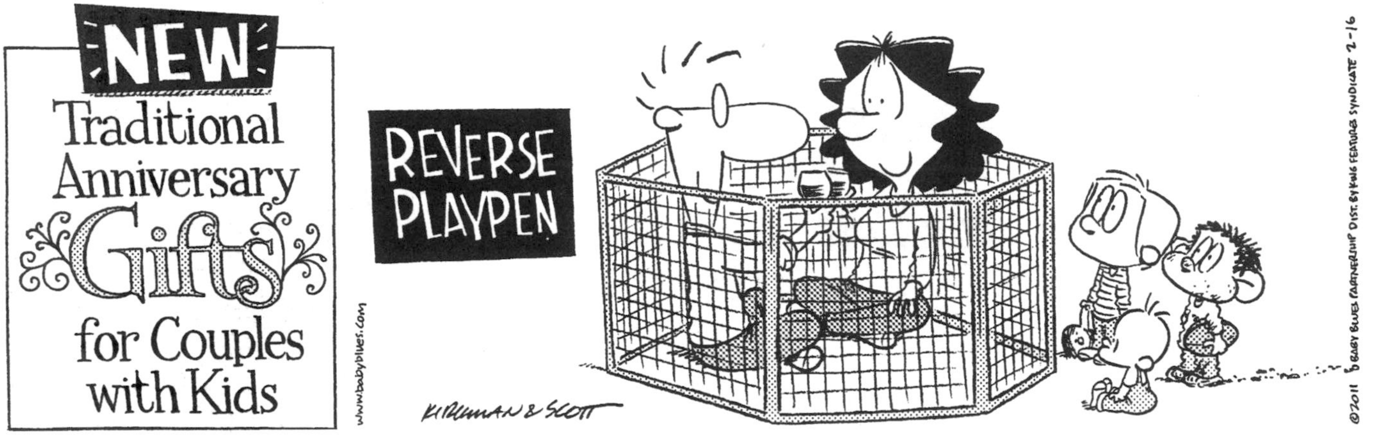
NEW
Traditional Anniversary Gifts for Couples with Kids
www.babyblues.com
REVERSE PLAYPEN
KIRKMAN & SCOTT
©2011 BABY BLUES PARTNERSHIP DIST. BY KING FEATURES SYNDICATE 2-16

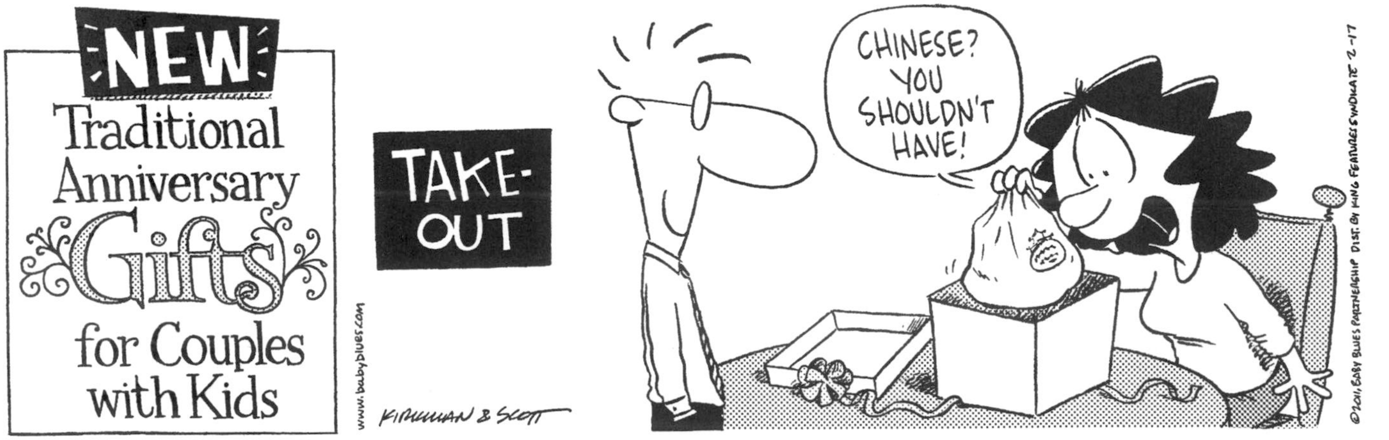
NEW
Traditional Anniversary Gifts for Couples with Kids
www.babyblues.com
TAKE-OUT
KIRKMAN & SCOTT
CHINESE? YOU SHOULDN'T HAVE!
©2011, BABY BLUES PARTNERSHIP DIST. BY KING FEATURES SYNDICATE 2-17

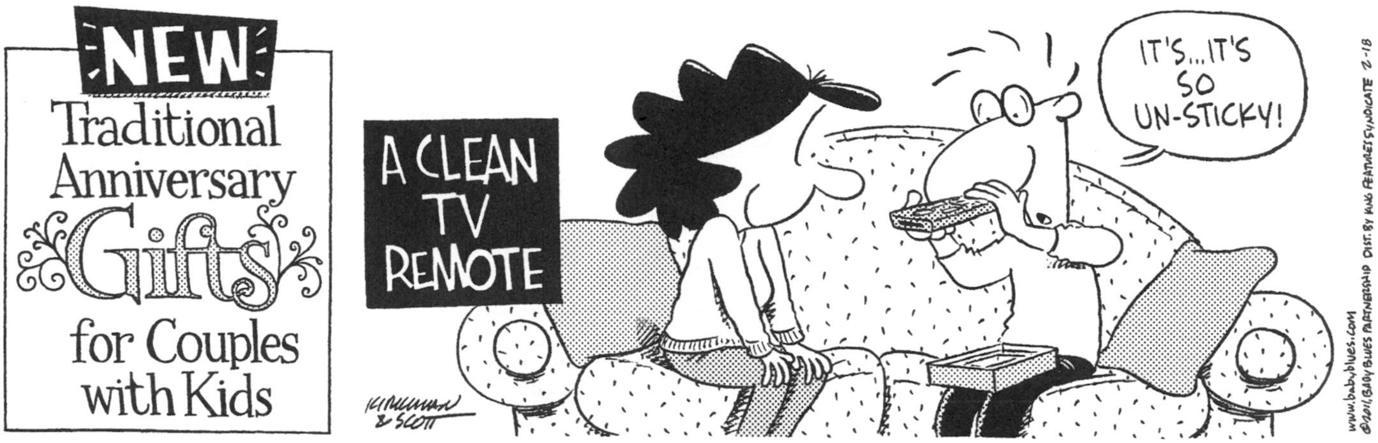
NEW
Traditional Anniversary Gifts for Couples with Kids
A CLEAN TV REMOTE
IT'S...IT'S SO UN-STICKY!
KIRKMAN & SCOTT
www.babyblues.com
©2011, BABY BLUES PARTNERSHIP DIST. BY KING FEATURES SYNDICATE 2-18

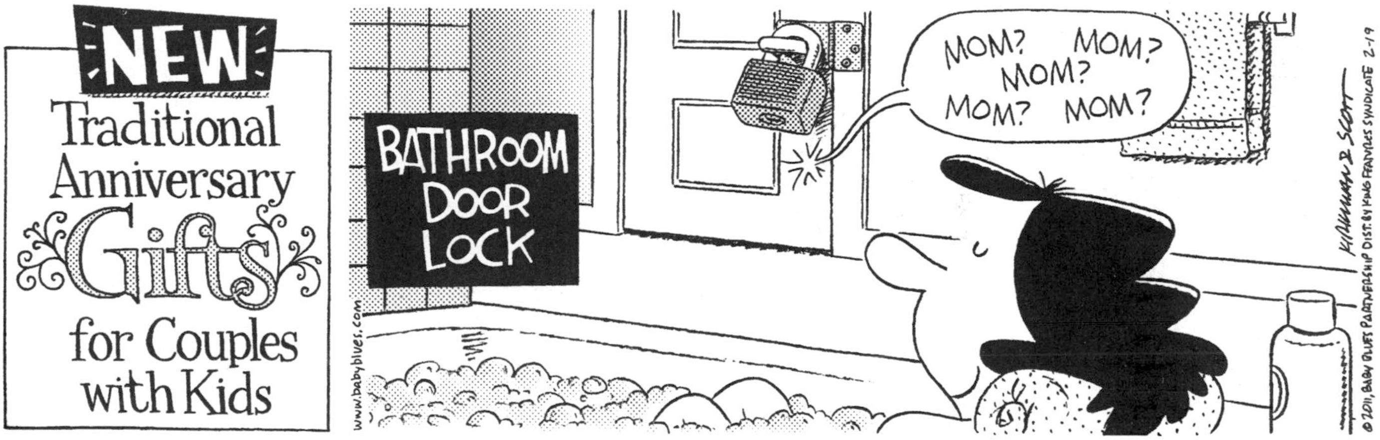
NEW
Traditional Anniversary Gifts for Couples with Kids
BATHROOM DOOR LOCK
MOM? MOM? MOM? MOM? MOM?
KIRKMAN & SCOTT
www.babyblues.com
©2011, BABY BLUES PARTNERSHIP DIST. BY KING FEATURES SYNDICATE 2-19

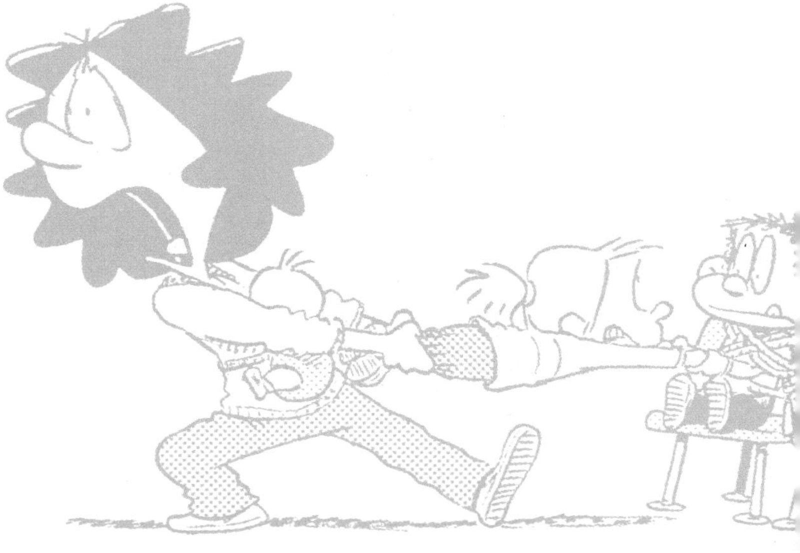

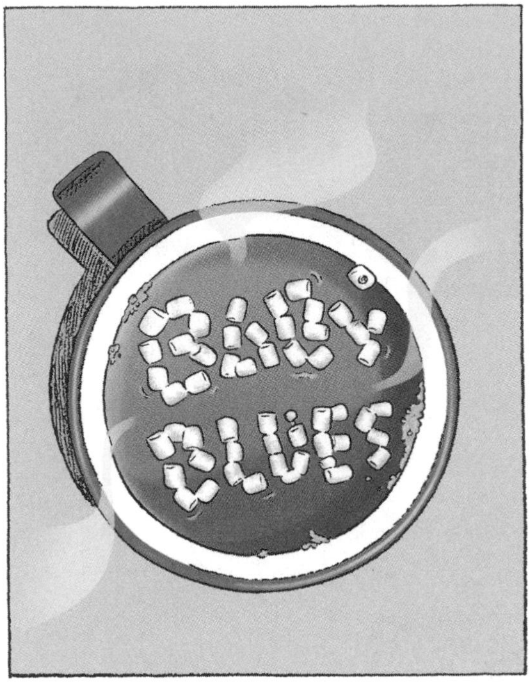
BABY
BLUES

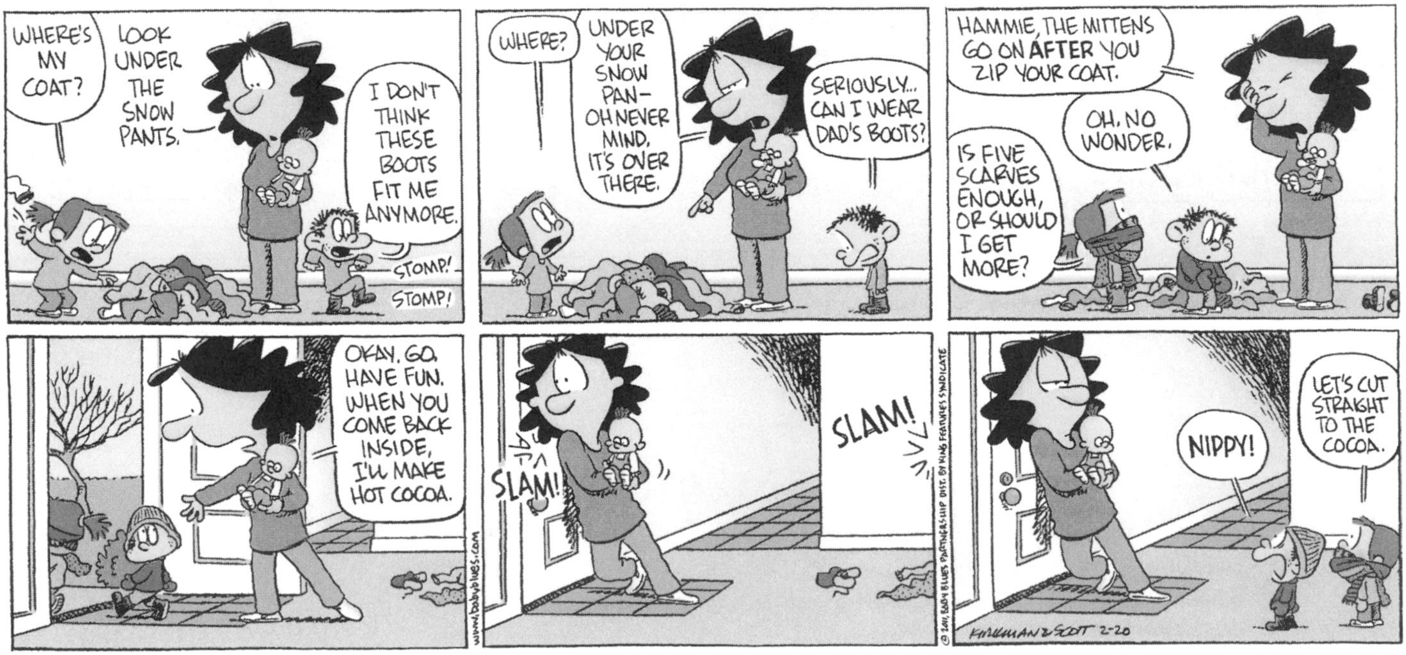
WHERE'S MY COAT?
LOOK UNDER THE SNOW PANTS.
I DON'T THINK THESE BOOTS FIT ME ANYMORE.
STOMP! STOMP!
WHERE?
UNDER YOUR SNOW PAN— OH NEVER MIND. IT'S OVER THERE.
SERIOUSLY... CAN I WEAR DAD'S BOOTS?
HAMMIE, THE MITTENS GO ON AFTER YOU ZIP YOUR COAT.
OH, NO WONDER.
IS FIVE SCARVES ENOUGH, OR SHOULD I GET MORE?
OKAY. GO. HAVE FUN. WHEN YOU COME BACK INSIDE, I'LL MAKE HOT COCOA.
www.babyblues.com
SLAM!
SLAM!
© 2011 BABY BLUES PARTNERSHIP DIST. BY KING FEATURES SYNDICATE
NIPPY!
LET'S CUT STRAIGHT TO THE COCOA.
KIRKMAN & SCOTT 2-20

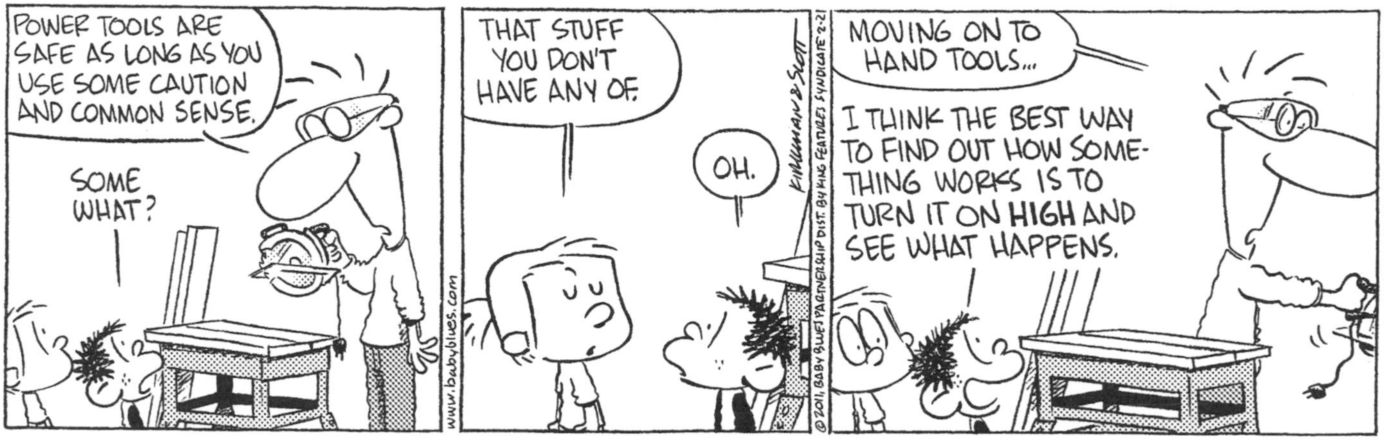
POWER TOOLS ARE SAFE AS LONG AS YOU USE SOME CAUTION AND COMMON SENSE.
SOME WHAT?
www.babyblues.com
THAT STUFF YOU DON'T HAVE ANY OF.
OH.
KIRKMAN & SCOTT
©2011, BABY BLUES PARTNERSHIP DIST. BY KING FEATURES SYNDICATE 2-21
MOVING ON TO HAND TOOLS...
I THINK THE BEST WAY TO FIND OUT HOW SOMETHING WORKS IS TO TURN IT ON **HIGH** AND SEE WHAT HAPPENS.

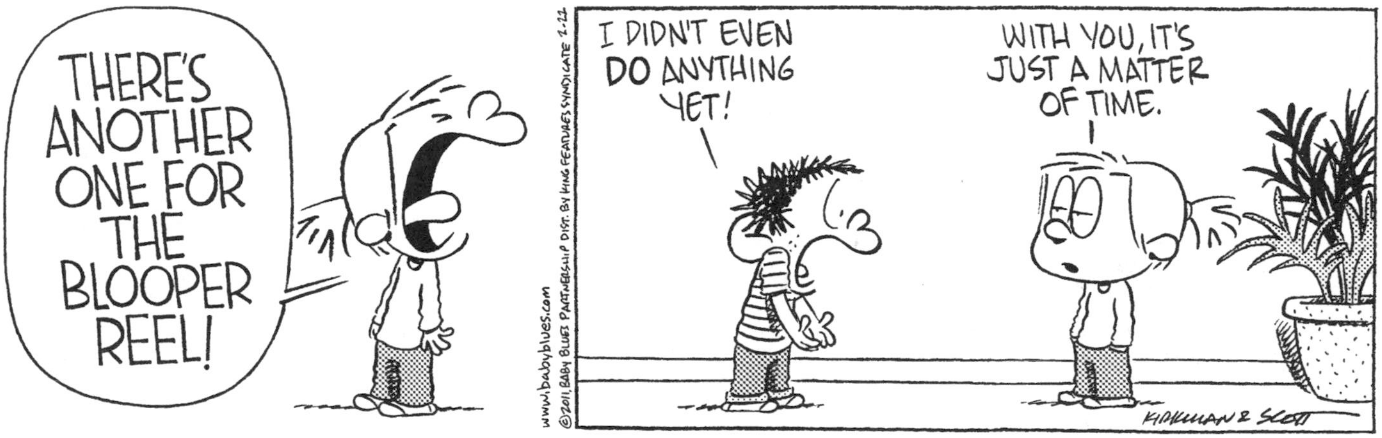
THERE'S ANOTHER ONE FOR THE BLOOPER REEL!
www.babyblues.com
©2011, BABY BLUES PARTNERSHIP DIST. BY KING FEATURES SYNDICATE 2-22
I DIDN'T EVEN **DO** ANYTHING YET!
WITH YOU, IT'S JUST A MATTER OF TIME.
KIRKMAN & SCOTT

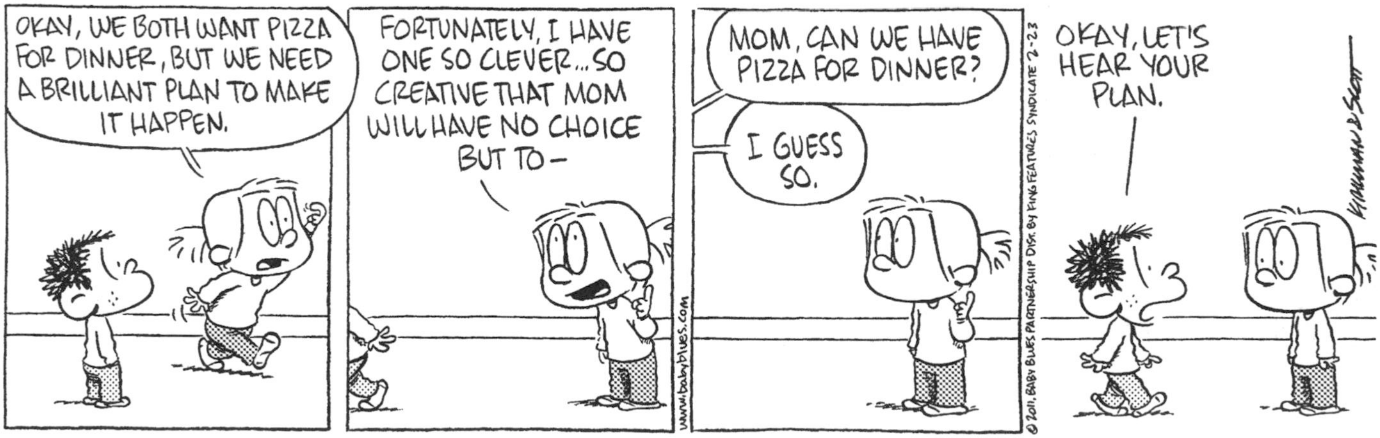
OKAY, WE BOTH WANT PIZZA FOR DINNER, BUT WE NEED A BRILLIANT PLAN TO MAKE IT HAPPEN.
FORTUNATELY, I HAVE ONE SO CLEVER... SO CREATIVE THAT MOM WILL HAVE NO CHOICE BUT TO –
www.babyblues.com
MOM, CAN WE HAVE PIZZA FOR DINNER?
I GUESS SO.
©2011, BABY BLUES PARTNERSHIP DIST. BY KING FEATURES SYNDICATE 2-23
OKAY, LET'S HEAR YOUR PLAN.
KIRKMAN & SCOTT

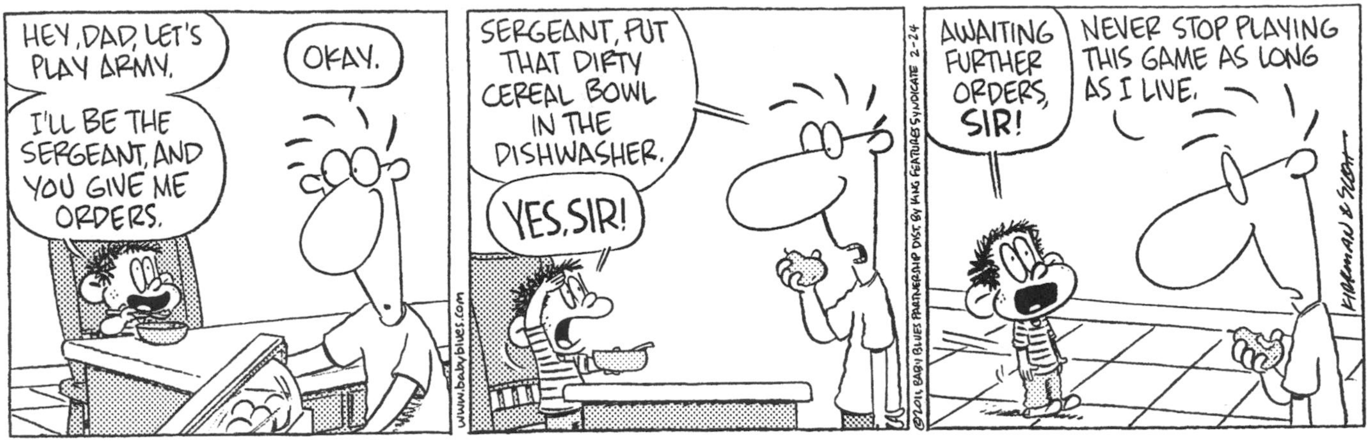
HEY, DAD, LET'S PLAY ARMY.
I'LL BE THE SERGEANT, AND YOU GIVE ME ORDERS.
OKAY.
www.babyblues.com
SERGEANT, PUT THAT DIRTY CEREAL BOWL IN THE DISHWASHER.
YES, SIR!
©2011, Baby Blues Partnership Dist. by King Features Syndicate 2-24
AWAITING FURTHER ORDERS, SIR!
NEVER STOP PLAYING THIS GAME AS LONG AS I LIVE.
KIRKMAN & SCOTT

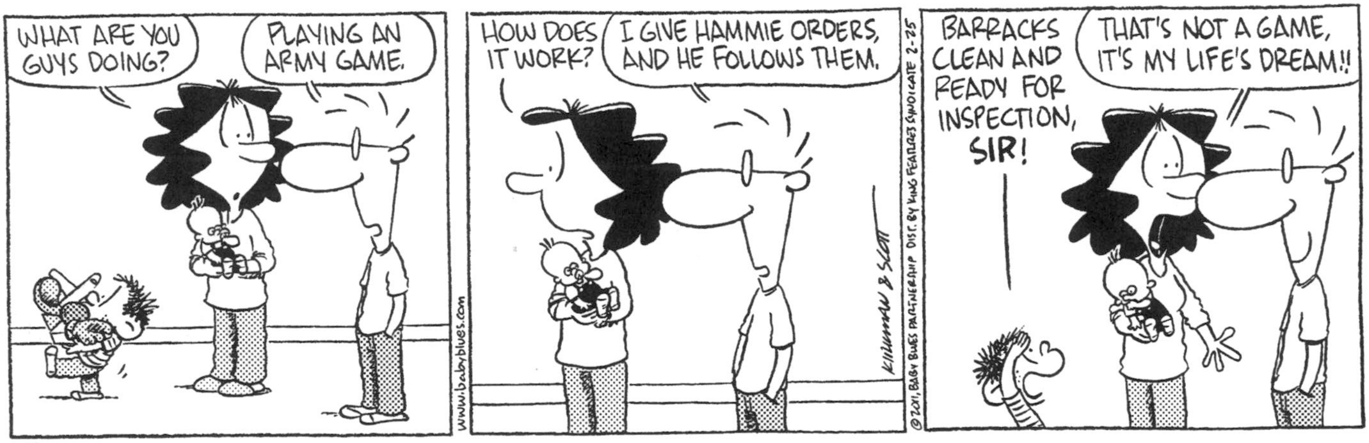
WHAT ARE YOU GUYS DOING?
PLAYING AN ARMY GAME.
www.babyblues.com
HOW DOES IT WORK?
I GIVE HAMMIE ORDERS, AND HE FOLLOWS THEM.
KIRKMAN & SCOTT
©2011, Baby Blues Partnership Dist. by King Features Syndicate 2-25
BARRACKS CLEAN AND READY FOR INSPECTION, SIR!
THAT'S NOT A GAME, IT'S MY LIFE'S DREAM!!

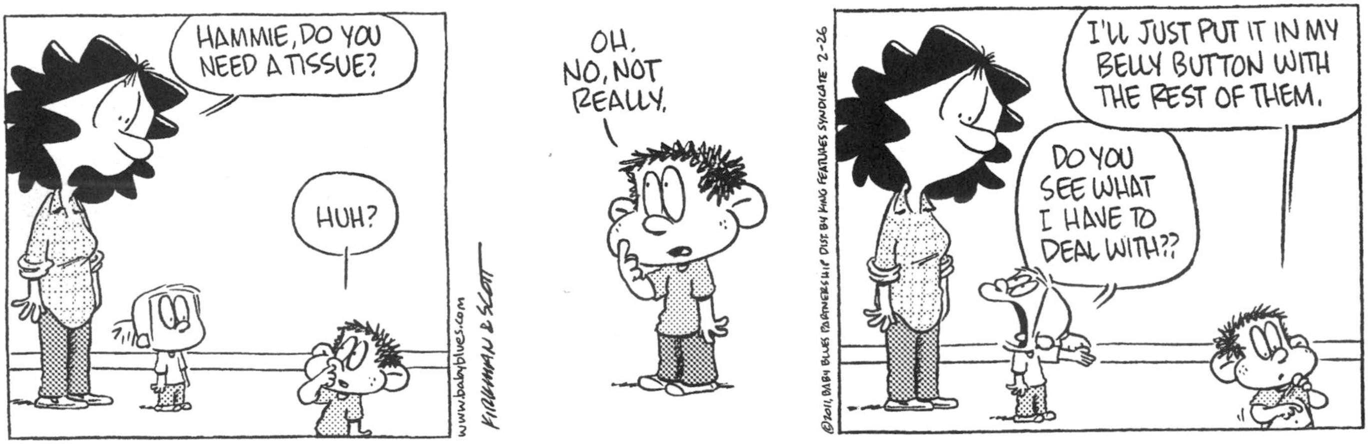
HAMMIE, DO YOU NEED A TISSUE?
HUH?
www.babyblues.com
KIRKMAN & SCOTT
OH. NO, NOT REALLY.
©2011, Baby Blues Partnership Dist. by King Features Syndicate 2-26
I'LL JUST PUT IT IN MY BELLY BUTTON WITH THE REST OF THEM.
DO YOU SEE WHAT I HAVE TO DEAL WITH??

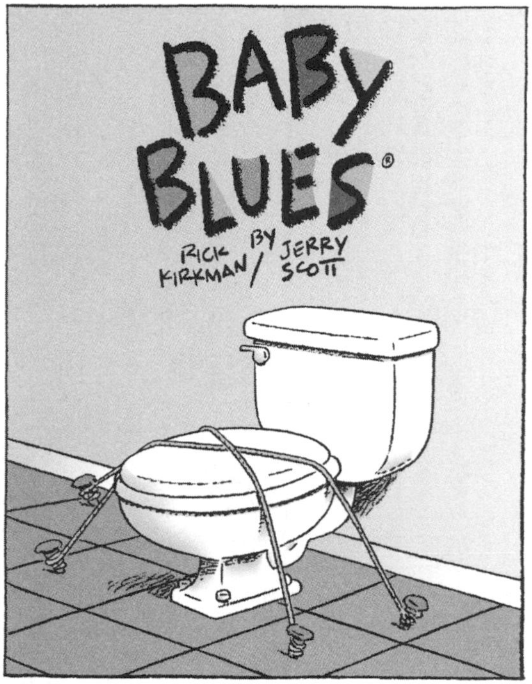
BABY BLUES®
BY
RICK KIRKMAN / JERRY SCOTT

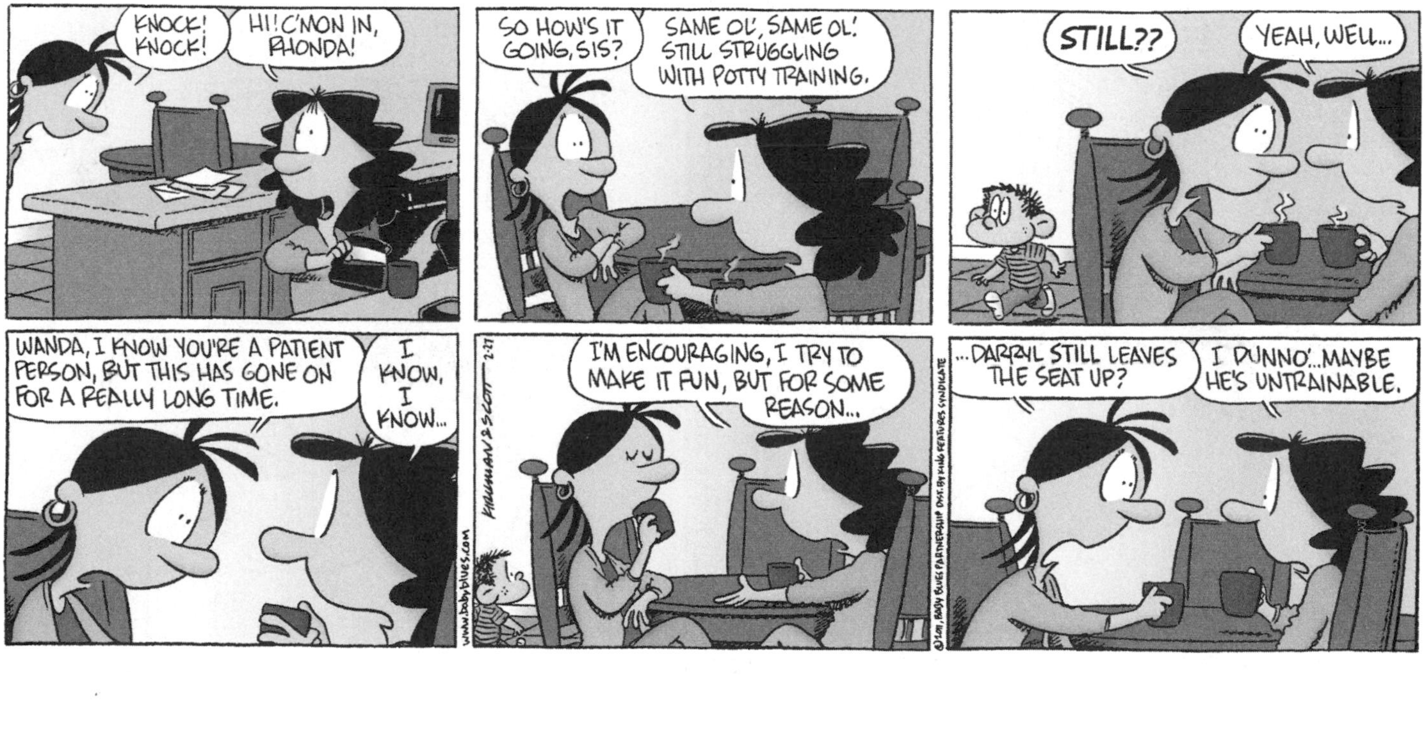
KNOCK! KNOCK!
HI! C'MON IN, RHONDA!
SO HOW'S IT GOING, SIS?
SAME OL', SAME OL'. STILL STRUGGLING WITH POTTY TRAINING.
STILL??
YEAH, WELL...
WANDA, I KNOW YOU'RE A PATIENT PERSON, BUT THIS HAS GONE ON FOR A REALLY LONG TIME.
I KNOW, I KNOW...
www.babyblues.com
KIRKMAN & SCOTT 2-27
I'M ENCOURAGING, I TRY TO MAKE IT FUN, BUT FOR SOME REASON...
©2011, BABY BLUES PARTNERSHIP DIST. BY KING FEATURES SYNDICATE
...DARRYL STILL LEAVES THE SEAT UP?
I DUNNO...MAYBE HE'S UNTRAINABLE.

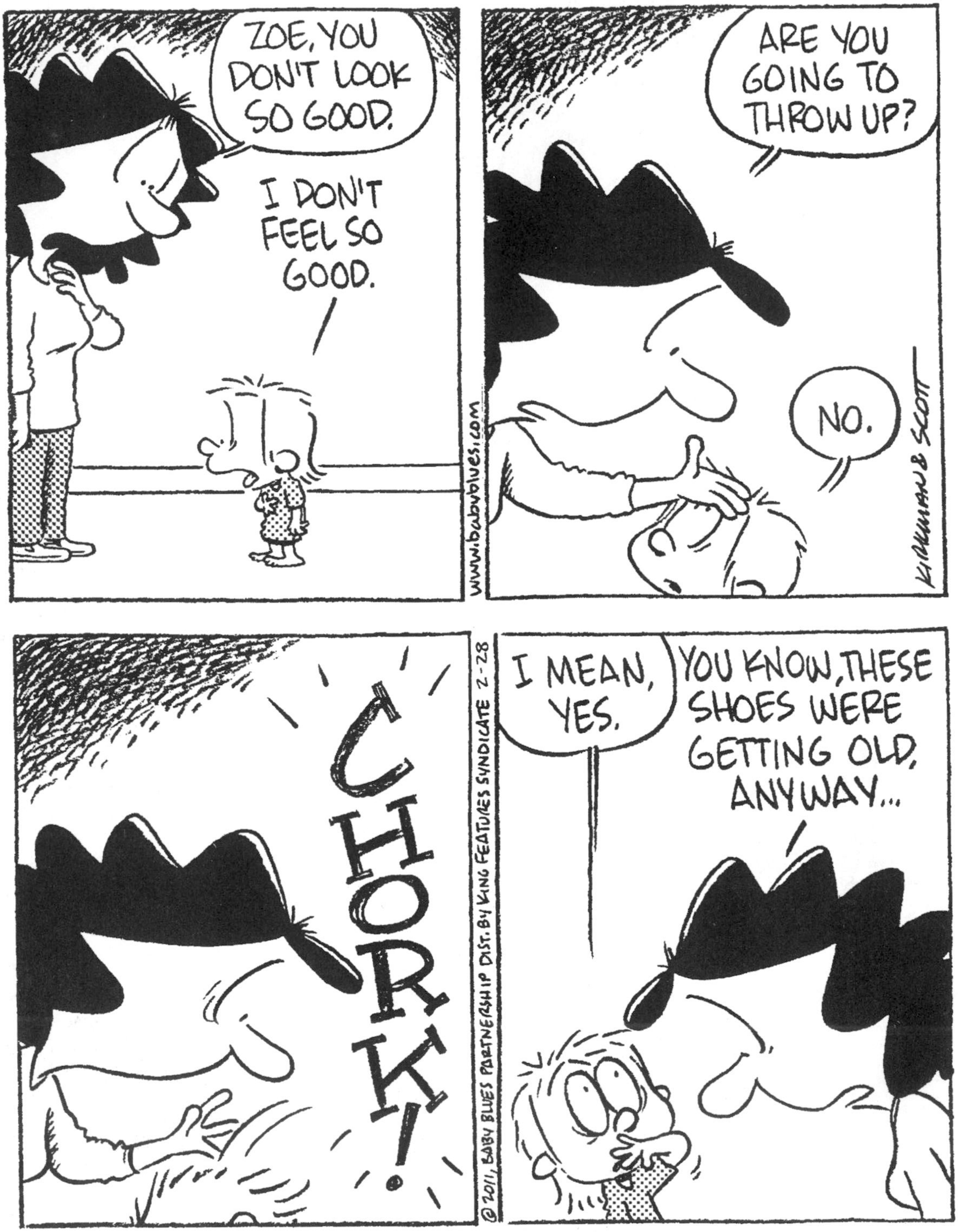
ZOE, YOU DON'T LOOK SO GOOD.
I DON'T FEEL SO GOOD.
www.babyblues.com
ARE YOU GOING TO THROW UP?
NO.
KIRKMAN & SCOTT
CHORK!
© 2011, BABY BLUES PARTNERSHIP DIST. BY KING FEATURES SYNDICATE 2-28
I MEAN, YES.
YOU KNOW, THESE SHOES WERE GETTING OLD, ANYWAY...

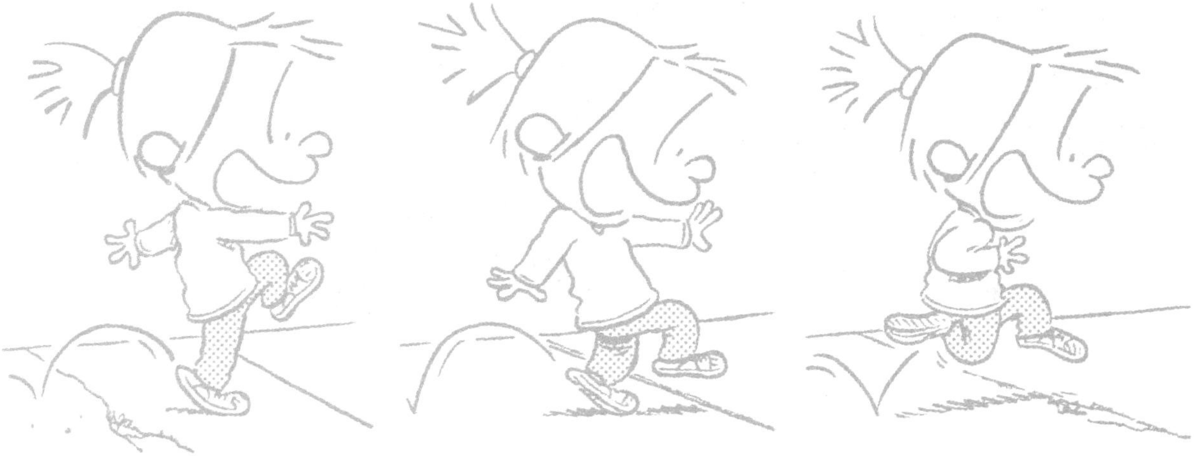

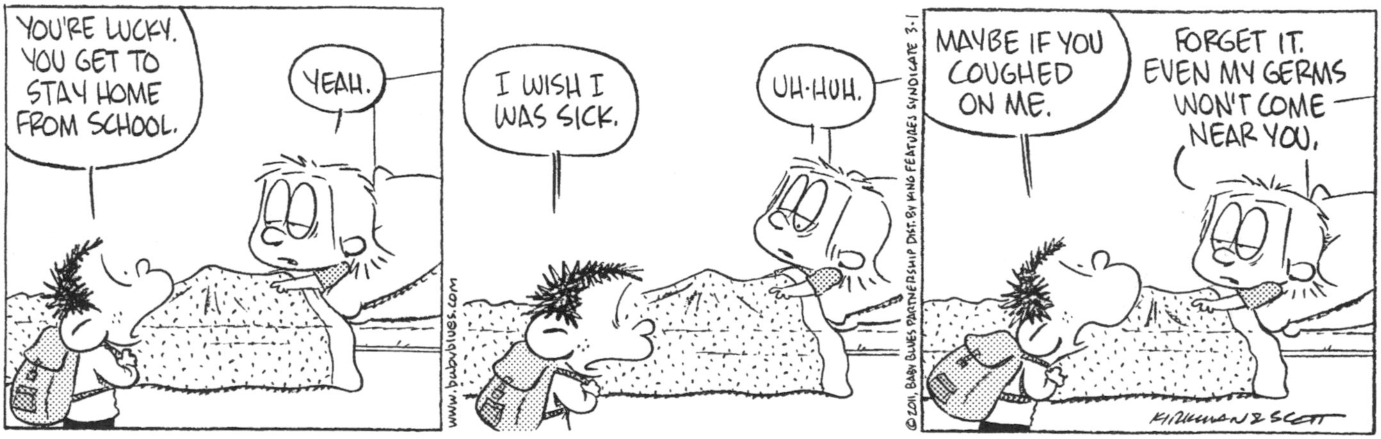
YOU'RE LUCKY. YOU GET TO STAY HOME FROM SCHOOL.
YEAH.
I WISH I WAS SICK.
UH-HUH.
MAYBE IF YOU COUGHED ON ME.
FORGET IT. EVEN MY GERMS WON'T COME NEAR YOU.
www.babyblues.com
© 2011, BABY BLUES PARTNERSHIP DIST. BY KING FEATURES SYNDICATE 3-1
KIRKMAN & SCOTT

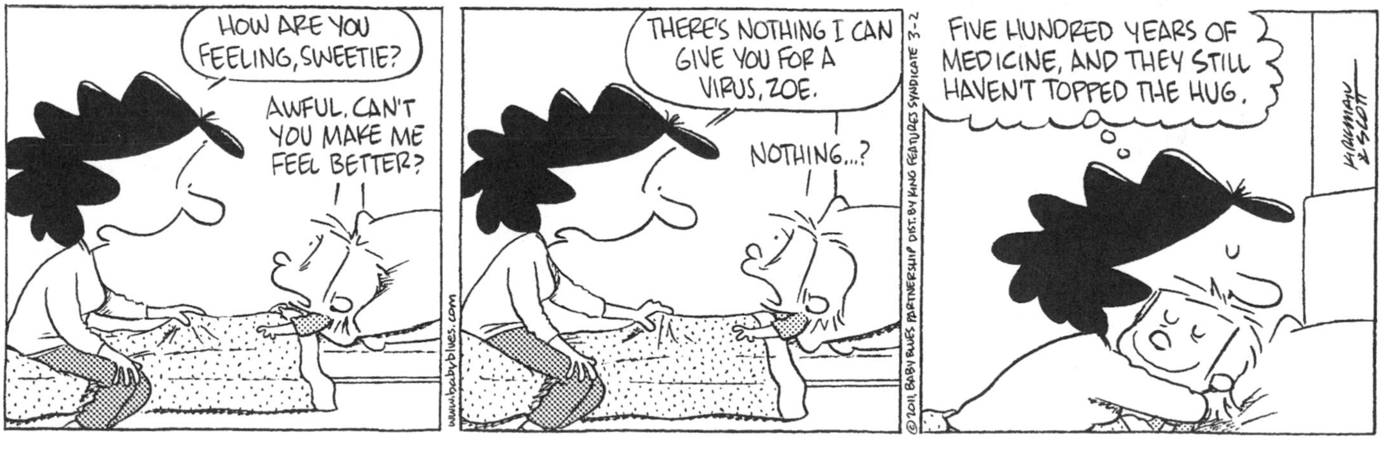
HOW ARE YOU FEELING, SWEETIE?
AWFUL. CAN'T YOU MAKE ME FEEL BETTER?
THERE'S NOTHING I CAN GIVE YOU FOR A VIRUS, ZOE.
NOTHING...?
FIVE HUNDRED YEARS OF MEDICINE, AND THEY STILL HAVEN'T TOPPED THE HUG.
www.babyblues.com
© 2011, BABY BLUES PARTNERSHIP DIST. BY KING FEATURES SYNDICATE 3-2
KIRKMAN & SCOTT

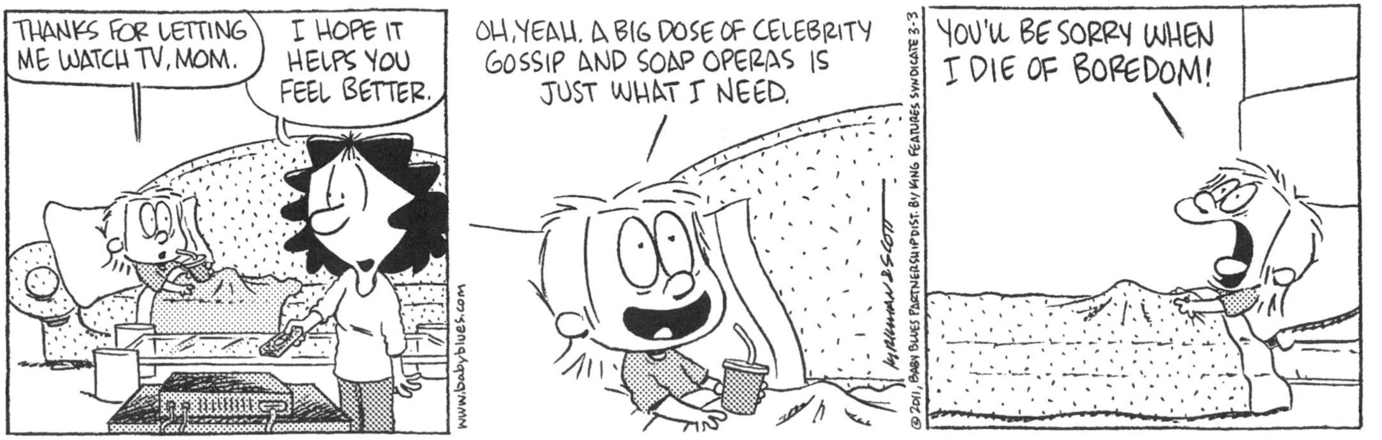
THANKS FOR LETTING ME WATCH TV, MOM.
I HOPE IT HELPS YOU FEEL BETTER.
www.babyblues.com
OH, YEAH. A BIG DOSE OF CELEBRITY GOSSIP AND SOAP OPERAS IS JUST WHAT I NEED.
KIRKMAN & SCOTT
© 2011, BABY BLUES PARTNERSHIP DIST. BY KING FEATURES SYNDICATE 3-3
YOU'LL BE SORRY WHEN I DIE OF BOREDOM!

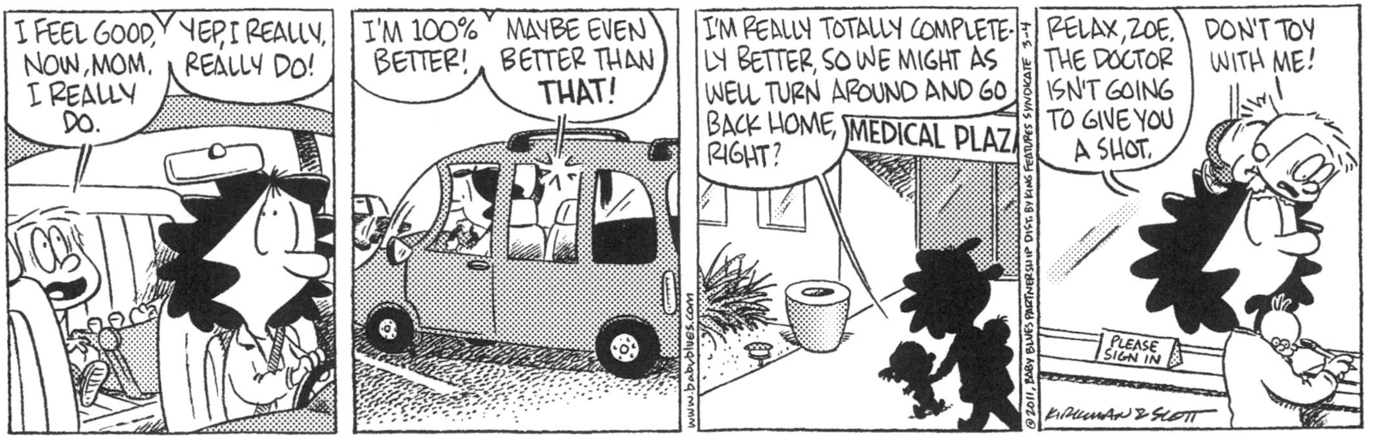
I FEEL GOOD, NOW, MOM. I REALLY DO.
YEP, I REALLY, REALLY DO!
I'M 100% BETTER!
MAYBE EVEN BETTER THAN THAT!
www.babyblues.com
I'M REALLY TOTALLY COMPLETE-LY BETTER, SO WE MIGHT AS WELL TURN AROUND AND GO BACK HOME, RIGHT?
MEDICAL PLAZ
© 2011, BABY BLUES PARTNERSHIP DIST. BY KING FEATURES SYNDICATE 3-4
RELAX, ZOE. THE DOCTOR ISN'T GOING TO GIVE YOU A SHOT.
DON'T TOY WITH ME!
PLEASE SIGN IN
KIRKMAN & SCOTT

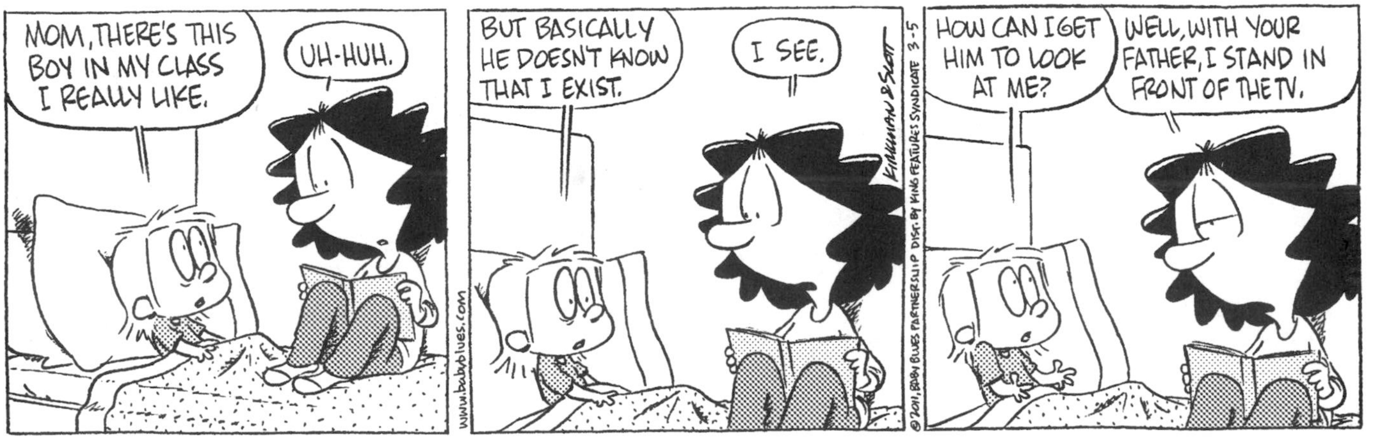
MOM, THERE'S THIS BOY IN MY CLASS I REALLY LIKE.
UH-HUH.
www.babyblues.com
BUT BASICALLY HE DOESN'T KNOW THAT I EXIST.
I SEE.
KIRKMAN & SCOTT
© 2011, BABY BLUES PARTNERSHIP DIST. BY KING FEATURES SYNDICATE 3-5
HOW CAN I GET HIM TO LOOK AT ME?
WELL, WITH YOUR FATHER, I STAND IN FRONT OF THE TV.

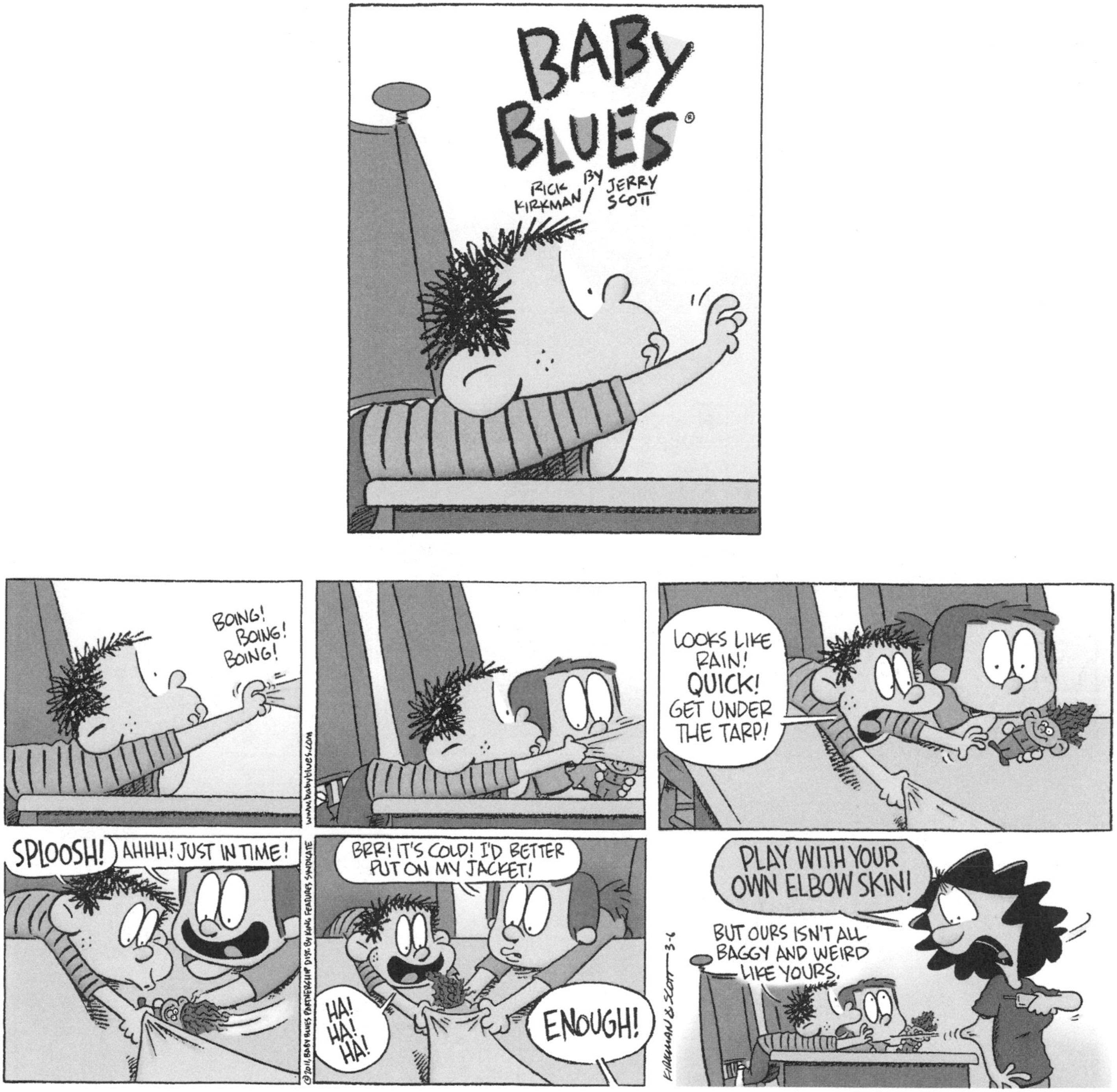
BABY BLUES®
BY RICK KIRKMAN / JERRY SCOTT
BOING! BOING! BOING!
www.babyblues.com
LOOKS LIKE RAIN! QUICK! GET UNDER THE TARP!
SPLOOSH!
AHHH! JUST IN TIME!
©2011, BABY BLUES PARTNERSHIP DIST. BY KING FEATURES SYNDICATE
BRR! IT'S COLD! I'D BETTER PUT ON MY JACKET!
HA! HA! HA!
ENOUGH!
KIRKMAN & SCOTT 3-6
PLAY WITH YOUR OWN ELBOW SKIN!
BUT OURS ISN'T ALL BAGGY AND WEIRD LIKE YOURS.

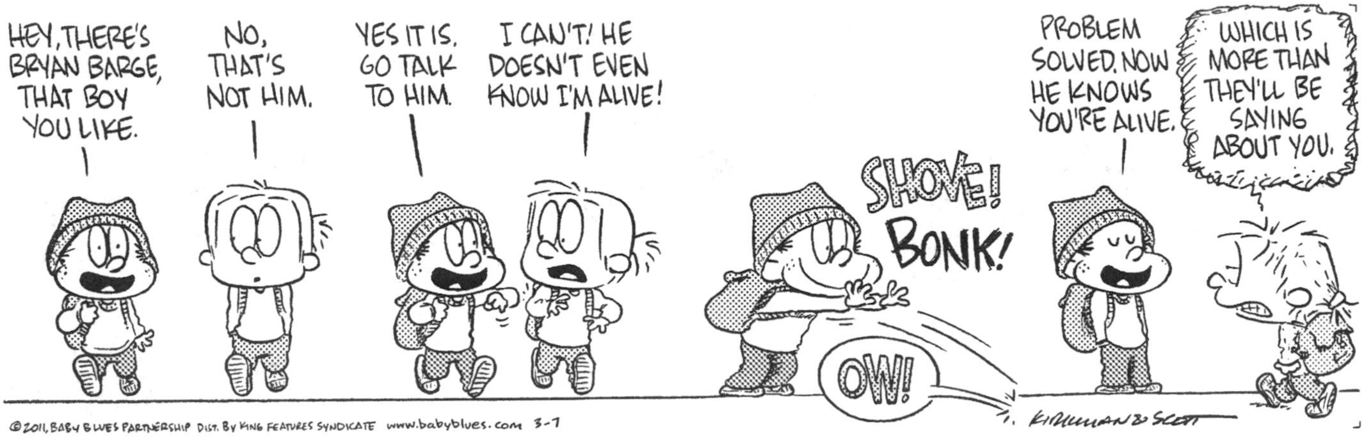
HEY, THERE'S BRYAN BARGE, THAT BOY YOU LIKE.
NO, THAT'S NOT HIM.
YES IT IS. GO TALK TO HIM.
I CAN'T! HE DOESN'T EVEN KNOW I'M ALIVE!
SHOVE!
BONK!
OW!
PROBLEM SOLVED. NOW HE KNOWS YOU'RE ALIVE.
WHICH IS MORE THAN THEY'LL BE SAYING ABOUT YOU.
©2011, BABY BLUES PARTNERSHIP DIST. BY KING FEATURES SYNDICATE www.babyblues.com 3-7
KIRKMAN & SCOTT

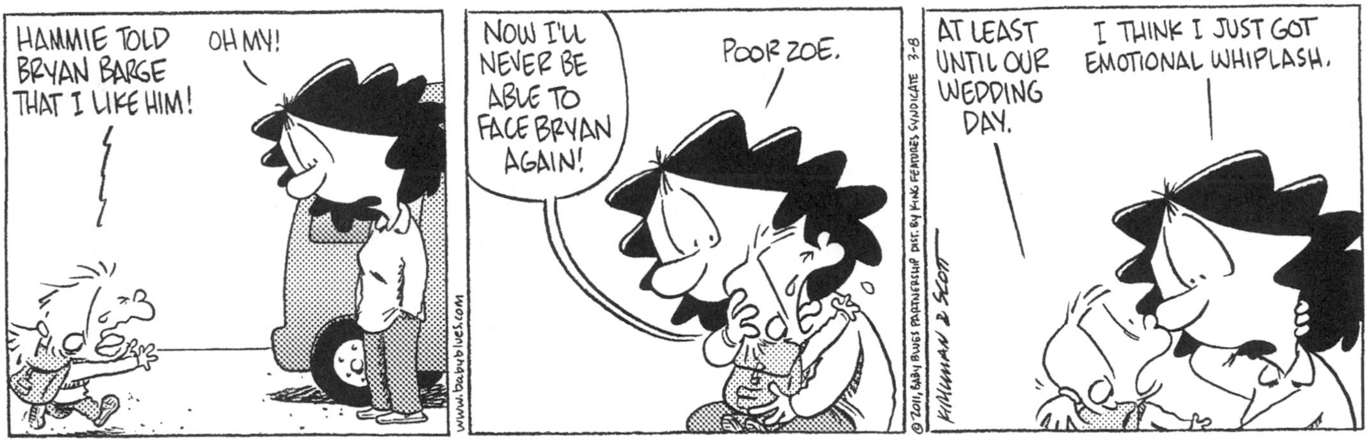
HAMMIE TOLD BRYAN BARGE THAT I LIKE HIM!
OH MY!
www.babyblues.com
NOW I'LL NEVER BE ABLE TO FACE BRYAN AGAIN!
POOR ZOE.
©2011, BABY BLUES PARTNERSHIP DIST. BY KING FEATURES SYNDICATE 3-8
KIRKMAN & SCOTT
AT LEAST UNTIL OUR WEDDING DAY.
I THINK I JUST GOT EMOTIONAL WHIPLASH.

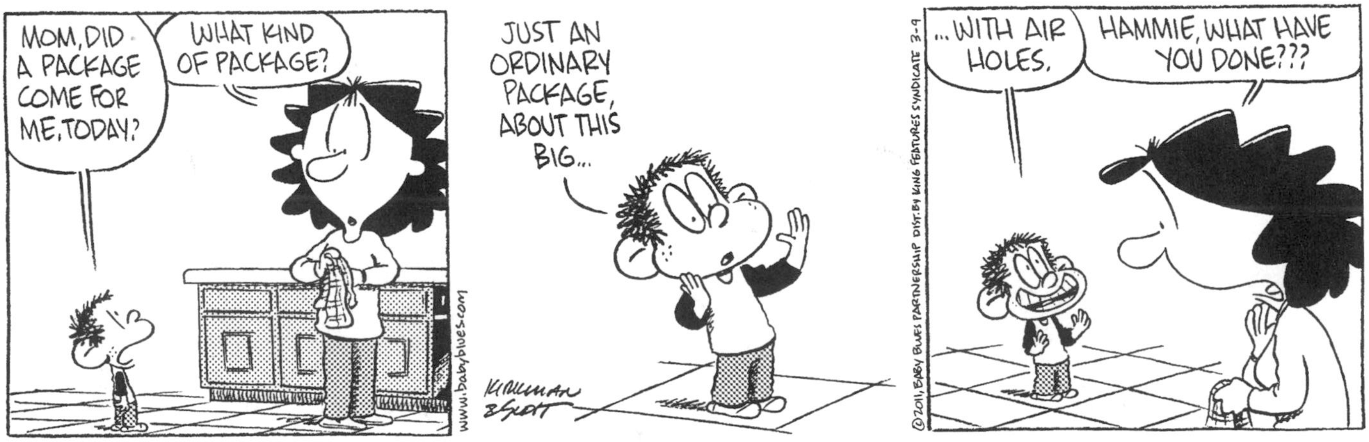
MOM, DID A PACKAGE COME FOR ME, TODAY?
WHAT KIND OF PACKAGE?
www.babyblues.com
JUST AN ORDINARY PACKAGE, ABOUT THIS BIG...
KIRKMAN & SCOTT
©2011, BABY BLUES PARTNERSHIP DIST. BY KING FEATURES SYNDICATE 3-9
...WITH AIR HOLES.
HAMMIE, WHAT HAVE YOU DONE???

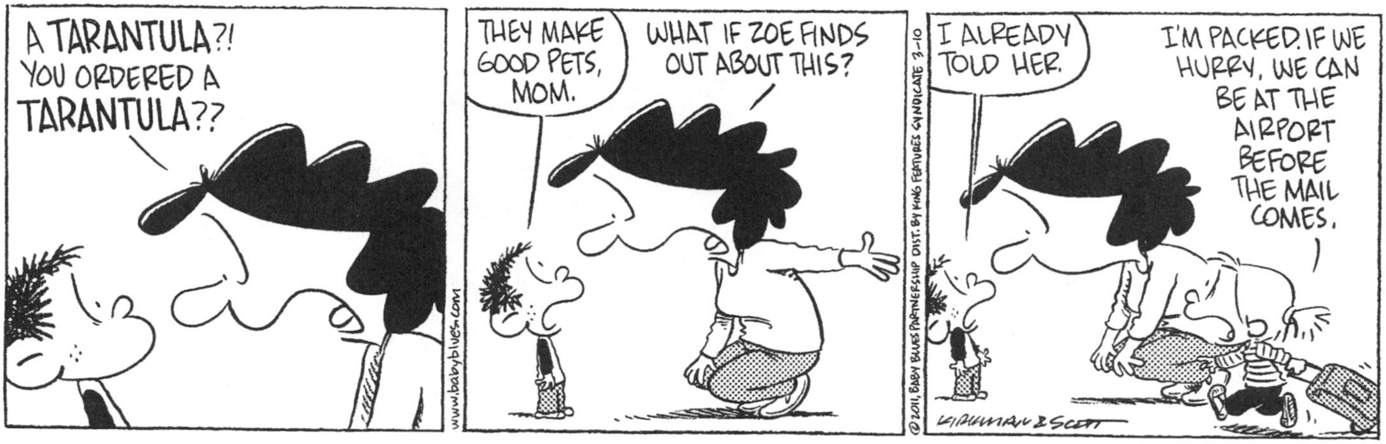
A TARANTULA?! YOU ORDERED A TARANTULA??
THEY MAKE GOOD PETS, MOM.
WHAT IF ZOE FINDS OUT ABOUT THIS?
I ALREADY TOLD HER.
I'M PACKED. IF WE HURRY, WE CAN BE AT THE AIRPORT BEFORE THE MAIL COMES.
www.babyblues.com
© 2011, BABY BLUES PARTNERSHIP DIST. BY KING FEATURES SYNDICATE 3-10
KIRKMAN & SCOTT

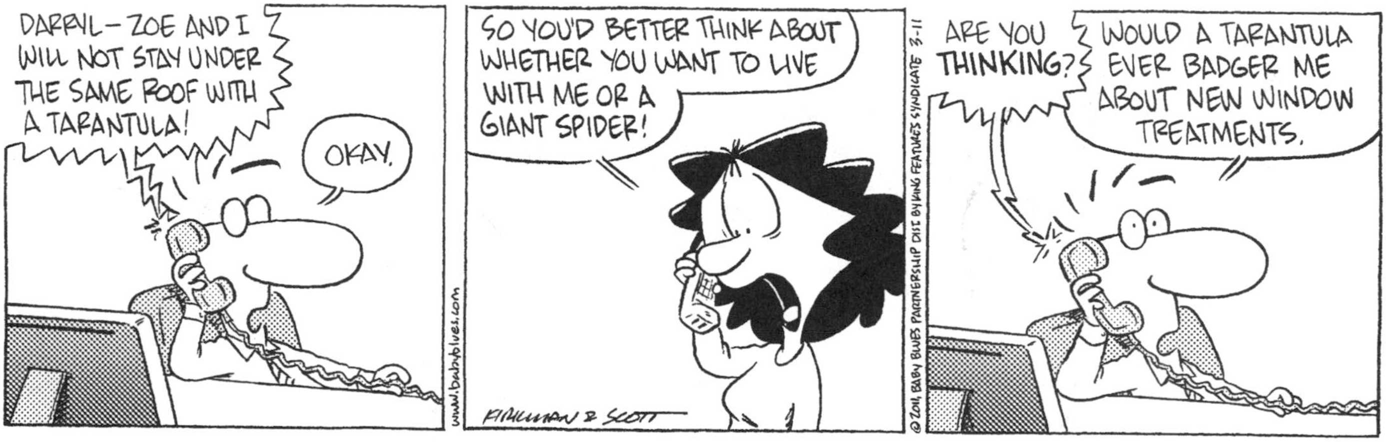
DARRYL – ZOE AND I WILL NOT STAY UNDER THE SAME ROOF WITH A TARANTULA!
OKAY.
SO YOU'D BETTER THINK ABOUT WHETHER YOU WANT TO LIVE WITH ME OR A GIANT SPIDER!
ARE YOU THINKING?
WOULD A TARANTULA EVER BADGER ME ABOUT NEW WINDOW TREATMENTS.
www.babyblues.com
KIRKMAN & SCOTT
© 2011, BABY BLUES PARTNERSHIP DIST. BY KING FEATURES SYNDICATE 3-11

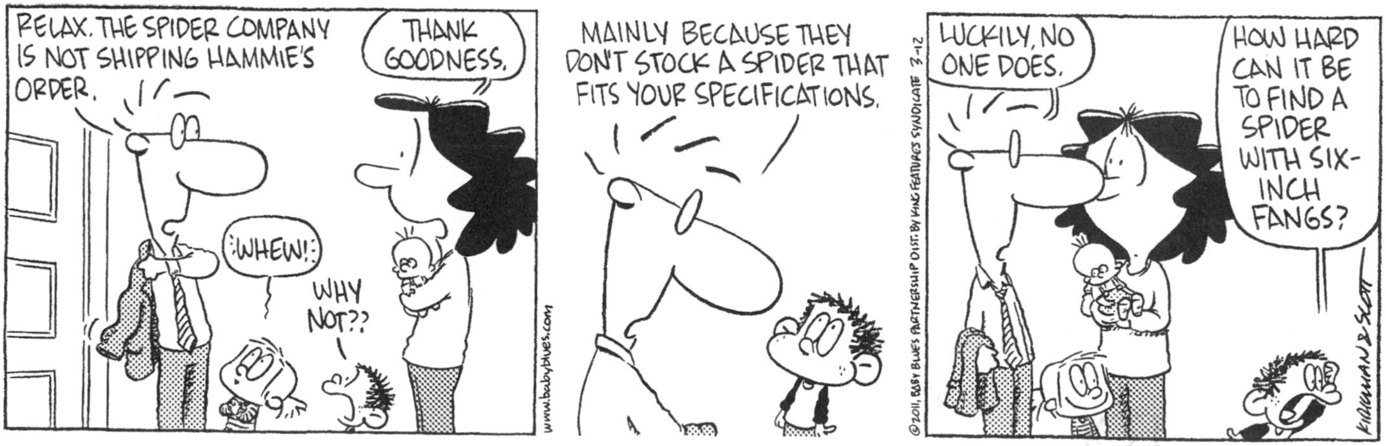
RELAX. THE SPIDER COMPANY IS NOT SHIPPING HAMMIE'S ORDER.
THANK GOODNESS.
WHEW!
WHY NOT??
MAINLY BECAUSE THEY DON'T STOCK A SPIDER THAT FITS YOUR SPECIFICATIONS.
LUCKILY, NO ONE DOES.
HOW HARD CAN IT BE TO FIND A SPIDER WITH SIX-INCH FANGS?
www.babyblues.com
© 2011, BABY BLUES PARTNERSHIP DIST. BY KING FEATURES SYNDICATE 3-12
KIRKMAN & SCOTT

BABY BLUES®
BY RICK KIRKMAN / JERRY SCOTT

READY... GO!
A-N-N-N-N-D... STOP!
GULPGULPGULPGULPGULP
GOOD. NOW STAY JUST LIKE THAT...
SHAKE SHAKE SHAKE
PHOO!
BWA-CHOOO
ISN'T IT WEIRD HOW SOME EXPERIMENTS ARE UNPREDICTABLE, AND OTHER TURN OUT JUST THE WAY YOU EXPECT?
MY WINDOW!
SNIF! UH-HUH.
www.babyblues.com
KIRKMAN & SCOTT

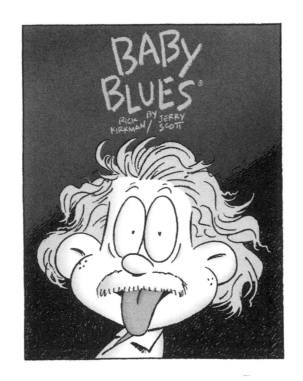